PLEASURE
AND THE NATION

SOAS Studies on South Asia
Understandings and Perspectives

PLEASURE
AND THE NATION

The History, Politics and
Consumption of Public Culture
in India

Edited by
Rachel Dwyer
Christopher Pinney

UNIVERSITY PRESS

OXFORD
UNIVERSITY PRESS

YMCA Library Building, Jai Singh Road, New Delhi 110 001

Oxford University Press is a department of the University of Oxford. It furthers the
University's objective of excellence in research, scholarship, and education
by publishing worldwide in

Oxford   New York

Athens   Auckland   Bangkok   Bogota   Buenos Aires   Calcutta
Cape Town   Chennai   Dar es Salaam   Delhi   Florence   Hong Kong   Istanbul
Karachi   Kuala Lumpur   Madrid   Melbourne   Mexico City   Mumbai
Nairobi   Paris   São Paolo   Shanghai   Singapore   Taipei   Tokyo   Toronto   Warsaw

with associated companies in   Berlin   Ibadan

Published in India
By Oxford University Press, New Delhi

ISBN 019 565090 5

Typeset in Adobe Garamond (10.5/12)
By Guru Typograph Technology, New Delhi 110 045
Printed in India by Pauls Press, New Delhi 110 020
Published by Manzar Khan, Oxford University Press
YMCA Library Building, Jai Singh Road, New Delhi 110 001

Contents

Introduction
Public, Popular, and Other Cultures[1]

CHRISTOPHER PINNEY

The place which an epoch occupies in the historical process is determined more forcefully from the analysis of its insignificant superficial
manifestations than from the judgements of the epoch upon itself . . .
The basic content of an epoch and its unobserved impulses recipro-
cally illuminate one another.

Siegfried Kracauer[2]

The line between the real and the filmic can be quite thin. [Amitabh]
Bachchan once said, 'When my mother dies I wouldn't know
whether I was really crying or just acting.'

Shah Rukh Khan[3]

IN A NATION as dramatically divided as India, there are some curious
places of shared desire: the melodies of Hindi film songs, the curves of
Amitabh's or Madhuri's body, the vivid materiality of popular visual
culture. Until a few years ago, the nation state would also have been a similar focus of pleasurable affirmation for many Indian citizens. The existence
of such areas (or more correctly, textures and styles) of convergent fixation
from diverse standpoints is illuminatingly paradoxical, and has consequences
for our understanding of the nature of South Asian society and of the particular forms of economic, political, and religious identity that seem to characterize it increasingly.

Before discussing in more detail some of the theoretical frameworks that help clarify the phenomenon under discussion, it may be useful to map out in general terms some common characteristics that bind together the representations and practices with which we are concerned. We can define the concerns of the chapters in this volume in a preliminary manner by noting that the public/popular culture with which they engage is inextricably linked to 'new' media and varieties of print culture, and to the rise and contestation of the nation state. However, the circulation of images and texts and the proliferation of cultural flows are of long-standing in India: the focus here is not solely on very recent electronic transformations, but rather on a deeper infrastructure of representational flows.

The creation and regeneration of the nation state in the face of its other is a central theme in many chapters. This can be through the generation of a new performative public sphere, the creation of communities of parallel consumers of film and television simultaneously engaged in mediating the nation, enduring channels of public discourse about cinema stars who have come to symbolize a national aspiration, or very direct migrations between the worlds of cinema and politics. All these different conjunctions between the public/popular and the nation are also mapped in domestic spaces, gendered domains of consumption and symbolization.

If the disparity of scale between the nation and the home is one fundamental tension informing popular discourses, then that between the urban and the rural is equally important. The metropolitan rarely exists on its own but is seen through the eyes of the ex-villager or the America-returned. Both Raj Kapoor confronting urban duplicity in *Shri 420* and Salman Khan returning to Bombay from the States in *Maine Pyaar Kiya* are bearers of a migratory liminality which seems to be central to public/popular cultural discourse. As Stuart Hall once argued, the popular can be seen as one response to attempts to re-engineer society—whether in the form of agrarian, industrial, or finance capitalism; public/popular culture has most to say, Hall suggests, during 'the active destruction of particular ways of life, and their transformation into something new' (Hall 1997: 456).

Walter Benjamin, so Adorno noted, had a 'preference for . . . everything that has slipped through the conventional conceptual net for . . . things which have been esteemed too trivial by the prevailing spirit for it to have left any traces other than those of hasty judgement' (Adorno, *Prisms*, cited by Bann 1989: 246). Hasty judgement has certainly in the past contributed to an unwillingness to address in the necessary way the cultural practices that form the focus of this book. However, rather than rehearsing old debates, this introduction will focus on the substance of the chapters that comprise this volume and the ways in which they can, collectively, lead us to a fuller understanding of the new forms of the political/aesthetic/cultural practices that characterize India and many other late twentieth-century societies.

What used to be called 'popular culture' is predicated on a sense of its own alterity, and its academic respectability is the result of the frisson of marginality. In the Euro-American academy, theorists recover a carapace of political legitimacy by allying themselves with what they claim are culturally disavowed (hence desirable) media and artefacts. The marginality of the everyday and the creative appropriations of consumers also invoked a new politics which appeals to those who have had to abandon earlier, more simplistic politics in the face of overwhelming evidence as to their irrelevance.

In India too, popular cultural forms (which, following Appadurai and Breckenridge, we will shortly designate 'public culture') are often consecrated with the blessing of a similar disavowal. It is strangely gratifying to read the complaint that the gyrations of Hindi film stars could reawaken the libido of an 'ailing pigeon' and to discover that this was intended as critique, not affirmation (Vasudev 1995: n.p.). When considering very accessible forms of popular entertainment, marginalization by a putative high culture becomes a means of endowing esoteric value. Rather as Montaigne once observed, monsters and storms must intervene in any voyage for the destination to have special value, the ghost of high cultural disparagement frames the subsequent discovery of cultural value in popular culture in a positive manner.

Perhaps we should then, be disappointed by the general lack of high cultural disparagement in India. Of course there are many vociferous critics (accurately recorded in their earlier writings by Sara Dickey and Rosie Thomas among others),[4] but they fail to connect with and consolidate any substantial alternative consumer base. The rantings of elitist critics abound in India, but these disappear in the wind, almost as quickly as they are uttered, finding receptive ears in only a few isolated institutions such as the Sahitya Akademi and the ICCR dedicated to a statist high culture of modernist progress, or its twin—folkloristic objectification.

Conventional models of popular culture presuppose a fundamental division between the elite and the popular. Indeed, Stuart Hall has suggested that the only viable definition of popular culture positions it 'in a continuing tension (relationship, influence, antagonism) to the dominant culture' (Hall 1997: 462). Such a position would appear congruent with the model of subalterneity which has emerged from Ranajit Guha's pioneering work for both 'popular culture' and the 'subaltern', born out of a previous misrecognition and invisibility. Within European history, 'popular culture' was the epiphenomenon of the discovery that history was not simply what

Peter Burke termed 'Ranke-type history, the political history of nation states' (Burke 1979: 69). Popular culture came to signify a broad non-elite focus: the 'attitudes and values of shopkeepers and factory workers, peasants and craftsmen, servants and fishermen, beggars and thieves' (Burke 1976: 69). Thus Christopher Hill, E.P. Thompson, and Carlo Ginzburg all became exemplars of this new engagement with popular culture conceived as 'unofficial culture' (Burke 1979: x).

Within South Asian history, subaltern studies emerged from the recognition that nationalist historiography reproduced colonial historiography in certain fundamental ways. A different elite was offered for contemplation, but it remained an elite. In Guha's formulation, this blindness to the mass of the people and their predicament reflected a more general 'failure of the Indian bourgeoisie to speak for the nation. There were vast areas in the life and consciousness of the people which were never integrated into their hegemony' (Guha 1997: xii). A parallel emerges between subaltern consciousness and 'popular culture', especially popular culture of the sort described by Carlo Ginzburg which was also born out of a fundamental absence of hegemony.[5]

'Subalterneity' has increasingly emerged—particularly in the work of Partha Chatterjee—as a characteristic of a supple culture of the colonized which manipulated eclectic signs against the dominant colonial structure. In later subaltern studies, subalterneity emerges not so much from the ground of an Indian authenticity but out of the translational slippage of the colonial encounter. It is in this context that Arjun Appadurai and Carol Breckenridge's claim that 'public culture' is an ally and footnote to subaltern studies, extending that perspective 'to India considered as a "postcolony"' (Appadurai and Breckenridge 1995: 4), makes sense. The sideways move from elite/popular distinctions proposed by public culture is, however, less easy to reconcile with Ranjit Guha's reassertion of a fundamental divide and, indeed, its growing intensification:

> That failure is self-evident from the difficulty which has frustrated the bourgeoisie in its effort so far at winning a hegemonic role for itself even after half a century since the birth of a sovereign Indian nation–state. The predicament continues to grow worse [Guha 1997: xiii].

This failure is vividly evident in the fear and miscomprehension that often characterizes the Indian urban economic elite's relationship to the rural population and the urban underclass, and which marks many secular intellectuals' apprehension of a popular religiosity (see Bharucha 1993). The alienated Indian's attempt to discover his/her 'own' culture (canonized in Nehru's *The Discovery of India*) is a continuing dilemma for many elite

Indians. A profound anxiety about a domestic *terra incognita* features prominently in Indian public discourse and as a foreign anthropologist conducting village fieldwork, one is frequently made aware of how utterly remote the rural is for many wealthy urban Indians.

In stressing the potential common ground of action that public culture constructs, I do not, therefore, wish to obscure the chiasmal cleavages to which Guha draws attention. What I want to capture—in some theoretically illuminating manner—is the mainstream authorized quality of much Indian public culture, and still leave room for the subaltern. It is important therefore to acknowledge that there are large sections of Indian society that do not readily participate in the public culture described here: we need to recognize the class specificity of *Stardust* and Shobha Dé's writing; and remind ourselves of the indifference (and hostility) to film and television that can be encountered in much of rural India. Further, it is vital that we grasp Indian public culture not as a homogenized whole but as a differentiated field with diverse audiences and agendas. Ashis Nandy's suggestion that Indian cinema presents a 'slum's eye view of the world' describes very pertinently the radical and questioning edge to movies such as *Deewaar* and *Coolie*, but cannot address the particular sentimental or class investments in films such as *Kabhi Kabhie* or *Hum Aapke Hain Koun . . .!*

However, while conceding that aspects of elite and subaltern culture remain mutually opaque, there is a middle ground of public culture that occupies a space which encompasses much of the 'middle class' and significant sections of small-town and rural India. Here, although different sectors may prefer one film over another and may be much more likely to see it in a rundown cinema than at home on video, all participate and become fluent in a shared grammar of cultural agency: a texture and style of expression and reflection occupy the central ground of public culture whose marginality is hard to discern.

This public culture occupies a new social space, one partially created by specific forms of media. Stuart Blackburn's chapter reveals a complicated relationship between different media and these new spaces: Tamil novels were able to bear messages that oral storytelling could not, but very few people could read them. Movies, by contrast, worked within, and extended, a pre-existing domain of orality, effecting a revolution from a space of familiarity. More specifically, Arjun Appadurai suggests that the 'community of sentiment' that emerges out of public culture is the consequence of the predominance of electronic mass media:

> Diverse local experiences of taste, pleasure, and politics can crisscross with one another, thus creating the possibility of convergence in translocal social action that would otherwise be hard to imagine [Appadurai 1996: 8]

Half the chapters in this volume are concerned with popular cinema which is unquestionably the driving force in creating the new space of public culture. Appadurai and Breckenridge note that 'film, television, and video technologies are at the heart of this new cosmopolitanism [and] contain models of celebrity and consumption that are pivotal to the new public culture' (1995: 10 & 8). M.S.S. Pandian has provided an invaluable historical investigation into Tamil culture elites' perceptions in the 1930s that cinema created a new space which threatened existing cultural hierarchies. Sandria Freitag provides a striking example of this from the 1927 Cinematographic Committee report in which one cinema owner reported the need to disinfect his premises after a showing of *Lanka Dahan* (Phalke's 1919 movie) in order to regain his usual western film-watching clientele. Pandian shows how such divisions were repositioned and partially elided as a result of cinema's equal popularity among the elite and the masses, and the elite's involvement in cinema as an industry. More importantly, however, Pandian isolates the citationality of film as crucial:

> Cinema as a medium was informed by what one may term [. . .] 'intertextual excess' whereby it could borrow both from high and low cultural universes at the same time and recombine them in unexpected ways [1996: 950].

This borrowing was apparent in the 'alliterative dialogue' which characterized the DMK genre of films critiqued for its lack of realism. This stress on 'realism' was one of the ways, Pandian argues, that the elite attempted to recuperate an idiom of cultural hierarchy within the medium itself. This however was a flawed project, subverted by the economy of the cinema with its dependence on a mass audience. Film's intertextual excess rebounded, and culturally arcane forms became signs to be manipulated in the ludic space of public culture. Pandian cites Revathi, an actress and dancer, lamenting that 'films can have a disco dance number in Bharatnatyam costume' (1996: 953). Similarly, hybrid film music incorporates Indian and western classical, Indian folk music, and western pop music in a new form that implodes genre distinctions.

Why 'Public'?

> Almost every fixed inventory will betray us. Is the novel a 'bourgeois' form? The answer can only be historically provisional: When? Which novels? For whom? Under what conditions? [Hall 1997: 462].

The editors of this volume follow Appadurai and Breckenridge in concluding that conventional notions of 'popular culture' have little analytical use in the context of a global modernity, and in the context of South Asia's position within that modernity. Empirical studies demonstrate that the assumptions behind both articulations of popular cultures in early modern Europe and the modern metropolitan practices beloved of cultural studies are so misleading that some new formulation which reworks the elite/popular divide is necessary. Late twentieth-century cultural flows have a quite different dynamic, Appadurai and Breckenridge suggest, and they propose the term 'public culture' as a way of naming that 'space between domestic life and the projects of the nation state—where different social groups [. . .] constitute their identities by their experience of mass-mediated forms in relation to the practices of everyday life' (1995: 4–5).

The chief problem with most conceptualizations of the 'popular' concerns its absent other—'the elite', and the sustainability of this divide. Whether one takes Adorno's regret at mass culture's simplicity and its lack of high modernist complexity, or the facile celebrations of the popular that have flourished in opposition to such elitist critiques, the 'popular' is always residual and apparently opposed to a (variously good or bad) other. Even the 'deconstructed' notion of popular culture as reluctantly advocated by Stuart Hall confines itself to what he terms 'the culture of oppressed, the excluded classes' (Hall 1997: 465). There would be no place here for the popular novels of Shobha Dé, or Zee TV (Dwyer 2000).

For Appadurai and Breckenridge writing in the first issue of their journal *Public Culture*, it is the historic changes contingent on modernity which undermine notions of both 'popular culture' and the metropolitan basis of Adorno's 'mass culture'. In India it is difficult to extract solid formations of 'high' and 'low' culture: in a post-colonial flux, categories are more fluid and mutually imbricated. Within this new context, the dialogue between elites and masses (terms they place under erasure) becomes infinitely more complex and demands a new—and correspondingly complex—theorization:

> The term *public* is not a neutral or arbitrary substitute for all these existing alternatives [popular, mass, folk, consumer, national or middle class]. Nevertheless, it appears to be less embedded in such highly specific Western dichotomies and debates as high versus low culture. With the term *public culture* we wish to escape these by now conventional hierarchies and generate an approach which is open to the cultural nuances of cosmopolitanism and of the modern in India [1988: 6].

The shift to public culture also forms part of an attempt to theorize new forms of transnational global cultural flows which make redundant 'traditional anthropological concepts of culture, which were designed for small-scale, well-bounded and stable societies' (Appadurai and Breckenridge 1988: 7). Thus, for instance, the impossibility of an isolationist village ethnography is paralleled by Appadurai and Breckenridge's recognition that 'folk culture is often a response to the competitive cultural policies of today's nation states' (1988: 8). A particularly spectacular example of the new cultural conjunctions that emerge within public culture has recently been documented by Rustom Bharucha in his description of Rajeev Sethi's 'Sarthi' (Bharucha 1997).

One crucial difference between public culture and popular culture is that the former presupposes processes of globalization within which the local operates. Globalization should not invoke a binary opposition between unity and diversity (Featherstone 1990: 2), but suggest, rather, the complex operations through which nomad technologies and ideologies become renegotiated and relocated in different locales. This is not a history of westernization or Americanization in which capitalist commodities triumph in the same form, but a much more complex process, what Homi Bhabha terms a 'performative, deformative' translation (Bhabha 1994: 241).

In an Indian context, although anthropologists had for long been studying 'non-elite culture', the emphasis was on rigorously local culture which excluded signs of a polluting modernity. One mark of this is the complete absence of discussions in most village ethnographies of the use of chromolithographs, which for many villagers are the most commonly used route to the divine. Where non-local culture was invoked, it was, understandably, a learned Sanskritic culture of religious texts. McKim Marriott's 1955 theorization of the nature of Hinduism's 'Little Tradition' argued for an equilibrium between the Great and the Little. He suggests that the Great 'lacked the authority to replace elements of the little tradition' (Marriott 1955: 218) but this was an argument for complementarity rather than opposition. There was little room here for an 'unofficial culture' embodying any radical alterity. Subsequently Dumont's stress on the encompassing nature of a singular ideology cast a consensual shadow which disavowed the possibility of radical subaltern perspectives. India, he claimed, was 'one': it was not multiple or contested, and his desire to elucidate a 'model' of traditional Indian society explicitly excluded signs of modernity.

Appadurai and Breckenridge's model of public culture defines it as a 'zone of contestation'. This is *a priori* compelling for we have all learned to pour scorn on earlier analyses that assumed consensus and agreement (usually arrived at by talking only to Brahmans). However, taken as a whole, the analyses in this book—and many elsewhere—do not support this claim in any strong sense. Appadurai and Breckenridge are certainly correct in starting with the assumption that all cultural systems operate on the basis of potential collapse and all emergent meaning is the result of negotiation in a zone of potential conflict. The chapters in this collection clearly bear this out. Several of them—particularly those addressing the debates over *Roja* and *Bombay*—also reveal exceptionally partisan positions and embroilments of the artefacts they discuss. It is also clearly the case that elements of Indian public culture also operate through an exclusion—through a blanking out of whole areas of many people's experience: for instance the bourgeois model of the family idealized in *Hum Aapke Hain Koun . . .!* does not fit in any obvious way with the aspirations and practices of economically marginalized groups. There is thus, at one level, ample evidence of erasure, of the elevation of particular dominant norms, alongside an ongoing debate about the nature of personal, community, and national identity. In this sense Indian public culture is without doubt a zone of cultural debate, rather than an arena of consensus and agreement. But, on the other hand, it is not a space characterized by the kind of massive cultural divide and miscomprehension that Carlo Ginzburg, or even Stuart Hall, mobilizes. This is, relatively speaking, a zone where consumers appear to share in a common language of cultural agency, a zone in which as Achille Mbembe has observed, diverse positions are inscribed in 'the same epistemological space' (Mbembe 1992: 14).

Why 'Culture'?

Much recent commentary has emphasized the ways in which the visible signs of India's public modernity have been put to partisan uses—televised Hindu epics inculcated in their viewers a new sense of the 'Hindu-ness' of the past, mass produced images of a muscular Ram have encouraged a new sense of Hindu agency, directors such as Mani Ratnam have been accused of a kind of 'fascism' and so on. All the chapters in this volume address in some way this current focus of debate, but collectively they suggest a set of conjunctions that other commentaries minimize. Rather than incommensurable interests structured around fundamental oppositions, there are differences ranged along a continuum. These chapters clearly document regional differences and identities, and radical shifts between the concerns of working-class Tamil film clubs and elite Bombay readers of *Stardust*, but these are different positions within a shared epistemological frame. The case studies collected here document a commonality against which the current manipulation of signs must be understood, and they place contemporary public modernity within a historical frame.

This sense of a certain shared epistemological space mobilized within public culture is one reason why it is useful to think of a popular visual 'culture'. Recently, in another context (that of colonial photography in Peru), Deborah Poole has advocated the use of the term 'visual economy'. She makes this suggestion because 'visual culture' suggested an inappropriate sense of 'shared meanings and symbolic codes that can create communities of people'. The term 'visual economy' on the other hand reflects much more accurately the Andean experience of fields of vision structured systematically in terms of inequalities and disadvantageous flows (Poole 1997: 8). Her point is well made, and yet in South Asia 'visual culture' retains a local saliency to describe the creation and maintenance of a set of overarching representational idioms which—as many papers in this collection suggest— are implicated in various partisan agendas, yet retain a powerful capacity to affirm common tropes, anxieties, and desires. One aspect of this consensual element was captured by Ashis Nandy when he pointed out that to argue that *Mother India* (Mehboob Khan's affirmation of an independent techno-democracy) is a 'Hindu' film (as indeed one could with some conviction) is to ignore the fact that it was directed by a Muslim—Mehboob Khan— and was narratively determined by a Muslim heroine—Nargis (Pinney 1995: 12). One is left with an irresolvable and productive paradox: everything about the disciplines from which analysts of non-elite culture come urges them to highlight dissent and the fragility of consensus; but the objects of their study and the practices entangling these objects habitually reveal an undergirding that fixes disparate groups in relationships of proximity.

The value of Nandy's observation lies not in any attempt to nullify the sectarian predisposition of an artefact through the documentation of the putative allegiances of its creator (after all we know that the BJP fields Muslim candidates in certain key constituencies), but rather to alert us to some common ground which cross-cuts both the productive infrastructure of public culture and its audience. The public culture with which this volume is concerned is without doubt an 'economy' driven by certain fundamental economic imperatives (we are continually reminded how many Bombay films fail at the box office every year), but this fiscal constraint is not shadowed by any parallel ideological or communal systematicity. Indeed there are grounds for supposing that—despite the debates over popular political imagery and films such as *Roja* documented here—the arena of popular cultural production remains one of the freest in India and a source for political optimism, rather than pessimism. In considering the domains of social action that Indian public culture helps open up there is, however, less reason to be optimistic.

'Deformations of Mastery' or 'Flashy Rags of Power'?

In India 'public culture' is only intermittently opposed to an authorized cultural discourse. It is not characterized at every turn by its fundamental ontological alterity (as in Bourdieu's formulation of a resistant anti-Kantian discourse—Bourdieu 1984), and the authorized discourse which very occasionally disparages it is—although it might be termed elite—hardly dominant. It is a discourse authorized in large part by state agencies but it has little authority and even fewer adherents.

This marginality of the 'non-popular' needs to be understood in the context of India's colonial encounter in the untangling of which the 'popular' was appropriated as part of the national struggle (Chatterjee 1992: 65). At the conclusion of the conference at which these papers were first presented, Ron Inden raised an important question concerning the nature of the middle class in a post-colony and its difference from the cultural/social formations around which conventional theories of 'popular culture' have been built. Another perspective on this is contributed by Ulf Hannerz who noted that in the Nigerian contexts with which he was familiar, popular culture 'appears to be above all a manifestation of metropolis-oriented sophistication and modernity'. Hannerz suggests that there are parallels between Nigeria—whose popular cultural forms drew their meanings from the centre and only secondarily from an opposition to an elite cultural practice—and early modern Europe where (and here Hannerz provides a contentious reading of Peter Burke), popular culture emerged as 'a field of activity more or less uniting elites and masses in shared pastimes and pleasures' (Hannerz 1992: 240–1).

A trope such as the journey from the village to the city (and vice-versa) is one of the ways in which diverse class and cultural experiences are overlapped in popular Indian culture.[6] The city—the central fixation of Indian public culture—operates as a space of experimentation and critique. In both Pramathesh Barua's *Devdas* (1935)—discussed in this volume by Ashis Nandy—and Mani Ratnam's *Roja*—discussed here by Nicholas Dirks—the opposition of village and city mobilizes a powerful framework of meaning and experience that elides popular/elite antagonisms. In Nandy's analysis, the city emerges as an uninhabitable place, but from which a return is never possible. In *Roja*, the eponymous heroine embodies a rural agency which ultimately secures the release of her kidnapped husband whose continuing incarceration was in large part a measure of the decay of the state. Here, as in *Shri 420*, Indian cinema's ongoing fascination with the city and the state as space of ambivalence, negativity, and more recently decay is very marked. Nandy also reveals in Barua's early work a sense of modernity turning sour, a theme which is also eloquently identified by Dirks.

Again in a Nigerian context, Hannerz further suggests that a 'metropolitan-orientedness' resulting from the realization that 'one can reach towards the charisma of the center at least as well through a greater investment in popular culture as through involvement with a more differentiated, less widely understood high culture' may also account for 'what is often referred to as the philistinism of the Third World elites' (Hannerz 1992: 240–1). Although Stuart Hall has urged that theoretical discussions of contemporary (western) popular culture should concern themselves with the period after the 1880s (Hall 1997: 458), studies of earlier periods retain a salience in comparative discussions and throw up unexpected conjunctions.

Hannerz perhaps simplifies Burke's position for, rather than suggesting an overlap of popular and elite practices which Burke was arguing for an asymmetry. This reflected the fact that although the elite had access to popular cultural practices (which were not yet fully stigmatized as lowly), in Europe the masses lacked the linguistic skills which would give them access to elite culture which was transmitted mostly in Latin. The continuities and discontinuities with India are worth briefly dwelling upon.

In placing these radically different societies side by side, one is immediately struck by the fact that the Indian public culture described in this volume has more in common with early modern European elite culture than 'popular culture', i.e. all that was excluded from the high learned culture. This is on the face of it rather amazing, and for this reason very instructive. One can think of all sorts of subaltern activities (aspects of popular Hinduism, untouchable possession activity, etc.) which do parallel early modern European popular culture, but this is something very different from the public culture analysed in the chapters in this volume.

The metropolitan aspiration described here with its encoding of empowering realms of knowledge and divinity is *projective*. Its orientation is to an outside, to a realm beyond the familiar: although the familiar is all around, it is recoded in the glamorous language of the outside. Indian public culture can be thought of as a citational praxis, or what Sumita Chakravarty termed 'impersonation' (1996: 4) and this citational impersonation, creates what Homi Bhabha terms a 'vernacular cosmopolitanism'. This cosmopolitanism mobilizes an accessible and fluid repertoire of signs that include dress and gesture which reverberate with other representational practices (for instance photographic studio portraiture). Unlike the case of Latin in early modern Europe, this grammar of practice requires no instruction, merely the eager ear of the movie goer and the repetitive citationality of popular cultural forms in which—as Frederick Jameson once noted—'nothing is heard for the first time; it is always half-heard in advance' (Jameson 1979: 135).

The Indian citational aspiration for the metropolitan strives, however, for a metropolis that is not American. The whole industry of cultural studies can be seen as a riposte to Adorno and Horkheimer for whom mass culture was inseparable from an American capitalism which threatened to enslave its victims as grotesquely as the Nazism from which they had fled. The metropolitan effect that Indian popular culture invokes, however, is one that operates independently of America and of a particular version of capitalism.

Foreign locales and 'foreign-returned' characters frequently feature in popular cinema, just as glamorous high-rise cityscapes are often the subject of calendar art depictions or used as backdrops in photographic studios. However, these usually connote an expanded domain of South Asian sophistication rather than the allure of a fundamental alterity. Rachel Dwyer has observed that in Shobha Dé's novels, 'foreign' is a place without foreigners for it is always peopled exclusively by South Asians. Rather as Michel Leiris travelled (in *L'Afrique Fantôme*) through Africa in a completely covered wagon (lest what he saw and experienced disturb the primacy of the voyage), so Dé's characters inhabit distant geographical locales stripped of any embodiments of alterity that might interfere with the primacy of Dé's characters' own metropolitan-ness. Shobha Dé's writing—like Bollywood itself—is a space of cultural debate in which the West is a mere cipher. Dé's novels invent a new zone of cultural contestation whose locale is Bombay. In the jostle of new elites, raiding other older elite's repertoires (Breckenridge 1988: 2), the West described by Dé is sketchy and unreal, a giant supermarket full of empty signs. As in Hindi films, the encounter with the West is in no sense dialogic; those who go there deal only with other South Asians. This contrasts powerfully with the English 'art' novel in India where the engagement with the West is frequently of major importance.

The same point is also made in Aditya Chopra's *Dilwale Dulhania Le Jayenge*. After he has made a particularly brilliant chess move against Amrish Puri, it is said about the character played by Shah Rukh Khan that 'the boy's not just a genius, he's indigenous'. This homonymic trumping of a transcendent universal cerebral quality (genius) by a localized identity (indigeniety) collapses linguistic form and content through its transformation of the English phrase—English being the medium of a global mass culture—into an onomatopoeic babble whose iconic quality outstrips its narrow semantic specificity. It is also a perfect example of Homi Bhabha's account in the conference's (n.1) concluding discussion of vernacular cosmopolitanism as 'an interruptive and questioning cosmopolitanism where there is a translation of symbols, a translation of sites . . . which confuses what is the general and what is the specific, what is the part and what is the whole'. It is this realm of a simultaneous persistence and transformation—what Homi Bhabha termed the 'circulatory and protean field of the popular in which artefacts are continually re-tooled, re-sited, re-located' that is also evoked in Kathryn Hansen's discussion of the enduring popularity and tenacity of the *Indar Sabha* story. Hansen traces the crossovers and migrations between media, and the citationality implicit in the paradigm of visual pleasure and spectatorship which the play/text/film invoked.

Public culture can be thought of as a nexus of overlapping discourses and interests that exist in a state of interruptive tension. For example, while the metropolitan exerts a phenomenal allure it is also, at the same time, deeply divided by a moral ambivalence. The retrospective eulogization of village life that is so apparent in Raj Kapoor's early films remains a strong feature of Indian public culture. Excluding 'America' from the metropolitan does not eliminate the moral dangers of a certain type of urbanism, the ambivalent fascination with which drives much public culture narrative as it explores what it might mean to be modern.

It is this interruptive tension at the heart of public culture's orientation to the metropolis, and the reconstruction of the metropolis that lies at its core, that makes it compatible with the field of influences and effects stressed so powerfully by Ashis Nandy in his earlier writings, although he stresses much more the marginality of these cultural forms. Nandy is particularly concerned with the ways in which Hindi cinema in particular articulates what he calls 'vestigial dialects' which outline a survival strategy of much greater use than anything to be found in the statist bourgeois sentiments of the editorial pages of the national dailies. Perhaps the clearest statement of his position is given in his remarkable Gandhi Memorial Lecture, 'The Discreet Charms of Indian Terrorism' in which he traces the events surrounding two hijackings of Indian Airline jets by Sikh militants in 1984. For Nandy the interior of a hijacked aircraft is a kind of laboratory in which the nature of modernity and morality can be tested. Within this claustrophobic space, external identities quickly erode and events then unfold within 'the limits imposed by another moral order' (Nandy 1995: 21).

A significant element in the articulation of this new morality was the meeting ground afforded by popular Hindi film music. A young hijacker sang 'melancholy songs of separation and love from Hindi films' and the passengers asked him to sing more. Nandy detects here a sub-strata of popular culture with dialogic possibilities:

The maudlin and comic aspects—which are certain to jar on the sensitivities of the Indian *haute bourgeoisie*—were exactly those that helped to establish the bonds among the three parties involved [1995: 21].

At this time of crisis, in which everyone was staking their lives, learned techno-rationalist codes were jettisoned and 'real convictions about the nature of the interpersonal world' (1995: 21) were tested. Nandy finds it enormously significant that at such times of duress, it is the sentiments found in commercial Hindi movies to which people appeal.

Nandy's reading of Hindi film's cultural agency as resistance is enormously appealing, but it is a reading that would find little favour with Achille Mbembe (1992). Nandy invokes something similar to the realm of the grotesque and the vulgar through which Bakhtin characterizes non-official culture's carnivalesque critique of official culture. Mbembe has explored the resonances of these tropes in the context of the (African) post-colony with startling effects, and much of what he proposes in the context of Cameroon, Togo, and Kenya raises key questions in theorizing public culture in post-colonial India.

The current fashion within cultural studies of the western metropole is to eulogize popular culture's positivity and productivity: consumers are transformed from passive victims of mass culture to endlessly creative appropriators of popular forms. One of the virtues of Mbembe's analysis is the space it opens for the re-acknowledgement of the negativity which also operates within much of the public/popular. In most cultural studies, Adorno's disparagements have simply been inverted and a general theory of consumption is emerging. The chapters in this volume suggest that one cannot have a 'general' theory of consumption, only an openness to the diverse outcomes of what happens after mass-mediated culture is made 'inalienable' (Miller 1987). A recognition of popular intelligence should not blind us to the power of capital—or in Mbembe's case the *commandement*—and the possibility that sometimes, at least, the mass media *does* produce the results which Adorno described so powerfully. Rather than argue over impossible binaries (e.g. people are stupid, or people are smart), detailed engagements with the nature of specific artefacts and the nature of the reception of different artefacts are required. The chapters in this volume exemplify this approach. Something of the nature of the unstable field of determinants and effects arising from such enquiries is captured in Ashis Nandy's suggestion that Hindi cinema asks 'the right questions but rarely produces the right answers' (Nandy, personal communication).

Whereas for Bakhtin the grotesque springs from the subaltern as a mode of parodying hierarchy, Mbembe is concerned to see it as a product of a very much more focused and compromised engagement in 'the places and times in which state power organizes the dramatization of its magnificence' and as a ludic field in which there are mutual investments—what he terms a 'promiscuous relationship' with 'convivial tension' (Mbembe 1992: 4–5). There is a 'logic of familiarity and domesticity' (1992: 5), he suggests, which explains why grotesque ludic performances by subalterns are not part of 'resistance', but instead participate in what Mbembe terms a mutual 'zombification'. A whole repertoire of signs through which the fluid post-colonial subject marks its fragmentation reveals not resistance or freedom, but rather the 'myriad ways in which ordinary people bridle, tick, and actually *toy* with power instead of confronting it directly' (Mbembe 1992: 22). The mass media and consumption practices are not, therefore, to be seen in the now conventional manner as routes to personal appropriation and the creation of inalienable resistant identities (Silverstone 1994: 126), but as part of a 'stylistic of connivance' (Mbembe 1992: 22). Bakhtin, Mbembe concludes, got it wrong it supposing that burlesque was produced exclusively by the subaltern with subversive intent:

> The real inversion takes place when, in their desire for splendour, the masses join in madness and clothe themselves in the flashy rags of power so as to re-produce its epistemology [Mbembe 1992: 29–30].

Perhaps the most challenging aspect of Mbembe's thesis for our purposes is the suggestion that the shared semiotics and gestures of a system 'inscribe the dominant and dominated within the same epistemological field' (Mbembe 1992: 14). One can easily produce numerous examples of this from Hindi cinema in which parodies of dress, gesture, and language permit characters to move through different social positions. This mimicry has the effect at some level of suggesting a commensurability between different (seemingly opposed) identities. It is this fluidity of subject identity and superfluity of mimicry which informs much popular photographic practice in which the local studio becomes a zone that can finesse the customer's body with the external signs of Gabbar Singh or Hema Malini (cf. Pinney 1997a).

There are, of course, other ways of reading these practices that would take us back nearer to the position mapped by Nandy, which might stress what Houston Baker terms 'the deformation of mastery'. The deformation of mastery in Baker's formulation is *phaneric*—it operates through adver-tisement and differentiation, rather than concealment or camouflage— and 'refuses a master's *nonsense*. It returns—often transmuting "stand-ard" syllables—to the common sense of the tribe' (Baker 1987: 51 & 56).

In a parallel manner, Sumita Chakravarty, writing about post-Independence Indian film, extrapolates the notion of 'impersonation' from Salman Rushdie's *The Satanic Verses*. 'Concentrated within this metaphor', she writes:

> are the notions of changeability and metamorphosis, tension and contradiction, recognition and alienation, surface and depth: dualities that have long plagued the Indian psyche and constitute the self-questionings of Indian nationhood [. . .] Impersonation subsumes a process of externatization, the play of/on surfaces, the disavowal of fixed notions of identity. But it also encompasses the contrary movement of accretion, the piling up of identities, the transgression of social codes and boundaries [Chakravarty 1996: 4].

Achille Mbembe and Houston Baker propose very different readings of the grammar of everyday action, but it is still possible to see in Indian public cultural practice elements which echo with aspects of both these contradictory paradigms: Indian ludic parody is frequently 'promiscuous' with power and often presupposes a common epistemological space of ruler and ruled; however, it is also frequently manifest through what Homi Bhabha—commenting on Houston Baker—terms the 'performative/deformative'. The 'stylistic[s] of connivance' (Bhabha 1995: 145) has a sting in the tail.

We must also note that in disassembling Adorno and Horkheimer as we try to theorize a public culture which was, until recently, without America we need also to record the transnational flows that take Indian popular cinema to West Africa,[7] West and South East Asia, the CIS, and to large Indian diaspora populations in Britain and the USA. Indian public culture is entangled in a global modernity, but it is one in which it is the agent, rather than the patient.

Cultural Agency

Rather than conventional politics, the cultural object in public culture participates in a grammar of cultural interrogation of which ordinary politics forms a small part. In a discussion that followed the conference, Nicholas Dirks suggested that the relationship between 'politics' and 'culture' had shifted in such fundamental categorical terms that it is still extremely unclear 'what a positive language of politics in the domain of cultural practice' might consist of. Here the term 'cultural agency' is used to articulate temporarily this new political/aesthetic/cultural domain. It connotes a field that exceeds both conventionally conceptualized 'politics' and 'culture', an extended field of intervention in the world in which the spectatorship and appropriation of commercial cultural artefacts play a central role.

This field of 'cultural agency' can be said to encompass a whole domain of potential interventions in the world through cultural practices, representational declarations, or cosmological hypotheses. 'Cultural agency' is intended to isomorphize the conventional political consequences (e.g. for voting patterns) of films which (say), depict an apocalyptic decay of the state, or the ruthless efficiency of the state in eliminating 'terroristic' elements, with representations such as advertising or domestic ritual images, which invite a certain kind of (different) heightened participation in the world but have no less political outcomes. 'Cultural agency' then becomes a way of conceptualizing diverse (and of course in many ways resolutely different) domains which share in common their positioning and articulation of individual and collective capability. As everyone wakes up each day in order to remake the world slightly differently, his or her desires and aspirations are mediated through—and articulated by—cultural strategies and idioms which necessarily imply the apportionment of power.

The media plays a centrally important role in this ongoing reapportionment, for it supplies, enhances, and elaborates many of the idioms and gestures through which social and political structures are reanimated at the start of each new day. Unless this media is understood to be at the centre of various overlapping domains (as opposed to a distinct field somehow set apart from the 'real' business of politics), it will always remain a puzzling anomaly to be explained as an obstacle, a hindrance in the way of a perfectly functioning polity.

Sudipta Kaviraj has noted the irony of attempts by analysts to demonstrate the existence of a public sphere in diverse societies, given the fact that Habermas' work 'shows precisely how a specific configuration of the idea of the public emerged in the modern West' (Kaviraj 1997: 86). In other words Habermas' project was only ever envisaged to be a theory about a particular European public space, rather than a global public sphere. Sandria Freitag's chapter delineates the various visual and performative registers and practices that created India's modernity. Like several of the other chapters here, it also suggests that although they may well be intensified and transformed by very recent developments, the 'new media' have a long history.

The European conception of orthodox politics which Dirks isolated as problematic and peculiarly unsatisfactory in this context is the outcome of a particular European history in which—in the Habermasian example—a public sphere emerges in which certain forms of communicative agency, debate, and resolution become routinized. Habermas' public sphere blossoms within a cognitivized (Meehan 1995: 3) chronotope (archetypically the coffee house where one could read and discuss *The Tatler*) within which a certain model of cerebral rationality is privileged. The cultural agency that Habermas embodies in this form of politics is linguistically overdetermined and is grounded in a notional dyadic interchange between two discoursing (and immobily seated) men. The theory of political culture that emerges from such constraints is structured by two absences which limit its powers of elucidation in the contexts discussed in this volume: the absence of any consideration of the bodies that produce these elocutions and of the performative element in these encounters. Freitag's work draws us towards the centrally important corporeal dimension of performance, the performative space of the procession, and the strangely neglected role of visuality, as constituents of the nexus of what in other contexts became the public sphere.

'Cultural agency' may merely sound like a clumsy term for old-fashioned 'ideology' whose effects via media practices have constituted the bread and butter of a generation of social scientists. However, 'cultural agency' implies a much wider field of symbiotic flows in which it is impossible to identify stable interests. Similarly, if on the one hand Foucault's stress on the pleasure within which the capillary forms of power subsist is appealing, on the other the residual sense of a totalizing order in whose interest this power ultimately operates is not. As Iain Chambers has written: 'If ideology is all around us . . . then we can no longer measure resistance and struggle for change along the yardstick of a non-ideological reality . . . we need to disrupt the presumed coherence of ideology, texts and images . . . That means living inside the signs' (Chambers 1986: 212).

Pleasure

Chamber's notion of 'living inside the signs' was echoed by Gyan Prakash's comments at the end of the conference in which he urged the necessity of 'losing oneself' within the objects of public culture. He was not arguing that analysts should merely celebrate these cultural products, just as there was little to be gained from an ideological critique from the outside. Rather, a strategy of investigation was needed which emerged from the implosion of the inside/outside opposition. This would be one solution to the dilemma voiced by Gramsci:

> The popular element 'feels' but does not always know or understand . . . the intellectual element 'knows' but does not always understand and in particular does not always feel . . . the intellectual's error consists in believing that one can know without understanding and even more without feeling and being impassioned [cited by O'Shea and Schwarz 1987: 109].

Gramsci emphasizes the incommensurality of an affective/corporeal encounter and a cognitive one and illuminates why it is that the field of popular cultural production has often been so problematic from the point of
view of 'aesthetic' discourse. The denigration of popular aesthetics has frequently pivoted on the popular aesthetic's immediacy and visual fecundity.
In 1978, Walter Spink provided a memorable condemnation of what he
termed the 'often excessively voluptuous popular poster art [which] seems
marvellously camp to the western eye bemused by such highly sentimentalized
and "realistic" religious productions' (Spink 1978: 92–3). Popular Indian
cinema has had to bear even more of these irrelevant dismissals as critics
have contrasted the worth of Satyajit Ray's neo-realist austerity with Bollywood's superfluity of corporeal affectivity (computed by the critics as a
deficit of aesthetic and imaginative worth).

Spink's stress on 'voluptuousness' as problematic isolates a particular
anxiety about the corporeality of the popular aesthetic. The figural density
of the image exceeds what ordinary language can address and the analyst
(searching only for what can be translated into discourse) is left uneasy. It
is in this context that we can understand why Didier Anzieu recently described the body as the 'repressed of today' (cited by Grosz 1994: 24).[8]

Another way of approaching this problem is suggested by Susan Buck-
Morss' distinction—in her reconsideration of Walter Benjamin's essay on
the 'Work of Art'—between 'aesthetics' and 'anaesthetics' (Buck-Morss
1992). She argues that the original field of aesthetics encoded in the Greek
aisthitikos connoted a broad domain of sensory reality. The 'modern
science of aesthetics', however, 'understood as detached contemplation
rather than instinctual cognition, functions as a form of anaesthetization, a
way for numbing the human sensorium, overwhelmed by the shock of war
or the shock of industrialization' (Efimova 1997: 75).

In a wonderful application of these ideas, Alla Efimova shows how
Soviet Social Realism mobilizes an aesthetics in its original sensory meaning.
'From this perspective, the aesthetics of Soviet everyday life no longer appear to be a paradox. As a powerful stimulation of the senses, by means of
pain, fear, or exaltation, life did not need to be beautiful or pleasing to
be "aesthetic" ' (1997: 78). The aesthetics of Socialist Realism, therefore,
are not of the anaesthetizing variety. They 'touch on the raw', and de-
anaesthetize.

Buck-Morss' archaeology of aesthetics is peculiarly useful for our understanding of public culture in India for here we encounter images produced
within and mediated by anaesthetizing discourses, and those produced
within and mediated by sensory—corpothetic—practices. It is the numbing

of the human sensorium which makes a certain style of early public culture so compatible with conventional art historical exegesis. Hence Ravi Varma and Guru Dutt can be written about 'aesthetically' in a way that Yogendra Rastogi and Manmohan Desai can not. It is the sensory immediacy of more recent film and popular picture production which makes it so intractable to conventional analysis and regard.

Similarly, the central Indian villagers—whose consumption of religious prints I have been researching for several years—do not surround these images with reified discourses. For an anthropology driven by the need to accumulate linguistic testimony, this is a severe problem. Buck-Morss' ideas, however, lead us to an understanding of a different dimension of significance in which it is not the efflorescence of words around an object that gives it meaning but a bodily praxis, a poetry of the body, that helps give images what they want (Mitchell 1996). Shifting the level of analysis from 'aesthetics' (i.e. 'anaesthetics' in Buck-Morss' terms) to 'corpothetics' discloses not a lack, but a rich and complex praxis through which villages articulate their eyes and bodies in relation to pictures. The 'meaning' of the images lies in their 'needs'—the necessity of worshipping them, in 'corpothetics' rather than 'anaesthetics'.

'Corpothetics'—like Lyotard's notion of 'figure'—transcends the artificial distinction between the visual and the linguistic. Lyotard opposed 'figure' to 'discourse' but not to denote a simplified opposition between the visual and linguistic artefacts for, following Merlau-Ponty, he saw poetry as powerfully figural for it resisted the 'linguistic philosophical closure' of discourse. Much discussion during the conference revolved around wider aspects of this question. Peter Van der Veer, alluding to Francis Haskell's work, urged caution in assuming that visual signs accessed some peculiarly privileged cultural domain since European thought had inherited this notion from nineteenth-century German Romanticism: the specificity of its genealogy should make us suspicious of its general claims (Haskell 1993: 365ff). Similarly, Paul Willemen was keen to stress the unavoidable imbrication of the visual in the linguistic. By addressing the power of figure as part of a praxis—simultaneously performative/visual/linguistic— 'corpothetics' provides a turning away from earlier binary contests.

A focus on 'corpothetics' would advance our understanding of both the vectors of pleasure, and how it is that people consume mass-produced artefacts so as to make them inalienable through pathways that are as much corporeal as they are intellectual or cognitive. However, many key questions remain. What are the strategies for analysing the consumption of early media which appear to have sunk beyond the horizon of historical recall?

What might the ethnographic strategies be that permit spectators' voices to transcend the already-theorized interrogation of the enquirer? What is to be the relation between exegetical enquiry and a phenomenology of the praxis of viewing and consuming? And most complex of all, if much of what we are writing about is part of a non-linguistic figural—corpothetic—realm that is opposed to discourse, what are the possibilities of capturing this figure in that self-same discourse?

Consumption

In commissioning and selecting these papers, a specific desire was to examine strategies in the analysis of 'consumption'. Although much ethnography has in a fundamental sense always privileged the consumer—inasmuch as it concerned itself with how cultural practice had value only within the terms specified by its own practitioners[9]—cultural criticism has frequently valorized the cultural artefact itself, reading it as some sort of text with a 'meaning' independent of its appropriation (other than by the critic). The chapters by Dickey and Uberoi renounce such an approach and apply specifically ethnographic methods to elucidate the diverse significations of cinematic practices among a wider field of consumers.

Uberoi explores the Delhi audience's responses to *Hum Aapke Hain Koun . . .!*, the highest grossing film in the history of Indian cinema. This 'family' film conjures a realm of consumer plenitude, of bourgeois gastronomic and sartorial excess: consumer goods, designer kitchens, yellow bathrooms, lavish childrens' toys, computers, open-topped jeeps. Nisha (played by Madhuri Dixit) displays pictures of herself eating ice-cream, and posters of sandwiches and milk shakes in her bedroom. Modern India's poverty and suffering are utterly absent. There is none of the philosophy of the masala here—it is a 'vegetarian' movie cleansed of all the psychic and existential predicaments that characterize so many Hindi films. The 'nation' (which looms so large in *Roja* and *Bombay*) appears to be completely absent in the film, and yet it is the nation which viewers reiterate as its fundamental subject. It is, they claim, about 'India' and 'Indian' values. Strikingly, the affluence of the filmic family seems to assist—rather than inhibit—diverse viewers' identification with it. There is what Uberoi calls a 'utopian' effect through which viewers recode their own family situations as echoes of the idealization on the screen.

The urban male poor who constitute the Madhuri fan clubs described by Sara Dickey inhabit a world that is very different. Yet there is a similar enthusiasm and endorsement of material success. The male film stars—such as MGR, Kamal Hassan, Rajnikant—who are the objects of film star club veneration, are viewed as successful members of an upper class, virile and heroic, the worthy beneficiaries of an upward cinematic mobility. The fans themselves have no desire to be glorified as the poor, preferring instead to see themselves as incipiently wealthy and possessed of a benevolent attitude to those beneath them. Dickey's chapter—as Ron Inden noted—touches on the vast domain of Indian 'street corner' society about which almost nothing is known.

Dickey's concern with the ways in which film, and its reception, have certain institutionalized forms and discourses outside of the cinema hall resonates with a celebrated analysis by Rosie Thomas (1990) which explores the ways in which the filmic text of *Mother India* was paralleled by—and read against—a field of informal knowledge about the stars that featured in that filmic text. There are echoes here of Nandy's consideration of Barua's existence as 'an urbane Devdas'. The artefact of the film is thus mediated by a dense ongoing discussion about personae for whom the film is an occasional meeting place. The ethnography of consumption ceases thus to be an 'event'—focused on particular individuals' reception of a specific film—but becomes rather an ongoing project 'living inside' the discourses which are perpetually maintained alongside filmic texts. Furthermore, the remarkable intertwining of filmic and everyday reality (in which Nargis and Sanjay Dutt become indistinguishable from their screen alter egos) defines one lineament of India's increasingly virtual existence configured by the ever growing invasion of a popular visual imaginary into everyday political choices.

This domain of cinematic discourses that thrive outside of the actual process of viewing films is further explored by Rachel Dwyer in the context of the film magazine *Stardust*. The prominence of the addressee in its text, and the social functions that are generated around the magazine suggest parallels with Dickey's working-class fan clubs. Film magazines—which in various languages and formats—occupy the middle ground of India's public culture have been the subject of intellectual hostility, Dwyer suggests, from academics who have been keener to study what have been identified as either 'elite' or 'subaltern' forms. Mirroring Rustom Bharucha's emphasis on the authorization of conspicuous middle-class consumption patterns in *Hum Aapke Hain Koun . . .!*, Dwyer discusses the interpolation of commodity consumption into the domain of filmworld glamour within publications like *Stardust*. If *Hum Apke Hain Koun . . .!* is about the family and shopping, *Stardust* is without doubt about sex and shopping. The magazine's Bombay-English (see 'Neeta's natter') also provides vivid examples of a 'deformation of mastery', but one that is—in Mbembe's terms—absolutely identical with the 'magnificence of power'.

If anthropologists have always had a methodological prejudice against formalism, analysts from other disciplinary traditions have approached consumption from the point of view of a more general critical dispersal of meaning away from the author onto other signifying agents, of whom—in cultural studies at least—the 'audience' acquired a supremacy, and whose primacy of interpretation underwrote the semantic indeterminacy of the authorial text.

But the chapters here, and the discussion they generated, suggests that such a shift throws up new problems. Ravi Vasudevan drew attention to the inextricable mutuality of reception and production in certain contexts. Tilak's production of a space for politicized Ganesh pujas in 1890s Bombay mobilized Hindu participants in a joint-communiqué from which it would be absurd to extract 'producers' and 'consumers' on opposite sides of a semiotic exchange. Vasudevan also draws attention in his chapter to the ways in which government censorship is simultaneously a form of reception and production. Similarly, and more insistently, Paul Willemen, speaking at the conference where these papers were initially presented, while acknowledging the limitations of purely text-based studies, critiqued the replication in many audience studies of a single stable point that guarantees meaning. In this sense, the failings of the authorial/textual model were replicated at a different site—that of the audience. There were also political implications in this, Willemen suggested. The historical moment of consumption-driven studies was significant, and the devolution of interpretation to the audience provided what he termed an 'academic alibi', an abdication of responsibility on the part of the intellectual *as part of the people*. Here Willemen rejected the notion of the intellectual's subjective apprehension as somehow incommensurably different from 'the popular' because 'all of the historical and cultural tendencies . . . that we see at work in the people we study and ask questions of are also at work in us'. While this could be appropriated in various ways—for instance as a neo-formalism that reinstitutes the primacy of the intellectual, or as a rallying call for a vanguardist interpretation that pays no attention to the non-affirmation of the masses—it productively connects with the new space of public culture in which the (elite) intellectual is not (necessarily) pitted against the popular. Bound by overlapping cultural flows and letting the signs play 'inside', the intellectual is positioned somewhat like a post-Geertzian anthropologist not concerned with maintaining an objectifying distance, but instead having to 'speak nearby' (to use Trinh T. Minh-ha's term) from a common ground in which interpretation becomes an imaginative probing within a set of shared (i.e. delimited) possiblities.[10]

This is the position from which Ravi Vasudevan and Nicholas Dirks assay their analyses of two Mani Ratnam films (*Bombay* and *Roja*) which have both been sources of a veritable efflorescence of critical discussion and anxiety in the pages of *Economic and Political Weekly*. Vasudevan responds as an engaged citizen, seeking to understand and acknowledge the basis of its existence as a mass-cultural artefact—its emotional power—and simultaneously keep watch over what Sunil Khilnani termed 'the pacts and complicities which the film requires for its success'. Vasudevan's own engaged response emerges out of an ethnography of 'the articulate strata of "the public", as expressed in the outlook of mainstream politicians, journalists and reviewers'.

Nicholas Dirks—discussing Mani Ratnam's earlier film, *Roja*—seeks to create a space of cultural analysis which—while ineluctably engaged—can complicate criticism. Many critics who commented on the film saw their existence threatened by a Hindutva tide of which *Roja* was perceived to be a part, and analysis was consequently predicated upon an urgent politicality and concern with 'effect'. Dirks agrees that the film is 'retrograde' and expressive of a new 'fascist' consensus. However, he writes not from the position of the Hindutva viewers of the film, or that of Indian intellectuals for whom criticism operated within very specific constraints, but from a space that permits him to attempt to understand the 'powerful and pleasurable effects' which films such as *Roja* evidently have. 'That cinema is all about pleasure . . . is part of the problem,' he notes.

The theme of pleasure as a central problematic—raised also by Dwyer—is continued in Asha Kasbekar's contribution. Kasbekar engages with the heterosexual male voyeurism which is one of the chief pleasures of popular Hindi film. Access to this pleasure operates within various constraints, however, and has to find a space that does not antagonize the state, female viewers, or the male viewer's own sense of propriety. One crucial strategy which appeases the latter is the fiction of the performance within a performance—often in a theatre, night-club or disco—which justifies the cinematic spectator's voyeurism because of the presence of a performance 'that *demands* to be looked at' and in which the diegetic spectator becomes the 'true owner' of this problematic gaze. The panoply of justifications that cloak pleasure in this instance also draw on citational strategies that have a long history within Indian public culture, for this internal framing of a performance within a narrative was also a central feature of the *Indar Sabha*.

Video Nights in Karimpur?

In November 1933, an Indian Airlines Airbus crashed in a paddy field near Tirupati. The plane was full of Tamil and Telugu film stars such as

Chiranjeev, Vijayashanti and Balakrishna (the film star son of N.T. Rama Rao). As they emerged through the emergency exists in a state of shock, they were greeted by local agriculturalists who worked on in their fields as though nothing had happened. As Balakrishna was to later explain, 'the villagers . . . thought a film shooting was going on and it took some time for them to realize that the accident was real.' He also noted that he 'was once given control of a flight, by a captain and [. . .] would love to do a similar role in [. . .] Telugu cinema' (*Indian Express*, 17 April 1993). Such delicious examples of the epistemological space—of expectation and obligation—that cinema creates, fit perfectly with accounts of India's lurch into postmodernity in which daily life is increasingly configured by cinematic images and the messages on billboards.

It is from such journalistic and anecdotal events that many a story of post-colonial simulation displacing reality is created. However, as Arjun Appadurai has noted, modernity, though decisively at large is 'irregularly self-conscious, and unevenly experienced' (1996: 3). There are two good grounds to suggest that simulation narratives run the danger of misleading. The first of these is a demographic question and concerns the extent to which the new velocity of image circulation through film and television has indeed produced qualitative change. The section heading 'Video Nights in Karimpur' refers to the UP village of Karimpur (known to anthropologists through the studies of Wiser and Wadley) and was chosen for its alliterative parallel to the location of Pico Iyer's 'Video Nights in Kathmandu', but in the absence of such mellifluous constraints any one of the other 700,000 villages of India would have served as well. This is intended to make a simple point: the majority of India's population is obviously not situated directly in the centre of the cultural melange that Iyer evoked.

A recent cartoon competition in India was won by an entry which depicted the Banaras funerary priests' umbrellas (which give the *ghats* their distinctive appearance) inverted. Thus transformed, they assumed the appearance of satellite dishes receiving a global modernity which the cartoonist wittily contrasted with the putative traditionalism of Kashi. Apart from its visual panache, the cartoon was no doubt chosen because the judging panel agreed with the Australian cultural commentator McKenzie Wark's slogan that today we 'no longer have roots, we have ariels' (or rather satellite dishes).

The cartoon speaks to a clear reality of modern India, but it is a reality in which not all of the population participates in. The Madhya Pradesh village that I have researched in intermittently since 1982 lies only 6 km from a stop on the main Delhi–Bombay railway line and its first satellite dish was installed in 1996 by the local liquor dealer. The dish, which sits atop his house, is an imposing presence, but during the first year he secured only a dozen village subscribers, and all of these were attracted by the promise of access to Hindi movies. For the small minority of villagers interested in this new opportunity, the incentive is the intensification of pre-existing pleasures—rather than anything qualitatively new—and our analysis of public culture must also record the profound disinterest of the majority.

Outside the metropolises, the electronic revolution is patchy and often difficult to discern. What is much more visible is the legacy of a set of media transformations that have a much longer history. In villages and small towns it is a popular visual and performative culture which is still experimenting within a framework established in the late nineteenth and early twentieth century which is most visible. Sandria Freitag and Kathy Hansen's chapters draw our attention to this historical moment and its ongoing legacy. Hansen documents a cultural artefact (the *Indar Sabha*) which traversed different media incarnations and demonstrated a remarkable persistence. Similarly the narratives generated around media manipulations of Hindutva have a late nineteenth-century precedent in the proliferation of Cow Protection literature and mass-produced visual imagery (Pinney 1997b). Stuart Blackburn's paper raises fundamental questions about the specific role of what are sometimes referred to as 'new media'. What is it that makes some media 'new', and what continuities exist between different idioms of articulation in the field that concerns us here?

In a related way, we might note that analyses of globalization which (rightly) emphasize the role of de-territorialized diaspora communities in generating and determining political trajectories within the Indian nation state usually ignore early twentieth-century analogues such as the Ghadr movement in San Francisco and British Columbia (cf. Singh and Singh 1966; Hans 1998) and Shyamji Krishna Varma's activities in London including the organization of the 'India House' and publication of the *Indian Sociologist* between 1905 and 1914 (Sarda 1954; Visram 1986: 102–8).

However, if on the one hand we might blur the temporal frame within which de-territorialized communities emerge, on the other it is simultaneously necessary to reassert the continuing primacy for many Indians of the 'nation' as the framework of agency (or its lack). Just this point has recently been argued by Partha Chatterjee and Rustom Bharucha in their (very different) critiques of Appadurai's vision of global flows.

The Nation (in Fragments)

We do not have the privilege [. . .] to imagine ourselves beyond the nation [Bharucha 1998: 177].

'Our India' was the first lesson in our social studies book in class three. It had a picture of the Red Fort, a map with a lady who looked like Hema Malini holding a flag, a picture of Gandhi, Nehru and Bose, a picture of a dam, a temple, a mosque, a gurudwara and a church, two children going to school, three stone lions on a pillar with a tiny horse, wheel and buffalo, a farmer and a sheaf of corn, a worker with a wrench and a soldier with a rifle. Everybody smiles, everybody gushes . . .

The other chapters had fewer pictures. America had the Statue of Liberty, Russia the Kremlin, England the Big Ben, Germany had a big road with cars, China had the wall, Australia had a kangaroo and all of Africa had a lion. Pakistan was a cricket team and a place down the corridor, you turned left, got in through a green door and stood staring at a blank tiled wall as you held your nose and kept your tryst with destiny [Sengupta 1997: 9].

This collection of essays develops the proposition that contemporary India cannot be understood if one excludes from one's analysis popular visual culture. It is in this visual culture, we suggest, that many contemporary Indians debate their present and their future. Perhaps future hindsight will reveal a shift from an earlier radical concern in Indian popular cinema with *kismet* and the vagaries of class inequality to a post-liberalization upscaling of cinema's epistemological space in which radical questioning was increasingly hard to spy among all the middle-class opulence. Alongside this, Indian public culture has documented a transformation of attitudes towards the state in which the innocent aspirations of *Mother India* have been transformed into the moral anomie and despair of *Sadak* (1991). In the 1957 *Mother India* a bountiful Nehruvian optimism elides the future of the nation with the efficacy of grand engineering schemes.[11] Three decades later, *Sadak* pits a heroic urban citizen against an utterly decayed post-colonial state and compromised civil society in which every successive source of salvation is revealed to be more corrupt than the last. Pleasure remains fundamental to popular film but it rarely erupts out of the project of the nation state.

Rustom Bharucha has argued that disaffection with the state stems not from its deprivation of its citizens' subjectivity, but from its atrophy: it is not 'violent efficiency' which is problematic (although as he notes the Indian state is often violent and, sometimes, efficient) but its inability to supply basic necessities. Alongside this, Bharucha continues, categories of language, blood, soil, race, and kinship[12] are 'the most tenacious categories, the residual narrative of community, which refuses to die, even as it is in the process of being fractured by very contradictory processes of citizenship' (Bharucha 1998: 177).

This sense of a state which is not adequate to the needs of its nation is a recurrent trope in recent Indian public culture. Its manifestation in Shankar's *Bharateeyudu* has recently been discussed by Tejaswini Niranjana and S.V. Srinivas. Whereas Mani Ratnam's films (which are often compared with Shankar's) are characterized by a 'relentless celebration of the new middle class' (Niranjana and Srinivas 1996: 3129), *Bharateeyudu* is characterized by a sombre angst about a nationalism that was deeply flawed in its inception. This critique is articulated through the elevation of Subhash Chandra Bose over Gandhi and Nehru.[13] The privileging of Bose and the Indian National Army validates 'direct solutions to present-day problems: fearless, violent struggle and instant justice' (Niranjana and Srinivas 1996: 3130).[14]

If one of the strengths of this collection is the longer historical frame within which it situates 'new media' and the rise of a certain sort of public culture, this *longue durée* should not blind us to the dramatic changes that have occured throughout this period. The trope of a modernity gone sour is clear in Barua's work in the 1930s, and in this respect the current figuration of this is not new. But the decay of the state and the necessity of its rescue by heroic representatives of the nation has, however, emerged as a qualitatively new theme. The emergence of this idealized model of political action signals the dangerous times that India and South Asia now inhabit.

A significant section of the history of this disillusionment is recorded in Raj Thapar's *All These Years*. Her account opens, however, with a memorable passage—sketched in a cinematic language—in which freedom blows from the Indian Ocean full of a delirious promise, and in which the career of the nation state entwines itself inextricably with the private and personal:

> I could never decide whether it was the Bombay of 1945 or my marriage in June of that year which made it a special time for me. The war was over and across that expanse of muddy sea to blue horizon you could decipher the outlines of Independence coming closer to the shore by the minute. As I sat dangling my legs over the windowsill of my new home, hypnotized by the monsoon waves pounding against the seawall in front, I could feel that same pounding within me, almost as if impatient to burst with the kind of fury which can only accumulate in that startling way in adolescence. And I was

an adolescent at that time, and though Indian Independence had yet to be born, its coming was marked by the same kind of impetuous energy [1991: 1].

From the gloomy vantage of a *fin-de-millennium* Indian cinema hall, Thapar's account looks like the faded nostalgic fantasy of an early Raj Kapoor movie.

NOTES

1. In addition to discussions with Rachel Dwyer, this introduction draws upon comments made by many participants during the conference at SOAS where these papers were presented. In particular I have made use of observations by Homi Bhabha, Gyan Prakash, Ron Inden, Paul Willemen and Peter Van der Veer. Ranajit Guha's subsequent provocative and critical reading of an earlier draft was especially useful. The agreement of any of the above or of volume contributors with the argument outlined here should not be assumed. I would like to thank the Centre for Cross Cultural Research, Australian National University, for providing the opportunity to complete this introduction.

2. Cited by Frisby (1985: 147).

3. Interview in *Filmfare*, November (1993: 38).

4. Cf. Dickey (1995: 133)—'Most critics refuse to discuss popular movies on the film's own terms—instead passing judgement from high culture perspectives.' My suggestion is that this may well once have been true, but it is invoked as rhetorical foil (to substantialize the alterity of one's own project); that it may not be true makes the phenomenon under investigation even more interesting.

5. I have in mind not only the position marked so clearly in *The Cheese and the Worms* and his later essay 'The Inquisitor as Anthropologist', but also some of the glosses of his remarkable essay 'Morelli, Freud and Sherlock Holmes: Clues and the Scientific Method'. When first published in *History Workshop* (Spring 1986), Anna Davin introduced it with these words: 'He is looking at "low" knowledge, the kind which "exists everywhere in the world, without geographic, historical, ethnic, gender or class exception", but which nevertheless is peculiarly the property of those who within a given society are not in a position of power. It is informal knowledge, orally transmitted, based on the everyday experience . . . and careful observation, which allows the observer to understand much more than can be directly seen' (1986: 6).

6. See also Dulali Nag's suggestion (in relation to the 1954 Bengali film *Agnipariksha*) that 'development'—the 'marriage' between the village and city was a means of 'eliminating class-difference in a national context' (Nag 1998: 787).

7. See for example Larkin (1997: 406), 'The sight of a 15ft image of Sridevi, dancing erotically on the screens of the open-air cinemas of northern Nigeria, or the

tall, angular figure of Amitabh Bachchan radiating charisma through the snowy, crackly reception of domestic television have become powerful, resonant images in Hausa popular culture'.

8. However, whereas Anzieu is suggesting that this repression characterizes the 'third industrial revolution', as will be apparent below, following Buck-Morss, I would trace this disavowal as contingent on the much earlier rise of a form of aesthetic lingusitic evaluation of the figural.

9. Although of course within anthropology there are/were pockets of resistance to this, such as doctrinaire structuralism.

10. Though of course this has its pitfalls. The intellectual's temptation to speak for the people, 'inside' the people, has to be continually scrutinized. See Crapanzano (1986).

11. 'India in the 1950s fell in love with the idea of concrete' (Khilnani 1997: 61).

12. The list is derived from Appadurai (1996: 161) for whom they are 'falsely "naturalised" categories propagandized by right-wing nationalists' (Bharucha, 1998: 177).

13. See Arjun Appadurai's commentary on the experience of his father (who was Bose's minister of publicity and propaganda in the provisional government of Azad Hind: 'To the end of their lives, my father and his comrades remained pariah patriots, rogue nationalists. My sister, brothers, and I grew up in Bombay wedged between former patriotism, Bose-style, and bourgeois nationalism, Nehru-style. Our India, with its Japanese connection and anti-Western ways, carried the nameless aroma of treason' (1996: 160).

14. See also Gupta (1996).

REFERENCES

Appadurai, Arjun, 1996, *Modernity at Large: Cultural Dimensions of Globalization*, Minneapolis: University of Minnesota.

Appadurai, Arjun and Carol A. Breckenridge, 1988, 'Why Public Culture?' *Public Culture*, 1(1): 5–10.

———, 1995, 'Public Modernity in India', in Carol A. Breckenridge (ed.), *Consuming Modernity*, Delhi: Oxford University Press.

Baker, Houston A., 1987, *Modernism and the Harlem Renaissance*, Chicago: University of Chicago Press.

Bann, Stephen, 1989, *The True Vine: On Visual Representation in the Western Tradition*, Cambridge: Cambridge University Press.

Bhabha, Homi K., 1994, *The Location of Culture*, London: Routledge.

Bharucha, Rustom, 1993, *The Question of Faith*, Delhi: Orient Longman.

———, 1997, 'When "Eternal India" Meets the YPO', *Third Text* 39: 39–58.

———, 1998, 'The Shifting Sites of Secularism: Cultural Politics and Activism in India Today', *EPW*, 24 January: 167–80.

Bourdieu, Pierre, 1984, *Distinction: A Social Critique of the Judgement of Taste*, trans. Richard Nice, London: Routledge.

Breckenridge, Carol A., 1988, 'Editor's Comments', *Public Culture* 1(1): 1–4.

Buck-Morss, Susan, 1992, 'Aesthetics and Anaesthetics: Walter Benjamin's Artwork Essay Reconsidered', *October* 62: 3–41.

Burke, Peter, 1976, 'Oblique Approaches to the History of Popular Culture', in C.W.E. Bigsby (ed.), *Approaches to Popular Culture*, London: Edward Arnold.

————, 1979, *Popular Culture in Early Modern Europe*, London: Temple Smith.

Chakravarty, Sumita S., 1996, *National Identity in Indian Popular Cinema: 1947–87*, Delhi: Oxford University Press.

Chambers, Iain, 1986, *Popular Culture: The Metropolitan Experience*, London: Methuen

Chatterjee, Partha, 1992, 'A Religion of Urban Domesticity: Sri Ramakrishna and the Calcutta Middle Class', in P. Chatterjee and G. Pandey (eds), *Subaltern Studies VII*, Delhi: Oxford University: 40–68.

Crapanzano, Vincent, 1986, 'Hermes' Dilemma: The Masking of Subversion in Ethnographic Description', in James Clifford and George E. Marcus (eds), *Writing Culture: The Poetics and Politics of Ethnography*, Berkeley: University of California Press: 51–76.

Dickey, Sara, 1995, 'Consuming Utopia: Watching Film in Tamil Nadu', in Carol A. Breckenridge (ed.), *Consuming Modernity: Public Culture in a South Asian World*, Minneapolis: University of Minnesota Press: 131–56.

Dwyer, Rachel, 2000, *All You Want Is Money. All You Need Is Love: Sex and Romance in Modern India*, London: Cassell.

Efimova, All, 1997, ' "To Touch on the Raw": The Aesthetic Affections of Socialist Realism', *Art Journal*: 72–9.

Featherstone, Mike (ed.), 1990, *Global Culture: Nationalism, Globalization and Modernity*, London: Sage.

Frisy, David, 1985, *Fragments of Modernity: Theories of Modernity in the Work of Simmel, Kracauer and Benjamin*, Oxford: Polity.

Grosz, Elizabeth, 1994, *Volatile Bodies: Towards a Corporeal Feminism*, Sydney: Allen and Unwin.

Guha, Ranajit, 1997, *Dominance without Hegemony: History and Power in Colonial India*, Cambridge, Mass.: Harvard University Press.

Gupta, Kanchan, 1996, 'Subhas Chandra Bose as a Mascot of Hindutva', in *BJP Today*, 1–15 May 1996 (also available on the BJP home page at www.bjp.org/history/htv-netaji.html).

Hall, Stuart, 1997, 'Notes on Deconstructing "the Popular" ', in John Storey (ed.), *Cultural Theory and Popular Culture: A Reader*, New York: Prentice Hall: 455–66.

Hannerz, Ulf, 1992, *Cultural Complexity: Studies in the Social Organization of Meaning*, New York: Columbia University Press.

Hans, Raj Kumar, 1998, 'Punjabi Press and Immigrant Culture in British Columbia between Wars', *EPW*, 18 April: 885–8.

Haskell, Francis, 1993, *History and Its Images*, New Haven: Yale University Press.

Jameson, Frederic, 1979, 'Reification and Utopia in Mass-Culture', *Social Text*, 1: 130–48.

Kaviraj, Sudipta, 1997, 'Filth and the Public Sphere: Concepts and Practices about Space in Calcutta', *Public Culture*, 10(1): 83–114.

Khilnani, Sunil, 1997, *The Idea of India*, Harmondsworth: Penguin.

Larkin, Brian, 1997, 'Indian Films and Nigerian Lovers: Media and the Creation of Parallel Modernities', *Africa*, 67(3): 406–40.

Marriott, McKim (ed.), 1955, *Village India: Studies in the Little Community*, Chicago: University of Chicago Press.

Mbembe, Achille, 1992, 'The Banality of Power and the Aesthetics of Vulgarity in the Postcolony', *Public Culture*, 4(2): 1–30.

Meehan, Johanna (ed.), 1995, *Feminists Read Habermas: Gendering the Subject of Discourse*, Routledge: New York.

Miller, Daniel, 1987, *Material Culture and Mass Consumption*, Oxford: Blackwell.

Mitchell, W.J.T., 1996, 'What Do Pictures Really Want?' *October* 77: 71–82.

Nag, Dulali, 1998, 'Love in the Time of Nationalism: Bengali Popular Films from the 1950s', *EPW*, 4 April: 779–87.

Nandy, Ashis, 1995, *The Savage Freud and Other Essays on Possible and Retrievable Selves*, Delhi: Oxford University Press.

Niranjana, Tejaswini and S.V. Srinivas, 1996, 'Managing the Crisis: *Bharateeyudu* and the Ambivalence of Being "Indian" ', *EPW*, 30 November: 3129–34.

O'Shea, Alan and Bill Schwarz, 1987, 'Reconsidering Popular Culture', *Screen*, 28(3): 104–9.

Pandian, M.S.S., 1996, 'Tamil Cultural Elites and Cinema: Outline of an Argument', *EPW*, 13 April: 950–5.

Pinney, Christopher, 1995, 'Hindi Cinema and Half-Forgotten Dialects: An Interview with Ashis Nandy', *Visual Anthropology Review*, 11(2): 7–16.

———, 1997a, *Camera Indica: The Social Life of Indian Photographs*, London: Reaktion Books.

———, 1997b, 'The Nation (Un) Pictured? Chromolithography and "Popular" Politics in India, 1878–1995', *Critical Inquiry*, 23: 834–67.

Poole, Deborah, 1997, *Vision, Race and Modernity: A Visual Economy of the Andean Image World*, Princeton, N.J.: Princeton University Press.

Sarda, Harbilas, 1954, *Shyamji Krishna Varma: Patriot and Perfect* [sic], Ajmer: Vedic Yantralaya.

Sengupta, Shuddhabrata, 1997, 'Identity Card and India Ink', *India Magazine*, May: 8–13.

Silverstone, Roger, 1994, *Television and Everyday Life*, London: Routledge.

Singh, Kushwant and Satindra Singh, 1966, *Ghadar 1915: India's First Armed Revolution*, New Delhi: R&K Publishing House.

Spink, Walter, 1978, 'The Ecology of Art: India and the West', in Mahadev L. Apte (ed.), *Mass Culture, Language and Arts in India*, Bombay: Popular Prakashan.

Thapar, Raj, 1991, *All These Years*, New Delhi: Penguin India.

Thomas, Rosie, 1990, 'Sanctity and Scandal in *Mother India*', *Quarterly Review of Film and Video*.

Vasudev, Arun (ed.), 1995, *Frames of Mind: Reflections on Indian Cinema*, New Delhi: UBSDD.

Visram, Rozina, 1986, *Ayahs, Lascars and Princes: Indians in Britain 1700–1947*, London: Pluto Press.

Visions of the Nation
Theorizing the Nexus between Creation, Consumption, and Participation in the Public Sphere[1]

SANDRIA B. FREITAG

Introduction: Theorizing the Role of the Visual

POWERFULLY EVOCATIVE VISIONS of the nation dominated the anti-imperial discourse of late nineteenth- and early twentieth-century British India. In the forms of posters, photographs, statuary, and, especially, live enactments in public spaces, South Asians explored and created a new visual vocabulary to express their alternative understandings of the world they inhabited. Yet historians have been astonishingly slow to theorize beyond the role of print in their efforts to interpret this complex past. They have treated the immensely rich visual primary-source materials simply as accompanying illustration for a narrative drawn solely from textual evidence.

This chapter is part of a larger examination that I have begun of the emergence over the late nineteenth and early twentieth centuries of a visual vocabulary of the nation in colonial South Asia. Although absurdly ambitious in its scope, I hope to compare a variety of visual media in order to explore new theoretical approaches to nationalism. Further, by relating the relatively new media of photography, poster art, and cinema to the established fount of live performance—with which they shared the visual vocabulary under study here—we can move beyond theoretical frameworks to beginning understandings about how this visual vocabulary worked to forge a sense of imagined community,[2] the basis for participation in the public sphere as well as the emergence of nationalist rhetoric. This then gives us an entrée to contemporary events as well.

For purposes of efficiency here, we must take as given many of the helpful advances made by recent scholarship on the nature of the public sphere[3] and the role assigned to civil society within it.[4] We will use as our working definition that provided by Charles Taylor, in which 'civil society in this sense exists over and against the state, in partial independence from it'. Its importance derives most, perhaps, from what it remains aloof from—'it includes those dimensions of social life which cannot be confounded with, or swallowed up in the state', on the one hand, and it is 'not the private sphere', on the other. At the heart of civil society lies the exercise of 'public opinion'—a notion that arose with the rise of modernity, in which issues 'commonly recognized as of common concern' are sharply debated (Taylor 1990). For civil society to operate effectively, information (in theory, at least) had to circulate freely and be equally accessible to all participants. Information did not, of course, emerge value-free and objective in form: it was created and circulated by interested parties in ways that attempted to persuade as well as elucidate. Located within the contestation inherent in this generation of information is the confluence of visual materials related to live performance, photography, posters, and cinema.

We must also beg treating in any detail the various aspects of the emergence of modernity that are equally important for our purposes, particularly the interrelated developments of western industrialization, global capitalism (in this early, imperial guise), and consumer culture. We will certainly touch on the technological developments that enabled mass production of visual media, and it will become obvious that these only became accessible through the action of a capitalism that linked far-flung parts of the globe. Most central to our discussion here, however, is the emergence of acts of consumption of popular culture artefacts, based as they are on 'the consumer's attachment of inner feelings to objects, and to his consequent ability to shape his own identity through the process of buying (consuming) those objects' (Gilmartin 1991: 130, n.10).[5]

Consumption as an act of identity formation lies, then, at the heart of our study; it directs our attention to the nexus between consumption and nationalism. Overlapping circles of activity at the turn of the century in British India, consumption and nationalism each prompted individuals to make choices that allied them with others—others who could be defined equally through these creative identity choices as fellow members of an ambiguously delineated but nevertheless shared group. The relationship of these developments in consumption and nationalism to changes taking place within the exercise and understanding of South Asian religion will emerge as crucial to our understanding—but this is a subject to which we will return later.

Analysts have had great fun in working through literary and architectural source materials for the emergence of consumer culture in turn-of-the-century France, especially the staging of world expositions to sell the goods of the world; the creation of underground shopping arcades to foster 'window-shopping' (to use the Americanism); the emergence of the bourgeois cultural world of the *flâneur* (urban stroller); and the development of the department store to provide a safe haven for the female shopper (see for instance Friedberg 1993; Williams 1982). Unfortunately for those of us interested in other parts of the world, the discoveries made by these scholars have been taken as an inevitable series of building blocks from the modern to the postmodern in ways that seldom make room for other norms or practices of cultural consumption.[6] Since these other practices may very well have emerged as oppositional forms to the metropolitan practices uncovered for industrialized/imperial France and England, it seems important to unpack the ways in which developments did or did not emerge in similar forms under the sway of global capitalism.

I want to argue here, for instance, that consumption as a practice defining individuals and groups in British India was a dialogic process that drew on several distinct sources, including indigenous forms of popular participation in public life as well as metropolitan forms of production. The ways in which consumption interacted with nationalism in this dialogic context simultaneously built on Indian forms of popular participation, especially in civic ceremonials, and imperial political institutions that rested on a metropolitan distinction (singularly incapable of being sustained in India) between public and private spheres. This argument will be explored in more detail when we return to a discussion of the three genres of visual media emerging at the turn of the century.

Beyond the Usual Eurocentric Analytical Framework

The purpose of this chapter is to begin theorizing about the role of the visual as an essential building block in shaping nationalism and other aspects of the modern world as emerged in colonized parts of the globe. To do this requires us to look with new eyes at the processes that have been analysed so exhaustively over the last few years. The analytical model provided by

Benedict Anderson may stand in for much of the work done on nationalism. In Anderson's model, the 'two forms of imagining which first flowered in Europe in the eighteenth century' were 'the novel and the newspaper'; these forms 'provided the technical means for 're-presenting' the *kind* of imagined community that is the nation'(Anderson 1991: 24–5).[7] These two forms proved important first, because of their form (print) and second, for their ease in reproduction (print capitalism). As print, both provided access to the same information for any number of readers/consumers, thus serving to link many individuals within the same imagined boundaries of the knowable and the known. To the extent that not just nationalism but the very exercise of civil society is generally assumed to rest on access to print information, we may also see implications in this Eurocentric model that from these shared sources flowed the information necessary to form public opinion, and the capacity of informed civil society to exercise surveillance over the state.[8]

Extending this model to its logical conclusions, Partha Chatterjee asked whether South Asian nationalism provided nothing more than a 'derivative discourse' dependent on western scientific rationalism for its intellectual underpinnings (Chatterjee 1986). Expanding this argument in his following book, Chatterjee traces this problematically derivative nature to the fact that the hegemonic frame for shaping the imagined community in post-colonial India is its intrinsic relationship (even if defined in opposition) to the Eurocentric model (Chatterjee 1993: e.g. p. 5). Chatterjee, too, looks at the forms of print capitalism that enable this culture of difference to emerge as the rallying cry for nationalism.

But few historians have looked beyond the printed text. Even the more innovative examinations of political activity have been curiously limited in their scope. A study of the 'public culture' of colonial Surat, for instance, analyses civic ritual, but does so from newspaper sources and assumes that the focal point must, by definition, be limited to those 'rituals' invented by the British (Haynes 1991: chapter 7). Similarly, work by one of the leading subaltern scholars seeks to move beyond traditional sources and into popular culture but, once again, relies predominantly on print materials (Pandey 1994).

Two recent theorizing innovations have made small steps away from print. In the first innovation, the links between reading, print, and orality have begun to be explored quite systematically. The most obvious implication of these links is the patterning of printed information along lines first shaped when information was retained through oral processes.[9] Broader in its applicability under this first innovation has been the recognition that even printed texts are not only read aloud, but that this exercise opens up other public and collective possibilities: 'reading in groups not only offers occasions for explicitly collective textual interpretation, but encourages new forms of association, and nurtures new ideas that are developed in conversation with other people as well as with books . . .;' this kind of 'social and intellectual empowerment . . . has had consequences in the realm of social action as well as ideas' (Long 1993: 194). In the second innovation, Mitchell has attempted to argue that the need in the public sphere for 'visual culture and literacy' is immensely important, and to suggest a methodology applicable to a 'postlinguistic, postsemoitic' society (Mitchell 1994), in which—as Ramaswamy has put it—central to the act of imagining a community is the pictorial image, where spectatorship meets creation in 'a complex interplay between visuality, apparatus, institutions, discourse, bodies, and figurality' (Ramaswamy 1994).

There is a third and interesting exploration worth mentioning in this context. Susan Horton's work on Victorian literature (which is probably not alone in charting these directions, but this is a field with which I have little familiarity) makes the argument that, even in the novels of this period, it is *vision* which dominates. She explores many of the scientific and entertainment developments of the period, linking them to a new sense of being an observer and observed subject that begins to orient novels of the period. The exercise of the gaze, that is, becomes textual as well as visual (Horton 1992).

Nevertheless, all of these analytical frames remain rooted in text. I would like to propose instead that we explore a framework that enables us to put the act of seeing at the centre rather than at the periphery of both the world of evidence that we examine and the kind of theorizing we do. There is a range of new theoretical approaches, spawned in several different disciplines including philosophy, art history, and the history of science, that begin to point the way—we will return to these in a later section. Most important to begin with, there are indicators from the sixteenth to the eighteenth centuries (as early modern India emerges) of fundamental experiences that enable Indians to shift the exercise and purpose of their gaze.

Sources for a New Theoretical Frame: South Asian Visual Practices and Processes

Although this work is still very preliminary, I would like to identify at least three realms in which 'visual images are the shapers and bearers of thought' (Eck 1985: 14)[10]—South Asian courtly culture; religious practices, including both the centrality of *darshan* and the special reshaping effected under *bhakti*; and live performance traditions. In each of these realms, visual vocabularies operate not as an extension or transmutation of oral or written words, but as basic building blocks in a process of 'knowing' that is achieved by acquiring and processing information through the eyes. In this section I will discuss the first two realms rather briefly (in the first case because not much work has been done on the subject; in the second, because too much work exists!) and concentrate especially on the third, as live performance serves as the fount for many of the crucial practices and elements of visual vocabulary central to the new media that emerged at the turn of the century.

Courtly Culture

Although little studied, the opportunity to gaze upon the king is recognized as an essential element in, for instance, Vijayanagara royal practice (Michell 1992, Stein 1989). Opportunities to gaze were provided both in the annual peregrinations of the ruler and in the elements in the Mahanavami Festival (developed as an integrative public ceremony staged annually at the capital). Significantly, processions functioned at the heart of these exercises: they not only provided occasions for physically integrating different constituencies within the same ceremonial whole, but also created the moment when ruled and ruler could exchange gazes. Justification for such practices harked back, usually, to the Cola period. Mughal adoption of the concept is related to earlier Hindu practices and, significantly, becomes concretized in the architectural detail included in each Mughal palace of the *jharoka-i daulat khana khass o 'amm 'amm* (ceremonial viewing balcony in the Public Audience Hall). That Aurangzeb discontinued the practice of appearing three times a day for the gaze of the public was regarded as a significant policy decision, marking a rejection of the distinctive Indo-Persian courtly culture created by his predecessors (see especially Asher 1992: xxvii, 253; 1995).

These visual aspects seem to have adhered as well to practices more often commented upon, such as the holding of daily *durbars* (audience) and, especially, the presentation of *khillat* in the exchange whereby ranked courtiers (*mansabdars*) made offerings (*nazar*) to the king, and the king reciprocated with gifts, usually articles of clothing. The emphasis on the body of the king in this exchange has been commented on both for the Mughals and for the seventeenth–eighteenth century Nayaka rulers in the south (successors to the Vijayanagara tradition); corporality and vision are deeply intertwined in this visual vocabulary.[11] Similar continuities can be traced among the Marathas, who adopted many Mughal practices.[12]

That performers served as central figures in each king's party at court also seems relevant in this context. The implications of live performance for communicating ideological positions will be explored in greater detail below. Here it may suffice to note that, with the king (or, in regional, sub-imperial centres, the king's chiefly supporters) serving as patron of performing artists, the messages conveyed in these performances proved particularly important. Including dancers, musicians, singers, and poets, these court parties of artists visually conveyed—in a vocabulary related to but often quite distinct from the written texts produced in these same circumstances—the values advanced by the ruling dynasty (Narayana Rao *et al.* 1992; Ramanujan *et al.* 1994; Erdman 1985).

What these various aspects of courtly culture suggest is that vision, and the exercise of the gaze as it became connected to royalty, set up certain expectations about the relationship between the font of power and the audience. Only the ruler could trigger the exercise of the gaze, but without the audience's physical proximity, he could not put the expected action into play. The exercise of vision in these circumstances also had a transactional quality: power was both reinforced and acceded and, in the process, partaken of; goods (both actual and notional) were exchanged; the exercise of the gaze became part of an integrative ceremonial process embedded with meaning (and, conceivably, layered with meanings that differed for each participant).

For the nineteenth century, and certainly by the turn of the century, these royal perquisites had become internalized in a society in which the rights accruing to patronage had devolved to lower levels in society. As other studies have shown (Freitag 1989a; Lutgendorf 1993; Bayly 1983; Freitag 1989b), patronage had first been taken up by the courtiers dispersed throughout urban centres and to regional successor state centres. Other urban leaders too (especially Hindu merchants), as part of their exercise of corporate control over local society, had taken up the responsibilities inherent in the role of patron. And, finally, by the late nineteenth century, popular patronage in the form of broad-based local participation in these visual opportunities had taken over increasingly large proportions of kingly perquisites. Necessarily these are all shorthand observations that deserve much greater exploration, but this must suffice for the moment. The implications of these changes will be explored in greater detail later in the chapter.

Religious Practices

Darshan and *bhakti* provide the central religious concepts/practices that illuminate the exercise of vision for our purposes. Myriad volumes have been devoted to these subjects; our task here is to treat them briefly in ways that underscore their significance in providing basic understandings and practices that become adapted to new media and new purposes under the expansion of mass media and its consumption.

Darshan, 'seeing the divine in an image, in a person, or in a set of ideas' emphasizes 'the interdependence of the visual and intellectual' (McDermott and Buck's introduction to Eck 1985). Indeed, 'the central act of Hindu worship from the point of view of the lay person', Eck tells us, 'is to stand in the presence of the deity and to behold the image with one's own eyes, to see and be seen by the deity. . . . Beholding the image is an act of worship, and through the eyes one gains the blessings of the divine' (Eck 1985: 3). Not just images, but places possess *darshan*, as do holy persons (*sants, sadhus,* and *sannyasins*). This is a mutual gaze: even as the believer sees the image, the image sees as well. And as with royalty, initiation of this mutual relationship is activated by the benevolence of the powerholder, the deity. But, dialogically, viewers must enables an image to see, through the application of specific ceremonies. Indeed, the deity's eyes must be 'opened' for the image to have sacral properties.[13]

That the exercise of the gaze in this respect gains one access to knowledge, that seeing 'is a form of knowing', underscores for us the importance of *darshan* in helping to create 'a basic cultural vocabulary and a common idiom of discourse' that rests on the visual (Eck 1985: 17). Eck explains that this is so, because two principal attitudes are embedded in the treatment of images—first, the image serves 'primarily [as] a focus for concentration'; second, the image is 'the embodiment of the divine' (Eck 1985: 45). Both aspects carry significant implications for our purposes. The processes of 'knowing' that relied on a visual focus for concentration became thoroughly adapted by the late nineteenth century to the needs of an emerging nationalism. Shorthand images such as that of the domestic goddess Saraswati, carried multiple meanings (just as a single sacred image had) that simultaneously conveyed a sense of the new nationalist home and its functions as a site of the individualized believer/participant in civil society (see section on posters, later). At the same time, the image as embodiment in the nationalist home became much more ubiquitous as two-dimensional images were mass produced and consumed. The meaning so embodied began to change in this period, just as the scale of consumption increased dramatically, and the increasingly individualized exercise of the gaze took on new functions.

Facilitating this shift, in part, was the connection between *darshan* and worship (*puja*). While puja could mean the elaborate rituals performed by priests in temples, it also included—more importantly for our purposes—'the simple lay rites of making offerings of flower and water, and receiving

both *darshan*, the "sight" of the deity, and *prasad*, the sanctified food offerings' (Eck 1985: 47). In the elaboration and extension of these simple lay
rites, performed by individuals at home in front of mass-produced posters
and images and without intermediaries, we may read a larger history that
connects important religious change with the capacity to invest new meaning and new fonts of authority in consumer products and their use by
individuals. At the heart of this innovation lay the continuing but refined
application of the gaze.

The shift to a conflation between consumption and religious exercise
was also facilitated in part by the expansion of *bhakti* (devotionalism).
'*Bhakti* comes from a Sanskrit verb which means "to share", and *bhakti*
is relational love, shared by both God and the devotee.' Significantly, the
saints of the *bhakti* movements (both modern and medieval) 'were, to a
great extent, anti-establishment figures who often championed the downtrodden and untouchables and despised brahmanical ritualism' (Eck 1985:
48, 71). This no doubt helps to explain the popularity, for instance, of religious posters among low-caste and untouchable groups.

Embedded in the Sanskrit word is also the notion of participation (Hess
1983: 173). Thus devotional religious modes—with their twin meanings of
devotion and participation—provided a special place for, and attributed
importance to, the acts of individuals in relation to larger constitutive entities. Within the very understanding of the nature of *bhakti*, then, were
brought together both the new emphasis on the individual as consumer of
religious and nationalist symbols, and the larger communities being constituted from collective acts staged by myriad such individuals. To understand
the nature of such collective acts, however, we must examine the contribution
made by live performance, particularly through public processions.

Live Performance
Public performances, at the turn of the century, were an expanding form of
urban visual communication. Privately organized performances often took
place in public spaces such as bazaars, street corners, open fields; these included street theatre, popular musical performances, textual exegesis, and
wrestling. Alongside such privately organized efforts were civic ceremonials,
ranging from local festivals staged in open squares and through urban
streets, to temple or mosque-based processions. Indeed, the distinction
between private and public observances was especially blurred for performance genres at this time—blurred in terms of patronage patterns, ideological
messages, and patterns of consumption (i.e. the interaction of performers
and audience).

As we have noted, a profound shift in the nature of patronage for such performances helps to explain why live enactments played such a key role at this time. In the eighteenth and early nineteenth centuries, patronage had moved from the regional courts that had succeeded the Mughals in the north and the Nayaka kingdoms in the south, to those increasingly responsible for local order and self-regulation in the larger cities, merchants and displaced courtiers. Those closer to popular culture—e.g. the heads of occupational groupings and neighbourhood or temple associations—began reshaping urban civic ceremonials and allied performance pieces toward the end of the century. This shift consolidated in ways becoming quite discernible by the early twentieth century, so that patronage increasingly resided in the consumers of the performances—the audience itself. Indeed, the unique tension that existed at the turn of the century between the influence of individual, wealthy patrons and the impact of the taste and values of middle- and lower-class/ -caste consumers must be seen as one of the most important alterations under way in this period, often affecting the kinds of ideological movements that emerged (e.g. the Cow Protection Movement).[14]

At the same time, we may discern an expansion in the use of *akhara* or *gharana* relationships to structure these privately organized performances (in which the leader, or *guru*, trained his *chelas* in a relationship based on absolute discipline and submission). From bands of musicians, the form came also to be used by wrestlers, acting troupes, and even physicians.[15] The *akhara* relationship provided a way not only to train new performers, but also to settle each year on a unique repertoire, and to establish a corporate image for the band of performers that was especially useful when competing against other troupes. The importance of competition, and the role played by the audience in these performances, cannot be overstated in its significance for our purposes here. Both street theatre troupes and folk/popular music *akhars*, for instance, usually set up competitions in open spaces, in which each group performed on a platform. First, the audience faced one group and then turned to face the other as they performed; at the end, the audience decided who had 'won' this contest. The various entertainment ploys by which the performing groups established links to the audience, in order to win its approval, ranged from creating lyrics or dramatic spoken asides that incorporated locally significant events and people, to public announcements of appreciation for financial contributions just made by members of the audience. Both the direct financial support, and the 'votes' cast regarding artistic merit, put the consumers in powerfully influential positions to shape artistic output. Consumption, in this context then, involved face-to-face participation by active observers, whose powerful gaze helped shape the content and pronounced on the quality of the art produced.

What was 'shaped' in this manner encompassed both subject matter and performance aesthetics. Subject matter is a complex issue that I will only be able to treat properly when the study is further along. Certainly it varied from region to region, but let us look briefly at characteristics identified by analysis of performances in the Bhojpur region of north India. *Svang* (a musical form of street theatre 'featuring full-throated male singers, loud, arousing drumming on kettledrums, and dancing by female impersonators') focused on stories of 'famous devotees', but also included historical stories about particular kings, or romances involving princesses and others. In the shift from saintly figures to romances, Hansen sees a new emphasis on victory in love and war. Although staged in public spaces using spontaneous and informal behaviour viewed as 'lewd and lascivious' by the middle classes, in fact *svang* messages were very conservative: they presented a 'highly moral universe, where good deeds and truthfulness are rewarded by the gods (*Raja Harischandra*); where kings yearn to become saints (*Gopichand Bharthari*); where even children are capable of exemplary devotion (*Prahlad, Dharu*). (Hansen 1989; Hansen 1991) Subject matter, then, reinforced the notion of active devotionalism and linked this with ultimate victory for a shared ideology.

No doubt this emphasis on activism in support of belief was reinforced by the aesthetics of live performance. In analysing two public song genres for this same cultural region, for instance, E.O. Henry noted that the most highly valued characteristic was the lyric and story of a song (rather than performance skill). Moreover, to the extent that skill was noted by members of the audience, it was judged primarily in the singer's ability 'to generate strong emotional response in the listener' (Henry 1988: 216–17). The consumer, in this context, expected to be implicated in the performance, and 'skill' was measured in the ability to achieve this goal. Yet the capacity of live performance to prompt strong responses did not depend on elaborate staging, relying more on costuming and make-up than on props or stage sets. Particular colours came to be identified with certain characters or personality traits (e.g. 'murky colours are appropriate for demonic beings': in Ram's story, the antagonist Ravana and 'his henchmen are seen in blue and black clothing' and the demons' armies have their faces blackened with soot, while Ravana's ten-headedness is always indicated). In general, the costuming conveys lushness and wealth for heroic figures (e.g. Ram wears gold-trimmed robes of rich red velvet and a distinctive headdress of gold; Sita wears a conventional but expensive sari and her special tiara; 'under the powerful illumination the silver and glass of their crowns glitter like stars', Hein 1972: 88, 20). Nevertheless, the fact that innovation played an important part in performance enabled these conventions to be harnessed to issues of local and immediate import, and was used by actors to convey emotion for new causes and figures.

Civic ceremonials occupied this same universe. In the list made by one scholar of performance genres presented annually in the north Indian pilgrimage centre of Mathura, for instance, the five forms included *jhanki* (tableau of living deities exhibited for worship and presented by travelling troupes); *kathak* (solo performance by a specialist 'which illuminates the words of narrative songs with fleeting impersonations and symbolic gestures,' usually performed within a temple complex); *ramlila* (large civic- or neighbourhood-sponsored enactments of Ram's story performed by local amateurs); and *raslila* (composite performance 'which brings together ritual enactment of a central Krishna myth in dance, with semi-operatic performance of any one of a vast number of peripheral stories' in the Krishna cycle, again usually organized on a civic scale by local performers) (Hein 1972: 13). In addition to these genres characteristic of many north India (in some cases, all-India) venues, a variety of local processions and ceremonial occasions also rose and fell in popular enthusiasms over time. Again, these waxing and waning patterns must be linked to the active roles filled by consumers. In the city of Agra, for instance, both a cow procession and expansion of a local festival honouring a swimming teacher emerged during the two tense decades before the turn of the century; these localized ceremonies served as ideological conduits that united urban space, local figures as signs of larger values, and visual imagery—from decorated cows to the devotional costumes donned by young boys.[16] Those who supported the festivals had to make explicit ideological choices and then act on them (this was especially true of the swimming fair, which came to be observed at two different times and in two different formats, stemming from contestations between representatives of two ideological stances). In the course of making these choices, consumers used active participation in the observances to put forward a visual vocabulary of sign and image that supported competing notions of community and values.

It is unfortunate that we lack space to discuss fully the range of live performances, for the connections to two-dimensional visual media are fascinating and astonishingly obvious. To make the point briefly, we shall look at *ramlila* and *jhanki*, two of the genres listed earlier for Mathura. In presenting *lilas*, the 'play' or 'sport' of the gods, residents of most towns and cities across north India staged selected episodes from Ram's story. Sometimes a city would choose to stage a 'complete' *ramlila*, drawing episodes from the entire storyline and designating different parts of the city as the geographical locales in which the action takes place (e.g. Ram's birthplace of Ayodhya,

Ravana's kingdom of Lanka, etc.), at other times particular neighbourhoods would gain fame for staging one particular episode each year. While Tulsidas' vernacular version serves as a touchstone, the story of Ram is an unbounded text, into which interpolations are freely made. Because each production selects out a unique combination of episodes and is controlled locally—financed by small sums contributed from a broad spectrum of society; acted by local boys (*svarups*); costumed and choreographed by amateurs marked by their 'passion' for the *lila*; organized by local devotees—it expresses well the participants' broader ideological concerns regarding the ideal civil society, couched in locally specific terms. Most important, however, was the point that these messages could change, depending on who controlled the decision-making that shaped the *lila*. Ambiguity and multiple meanings were carried especially well by this genre because it included several tellings of the same event: reciters repeated verses from Tulsi's poetry; the *svarups* enacted with broad gestures; many scenes would be replayed with gigantic paper replicas that torched for a dramatic climax.

On the face of it, *jhanki* might appear to differ significantly from *lilas*. In these tableaux vivants, the actors make the message accessible to audiences without any assistance from written text or oral commentary. For an hour and a half to two hours, actors are displayed in a single scene that has to carry within it its own narrative and signification. In Mathura, for example, Ram and Sita sit in state as though holding a typical ruler's 'durbar'. In Banaras, the reunion of Ram with his brother Bharat is enacted.

> *Jhanki* thrives in a little frequented frontier of representational art where drama and image worship meet . . . Witnessing the display can become a form of *puja* for the Vaishnava because of his belief that an actor, while wearing the special costume and crown of a god or goddess, is not merely the living similitude of the deity represented, but is in fact the abode of that divinity. . . . The very name *jhanki*, meaning 'a view, a glance' has a special religious sense and refers to the fact that in the drama the devotee sees physically the god of his devotion [Hein 1972: 17–18].

As we shall see, not only the signs and symbols of this performance genre, but the very relationship between viewer and vision will be transferred to two-dimensional form when 'god-posters' emerge as a new consumable.

Perhaps the most crucial aspect of live performance, however, was the central role assigned to movement and to audience participation in that movement. Processions moved the action from one locale in *ramlila* to another; processions accompanied Ram and Bharat as they moved to meet in a large field in Banaras. A wide variety of liminal and structural purposes

were served by these processions, which united urban places and their participants. Given our theoretical interests, we may focus here on the mobility
of the viewer/ participant, and the ability of the mobile viewer's gaze to consume both concentrated and diffused visual messages. This mobility inherent
in the very nature of performance was echoed, significantly, in the two
other major South Asian forms of participatory 'entertainment', pilgrimage
and tourism. Although there is no space here to explore the interconnections,
we should at least note them and the general trend toward the mobile gaze
that became expanded at the turn of the century.

Thus it is the gaze every bit as much as it is printed text that provides information and serves as the basis for individual choice (and motivation for
action) as consumer society expands in the later part of the nineteenth century. We have noted in passing the devolution of patronage from royal
courts to new intermediary/middle classes and thence to popular audiences.
Through the consumption of goods as well as experiences (souvenirs from
pilgrimage; posters for use in domestic spaces; participation as members of
processions or audiences who decided the 'winners' of musical performances-
cum-contestations), an ever-broader public focused its gaze upon visual
vocabulary that expressed increasingly complex notions about civil society
and its relationship to the state.

In ways different from but akin to developments in the metropoles, the
social formations of modernity therefore became increasingly mediated
through the image. The centrality of the procession in Indian civic life
would have guaranteed this development in any case; participation in the
polity had long been linked to active interaction with patrons and their
local deities paraded through urban streets. As contestation about the values
and meaning of modern life increased, so too did civic ceremonials that pitted one worldview against another, one group of local notables against
another. But the ways in which civic and religious stories were told through
enactment (e.g. *ramlila* and Muharram in the north) expanded in this
period, and the expansion incorporated ever-larger roles for images and
visual vocabulary.

In these and similar developments we may trace a changing exercise of
the gaze in early modern South Asia. Vision thus operated at the centre of
a number of public activities, all of which became available for transformation
in the service of nationalism and the operation of a specially shaped civil
society under imperial rule. As the mobile gaze[17] expanded its repertoire, it
also began to envelop a range of new materials and technologies brought to
the subcontinent under the impulse of the global market made possible by
imperialism. For our purposes, the crucial linkage in nineteenth-century

India brought together previous exercises of the gaze with a dramatically increased scale of consumption made possible by India's place in a global market. The nexus between consumption and nationalism thus makes important for India the kind of reformulations under way in Europe around a new emphasis on ocularcentricity.

Sources for a New Theoretical Frame:
New Consumption in the Global Market

Philosophers and intellectual historians have begun to examine what they call the 'ocularcentricity' or the 'epistemological privileging of vision that begins at least as early as Plato's notion that ethical universals must be accessible to "the mind's eye" and continues with the Renaissance, the invention of printing, and the development of the modern sciences' (Levin, 'Introduction' in Levin 1993). For Heidegger, the modern period is distinguishable from its Greek beginnings in the nature of its ocularcentricity, as 'in this "new epoch" the ocular subject finally becomes the ultimate source of all being—and the reference point for all measurements, all calculations of the *value* of being'. Similarly, for Foucault, the 'ontological reductionism' of modernity yielded a 'modern hegemony of vision, modern technology, and modern forms of governmentality': within the exercise of the gaze thus became united 'the technologies of production, the technologies of sign systems, the technologies of power [and] the technologies of the self'.[18] Vision thus rested at the centre of many western philosophic explorations over the last century (including—beyond Heidegger and Foucault—Hegel, Nietzsche, Sartre, Merleau-Ponty, Derrida, and Benjamin).

In any case, the centrality of vision and the impact of the gaze certainly came to the subcontinent in this guise, in the train of western industrialization. The fit, while not perfect, displayed a reasonable convergence. As we have noted, rather than the *flâneur* it is the processionist who takes centre stage in this South Asian history of the 'mobilized gaze'. And, as Anne Friedberg has noted, 'forms of commodified visual mobility, once only available in the imperial cities of the first world, gradually became a global standard of modernity,' so that developments emerging from local culture in the subcontinent became reinforced under the expansion of consumer society (Friedberg 1993: 4). Indeed, 'the second half of the nineteenth century lives in a sort of frenzy of the visible. It is, of course, the effect of the social multiplications of images . . . the effect also, however, of something of a geographical extension of the field of the visible and the representable: by journeys, explorations, colonizations, the whole world becomes visible at the same time that it becomes appropriatable.'[19] Taken together, then, these influences created (particularly in the increasingly urbanized spaces that began to dominate colonial India in the last half of the nineteenth century) cultural contexts for 'commodified forms of looking [linked to . . .] the experiences of spatial and temporal mobility' (Friedberg 1993: 7), and resulting in the 'mobilized gaze' of a consuming public. The philosophical and consumption aspects of the exercise of the gaze are related more than coincidentally. The developments of the nineteenth century may be characterized, as Jay (1993) has put it, as a 'spectatorial and intellectualist epistemology based on a subjective self reflecting on an objective world exterior to it'.

The philosophical and consumer implications of the exercise of the power of the gaze thus lie at the heart of my argument, and it is worth taking a moment to explore these implications for studies of the visual in popular culture. Much has been made in the history of imperialism (as in the history of modernity) of the emergence of the 'panoptican gaze'—by which Foucault meant the overpowering of the positivist tendencies (described above by Jay) through a process by which vision became supervision, and in which governmentality (organized by supervision) emerged as the prime force in society. But if we examine the evidence from colonial India, I think we discover that the result of the complex new developments—related to philosophical reinterpretations of how the world worked and linked to the development of a consumer culture—was a gaze that simultaneously shaped and reflected; it was at once both a 'panoptican gaze' and a 'mobilized gaze'. That is, governmental supervision was quite successfully *contested* by the surveillance exercised by civil society.[20]

Such surveillance, nourished by the flow of information and functioning through the expression of public opinion, became integrally linked to the exercise of consumption. In South Asia, this exercise of consumption linked the new global focus of the consumer's gaze with local visual practices in new ways. The empowerment of alternative interpretations, based on new information presented and consumed visually, pushed back against the state. Consequently, this alternative gaze is not constrained by the panoptical capacities of those in power; on the contrary, it gains its force by the very nature of its mobility—its capacity to encompass within its frame a wide range of viewer-defined materials and values; its ability through movement to incorporate many practices and practitioners; its rejection of a single orthodoxy or sociology of knowledge in favour of an ambiguous and unbounded sense of the whole. Perhaps most significant for our purposes, the mobile gaze that emerged from aggregate acts of consumption could not be controlled by the didactic or ideological desires of the state: composed of a series of individual choices, these aggregated acts added up to a different vision of the nation than that advanced either by middle-class anti-imperial ideologues, or later by the nation state itself. We will return to the implications of this alternative gaze when we discuss the three emerging mass media; for the moment, let us continue our examination of late-nineteenth-century developments for the context they provide.

This emphasis on the gaze of the consumer is hardly surprising, as vision and the eye also loomed large in scientific discovery in this period. The impact of 'science' was, however, quite ambiguous. On the one hand, this was the era of rampant social Darwinism, when 'scientific observation' became the bedrock for much of the social science construction of knowledge— within which knowledge could be divided up into small and isolatable bits that, once captured, could be recombined and reconfigured for a variety of pseudoscientific end-purposes.[21] In the train of this influence, the eye and observation became reliable sources of information that structured the sociology of knowledge about the universe. On the other hand, a number of scientific discoveries of the period put the information provided by the eye in doubt. By mid century, for instance, the earlier experiments of Goethe on the physiology of the eye had become common knowledge through translation and biography; the lesson Goethe drew from these experiments was that the information received by the brain through the eye depended not on the nature of the external object being observed, but on the nature of the sensory nerves that processed the information.[22] This new 'science of optics', then, simultaneously 'augment[ed] the power and prestige of vision' while it underscored the 'deceptiveness' of vision, and the inherent danger that perception could unduly affect reason ('Introduction' to Levin 1993: 9).

The explosion of forms of ocular-based entertainment characteristic of this period rested most often on a similar tension, in this case between verisimilitude and the deceived eye. This is not surprising, since they were (in the words of an art historian) embedded 'in a much larger and denser organization of knowledge and of the observing subject'.[23] Under the diffusion possible through global capitalism, these forms of entertainment through export directly connected metropole and colonies. Such entertainment included the panorama, diorama, eventually the camera obscura and magic lantern (as publicly consumed forms), the stereoptican and kaleidoscope (as privately consumed forms), as well as museums and international expositions. Panoramas presented oversized 360-degree paintings, specially lighted; they filled a building and managed, optically, to 'transport' a viewer (through an '*imaginary* illusion of mobility') to another place and/or time, thus providing 'a spatial and temporal mobility—if only a "virtual" one'. With this new sense of time and place, the panorama could become 'the bourgeois public's substitute for the Grand Tour'. (In this respect, it is important to note that representation in the panorama rested on a new sense of perspective, fostered earlier by the overviews discovered in hot-air ballooning, and on immensity in scale made possible by devoting entire buildings to the presentation of panorama paintings.)[24] Louis Jacques Mande Daguerre, who would later invent the photographic process called the daguerreotype, in 1822 introduced into the panorama a new viewing device that manipulated light through a transparent painting. Using a platform that periodically rotated 73 degrees to open up a new scene, the diorama also served to transport viewers in a number of European cities to other imagined places and times. With hand-held devices such as the stereoptican, this ability to be transported to an 'imagined elsewhere' (as Chris Pinney has so aptly phrased it) could be brought home.[25] Christoph Asendorf has argued that what most characterizes these viewing experiences, and links them to the offerings of the museum and exhibition, was the 'encyclopedic offering' of 'social or historical reality' in ways that demanded of the viewer a new way of looking (or absorbing the information on offer)—one that included both concentration and diffusion. Asendorf calls this new way of looking 'a new perceptual task', in which the nervous system had to 'operate selectively and not simply collapse under the assault of impressions' (Asendorf 1993: 47, 61).

Mastering this new perceptual task is what enables the act of consumption, and thence the truly mobile gaze of the consumer. Asendorf implicitly links this development in entertainment and popular culture to the larger context of industrialization and expansion of capitalism, calling our attention to observations by Marx. It is here, Asendorf argues, that we can trace a change in the perception of things, 'now spatially displaced in generalized circulation or under the gaze of the natural sciences and pushed out of the domain of habitual experience. Things no longer inhabit a spatiotemporal continuum but exist only momentarily and in isolation'. For Asendorf, and I would argue for us, it is in this process of changing perception that we can locate the fundamental shift that makes possible the amalgam of nationalism and consumption: 'the transformation of materiality into abstraction'. Thus philosophic, scientific, and commercial interests coalesced around an 'abstraction of the world of things and social relations in commodity circulation'. The reaction was a 'search for new forms of perception and communication' (Asendorf 1993: 5, 6, 192)—and the emergence of the alternative gaze of the mobilized consumer who was also a participant in the public sphere.

Evolution of Mass Consumption Visual Media
in South Asia

Thus two influences converged in late-nineteenth-century South Asia, to emerge in new forms of perception and communication: (1) the material conditions of technological innovation related to print production and how these altered to enable mass consumption; and (2) the visual vocabularies and spectator conventions invoked by previous cultural experiences in exercising the gaze. In the sections that follow we will examine briefly in turn the particular media that generated the shared visual vocabulary about which we theorize. For our purposes, however, the effect these media had in the aggregate matters much more than the developments within a single medium. How did the casting of a mobilized gaze create a shared understanding by participants in the British Indian polity? Chris Pinney has suggested an immensely important element in this process, when he notes that 'popular Indian visual semiosis creates instead what might be termed a sense of the "elsewhere", and it is this—operating within a quite different configuration of cultural factors—which allows many Indians to "think" their nation' (Pinney 1994: 9). The 'instead' to which he refers is an alternative to Anderson's characterization of the process by which the nation becomes imagined; Pinney's argument about the 'imagined elsewhere' embedded in visual representations of community draws our attention to the ambiguity and multivalent possibilities in visual evocation that relies on the viewer's gaze for meaning. That is, single images or icons can carry within them multiple meanings. The fact that they stand as a single representation, however, implies a single and shared meaning. Negotiating this ambiguity becomes the task of the viewer, the assignment of the member of the nation. Viewers brought to this perceptual task a great deal of experience, however—experience gained as active participants in live performance.

Painting and Posters
The decades around the turn of the century are the 'moment' when a popular commercial art, and the mass production of pictures, can be said to have emerged. This new pattern of consumption, in turn, contributed to an expanded sense of the public: this was a public that participated in shaping visual expressions both as critics and as consumers. As the scale of this new market increased alongside technological advances, the interaction between consumer and producer dialogically produced a visual discourse inherently multivocal in its nature. This dialogic process can be traced, for instance, in

the shifts in Calcutta through the one-off Kalighat paintings for pilgrims, to a mass market of printed mythological pictures and cheap book illustrations; and in western India, in the emergence of a new mode of (what has come to be called) 'calendar' or 'pavement' art (for its point of sale), made possible by the new technology of mass lithographic production. Given the work of Guha-Thakurta and Uberoi, I need only note briefly that in both Calcutta and Lonavala (where Ravi Varma eventually settled his lithographic press), artists first mastered a European aesthetic and compositional style: Ravi Varma of Travancore's royal family gained renown for his oil painting (Uberoi 1990: WS42–3; Mitter 1990: 361–7); in Calcutta, graduates of the Government School of Art formed the Calcutta Art Studio, again mastering oil painting and winning awards in 'fine art' exhibitions. But in both places, the 'booming indigenous market for picture prints, and book and magazine illustrations' attracted artists to move from elite to mass cultural production when they could not break through the imperial barriers of the 'high art' world.[26] Thus the dialogic interchange in this process appears to contain at least two parts, in which Indian artists simultaneously made technological breakthroughs to reach a mass audience, *and* tapped into the new avenues of communication that were fostering a middle-class aesthetic.

While the technological changes involved in printing were essential for this dramatic change, the characteristics of oil painting proved crucial as well. (That is, the visual conveyance of messages was not simply in the signification but in the very nature of the medium, as well.) Much has been made of Indian efforts to 'prove themselves' in this distinctly European medium (Guha-Thakurta 1992). But the qualities of oil painting met Indian aesthetic demands as well. Oil painting in the new style 'contained the double allure of colour and tactile illusionism: of the simulation of tones, textures, substance and atmosphere . . . [yielding] the "fleshing out" of gods and goddesses, the "animation" of gestures, the dramatization of episodes . . .' (Guha-Thakurta 1991: WS92). The 'highly tactile means [enable oil painting] to play upon the spectator's sense of acquiring the *real* thing which the image shows' (Berger 1972: 140–1), when the popularity of photography in India had created a desire for 'reality' that produced profound shifts in aesthetic expectations. Such shifts affected, for instance, the three-dimensional quality of the compositions, with a new depth and dimension introduced as images receded into an imaginary distance. Around the figures the dense use of light and shade lent a voluptuousness to layers and folds of fabric that conjured up the treatment of the three-dimensional icons of gods (not least in performance and other processions). As Pinney has so aptly written, 'It is through the conversation between the idioms of oleography, theatre, and photography—together with strategic alliances between these representational forms and the realms of religious authority and nascent ideas of the "nation"—that "realism" was able to triumph . . .' (1995: 4).

These figures were now also placed in tangible settings of historical palaces or pretty landscapes ('scenics') whose features had been made familiar through photography.[27] The expanded understanding surrounding the use of landscape has also been explored by Pinney, who argues that the meanings attributed to landscapes in mass-produced prints have always included complementarily antithetical notions of 'space' and 'place' (Pinney 1995: 78–113). That is, in most prints utilizing landscape, ' "place" is connoted by the foreground which exists in a state of mutual dependence with a "space" connoted by the horizon'. The backgrounded space often references 'epochs and kingdoms' through signifiers of 'classical elegance and sobriety' that also attach a meaning to nation. The foregrounded figures—be they goddesses, housewives, heroic figures, or mythic subjects—negotiate this background, often by negating it and thus setting up a tension that must be resolved by the viewer (ibid.). A similar function is supplied by the ubiquitous use of the proscenium arch as a framing device. (This is perhaps not surprising, given that commercial art studios, such as the Calcutta Art Studio, advertised a wide variety of work, including 'Portrait painting, Landscape painting, oil painting, water painting, all kinds of decoration and lithographic works . . . Hindoo Mythological and Historical pictures, and also Stage Scenes and Prosceniums.')[28]

Finally, the use of colour, while it added a 'realistic aura' also had strong iconic overtones; it was 'stretching beyond the parameters of the real and temporal into a world of gaudy and glittering splendour. Realism appeared to have dissolved itself at many levels, to create its own stereotypes of mythic fantasy' (Guha-Thakurta 1988: 13). To use the term Dean MacCannell coined for the commodification of place through tourism, such techniques enabled a 'staged authenticity' to be put forth and consumed where the consumer's gaze knowingly colluded in this new kind of artificial invocation.[29]

We can only retail briefly the important characteristics that emerge in the visual idioms introduced by posters. First was the ability of this idiom to fit 'regional' aspects of the genre within a pan-Indian or national frame, both in terms of visual referents and in terms of production. Ravi Varma's oil painting of eleven Indian women musicians, 'The Galaxy', for instance, well illustrates a type of presentation in which women from different regions and communities form a tableau, 'each an authentic physical type and

dressed in a recognisably regional apparel but subject to a single aesthetic' (Uberoi 1990: WS44). A tension in the interaction between regional
and pan-Indian contributions continued to mark the calendar art genre as
it developed: local artists at various centres throughout the subcontinent
produced paintings and then sent them to the centre in Lonavala to be reproduced as part of this emerging 'Indian' discourse, often in sublimated
resistance to it. Despite Ravi Varma's attempt to use such images as regional
women united in a single national whole, then, no effort to create a hegemonic discourse on 'the nation' could be expected to fully succeed when the
mechanics of creation, production, and distribution moved so easily back
and forth.

A second characteristic was the 'domestication' of divinity: 'the figures
of Durga or Parvati, as she appeared in the guise of a real-life woman, was
also cast into a contemporary social mold of daughter, wife or mother'
(Guha-Thakurta 1988: 12). The juxtaposition, if not blurring, of the categories of the religious and the domestic was a particularly strong aspect of
this new medium—which conflated public and domestic subjects; produced
and marketed items in intensely public venues for use in domestic spaces;
and which posed a visual commentary on the changing understandings of
both 'nation' and the respective roles to be played by men and women within it and the new (and aspiring) middle-class home.

A third related characteristic is the use of woman as signifier for some
other thing or quality, especially as a trope for 'the nation'. The corpus of
work by Ravi Varma and his followers is dominated by figures of women;
Uberoi argues that Varma's popularity with a pan-Indian audience emerged
in part because of his project of creating a national identity through the
construction of the ideal Hindu woman. Her most important point for our
purposes is her argument that 'the sacred and secular poles [of a continuum
that links the two] appear to be mediated by the patriotic [theme], as in the
figure of Mother India' (Uberoi 1990: WS44). The patriotic, that is, comes
to gloss many of the categories of calendar art prints that emerge, including
the mythological. And the patriotic is most often expressed by the trope of
'woman'. We can see this, as well, by looking at the succession of cheap
prints created in Calcutta in this period. From the quickly executed one-off
paintings sold at the Kalighat temple, to the woodblock printings of Bat-
tala, into the calendar art-style lithography that displaced the other two, the
figure of woman serves as the central vocabulary for expressing a wide range
of aspects of 'the nation': She is powerful enough to trample her patron or
bring down a temple priest and two *bhadralok* families, even while she
represents the vulnerability of domestic honour (prints illustrating the

Tarakeshwar scandal); she stands as a trope for both heroic efforts in resisting foreign invaders (e.g. the Rani of Jhansi), and the seductions of the modern world of easy money and easy vice (many of the Kalighat pictures and Bat-tala woodcuts show the Babu and his courtesan); most particularly, she enables the personification of the nation through the goddess/mother figure—to be revered and defended at all costs.

Much attention has been devoted of late to the process by which female figures stand in for domestic values that then become abstracted to stand in for the nation. Certainly the ways in which the movement on behalf of the Tamil language/cultural region became focused through the goddess Tamilt-tai illustrates most convincingly the efficacy of this strategy (Ramaswamy 1992). Guha-Thakurta has put it most succinctly:

> In the new urban art forms of modern India, the woman's form had undergone a striking metamorphosis, posing a new configuration of the 'modern' and the 'traditional'. While its form was 'modernized', the concepts and ideals it signified always harked back to 'tradition'—to Hindu mythology, Sanskrit literature, regional customs or Indian values and ethics. . . . Over the late 19th and early 20th century, such pictorial representations of women coincided with a new powerful set of equations made by nationalist discourse between 'tradition' and 'feminity', between the 'nation' and the mother-goddess.[30]

Nevertheless, I think it is possible to overstate the role of the woman-as-sign in this process of envisioning the nation. Other symbols of the domestic—most notably well-fed babies and young children—also serve this rhetorical function. And present as well among the topics sold as calendar art are representations of local heroes and kings, regional saintly figures, and even pictures of places. It is the visual universe in its entirety—in which a variety of representations stand in for localities and for the nation as whole—that should attract our attention, not simply the trope of woman. Indeed, this larger universe underscores the final point to be made about this new commercial print world at the turn of the century: the emerging articulation of a national cultural 'tradition' through the conflation of 'cultural' and 'religious' meanings. On this last point Patricia Uberoi draws our attention to the inability to separate sacred and secular (which she posits as forming a continuum). She argues that this continuum derives in part from a constant 'resacralizing process' that can be discerned in these prints from the very beginning (Uberoi 1990: WS43–4, WS46). It is not only that, as many analysts have noted, characters from the epics come to stand in for values (including domestic values) shared nationally—Ram as ideal ruler,

Sita as ideal wife, Hanuman as perfect devotee. It is also that the very form of discourse becomes appropriated to express a pan-Indian idea of the nation. This appropriation is undoubtedly linked to similar developments in performance, in which devotionalism and passionate activism become conflated, and through which iconic vocabulary conflates sacred figures and the state.

This conflation of cultural and religious meanings to create a national cultural tradition has been attributed to a 'nationalist project' perpetuated by a new middle-class elite. Certainly, as Guha-Thakurta has shown, if we understand the creation of a visual vocabulary to be shaped by the creators of the posters themselves, the textual evidence they left behind supports this view of a hegemonic project. But it seems to me very important to recognize the active role played by consumers in this process. The effort to create a new national vision from religious and cultural materials succeeded—especially in the commercial realm—*precisely because* the ordinary users of the icons needed 'to pay little attention', since they already knew 'the significance of the situation of which the icon was a part, a significance in fact constructed by the icon and by the space to which it belong[ed]' (Summers 1991: 208). Indeed, the very design of 'the space to which it belonged' can be seen as an active contribution made by consumers. In shops and homes, favourite posters came to be framed and mounted on the walls, to serve as the centre of small and personalized shrines. Various forms of worship—from *arati* to garlanding—were adapted from temple practices, now without benefit of religious specialist as intermediary. Often several posters would be combined in the shrine, conveying a message distinctly individual in its vision. That this idiom worked both in a domesticated sacral context, and to convey visions of the future nation, reiterates for us the close connections achieved between personal devotion and political activism: the individual becomes an actor whose choices—whose mobilized gaze—profoundly affect the dialogic processes that worked to create the nation.

Before turning to another medium, it is important to note that this visual vocabulary was not exclusively Hindu, as the foregoing examples might seem to imply. The poster form was also used, although apparently on a much smaller scale, by Muslims. Much more work is needed on this aspect in order to explore the similarities and differences in the rhetorical devices developed and the discursive stances adopted by Muslim consumers. (Muslim artists, of course, often produced the distinctively Hindu-ized national art previously described.) From the small sampling I have done thus far, it seems accurate to note that Muharram motifs feature large in this repertoire, and can be traced from *jadupatua* scrolls to contemporary south Indian poster art.[31] Taziahs and the figure of Duldul the horse, seem especially popular. This visual vocabulary is quite consistent with the pattern I have traced for ceremonial performance and oratorical motifs for this period as well. If this consistency holds up when I've examined many more examples, it will be possible to argue that, within the same genres, the visual messages conveyed are in fact quite different for Muslim consumers, focused especially on martyrdom at a time when Hinduized nationalists are asserting a triumphant new ideology of resistance to imperialism.[32]

Photography

The representation of India in photographs was well developed by the end of the century. As an art form, this discursive mode had been shaped long before by European aesthetics around the picturesque and notions of the ideal landscape. True to these aesthetic conventions, photography selected out certain key objects to capture, especially dramatic landscapes and historical monuments. (Eventually, the subject matter expanded to include an ethnographic catalogue of 'the peoples of India', a project shared with and extended from Company painting.)[33] We are not interested, however, in the photography of prestigious fine art photographers; many of them moved on to a 'realistic' style of photography that soon eclipsed the picturesque.

More to our point, if we wish to understand the photographs prepared for mass consumption, is the cultural production located in the ubiquitous local photography studios that became established in virtually every good-sized town and with itinerant photographers who set up along pilgrimage routes and other main thoroughfares or sites where crowds gathered. The studios, run by Indians, prepared formal portraits (for weddings and other special occasions); captured the local civic leaders at annual meetings in photographs that appeared in local newspapers; photographed local scenery of renown; and documented the changes in local families. Itinerant photographers, with lower overheads, brought the medium to quite ordinary people. Setting up their brightly covered backgrounds against buildings, ox carts, or the trunks of trees, they could photograph anyone in a way that situated the subject visually within a shared, even common discursive context both evocative and ubiquitous in its nature.[34]

The persuasiveness of the European aesthetic of the picturesque captured most of this field, but became indigenized in subtle and important ways. I will need to know much more about studios and middle-class patronage as well as the uses made of itinerant photographers; nevertheless, it is possible to discern even now some differences of composition and aesthetics between Indian and European photographers even before the turn of the century. The interplay between market, production, and distribution seems

particularly complicated to sort out *vis-à-vis* the influence exercised by
Indians in the shaping of photographic subject matter and composition for
mass consumption. For instance, Indian princes' presentation albums did
more often use full-size figures of Indians, often in the foreground, posed
informally to suggest their 'naturalized' presence and, even, individuality.
Photographs on postcard stock purveyed by Saeed Bros. of Banaras (printed
in Berlin) provide another example of startling Indian bodies in the foreground. Similarly, the substitution of events (such as Muharram or civic
processions) for scenic displays or historical monuments also tended to be
made by Indian photographers such as Gobindram and Codeyram of Jaipur or H.A. Mirza and Sons of Delhi.[35]

Like the world of cheap prints, this is very much a world of individual
entrepreneurs—in the case of Indians, most often father and sons, or brothers. The photographs pictured a world public in access, conveying an array
of public spaces and monuments linked within a single, shared vision of all
India. At the same time, the studio-based photographers also marketed
other forms of their craft, uniquely combining the local and the all-India,
the domestic and the public. They produced family portraits for both the
British and middle-class Indians, even setting up '*zenana*' studios with
women photographers for Indian women in purdah. They also documented
(and sold) important political events, such as Curzon's Delhi Durbar of
1903. And they assembled 'albums' of subjects: in 1895, Raja Deen Dayal
and Sons' catalogue included a 'Tour of Bundelkhand', 'Views' of Rajputana
and Mewar, a projected four-volume work on 'Places of Interest in India',
and various 'souvenirs' of state visits by European royalty to Hyderabad.[36]
The albums themselves gained currency as 'presentation' gifts that could be
calibrated in size (both the numbers of photographs and their measurements)
to reflect the status of the recipient. Individual prints could be purchased
as well.

As a reflection of a new and mobilized gaze, this history of the mass-
consumed photographic print could hardly provide a better illustration.
The single photograph by the itinerant photographer, the presentation
album, even the prints of familiar and local civic events, certainly became
by the end of the century 'commodified forms of looking*[linked to . . .] the
experiences of spatial and temporal mobility'. The nation implicitly 'becomes
visible at the same time that it becomes appropriatable'.[37] To the extent that
far-flung places became part of the same visual whole, photographic representations reinforced the expanding urge of tourism; together, the two
visual phenomena provided the opportunities for movement and consumption in ways that reinforced the notion of unity, of nationalism.

Notably, this is a world with a rather different visual idiom: the trope is not woman, but place. The medium—smooth and continuous—'inhibits the viewer's attending to tactile qualities', (Shiff 1991: 147) an attribute that had been central to painting and print. Despite the lack of tactile representation, however, the transfer of patterns of light points from one surface to another enabled the viewer to make a 'visual passage from one depicted object to another[,] facilitated by the perceived continuity of the "real" space represented' (Summers 1991: 208). The assumption that 'reality' was pictured, and that this reality included a number of particular places all captured within the same two-dimensional formats, worked together to create a distinct visual idiom. Connected to this was the need, occasioned by the plurality of images, to create an integrative narrative frame for these bits of reality—one that posed a 'nation' to integrate diversity and difference. Although I am not yet sure how far this contrast can be pressed, it seems to me that the implicit visual vocabulary used in photography poses a contrast to prints that is almost gendered in its nature: what we see in this medium is a mastery of the landscape that is virile, that is interested in control and manipulation in a distinctly masculine way.

At the same time, there are certain continuities of imagery and modalities that make it possible to see how a single, shared visual vocabulary could arise from medium to medium. One example must suffice, given the length of this chapter. Up until fairly recently, almost all the brightly painted backdrops carried by itinerant photographers were framed by a proscenium arch. They also included a number of other referents borrowed from painting and posters, and from the storylines used in live performances.[38]

Finally, we should note the role of the production in effecting a mobilized gaze. Before the turn of the century, a number of photographers were sending their photographs to Europe (Germany, Saxony, Luxembourg, and the like) for mass production. This is much the same process, of course, as that by which calendar art became a mass commodity when the Bengal painters sent their paintings to Europe to be turned, through the oleographic printing process, into prints. Almost a century earlier than we might expect, we had (quite literal) transnational flows in cultural production.

Cinema to 1929[39]

Early cinema in India provides a fascinating counterpart to the other visual media we have briefly examined. Like photography and poster art, silent film tried to fulfil popular aesthetic expectations nurtured by live performance, especially the regional folk drama traditions (ranging from Bengali *jatra* to Punjabi *svang*, the *kathakali* of Kerala, and the like).[40] With the other two, it built on technological innovations brought from the West, relying on Indian entrepreneurs to gain access to both machinery and expertise, and receiving its shape through astonishingly rapid influences from world capitalism.

Bombay city witnessed the beginning of Indian film history on 7 July 1896, when the Lumière Bros. presented a series of short films composed of 'living photographic pictures in life-sized reproductions'. Significantly, Bombayites shared this sensation with urban dwellers throughout the world, for similar openings took place at much the same time in Russia, China, Australia, and South Africa; European and New York audiences had been exposed only a few months earlier, suggesting the rapid pace of technological dispersion possible in this capitalistic context. Their campaign succeeded spectacularly because the machines served as cameras as well as projectors and printing machines. Far-flung operators could create new material even as they showed the old. This enabled them not only to regularly offer a 'change of programme', but by sending their new material back to the Lumière Bros.' home base, also to very quickly build up a repertoire of worldwide dimensions. This was a mobile gaze with a vengeance!

The pace of change within India was equally rapid: within just two-and-a-half years, viewers could see local events such as 'Poona Races '98' and 'Train Arriving at Bombay Station', and by 1902 the rudiments of the first film empire—encompassing production, distribution, and exhibition—had been established in Calcutta by Jamjetji Framji Madan.[41] Similar patterns of technology transfer had taken place around photography and oleography as well. But the scale of financing needed to fund filmmaking tied this process much more closely to world capitalistic processes for a much longer period. It was not only that training and technology continued to be sought by Indians in Europe (e.g. the first feature filmmaker, Dadasaheb Phalke, still felt the need to travel to England in 1911 to meet with leading filmmakers before launching his studio work in Nasik); it was also that, to recoup the costs of producing a film, filmmakers had to have fairly far-flung distribution of their films. For viewers in India, this meant that they were offered an extraordinarily international fare, with the bulk of films before World War I coming from France, as well as England, the United States, Italy, Denmark, and Germany. (As a result of the first World War, the source of such international fare shifted, with American films dominating worldwide distribution networks by the mid-1920s.) In the case of Indian filmmakers distributing their wares outside the subcontinent, they easily found audiences in Burma and Ceylon (administered as part of the same sector of the British empire), but also throughout South-east Asia as well as

East and South Africa (presumably many consumers in these places were overseas Indians especially).[42]

Nevertheless, what is striking within this global capitalism frame is the extent to which cultural specialization emerged almost immediately in order to satisfy desires in this particular cultural region. Such specialization affected marketing, financing, and the content of the films themselves. It only took a few days in Bombay during the initial offering by the Lumière Bros., for instance, for the theatre manager to change from a single (Re 1) price to a broad scale of prices, from 4 annas to 2 rupees. At the same time, he introduced 'Reserved boxes for Purdah Ladies and their Families'. These conventions have continued to be extremely important in making filmgoing in India the broadbased activity it is (Barnouw and Krishnaswamy 1980: 5). Similarly, as the film industry became established in India, it attracted investment from a variety of Indian industrialists who were acquiring wealth from their participation in the global economy in such areas as textiles. Most interested in owning part of the action, of course, were theatre owners, who soon began to create empires that encompassed all aspects of cinema from production through distribution to actual viewing.[43]

Once again, however, it is consumption that marks Indian participation in this global economy as active rather than passive. In part this is a result of the very nature of the medium, in which the desires of the viewer—the intent, as it were, behind the gaze—were presumed to matter, even from the beginning. It is striking, for instance, that when Phalke took his films to England as early as 1914, those interested in the medium recognized the localized nature of the market he addressed. An article in the London-based periodical *Bioscope* begins: 'Since one of the greatest and most valuable possibilities of the cinematograph is the circulation throughout the world of plays dealing with national life and characteristics, acted by native players amidst local scenes, it is with no small interest that one awaits the appearance in this country of Mr D.G. Phalke's first Indian films.' But in part it relates, as well, to the very nature of film as a visual medium. Of great significance for us, then, is the point made later in the *Bioscope* article, which goes on to argue that cinema is uniquely qualified in this respect: 'In a film version of a story, the whole beauty of the original may be retained so far as its action and characterization are concerned, whilst it is possible to realize local colour and scenic detail in a manner which would be quite out of question in any purely literary form, or even in the most lavish state production.[44]

Thus influences relating to both the global-but-localizing nature of the market for cinema, and the ability to harness the medium's unique properties, led almost immediately to Indian efforts to create films that met Indian viewers' interests. As suggested by the *Bioscope* writer, these efforts began by using the technique, already developed in photography, of reproducing local scenery that could simultaneously invoke interest in a singular place and be linked to a larger notion of a nation. Phalke's pioneering contribution soon moved Indian filmmaking beyond this initial strategy, however, by capitalizing on stories well-known to his audiences. This genre came to be known as 'the mythological', and he began with the tale of Raja Harischandra (a story also regularly featured in popular live theatre performances). He then moved on to stories excerpted from the epics (his intention from the start), including *Lanka Dahan* (The Burning of Lanka), *Krishna Janma* (The Birth of Krishna), and the like.[45]

These films had an immediacy and appeal for Indian audiences that the very foreign films from the West lacked. Indeed, from their inception, such homegrown productions 'earmarked for the Indian film an area of subject matter that won for it an immediate and powerful hold in India and neighbouring countries—and at the same time shut it off from others'.[46] The audience quickly became different and distinguishable from that attending western films; as one theatre owner put in his testimony to the Indian Cinematograph Committee in 1927:

> The type of people who like Indian pictures, their way of living is quite different and generally they are people who chew betel leaves . . . let me give you an example. I did show an Indian pictures at my Western theatre, *Lanka Dahan*, and I made 18,000 rupees in one week. But it ruined my theatre altogether.
>
> Q: You mean you had to disinfect the cinema?
> A: I had to disinfect the hall and at the same time I had to convince my audience I had disinfected it. . . . Till that time I went on losing money.[47]

The familiarity of the storylines and the aesthetics involved enabled this fledgling medium to cater to, as well as create, a single, shared, national culture.[48] The relatively simple addition of several sets of subtitles in different languages allowed silent film to 'speak' to a huge audience through the shared visual vocabulary on the screen. The 'common cultural legacy' of the epics, particularly given their unbounded nature and their previous histories of having been recounted in a wide range of performance genres throughout the subcontinent, provided a shared basis for understanding how the world worked. When this shared content became linked to new commodities in the new context of cultural consumption as an act of participation in the public sphere, a new form of nationalist activism became possible. Individuals as consumers became linked through common activities of viewing;

the mobile gaze became the shared activity of surveillance. Values conveyed through visual evocation became the grounds for consensus as well as contestation.

The most obvious change was the introduction in the late 1920s of talkies. For cinema, this changed quite utterly the aesthetics and visual strategies used in films. On the one hand, it enabled the introduction of song and dance into cinematic presentations—strong components of live performance and technologically problematic in silent film. The obvious connections between photography, poster art, and cinema became, as a result of this change, much more oblique and less direct, even as the extremely important aesthetics of live performance became more immediately transferable to film. On the other hand, sound also introduced the complications of language in a way never before encountered, so that filmmakers suddenly found their markets reduced to a tenth of their previous size, while economies of production in a few dispersed centres were fragmented by the need to create films catering to specific regional/linguistic cultural areas.[49]

This was also a period in which the content of nationalism became much more overtly contestable and contested. Not surprisingly, the ability to convey through a visual vocabulary certain shared aspects of identity and community formation became problematized in new ways at this point. Regional cultures, as well as alternative religious communities, became sources for new evocations of identity in ways that could, through film as well as posters, be visually compelling but also fragmenting.[50] Images that had previously been viewed as integrative—including *Mother India* and the characters of the *Ramayana*—now could be seen as posing the threat of a hegemonic visual discourse and political domination. Exercising the gaze became an act that forced a viewer to choose one of several alternatives posed visually; consumption of an image became a political act of great import. For some, these political acts continued to be anti-imperial in nature; for others, they became forms of resistance by those who could see themselves cast in subaltern roles to indigenous powerholders who attempted to dominate on the basis of regional, caste, class, or gender identities. That visual strategies continued to lie at the heart of this activism seems indisputable. But theorizing how this worked is clearly more complicated, not least because of the introduction and elaboration of aural culture along with the visual.

Conclusion

Turning back, then, from specific genres to a theorizing framework, I would like to argue that the emphasis on the exercise of the gaze reminds us, when looking at the visual evidence itself, that we need constantly to keep in mind the tripartite process by which the creation, production, and consumption of forms of popular culture interacted dialogically to enable the consumer to make choices among a new and overwhelming range of information sources. For historians, particularly, the need to keep in mind the impact of consumption provides an immensely useful corrective to an over-reliance on textual evidence. At the same time, such an emphasis moves us beyond the traditional constraints in art history that tend to limit meaning to the iconic conventions utilized by the artist in the process of creation. By considering a range of media together for both the overlap and the distinctions in the ways they communicate visually, we can begin to discern the extent to which the very use of such conventions enables consumers to take certain things as given, and then to go on to create for themselves new meanings around the images and icons.[51]

Part of the power of this theoretical framework, I think, is that it also enables us to look beyond visual evidence to other, allied media of communication. Cinema, for instance, is also intimately connected to billboards, as well as to fan magazines, cassettes of filmi music, and the like. All of these are immensely important in understanding the interactive relationship between consumers and producers of cinema,[52] and thus in delineating the active ways that consumers negotiate their way through the choices thrown up before their gaze. Thus a focus on the gaze does not prevent us from dealing, as well, with textual materials (at one end of the spectrum anchored by visual media in the middle) or with aural ones. But it does frame this range differently than would a focus on text or print capitalism—and provides at least one important side benefit, which is the inclusion of a much larger audience than would be possible with a focal point solely on print media (whatever the extension of that form of communication through reading aloud and the like).

When looking beyond the specific pieces of evidence to the larger picture, this theoretical frame also requires us to think about the cumulative effects when the mobilized gaze is exercised. It is this which leads us back to the public sphere. For South Asia, there is much evidence that what has passed for the public sphere in the twentieth century has had rather different contours, not least for the need to deal with an imperial state before Independence, and the rather distinctive post-colonial state since 1947.[53] The trope for this public sphere, particularly as it relies on the mobilized gaze for its surveillance of the state (both before and after 1947) should certainly be the processionist (joined by the pilgrim and the participant/audience for live performance). As with the trope of *flânerie* in France, this mobile viewer 'delineates a mode of visual practice coincident with—but antithetical to—the panoptic gaze. Like the panoptic system, [this mode] relied on the visual register—but with a converse instrumentalism, emphasising mobility and fluid subjectivity rather than restraint and interpellated reform'. With this 'increased priority of the visual register' (Friedberg 1993: 16), that is, participants in South Asian civil society are presented with more flexibility, not less; with more capacity to shape and influence the values presented and the interpretations constructed. The very ambiguity of the visual mode of communication—the very ability of the viewer to bring to his or her gaze individual interpretations and contextualization—provides much room to manoeuvre and negotiate in the relationship to the state within the public sphere. In these circumstances, we are bound to encounter multivariant ways to visualize the nation.

NOTES

1. Earlier versions of this chapter were presented in June 1995 to the SOAS conference resulting in this volume, and to a conference in Amsterdam, sponsored by the Max Planck Institute and the Research Centre on Religion and Society at the University of Amsterdam, in November 1995. I am grateful for comments on these versions at the conference (especially by Christopher Pinney, Peter van der Veer, and Patricia Uberoi) and since then, by Jim Masselos, Sumathi Ramaswamy, David Gilmartin, and Sumit Guha.

2. While drawing on Benedict Anderson's useful term, this study reveals, in fact, that many of the sinews identified by Anderson as essential for the development of nationalism—especially the use of print to foster shared identity; the replacement of shared religious values with secularism; and the substitution of the novel for the epic—are not characteristic of the colonized parts of the world (Anderson 1991).

3. Elaboration of the Frankfurt School's examinations of the public sphere, particularly by coming to grips with the arguments put forward by Jürgen Habermas, has become a growth industry in the last few years. For the fount of this work, see Habermas, 1989; for explorations regarding the impact of imperialism on development of the public sphere in South Asia, see the special issue of *South Asia*, June 1991—which also cites a number of other important works on the public sphere.

4. For a detailed discussion see Freitag (1989a).

5. Gilmartin's argument has been influenced especially by the work of Jean-Christophe Agnew (1983).

6. Many of the essays in *Public Culture*, for instance, rest on the assumption that there is now a shared, global or transnational cultural production process in

which participants are equally active. This seems to me to beg the very central question. For a recent essay exploring the implications for contemporary India of the failure of this distinction between public and private, see Freitag (1996b).

7. Indeed, from the nature of the kinds of questions traditionally asked by those working on political developments in British India, it seems clear that these South Asian studies, like Anderson's work, have been informed by the western European model of the emerging public sphere. Though Anderson denies this Eurocentric influence and insists that nationalism was 'born' under colonialism, his model does not in any way fit developments in virtually any part of the Third World—or elsewhere outside England and, perhaps, France.

8. It is Habermas who argued most convincingly that English civil society emerged with *The Tatler* and coffee houses in which to read it; Thomas Crow posits a parallel development with the printed critiques of the crown's official exhibitions of paintings, Crow (1985).

9. This is the organizing principle behind Sweeney (1987).

10. Eck is commenting on Rudolf Arnheim's work, especially his *Visual Thinking*, chapter 2.

11. See, for instance, Buckler (1927–8: 239–41): discussed by Bernard Cohn (1987: 636). These comments are Cohn's, with the embedded quotations from Buckler: 'The king stands for a "system of rule of which he is the incarnation . . . incorporating into his body . . . the persons of those who share his rule." Those thus incorporated were not just servants of the king, but part of him, "just as the eye is the main function of sight, and the ear in the realm of hearing." . . . These acts, seen from the perspective of the giver of nazar and the acceptor of the khelats, were acts of obedience, pledges of loyalty, and the acceptance of the superiority of the giver of the khelats.' For the Nayakas, see Narayana Rao (1992, especially chapter III): 'The svari might be said to be the king's primary public business. . . . He has to show himself to his people outside the palace; this he accomplishes by a regal procession' (p. 60).

12. Thanks to Sumit Guha for this point, personal communication.

13. Eck (1985: 7, 53). Rich Freeman points out that possession rituals also involve this exercise of the gaze of the deity—the performer must look into the mirror to draw the deity's gaze to his own face, and thus activate possession. Sumathi Ramaswamy also commented that in her studies of Tamilttay statues (serving as personifications of linguistic identity), she has been told explicitly that they were not deities because their eyes had not been 'opened'. Personal communications.

14. For histories of changing patronage see, for instance, Lutgendorf (1993); R. Chatterjee (1990).

15. For a description of the *gharana* form of organization, see Neuman (1980); for the variety of performance genres now ordered by *gharana* or *akhara* relationships, see discussions in the essays included in Freitag (1989b).

16. For more detail, see chapter 4 of Freitag (1989a).

17. This term is used in the way art historians and philosophers have used it—to mean the literally uprooted gaze capable of mobility. This meaning inheres in the ability of the viewer to move about, to select from among competing images in constructing meaning. In this the term differs distinctly from that used in film theory in relation to the camera's perspective.

18. Jay in Levin (1993: 143). The point to Jay's essay is that Sartre and Merleau-Ponty were the first of the twentieth-century French philosophers to try to break up the hegemony exercised by vision; the logic of their attacks led, ultimately, to Foucault's insistence on the 'panoptican gaze' (see later discusssion in the chapter).

19. Jean-Louis Comolli, 'Machines of the Visible', in *The Cinematic Apparatus*, edited by Teresa de Lauretis and Stephen Heath (NY: St. Martin's Press, 1980), pp. 122–3, quoted in Friedberg (1993: 15).

20. Habermas' contribution to this recognition of complexities is noted by Levin when he describes the refinement introduced by Habermas as positing a replacement for the emphasis on the traditional ocularcentrism of the singular observer with democratic participation (i.e., the surveillance of the state exercised by civil society). This Habermasian shift in the paradigm, Levin argues, releases 'the modern subject from a terrible double bind. For, in the objectivist paradigm . . . the subject is invariably positioned either in the role of a dominating observer or in the role of an observable object, submissive before the gaze of power', Levin (1993: 4, Introducton).

21. Perhaps the most striking example of this exercise for me was the ethnographic/administrative uses to which the materials generated earlier by W.H. Sleeman on the Thags were put. By the end of the century, snippets of the documentation Sleeman had produced as participant-observer in the 1830s (*Ramaseeana* and the like) were being culled, to be reprinted under appropriate ethnographic headings such as 'wedding ceremonies' in *North Indian Notes and Queries*, the serial publication of the late nineteenth century.

22. Goethe's *Theory of Colours*, for instance, used the exercise of shifting back and forth between a blue circle and a yellow one, which led the eye to 'see' a green circle that did not exist. Popular, often reprinted, volumes included the translation into English of *Theory of Colours*, as well as George Henry Lewes' *Life and Work of Goethe*, which appeared in 1855. Cited in Horton (1992).

23. Jonathan Crary, 'Modernizing Vision', in Foster, Hal (ed.), *Vision and Visuality*. Dia Art Foundation Discussions in Contemporary Culture, vol. 2 (Seattle: Bay Press, 1988), quoted in Horton (1992: 8).

24. These observations are from Friedberg (1993: 20); the final quotation she has drawn from Richard Altick, *Shows of London*, 180.

25. It is ironically interesting that the stereoptican disappeared from Victorian

parlours after it became clear that the subject matter that lent itself most effectively to such viewing was the nude.

26. Most had been relegated to 'second-tier jobs as drawing masters, draughtsmen, engravers and lithographers'. Tapati Guha-Thakurta (1988: 11).

27. See discussions of technique in Uberoi (1990) and Guha-Thakurta.

28. Advertisement in the *Bengalee*, 8 November 1879, quoted in Guha-Thakurta (1992: 79).

29. Dean MacCannell, *The Tourist: A New Theory of the Leisure Class* (NY: Schocken, 1989), II, quoted in Friedberg (1993: 61).

30. Guha-Thakurta (1991: WS–95). I would, however, disagree with the conclusion Guha-Thakurta draws from this evidence, when she argues that this emphasis led to a new distinction between public and private. On the contrary, it seems to me quite clear that this new role for woman iconography profoundly conflated public and private, and politicized a wide range of ostensibly domestic activities so that Indian males could contest each other's in control over them and the ideological values for which they stood.

31. For examples of the former, see Mildred Archer (1977). For the latter, see The British Council (1995).

32. This argument is explored in some depth in Freitag (1989: chapter 6). New work on the Muslim market for posters is explored in Freitag (1996).

33. The aesthetics developed especially around the Grand Tour and became expressed in painting as well as photography. Worswick (1976: 1–2). The ethnographic project is well delineated in Pinney (1990).

34. See the fascinating collection of painted backgrounds and photographic portraits of George Berticevich, photographer and collector based in California. Recent exhibition at the Halsey Gallery, School of the Arts, College of Charleston.

35. I am not, however, convinced by the elaborate argumentation of Judith Gutman that this quite distinctive photographic style grows out of classical philosophy and art history canons fostered especially by the princely states. On the contrary, embedded in Gutman's own presentation is significant evidence that Indian photography differed according to audience/consumers, and that it was fundamentally affected by other media. I would argue that those influences included posters, something she resolutely tries to ignore (in favour of miniatures produced more than one hundred years earlier), Gutman (1985).

36. Appendix to Worswick (1980). The fact that Deen Dayal became the official photographer for the Nizam of Hyderabad helps to explain the especially broad inventory and, of course, the presence of presentation albums.

37. Freidberg (1993) and Friedberg quoting Jean-Louis Comolli (1993: 15). See above.

38. Examples from the George Berticevich collection.

39. I am hesitant to include this section as I have done no original work on this portion of the project yet and can only present here conclusions from secondary

sources. But as the first sentence suggests, the medium is a critically important part of the mix if we are to understand what was happening in these decades.

40. Barnouw and Krishnaswamy (1980: 72–3). However, Barnouw and Krishnaswamy presume that these folk theatre traditions had enjoyed uninterrupted careers for many centuries; recent studies at least of *kathakali* and *svang* suggest, instead, that they, too, were part of a cultural renaissance of relatively recent times. More work is undoubtedly needed on the ways in which these aesthetic expectations were kept alive after *c.* AD 1000.

41. Barnouw and Krishnaswamy (1980: 1–2; quoting *Times of India* advertisement, 7, 8).

42. Generally the cost for producing a feature film was calculated by the 1920s to run to about Rs 20,000. Indian producers had to recoup these costs primarily from their Indian audiences. By contrast, overseas producers recouped their costs at home and could therefore offer their wares to Indian theatre managers for much reduced fees. This put homegrown productions at a distinct disadvantage that clearly grew from their position in the world market. Barnouw and Krishnaswamy (1980: 41).

43. Perhaps because of the connections established among these functions by the original machinery of the Lumière Bros., even filmmakers found themselves from the beginning involved in distribution. These producers often had to take up tents and tour with their work in order to raise the capital to pay off their bills and move on to the next project. See description of Phalke's activity, Barnouw and Krishnaswamy (1980: 15).

44. *Bioscope*, 4 June 1914, reproduced in its entirety in Barnouw and Krishnaswamy (1980: 21).

45. The mythological dominated early movie making in India, but two other main genres—the 'social' (with its contemporary background) and the 'historical' (with its focus on actual figures from the past)—had also emerged by the 1920s.

46. Barnouw and Krishnaswamy (1980: 20). This appeal operated, it should be remembered, in a context in which only 15 per cent of the films viewed were made in India, while the other 85 per cent came from overseas (predominantly America). Figures from Indian Cinematograph Committee, *Report*, p. 188.

47. Indian Cinematograph Committee, 1927–8. *Evidence*, vol. I, p. 21 (Government of India Central Publications Branch, 1928); quoted in Barnouw and Krishnaswamy (1980: 48).

48. The capacity of the medium to effect this national consensus was not lost on early nationalists, such as Debaki Bose in the 1920s. See Barnouw and Krishnaswamy (1980: 30).

49. For details of these predicaments, see Barnouw and Krishnaswamy (1980: chapter 4 and beyond).

50. The development of the Tamil film industry as a direct source of popular political support is but the most obvious example of this change. Another early

example of this potential was the making of 'Razia Begum' in Hyderabad by Dhiren Ganguly: the film attempted to tell the historically accurate story of a Muslim queen in love with a Hindu subject. Released in an atmosphere of a Hindu–Muslim communal tension, the movie immediately incurred the wrath of the Nizam of Hyderabad who forced Ganguly and his partners to close up their two theatres, pack their equipment, and leave the Nizam's dominions within twenty-four hours. Barnouw and Krishnaswamy (1980: 28).

51. It may well be, of course, that the 'readings' we make of the forms of consumption created by individual gazes may be distinctive to particular genres. See, for instance, the different kinds of readings applied to photographs and to wall decorations in Norway, Reme (1993) and Reiakvam (1993).

52. The interaction between fans' knowledge about the lives of the stars, and their characters on-screen, is explored in Rosie Thomas, 'Sanctity and Scandal: the Mythologisation of Mother India', unpublished paper circulated to conference on Public Culture, 1988.

53. In my own work I have tried to capture that difference by referring to the 'public arena'; the implications for negotiations in the nature of the civil society in post-colonial India are explored in Freitag (1966).

REFERENCES

Agnew, Jean-Christophe, 1983, 'A Touch of Class', *Democracy*, Spring: 59–72.

———, 1990, 'Coming Up for Air: Consumer Culture in Historical Perspective', paper presented to a symposium on Popular Culture/Public Culture, North Carolina State University.

Anderson, Benedict, 1991, *Imagined Communities: Reflections on the Origin and Spread of Nationalism*, London: Verso, 1991, revised edn.

Archer, Mildred, 1977, *Indian Popular Painting in the India Office Library*, London: HMSO.

Asendorf, Christoph, 1993, *Batteries of Life: On the History of Things and Their Perception in Modernity*, trans. by Don Reneau, Berkeley: University of California Press.

Asher, Catherine, 1992, *Architecture of Mughal India*, vol. I.4 of *The New Cambridge History of India*, Cambridge: Cambridge University Press.

———, 1995, 'Mapping Hindu–Muslim Identities through the Architecture of Shahjahanabad and Jaipur', paper presented to the Indo-Muslim Identity workshop, Duke University.

Barnouw, Eric and S. Krishnaswamy, 1980, *Indian Film*, NY: Oxford University Press, 2nd edn.

Bayly, C.A., 1983, *Rulers, Townsmen, and Bazaars*, Cambridge: Cambridge University Press.

————, (ed.), 1990, *The Raj: India and the British, 1600–1947*, London: National Portrait Gallery Publications.

Berger, John, 1972, *Ways of Seeing*, London: Penguin Books.

The British Council, 1995, 'A Shifting Focus: Photography in India 1850–1900', catalogue for travelling exhibition.

Chatterjee, Partha, 1986, 'Nationalist Thought and the Colonial World: A Derivative Discourse?', London: Zed Books.

————, 1993, *The Nation and Its Fragments: Colonial and Post-colonial Histories*, Princeton: Princeton Studies in Culture/Power/History.

Chatterjee, Ratnabali, 1990, *From the Karkhana to the Studio: A Study in the Changing Social Rules of Patron and Artist in Bengal*, New Delhi: Books and Books.

Cohn, Bernard, 1987, 'Representing Authority in Victorian India', in *An Anthropologist among the Historians*, Delhi: Oxford University Press.

Crow, Thomas, 1985, *Painters and Public Life in Eighteenth-Century Paris*, New Haven: Yale University Press.

Eck, Diana, 1985, *Darsan: Seeing the Divine Image in India*, Chambersburg PA: Anima Books, 2nd revised and enlarged edn.

Erdman, Joan, 1985, *Patrons and Performers in Rajasthan*, Delhi: Chanakya.

Freitag, 1989a, *Collective Action and Community: Public Arenas and the Emergence of Communalism in North India*, Berkeley: University of California Press.

————, (ed.), 1989b, *Culture and Power in Banaras*, Berkeley: University of California Press.

————, 1996a, 'Indian Muslims: The Islamicate World, and the Visual Language of the Nation', paper presented to the Second Rockefeller Conference on the Muslim World, Research Triangle North Carolina.

————, 1996b, 'Contesting in Public: Colonial Legacies and Contemporary Communalism', in Ludden 1996.

Friedberg, Anne, 1993, *Window Shopping: Cinema and the Postmodern*, Berkeley: University of California Press.

Gilmartin, David, 1991, 'Democracy, Nationalism, and the Public: A Speculation on Colonial Muslim Politics', *South Asia*, 14(1), pp. 123–40.

Guha-Thakurta, Tapati, 1988, 'Artists, Artisans and Mass Picture Production in Late 19th and Early 20th Century Calcutta', *South Asia Research*, 8 (1).

————, 1991, 'Women as "Calendar Art" Icons: Emergence of Pictorial Stereotype in Colonial India', *Economic and Political Weekly*.

————, 1992, *The Making of a New 'Indian' Art: Artists, Aesthetics and Nationalism in Bengal, c. 1850–1920*, Cambridge: Cambridge University Press.

Gutman, Judith Mara, 1985, *Through Indian Eyes*, Oxford University Press.

Habermas, Jürgen, 1989, *The Structural Transformation of the Public Sphere*, trans. Thomas Burger, Cambridge, Mass: The MIT Press.

Hansen, Kathryn, 1989, 'The Birth of Hindi Drama', in Freitag (1989b).

Hansen, 1991, *Grounds for Play*, Berkeley: University of California Press.

Haynes, Douglas E., 1991, *Rhetoric and Ritual in Colonial India: The Shaping of a Public Culture in Surat City, 1852–1928*, Berkeley: University of California Press.

Hein, Norvin, 1972, *The Miracle Plays of Mathura*, Delhi: Oxford University Press.

Henry, Edward O., 1988, *Chant the Names of God*, San Diego: San Diego State University Press.

Hess, Linda, 1983, '*Ram Lila*: The Audience Experience', in Monika Thiel-Horstmann (ed.), *Bhakti in Current Research, 1979–1982*, Berlin, Dietrich Reimer.

Horton, Susan, 1992, 'Were They Having Fun Yet'? paper prepared for the UC Santa Cruz annual Dickens Conference.

Jay, Martin, 1993, *Downcast Eyes: The Denigration of Vision in Twentieth Century French Thought*, Berkeley: University of California Press.

Kemal, Salim and Ivan Gaskell (eds), 1991, *The Language of Art History*, Cambridge: Cambridge University Press.

Levin, David Michael (ed.), 1993, *Modernity and the Hegemony of Vision*, Berkeley: University of California Press.

Long, E., 1993, 'Textual Interpretation as Collective Action', in J. Boyarin, *The Ethnography of Reading*, Berkeley: University of California Press.

Ludden, David (ed.), 1996, *Contesting the Nation*, Philadelphia: University of Pennsylvania Press.

Lutgendorf, Philip, 1993, *Life of a Text*, Berkeley: University of California Press.

Michell, George, 1992, *The Vijayanagara Courtly Style: Incorporation and Synthesis in the Royal Architecture of Southern India, 15th–17th Centuries*, New Delhi: Manohar/AIIS.

Mitchell, W.J.T., 1994, *Picture Theory: Essays on Verbal and Visual Representation*, Chicago: University of Chicago Press.

Mitter, Partha, 1990, 'Artistic Responses to Colonialism in India: An Overview', in Bayly.

Narayana Rao, V., D. Shulman and S. Subrahmanyam, 1992, *Symbols of Substance: Court and State in* Nayaka *Period Tamil Nadu*, Delhi: Oxford University Press.

Neuman, Daniel, 1980, *The Life of Music in North India: The Organization of an Artistic Tradition*, New Delhi: Manohar.

Pandey, Gyanendra, 1994, 'The New Hindu History', *South Asia*, XVII, Special Issue, pp. 97–112.

Pinney, Christopher, 1990, 'Colonial Anthropology', in Bayly.

———, 1994, 'Nationalist Icons: Visual Propaganda from the Cow Protection Movement to the Indian National Army', presentation September.

———, 1995, 'Moral Topophilia: The Signification of Landscape in Indian Oleographs', in Eric Hirsch and Michaels O'Hanlon (eds), *The Anthropology of Landscape: Perspectives on Place and Space*, pp. 78–113.

————, 1995, 'An Authentic Indian "Kitsch": The Aesthetics, Discriminations and Hybridity of Popular Hindu Art', *Social Analysis.* September

Ramanujan, A.K., V. Narayana Rao, and David Shulman, 1994, *When God is a Customer: Telugu Courtesan Songs by Ksetrayya and Others*, Berkeley: University of California Press.

Ramaswamy, Sumathi, 1992, 'En/gendering Language: The Poetics and Politics of Tamil Identity, 1891–1970', Berkeley: University of California, dissertation in history.

————, 1994, 'An Image of Her Own? Visualizing Tamil', unpublished presentation.

Reiakvam, Oddlaug, 1993, 'Reframing the Family Photograph', *Journal of Popular Culture*, 26 (4).

Reme, Eva, 1993, 'Every Picture Tells a Story: Wall Decorations . . .', *Journal of Popular Culture*, 26 (4).

Stein, Burton, 1989, *Vijayanagara: The New Cambridge History of India*, Part 1, vol. 2, Cambridge: Cambridge University Press.

Shiff, Richard, 1991, 'Cézanne's Physicality: The Politics of Touch', in Kemal and Gaskell.

Summers, David, 1991, 'Conditions and Conventions: On the Disanalogy of Art and Language', in Kemal and Gaskell.

Sweeney, Amin, 1987, *A Full Hearing: Orality and Literacy in the Malay World*, Berkeley: University of California Press.

Taylor, Charles, 1990, 'Modes of Civil Society', *Public Culture*, 3 (1), pp. 95, 108, 109.

Uberoi, Patricia, 1990, 'Feminine Identity and National Ethos in Indian Calendar Art', *Economic and Political Weekly.*

Williams, Rosalind H., 1982, *Dream Worlds: Mass Consumption in Late Nineteenth-Century France*, Berkeley: University of California Press.

Worswick, Clark, 1976, *The Last Empire: Photography in British India, 1855–1911*, NY: Aperture Books.

————, 1980, *Princely India*, New York: Knopf.

The *Indar Sabha* Phenomenon
Public Theatre and
Consumption in Greater India
(1853–1956)[1]

KATHRYN HANSEN

I N THE DECADES following 1850, vibrant public theatre emerged in
several metropolitan centres of the South Asian subcontinent, most
notably Bombay and Calcutta. Triggered by the mid-Victorian encounter of urban elites with colonial culture and education, theatre became a site
for the consolidation of a set of disparate, localized performance practices
into a widely circulated pan-Indian style. With its emphasis on spectacle
and song, it fostered modes of visual and aural discrimination that were
linked to pre-existing forms, yet afforded new pleasures by means of technological innovations that conveyed the feel of modernity. This performative
grammar together with an evolved typology of narrative later infused into
Indian cinema the character of a national idiom. The early modern theatre,
both as a temporal link to deep sources of cultural authority, and as a spatial
connector mediating scattered genres of poetry, music, and dance, laid the
ground for a shared expressive life, playing a critical role in the history of
public culture in India.

This chapter traces the theatrical legacy through a specific text, the *Indar
Sabha*, a work whose phenomenal success helps elucidate the transformations
in cultural consumption occurring toward the end of the nineteenth century. An early example of the crossover, the drama quickly moved out of its

courtly milieu to inhabit a large public domain. As it migrated, the story moved across media, taking shape as a popularly printed text, a stage drama, a rare book, a set of recorded songs, and as film. It traversed not only the distance from the provincial world of the Nawabs of Lucknow to cosmopolitan Bombay, it travelled across continents. While this chapter documents the mobility of the drama and its fluidity of format, it is centrally concerned with the elements of visual pleasure that underlay the text's wide circulation. Moreover, it focuses attention on the paradigm of spectatorship embodied in the central character of King Indar. Even as he reminded audiences of a bygone era, his position within the drama as patron and observer helped to construct the imagined self of the new consumer of popular culture. The transportation of the monarchical *mise en scène* to stages across the subcontinent and beyond extended the paradigm of royal consumption, establishing Urdu as the lingua franca of popular theatre and prefiguring the historical and mythological spectacles of the twentieth-century cinema.

The *Indar Sabha* (The Assembly of King Indra or in popular parlance Indar, hereafter IS) appears at a transitional moment in the history of northern India. On the most widely accepted account, it was composed in 1853 by Agha Hasan Amanat (*aka* Amanat Ali 1816–59), a poet attached to the court of Wajid Ali Shah at Lucknow (Illus. 2.1). The rule of the Nawabs of Awadh, arguably the most celebrated of the successor states that followed the Mughal dynasty, was to come to an inglorious end within a few short years. The bloodless annexation of Awadh in 1856 besmirched the king's reputation permanently and left later Indian nationalists with acute memories of loss and guilt. A series of uprisings in 1857 challenged British dominance, but this revolt was resoundingly suppressed, and in 1858 Queen Victoria assumed new powers as the Empress of India. Nonetheless, during the decade of his reign Wajid Ali was considered a generous and creative patron of the arts, who not only provided for the maintenance of performers but through his personal involvement advanced artistic development in several fields. He nourished *kathak*, the distinctive Indo-Muslim style of dance, embellished the light classical song form *thumri*, composed poetry in several languages, and adapted both Persian-style romances (*masnavi*) and dramas based on stories of the god Krishna (*lila*) for his own royal stage. Famed for his hedonistic habits, among the British he gained notoriety for spending more time in his harem, which he called a *parikhana* or 'house of fairies', than attending to affairs of state.

Apparently affected by the eclectic activities at his patron's salon, the poet Amanat Ali created the IS, an original work that assimilated Urdu *ghazals*, Braj Bhasha *thumris*, and Awadhi folk songs to a narrative base

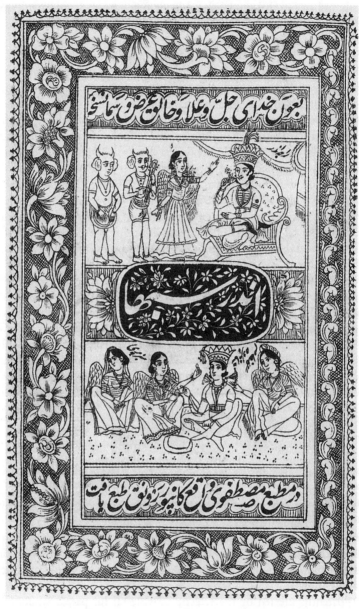

2.1. Title page of 1853 Urdu edition of Amanat's *Indar Sabha*.
Reproduced with permission from the British Library.

drawn from several popular *masnavis*. Composed entirely in verse, having no division into acts and scenes, and constructed as a pageant of song and dance connected by a thread of a story, the IS lacked the characteristics of modern drama that critics would subsequently delineate. Yet this premodern literary text became a performance phenomenon that remained a favourite on the stage and in cinema for more than a hundred years, well into the modern period. Now viewed by scholars as the first Urdu drama, the IS was such a novelty that it became a nineteenth-century bestseller. It was multiply reprinted in Urdu, transliterated into Hindi, Gurumukhi, Gujarati, and even the Hebrew script, and published in Tamil, Sinhala, Malay, and German translations. Moreover, as a standard item in the repertoire of the Parsi theatrical companies, it was carried to all corners of the subcontinent and even beyond, and it spawned a legion of imitations and adaptations into other languages. In the twentieth century, songs from the IS were among the first wax recordings made; several successful screen versions are known. The IS is thus both a landmark in the canons of literary history and a foundational moment in the evolution of the popular culture of South Asia.

Royal Patronage and Historiography

Before proceeding to Amanat and his contested career, let us briefly review the north Indian landscape and the development of courtly drama between 1600 and 1850 in the languages that came to be collectively referred to as 'Hindi'. Braj Bhasha adaptations of Sanskrit plays were written and possibly performed under royal patronage beginning with *Hasyarnava* of Rasarup in 1689. In Rajputana, princely patronage spurred the Khyal theatre, linked to martial and romantic ballads of the region, from around 1750. Meanwhile a flourishing Vaishnava court theatre developed under the ruling dynasties of several regions in the north and east, including Mithila, Nepal, Bundelkhand, and Assam. Dramas like *Harishchandra Nrityam* (1651), *Raja Gopichandra* (1712), *Krishnacharitopakhyan Natakam* (1835), all manuscripts found in Nepal but written to varying degrees in Hindi, establish the significant patronage of the Malla court in Nepal.[2] In Varanasi, the *Ram Lila* as staged at Ramnagar was massively reworked under Maharaja Ishvariprasad Narayan Singh (1835–89). The Rani of Jhansi's husband, Gangadhar Rao (r. 1835–53), presented *Shakuntala* and *Harishchandra* at court and occasionally appeared on stage himself. Contrary to the notion that Muslims eschewed theatrical entertainment, different groups of players known as Bhagatiyas, Bhands, Nats, and Naqqals found favour in the Mughal and Nawabi courts at Delhi and Lucknow (Hansen 1992: 56–75).

Wajid Ali Shah's theatrical interests summed up a number of these trends. Before he attained the throne, he penned a drama *Radha Kanhaiya ka qissa* based on the amours of the Hindu cowherd god; it was performed in Huzur Bagh in 1843. As king, he spent large sums to maintain a *rahas-khana*, or drama hall, named after the *rahas* or *ras lila* tradition of Vaish-nava devotional drama. Singing and dance formed integral parts of these productions, for which a large corps of concubines was especially recruit-ed and trained, and legend has it that Wajid Ali himself played the role of the god Krishna. Although it is often assumed that temple dramas of the Vrindavan area were influential in this construction, courtly traditions of Krishnaite pageantry elsewhere in the region may have been more important. The meaning of the word *rahas* gradually mutated to embrace all of the theatrical entertainments at the Lucknow court, regardless of topic. Wajid Ali additionally adapted three Persian romances (*masnavi*) for the stage and sponsored performances of them in Qaisar Bagh during his reign (Hansen 1992: 75–6).

Despite the obvious importance of this courtly dramatic activity, scholar-ship on the IS has long been divided on the question of Amanat's relationship to it. One body of opinion asserts that Amanat was commissioned to write the IS by the Nawab, that he was inspired by the model of western opera, and that the first performance of the drama occurred on the royal stage in Qaisar Bagh. Some commentators claim that Wajid Ali Shah played the title role of King Indar in the debut. This view stems from Nur Ilahi and Muhammad Umar's *Natak sagar*, a compendium of world drama and, pub-lished in 1924, the first such to be written in Urdu. The various notions of a royal commission, a western model, and/or a court performance are ac-cepted by the major Urdu literary historians writing in English, Ram Babu Saksena (1940), Annemarie Schimmel (1975), and Muhammad Sadiq (1984), as well as by a host of scholars writing in Urdu. The passage upon which they rely is as follows:

Who is not familiar with the circumstances of Wajid Ali Shah of Awadh? The tales of that era still cause tears of blood to flow from the eyes of sensitive souls. But a detailed description of all that is beside the point of this essay. It is sufficient to say that the court at that time was the cradle of luxury and pleasure. And every innovation at Qaisar Bagh, every royal order, indeed every new scheme raised a furor of excitement. Each member of the court was absorbed in the project of devising some new form of entertainment for Rangila Piya [the king]. Gradually all their powers of invention were ex-hausted, and the courtiers began to fill new bottles with old wine. In this connection a French attendant introduced a model of the theatres in the

west. This attracted the attention of some of the Hindustanis, and they compared the prevalent forms of theatre with western dramas. This was the time
when . . . [not only] France but Europe in general was becoming converted
to *opera* (meaning, that drama performed entirely by means of singing and
dancing). Therefore the kind of French drama that was mentioned in the
presence of the king was *opera*.[3] Singing and dancing were already favourite
items, thus it was suggested that an opera be prepared conforming to
Hindustani taste. By drawing lots, Amanat's name was chosen, and he fulfilled this duty in the manner of an obligation in 1270 H [Ilahi and Umar
1982: 354–5].[4]

Opposing this, Abdul Halim Sharar maintained that Amanat, rather
than taking orders from the Nawab or any foreigner, had on his own initiative imitated the courtly enactments of the dalliance between Radha and
the *gopis* with Lord Krishna, in which the king reputedly acted with his
favourite. Interestingly, Ilahi and Umar's remarks had already come under
attack by Abdul Halim Sharar, and in the *Natak sagar* itself they incorporated
a long passage from Sharar's essay in *Dil gudaz*, together with a detailed re-
futation. Another article by Ilahi and Umar, published in the journal of the
Anjuman-i Taraqqi-i Urdu in 1924, provoked a similar counter-response
by Sharar. Sharar's pieces were later collected in his chronicles of nineteenth-
century Lucknow culture and society, published as *Guzashta Lakhnau* in
1927 and translated as *Lucknow: The Last Phase of an Oriental culture.*

In 1927, Masud Hasan Rizvi 'Adib' added his voice to Sharar's, basing
his arguments on what he considered the first edition of the play, to which
Amanat had appended a commentary (*sharh*). Later research by Rizvi took
shape in two lengthy volumes under the title *Urdu drama aur istej* (1957).
Bristling at the notion of western influence, Rizvi rather sweepingly asserts
that no European had access to the Nawab. He denies that Amanat was ever
present at court, citing Fasahat, Amanat's younger son, who in 1926 wrote
that apart from his father's attachment to a Sufi sanctuary from which he
received a stipend, he had no connection to any *darbar* (Rizvi 2, 1957: 42).
Further, Rizvi appends evidence from *tazkirahs* and the poet's oeuvre to
show that Amanat suffered paralysis and from the age of twenty could not
speak. In the commentary to the IS, for example, Amanat wrote that he had
become housebound because of his condition, and from this Rizvi attempts
to establish that he was never present at court. Finally, Rizvi quotes Amanat's first son Latafat, to the effect that his father composed the IS at the request of his own friends (Rizvi 2, 1957: 44). In the absence of any mention
of Amanat in Wajid Ali's many writings, Rizvi concludes that there was no
royal command behind the drama and no court performance.

Rizvi's position has been influential among the newer generation of Urdu scholars, who perhaps are more eager than their forebears to establish the Indian roots of the IS. It is not difficult to see how denying foreign contact, particularly at the moment of origin, fits a particular kind of nationalist narrative. Without belabouring the issue further, it seems likely that both views contain some truth. The event of composition might have occurred over a period of time and amidst a combination of circumstances: Amanat's probable presence at court (whether mute or no), suggestions circulating about a new operatic style, his desire to capture the Nawab's favour (possibly unsuccessful), and performances inside and/or outside the royal circle. The disgrace attached to the Nawab's name by nationalists could explain the disavowals of Amanat's sons. Perhaps they were attempting to legitimize their father's achievement.

Regardless of the merits of the two sides' claims, what stands out most strikingly is the fact that public opinion until the 1920s firmly associated Amanat and the IS with the Nawab of Lucknow, Wajid Ali Shah. Although in 1924 the issue of the drama's origins did become a topic of debate within a small scholarly coterie, in the period of its greatest public following the IS carried with it a history that linked it to the court at Awadh and to the flamboyant personality of the Nawab. Writing in 1889, John Campbell Oman, a professor of natural science at Government College, Lahore, reported after viewing a performance of the IS in Anarkali that it was 'composed, it is said, by a Mussulman poet, by command of Wajid Ali Shah'.[5] The opinion of *Natak sagar* authors Ilahi and Umar was based largely on the traditions of Khurshedji Baliwala, a famous actor of the nineteenth-century Parsi theatre (Ilahi and Umar 1982: 359; Saksena 1940: 351). In 1917, A. Yusuf Ali, in an article for the Royal Society of Literature in London, called Wajid Ali Shah and Amanat 'co-founders' of the modern school of Hindustani drama (Yusuf Ali 1917: 91).

The publicly shared perception of royal origins must be counted as a significant factor in the popularity of the IS, insofar as spectators believed they were beholding a direct link to the Awadh court and its sumptuous ambience. The famous drama enjoyed the reputation of offering something real, something historically verifiable about the monarchical past. For many viewers, the tableau of Indar enthroned also had religious resonances, a point I will soon develop. In any event, what the stage delivered was a past transformed, brought closer to the audience by having crossed an imagined boundary between court—where it had its putative origins—and populace—where it was presently situated.

Narrative and Linguistic Convergence

The text of the IS, although not demarcated by Amanat into acts or scenes, naturally divides into two parts; the second of these comprises the story proper. The events take place in the court of Indar, king of the gods, who sits in state flanked by beautiful fairies. The Emerald Fairy (Sabz Pari) falls in love with an earthly prince (Gulfam), and with the assistance of the Black Demon (Kala Dev) she smuggles Gulfam into Indar's heaven. Displeased at this infraction, Indar casts Gulfam into a well and clips the wings of the Sabz Pari, who plunges to earth. Undaunted, she disguises herself as a female mendicant (*jogin*) and, singing irresistible songs of separation, gains readmission to the heavens, whereupon she wins the king's favour, and eventually earns her lover's release. Indar grants his blessings to the couple and they are reunited amidst general celebration.

By late medieval times the Vedic deity Indra/Indar had evolved into an emblem of the lordly monarch, and his entourage of beautiful dancing girls, whether known as *apsaras* or *paris*, symbolized his potency and dedication to sensual pleasure (*vilas, kam*). This figurehead of the Hindu pantheon is wedded in the IS to the theme of romance between a fairy and a mortal, long a staple of narrative genres in Urdu and Persian (*qissa, dastan, masnavi*). Amanat probably modelled his plot on two specific *masnavis* that achieved renown earlier in the nineteenth century. The romance of prince Benazir and princess Badr-i Munir as told in *Sihr ul-bayan* by Mir Hasan (1727–86) was, in 1805, one of the first Urdu books ever printed. It could have been the source for such scenes in the IS as the fairy's first encounter with the sleeping prince, his befuddled awakening in the fairy world, his imprisonment in the well, and the disguise of the fairy as a *jogin*. A later work, *Gulzar-i nasim* by Daya Shankar 'Nasim' (1837), itself a reworking of the prose tale *Gul-i bakavali* or *Mazhab-i ishq* by Nihal Chand, was said to be an effort at repeating Mir Hasan's success (Schimmel 1995: 199). From it Amanat may have borrowed the description of Indar's court, the king's anger upon learning of the fairy's love for a mortal, and other such passages.

What sets the IS apart from its antecedents is the very simplicity of the storyline. Whereas long *dastans* contain embedded worlds with innumerable conquests and love affairs, even the shorter tales generally include a subplot with a second pair of lovers, useful for complications such as jealousy, mistaken identity, and so on. The IS storyline is restricted to a single pair of lovers, and the only serious obstacle they face is the king's hostility, which is readily overcome by the fairy's enchanting singing.

One aspect that the IS shares with the earlier narratives is the presence of an active female *ashiq* (lover) in the character of the *pari*. Fairies in these stories pursue their male love-objects, declare their infatuation openly, carry them away through the air, and kiss or touch them on their own initiative. Born of fire, possessed of the ability to appear and disappear at will, they exert a powerful control over the hero, not unlike the demanding, high-status Beloved of the Urdu *ghazal*. The difference is that the Beloved of the *ghazal* remains Other—distant, veiled, unobtainable except in death. The *pari* is all too near, forward, and potentially overpowering.

The compression of the narrative and, possibly, the construction of feminine agency suggest a rudimentary form of realism, a reading buttressed by the popular commentarial tradition. For generations, it has been maintained that the character of Indar in the drama is based on the historical figure of Wajid Ali Shah. Some commentators extend the verisimilitude to the other characters as well. Gulfam's tenderness and passivity are hereby explained as the character traits of his real-life counterparts, the princes at the court. The effete environment in which they moved supposedly deprived them of manliness and fortitude. The Sabz Pari similarly is said to resemble the courtesans of Lucknow. In contrast to the princes, she is depicted as full of daring, vision, and determination. Additionally, she uses a form of women's speech (*zanani boli*) that identifies her as a member of a particular stratum of Lucknow society (Husain 1990: 22–3).

This interpretation gains support from the first (and in certain ways more original) part of the drama, in which Amanat recreates a court that resembles Wajid Ali Shah's own. In the opening scene, Indar is displayed enjoying himself as he is entertained by a succession of lovely fairies who enter one by one. Each performs a set of songs and dances before him. This royal assembly is designated within the text by terms such as *sabha, majlis, mehfil,* and *jalsa*, all of which convey the general sense of a public function, recital, or performance. These usages refer to the cultural gatherings held in the outer, public rooms of wealthy patrons, wherein poetry was recited and/or dance and musical expertise displayed. Such celebratory events establish a context in which public honours may be distributed or denied, and in which the mutuality of regard (or its lack) between the performer and the patron may be magnified in intensity by the potential rivalry of the others present within the circle. This could be called a kind of public sphere, but it is one filled with strong currents of personal and at least partially covert feeling.

Within the *sabha*, through the poetic vocalizations of the fairies, the character Indar is serially addressed as deity, king, patron, poet, and lover. One moment a fairy takes on the voice of a *gopi* in a Hori, a Braj Bhasha song genre celebrating the Holi festival, and chides the playful Shyam (Lord Krishna) for drenching her:

Pa lagi kar jori
Shyam mo se khelo na hori.

Clasping your feet I beg of you,
Please Shyam, don't play Holi with me.

Gauven charavan main nikasi hum sas nanand ki chori
Sagari chunar rang men na bhijovo itni suno bat mori. (#9)[6]

I came out to graze the cows, stealing away from my in-laws.
Don't drench my whole garment in dye—this much I ask of you.

Next she mourns the absence of her lover (*piya*, 'beloved', one of Wajid Ali's pen-names) in the genre specific to the rainy month of Savan:

Bin piya ghata nahin bhave
Rah rah dil raund ho ave
Bijari ki chamak tarpave darave
Bin piya ghata nahin bhave. (#28)

Without my Beloved/Piya, I cannot endure the rainy season:
My heart is oppressed with longing.
The lightning crashes—my body thrashes.
Without my Beloved/Piya, I cannot endure the rainy season.

Or in the characteristic masochistic pose of the *ashiq* or lover in an Urdu *ghazal*, she complains of her beloved's haughty neglect and threatens suicide:

Takara ke sar ko jan na dun main to kya karun
Kab tak firaq-i yar ke sadme saha karun. (#11)

What should I do but dash out my brains?
How long can I bear the blows of separation from the Beloved?

He, the passive but powerful Beloved, emerges as a multivalent object of desire.

The language of the songs moves back and forth easily between Urdu, Braj, Awadhi, and Khari Boli. 'Hindu' and 'Muslim' referents overlap as the king's identity slips between Indar, Krishna, and Nawab. Whether one chooses to think of the IS as a self-consciously syncretistic work or an unpremeditated reflection of the hybrid culture of the Lucknow court, the distance between it and its sectarian antecedents—the Vaishnava drama and poetry, the Sufi romantic allegories—is striking. Mystical overtones are absent or converted into erotic pleasure bordering on the comedic. Although the current understanding of secularism hardly existed, the IS could be considered a secular text insofar as it was consumed by heterogeneous groups without regard to its religious references. The potential for this pluralistic pattern of consumption is specifically encoded in the play's language, its most fundamental means of representation.

Indar's very presence on the stage invites the spectator into the generic courtly setting within which the drama unfolds. Given the structure of the play within the play, the audience's sense of being a witness—indeed a participant—at court travels with the performance regardless of where the stage is set or who enacts the role of Indar. The text herein exemplifies a recurring feature of nineteenth-century popular culture present in sundry expressive media. This is the fascination with royal power and its symbolism of splendour and sensual pleasure, even as the political fortunes of the aristocracy were on the decline. The courtly aesthetic with its opulent sets, costumes, etiquette, diction, and abundance of feminine beauty dominate the era, providing a point of identification initially for the pleasure-seeking nobility but eventually for spectators of more humble origins.

With the breakdown of the structure of royal patronage after the annexation of Awadh and the post-1857 consolidation of British power, sophisticated styles of music, dance, and poetry moved out through the mediation of popular theatre into a restructured entertainment economy. Earlier, in the days of Shuja ud-Daula, Lucknow had witnessed an enormous influx of musicians and singing courtesans, a process which accelerated in Wajid Ali Shah's time. After the fall of Awadh, there ensued an exodus of the court and the harem to Matiya Burj in Calcutta. With performers formerly employed at court turning to the rapidly-growing theatre industry (and later the cinema) for economic reasons, dance and song genre such as *kathak* dance, *thumri*, and *ghazal* singing entered the popular arena, where they were readily consumed by audiences attracted by their aura of prestige. Indeed, the post-feudal aesthetic would prove to be far more persuasive with the larger populace than the shifts in literature and art towards depiction of the new urban elite and its concerns. Middle-class reformists may have spurned this nostalgia for the monarchical past and devalued works of popular theatre that represented it, but feudal attachments remained strong among the public well into the twentieth century.

The Spectator as Consumer of Visual Pleasure

Searching the text for clues to its realization in performance, one is struck by the strong visual element which is conveyed at two levels: 1) through the speeches of the characters, with concomitant suggestions of movement, lighting, and costume; 2) through illustrations to the various printed editions. (No stage directions were published in the early editions of the text.) The illustrations call for a separate treatment, to which I will return. A striking element of colour coding is contained within the IS and was carried into production by the stage directors.[7] In the first part, the *sabha* section per se, the four fairies are named after monocoloured gemstones: *Pukhraj* (topaz), *Nilam* (sapphire), *Lal* (ruby), and *Sabz* (emerald). Each is attired in clothes appropriate to her colour and signs songs that describe her beauty, referring to that colour and its association with seasons, festivals, flowers, trees, and other elements of nature. Thus the Topaz Fairy signs an item known as Basant (spring) in the *raga* Bahar (spring) celebrating her yellow outfit and referring to marigolds and the new blossoms of the mustard plant (*sarson*).

Rut ai basant ajab bahar
Khile jard phul birvan ki dar
Chatko kusum phule lagi sarson
Phapakat chalat guhun ki bar. (#7)

Spring has come, that wondrous season!
Yellow blossoms hang from the tree branches.
Clusters of bright mustard flowers burst forth,
Sheaves of new wheat rustle and sway.

Beginning in the 1870s, special lighting was added to accentuate each fairy's colour when she first appeared on stage. According to Memuna Dalvi: 'To create the effect of the marvelous, *lime light* was used, so that as each fairy entered Raja Indar's court, the entire scene was bathed in the light of that fairy's garments. The spectators were beside themselves and burst into spontaneous applause.'[8]

As the pageant proceeds, the fairies assembled on stage form a rainbow. Their songs suggest an abbreviated *barahmasa*, a favourite song genre of the nineteenth century depicting the erotic possibilities of the cycle of twelve months. These serial performances construct a fashion show, an early Miss India contest, wherein acting and singing talent are joined with contrasts in appearance and style. The IS's prologue also prefigures the variety show, now a ubiquitous genre of the subcontinent's transnational popular culture. The practice of submitting performers to a dignitary for judgement is still prevalent. Karen Leonard reports that at a Hyderabad Association dinner in Fremont, California, girls from one Mrs Saxena's Dance School performed on stage before a community leader identified as 'Nawab', seated on a red velvet sofa (Leonard 1996). The VIP-as-Indar/Nawab model helps a group construct a sense of identity through enacting binary relationships to a central authority.

In reference to the art of traditional narrative, the IS charts a movement away from *dastan* with its emphasis on episodic elaboration, extension through itemization, and verbal exhibitionism, to the late nineteenth-century genre of musical drama that characterized several regions of South Asia. Here narrative is attenuated, the action being not plotted so much as incidental to set pieces of song, dance, and poetry that seek repeated rounds of audience applause. The second movement is the accompanying shift from a private space to a public arena for entertainment, and with it a move from an aural/oral to a predominantly visual manner of consumption. *Dastans* with their endless illusions (*tilasm*), although recited in company, were often enjoyed within the realm of personal fantasy, aided by ingestion of opium.[9] The theatre replaced the visions in the mind with visions on the stage.

Several 'gazes' or types of viewing relationship were thereby constructed: that between performers on the stage, that between performers and the public, and that among members who constituted that public.[10] In the IS, the fairies perform for and bestow their 'sidelong glances' (*tirchhi nigahen*) not only upon the king but also upon the audience. Audience members direct their sights and desires towards the king and the entertaining fairies, as well as at each other. And Indar presides and gazes upon all those assembled. As patron and admirer of a bevy of colour-coordinated beauties, the position of Indar blurs with that of the spectator. While they may not completely elide, a bond of 'erotic complicity', as Anuradha Kapur calls it, pulls the chief performer and the spectator into close alliance (Kapur 1995: 407).

In this manner, the figure of Indar served to link premodern and emerging modern modes of spectatorship. With his valences as omniscient observer, lover, deity, and royal patron, he mediated the disparate cultures that once separated court and populace. When actual power passed to the British, many Indians clung to nostalgia for the throne and a king involved in dance, song, and poetry. A section of colonial society was persuaded by reformists that these displays of indigenous expressive culture were immoral, but the majority continued to treasure them and the ideal of a hedonistic patriarch. Moreover they found in him a new self-image. In this sense Indar's function was more than nostalgic; it was in a certain sense pedagogical. He instructed his audience in the art of ocular consumption. His position in the drama as focus of desire and his royal status as pre-eminent consumer or *mahabhogi*, constructed an imagined self for the emerging spectator. It generated pleasure in the consumption not only of theatrical entertainments but, by extension, of twentieth-century cinema, print journalism (film and fashion magazines), and romantic fiction.

Proliferation of Performances

The transformation of the IS into a phenomenon of the public stage owes a great deal to the Parsi theatre, a broadly based commercial network whose appeal and influence extended far beyond the community of Zoroastrians from which it took its name. Polyglot, panregional, and culturally hetero-geneous, the Parsi theatre encompassed performance in English, Gujarati, Marathi, and other Indian languages, although its primary languages were Urdu and, in the early twentieth century, Hindi. Its repertoire at first comprised heroic legends from the Persian *Shahnamah*, Indo-Islamic fairy romances, and adapted Shakespearean comedies and tragedies. By the late nineteenth century, content had come to focus on Indian historical epics, Hindu mythologicals, and contemporary social dramas.

Parsi-led amateur student groups emerged in Bombay around 1850. Shortly thereafter, Parsi business managers and shareholding actors organized some of the theatrical clubs into professional touring companies. The success of these companies can be attributed to several factors: new marketing techniques like newspaper advertisements and printed handbills; exotic names that evoked the British monarchy ('Empress Victoria Theatrical Company', 'New Alfred Company'); the novelty of the proscenium stage with its elaborate painted scenery and special effects; the allure of 'operatic' singing and declamatory acting techniques; and a sudden desire among the urban populace to be seen and to see one another in the theatre.

Parsi theatre was the most widely circulated form of dramatic entertain-ment available to urban audiences in greater India until the advent of sound films in 1931.[11] The Bombay companies regularly toured Lahore, Karachi, Peshawar, Delhi and the Gangetic plain, Calcutta, Dacca, Hyderabad, and Madras. In each of these cities spinoff troupes emerged, imitating the style and even the names of the prestigious Bombay companies. Through a pro-cess of selection and adaptation in contact with local forms, the Parsi theatre influenced a number of regional styles of musical theatre, including the Maharashtrian Sangeet Natak, the Company Natak in Karnataka and Tamilnadu, the Nautanki in northern India, and the Calcutta Theatres in Bengal. It also exerted a major impact on new urban drama in Hindi, Mara-thi, Gujarati, Bengali, and Tamil. Reaching even beyond the 'black waters', in the 1880s Parsi companies carried Indian languages and songs to Ran-goon, Colombo, Singapore, and London. Like Nautanki, the 'folk' form about which I have written at length (Hansen 1992), the Parsi theatre was an important conduit in the cultural flow connecting distant urban areas with each other and with the hinterland. The difference was chiefly one of audience. Whereas the Parsi theatre appealed, at least in its first half-century, to a sophisticated urban clientele, the Nautanki audience was drawn primarily from the agricultural and artisan groups in villages and towns.

From highlights of the IS's stage life preserved in various sources, it is possible to assemble a partial chronology of performances of the long-lived play. Most commentators note that Amanat's drama earned immediate fame and soon appeared on stages all over India. Yet there is a gap between the IS's initial date of publication, 1853, and what appears to be its first performance by a Parsi theatre company in Bombay in 1864. One can only conjecture how the play reached Bombay from Lucknow. Rizvi, referring to a *qita* of Amanat's in the first edition of the IS, maintains that the drama had already become famous by the time it was published and was being imitated and committed to memory. He suggests that professional troupes based in Lucknow fanned out into the towns and villages in order to perform it. Performances were known by the names of the troupe organizers, e.g. *The Indar Sabha of Hafiz, The Indar Sabha of Jawahar.* Competitions were held, in the manner of simultaneous shows on opposite sides of the Husainabad tank, to see which troupe could attract the largest crowd (Rizvi 2, 1957: 119–20). Rizvi's assertions are consonant with his interpretation of the IS as an essentially *awami* (people's) phenomenon. However, he fails to address the disturbances in Lucknow in the period 1856–8, resulting from the annexation of Awadh and the so-called mutiny, and the effect they may have had on play production and attendance. Saksena implies that these events caused the migration of the IS, asserting, 'With the deposition and deportation of Wajid Ali Shah festivities and frolics at Qaisar Bagh came to an end. *Inder Sabha* found no home at Lucknow with its turmoil and tribulations and it travelled forth to Bombay' (Saksena 1940: 353).

According to Abdul Alim Nami, the first Bombay performance was presented by the Alfred Natak Mandali (theatrical company) in 1864. This Parsi company was one of the first to switch from English and Gujarati plays to Urdu, retaining Muhammad Ali Ibrahimji Bohra as scriptwriter. The troupe also toured Hyderabad and Madras and began regular tours to Delhi, Agra, and Lahore in 1861. Although Nami offers no details about the IS performance, he observes that the Alfred was also the first company to employ mechanical devices to create special effects (Nami 1975: 44–9). Another chronicler, Masihuzzaman, does not name the company, but he confirms that an 1864 Grant Road performance was the first in which the

IS was presented on a proscenium stage with a frontal curtain. He indicates that the play had been adapted for this purpose by being divided into five scenes or acts.[12]

The next memorable performance was the 1873 Bombay production by the Elphinstone Dramatic Club under the direction of Kunvarji Nazir (*aka* C.S. or Cooverji Sohrabji Nazir). This production was famed for its special innovations in lighting, cited already. The music also received special attention, with the whole play apparently being performed in one 'rag-ragini' (Ibrahim Yusuf 1980: 57). Gulfam was played by N.N. Parakh, Sabz Pari by Shyavaksh Rustamji Master, and Indar by Khurshedji Behramji Hathiram (Gupta 1981: 135).

If Somnath Gupta's dates are correct, it was in the following year that Nazir introduced the IS to Calcutta theatre audiences during a tour of the Victoria Natak Mandali, the most successful Parsi troupe of this period. In Bombay, the company had already earned considerable fame by presenting Gujarati plays directed by K.N. Kabra. When Dadi Patel took over in 1871, he began experimenting with dramas in Hindustani, often translations from Gujarati of plays by Edalji Khori. The concept 'Urdu opera' achieved popularity with the company's 1871 production of *Benazir badr-i munir*, starring Khurshedji Baliwala and Pestanji Framji Madan. In 1872, at the invitation of Sir Salar Jang, Dadi Patel led the troupe on a royally sponsored visit to Hyderabad in the Deccan, which included a special performance in the palace harem.

In 1873, C.S. Nazir took over the company (Gupta 1981: 105–10). The circumstances of the Calcutta performance were the following:

> From Lucknow the troupe arrived in Calcutta, where they stayed in a Parsi family mansion. Before 1874, no Parsi theatrical company had visited Calcutta. Nazirji rented the Lewis Theatre on Chowringhee Road, later known as the Royal Theatre.
>
> Bengalis are of course extremely fond of music, and they awaited the Parsi singers with utmost eagerness. Several eminent Bengali singers invited the Parsi singers to their homes, where they discussed a number of matters pertaining to music. At that time in Bengal, the *organ* was commonly used, whereas in Bombay the tabla and sarangi were favoured, with only occasional use of the *fiddle*. The effect of these discussions was that the Parsi musicians were deemed deficient in their knowledge of classical music, leaving a bad impression on the Bengalis. Baliwala clearly indicated this deficiency to Kunvarji Nazir, and he became disheartened and perplexed. Then he took the bull by the horns and began preparations for the opera IS. He sent telegrams to Delhi summoning Dadabhai Ratanji Thunthi, Dr Narsharvanji

Navroji Parakh, and Dosabhai Dubash. The speciality of these three was that they could enact the IS anywhere, under any conditions. They had particular expertise in this drama.

The IS was performed successfully in Calcutta. The part of Raja Indar was played by Dadi Thunthi, Gulfam by Dr Parakh, and Lal Dev by Dosabhai Dubash. Dadabhai Thunthi's singing, acting, and attractive appearance impressed the audience tremendously. But jealousies cropped up among the actors. Dosabhai Mangol and Khurshed Baliwala, who ordinarily played the roles of Indar and Gulfam respectively, were upset that they did not get a chance to perform [Gupta 1981: 111–12].[13]

After Calcutta the troupe performed in Banaras, where the Hindi author Bharatendu Harishchandra was a disgruntled spectator of a performance of *Shakuntala* (Hansen 1989: 85). Dadabhai Thunthi assumed the Victoria's directorship in 1876, and one of his innovations was to stage a *jalsa* or musical prelude before every drama, in which each member of the cast presented a song and then all joined together in a chorus. This practice, obviously imitated from the IS, caught on with the audience and was adopted by other Urdu-language companies (Gupta 1981: 114, 176). In 1876, the Victoria Theatrical Company toured Calcutta, Banaras, Delhi, Lahore, and Jaipur. In 1878, the company went as far as Rangoon and Singapore, and in 1881 they performed for the King of Mandalay. They also enjoyed the patronage of the maharajas of Jaipur and Patiala.[14]

The charismatic actor Khurshedji Baliwala was now at the helm, and following on these successes, he led the troupe to London in 1885 for a colonial exhibition. It is not known whether the IS was performed in the company's brief run at Gaiety Theatre. Because they had not obtained a government licence, a large fine was levied against the players, and they were forced to empty their coffers on the banks of the Thames and return to India empty-handed (Namra 1972: 62). Their first tour of Ceylon was in 1889, where the IS was among a number of popular Urdu plays performed. In the same year, the company had two dramas translated for performances in Sinhala; they returned to Ceylon in 1916–17 (Gupta 1981: 117–18).

The accounts of casting assignments establish that the fairies' roles, the only female parts in the IS, were consistently played by men until the 1870s, with male and female performers competing for these roles thereafter. In Lucknow itself, a contemporaneous account by Sa'adat Ali Khan Nasir establishes the early connection between the IS's popularity and the attraction of cross-dressed youths:

Miyan Amanat wrote a Masnavi [*sic*] called 'Indar Sabha' in the manner of a Rahas. . . . After hearing it, Pandit Kashmiri, Bihari Kahar and Mir Hafiz selected a few beautiful youths who were beardless, moon-faced, and beautiful. They gathered them together, had them memorize the Masnavi and taught them *raga* and dance, and thus they staged a Rahas. . . . In short, this IS became a big hit and was renowned among the populace. Just as having read Mir Hasan's Masnavi, thousands of women became debauched, similarly from this Masnavi IS, thousands of men became sodomites and pederasts, and pederasty began to enjoy great currency [Nasir 1970: 231].[15]

Once the IS was taken up by the Parsi theatrical companies, the female roles were routinely played by men. In the early days, young men of high social standing performed female dramatic parts in the cosmopolitan setting of new institutions like the Elphinstone College. D.N. Parakh, later a medical doctor and lieutenant colonel in the Indian Medical Service, who was a close associate of Nazir, featured in notable roles such as Portia in *The Merchant of Venice* and Mrs Smart in G.O. Trevelyan's *The Dawk Bungalow*. After 1870, the Parsi theatre entered a stage of increasing professionalization, and young men were systematically recruited and schooled to play women's parts. Pestanji Jijibhai Batliwala, an outstanding female impersonator, was known as Pesu Pukhraj, on account of his part as the Topaz Fairy in the IS (Gupta 1981: 144). Similarly Nasharvanji Framji Madan, a member of the Madan clan which came to exert financial control over a vast Parsi theatre empire, became famous as Naslu Tahmina for his performance as Sohrab's mother in *Rustam and Sohrab* (1868).

When Jehangir Khambata founded the Empress Victoria Theatrical Company in Delhi in 1877, he took full advantage of the talents of a popular female impersonator known as Naslu Sarkari (Nasarvanji Ratanji Sarkari). Famed for his sweet, cuckoo-like voice (*kokil kanth*), Naslu played the Sabz Pari to Kavas Khatau's Gulfam in the IS. Although a few Anglo-Indian women began to appear in female roles in the 1880s, resistance to the employment of women on stage continued well into the twentieth century, most notably in the New Alfred Theatrical Company which for over forty years upheld a ban on actresses. Not surprisingly, the New Alfred acquired the reputation of being one of the most 'respectable' Parsi troupes, and it attracted the likes of Madan Mohan Malaviya and Motilal Nehru to its performances. A number of female impersonators were associated with the New Alfred—Amritlal (Ambu), Narmada Shankar, Master Nissar (who later played opposite actress Kajjan in films), and Motilal.

Male company proprietors feared the stigma that would attach to their shows if women from the singing and dancing trades were allowed onto the stage. But professional women were eager to join the Parsi companies. While the Victoria company was away on tour (in 1872 or 1874), the Parsi Natak Mandali put on a performance of the IS with Latifa Begam, an accomplished courtesan, presumably in the role of the Sabz Pari. At the play's conclusion, just as she entered the wings, she was abducted by a Parsi man. Throwing his overcoat over her costumed body, he whisked her into his waiting carriage. The company owners did not have the courage to confront him. Latifa's disappearance created a sensation and was widely discussed in the newspapers, as a result of which the introduction of women on stage received a setback. But soon Amir Jan and Moti Jan, two Punjabi sisters, replaced Latifa with the company (Gupta 1981: 140).

Baliwala's chief rival, Kavasji Palanji Khatau, came to fame on the strength of his performance in the IS. Jahangir Khambata and Khatau employed a Bohra scribe to adapt the IS for the Empress Victoria Natak Mandali, founded in Delhi in 1876. The cast consisted of Khatau (Gulfam), Naslu Sarkari (Sabz Pari), Dorab Sachin (Pukhraj Pari), Kau Kalgir (Lal Dev), and Kavasji Handa (Indar). The Delhi IS was a huge hit and was followed by *Laila Majnun, Gul bakavali,* and *Khudabakhsh.* It was at one of these performances of the IS that Khatau and Miss Mary Fenton, the daughter of an Irish soldier, had their fateful meeting. When Khatau took over the Alfred Company in 1886, Mary Fenton became his chief actress, creating controversy but also attracting much attention to her renditions of Hindustani songs (Gupta 1981: 120; Saksena 1940: 354).

Another renowned Anglo-Indian actress was Patience Cooper, who frequently played in the dramas of Agha Hashra Kashmiri. As women joined the Parsi stage in greater numbers, a premium remained on the exoticism of fair-skinned, seemingly foreign heroines. Handbills for Pandit Narayanprasad Betab's plays in the 1920s advertise 'White misses [*gori-gori misen*] who will present enchanting songs and dances' (Singh 1990: 61). Records include mention of the Indian Ladies Theatrical Company (Bombay) which featured Jamila, a Jewish woman who played the role of the Sabz Pari, allegedly surpassing all competitors (Ibrahim Yusuf 1980: 310–12). While earlier male-to-female impersonators gained fame for their successful cross-dressed performances, somewhat later Mai Rajul, the director of the Sindh Theatrical Company, became well-known for her portrayal of Raja Indar in the IS (Singh 1990: 169).

A number of other troupes were celebrated for their performances of the IS. The Star of Punjabi Theatrical Company of Lahore, founded in 1875

and owned by Babu Nabi Bakhsh, had the IS as its most successful production. The IS was the most popular play of Shining Star Theatrical Company of Karachi. The Empire Theatrical Company of Burma staged the
play in Singapore in 1912. In the 1920s, the IS was regularly featured by
the Great Eastern Parsi Theatrical Company and the Nizam Theatrical
Company in Rangoon. As late as the 1940s, companies in Bombay such as
the B.N. Theatrical Company and the Sun Moon Light Theatrical Company
were distinguished by their performances of the IS (Ibrahim Yusuf 1980:
310–12).

Such an enumeration can only be considered partial, for theatre companies
were established in every major city in the subcontinent from Peshawar to
Madras to Dacca.[16] And wherever Parsi theatre was found, the IS was not
far behind. The IS phenomenon dominated the popular theatre world until
the era of the talking cinema. When the Parsi companies did not produce
it entire, they used a scene or two as a curtain-raiser (Gupta 1981: 229). In
1917, A. Yusuf Ali, a Fellow of the Royal Society of Literature in London,
reported that the IS 'still holds its own on the Hindustani stage after a run
of seventy years, and its universal popularity is proved by the numerous but
unsuccessful imitations made of it. Most companies even now include it in
their repertory' (Yusuf Ali 1917: 91) (Illus. 2.2).

Moreover, touring troupes reached Nepal, Guyana,[17] and, as already
mentioned, England, Singapore, and Ceylon. The eminent Nepali dramatist
Balakrishna Sama (1903–81) recounts in his autobiography growing up in
a well-to-do Rana family where Parsi troupes performed in the palatial resi-
dence of his grandfather, General Dambar Shamsher (Pradhan 1980: 5;
Onta 1997: 75–6). Submitting a petition to the Prime Minister of Nepal
in 1932, Sama reported that Hindi and Urdu-language plays were taught
and performed in the Rana palaces, among first on the list of these plays he
named the IS (Sama 1972: 340).[18] Another source indicates that a performance of the IS was staged at the Royal Imperial Opera House in Kathmandu
in 1901 by one Manikman (Das 1991: 237).

The IS was similarly carried to Singapore and Malaya by Indian performers. According to Indonesian scholars, theatre troupes known locally as
Wayang Parsi employing men and women arrived as early as the 1870s
(Hussain 1992: xxii).[19] The performance of the IS normally took two
nights, evidently corresponding to the two parts of the drama. The songs,
set to Hindustani melodies but using Malay words, became so popular that
the play was widely enacted not only at weddings and celebrations of high-
level officials but among the people. The Parsi theatre style was incorporated,

Long awaited Programme

At 9-45 p. m. From Saturday 11th June 1938 At 9-45 p. m.

At SHIVANANDA THEATRE

The New Parsi Coronation Theatrical Co., of Calcutta,

Proudly presents

Indra Sabha

(IN HINDUSTANI)

Featuring:-

Master Nissar,

Miss. Mukhtar Begum,

Miss. Ramdulari,

Miss. Sultana,

Miss. Alquab,

Miss. Razia,

Mr. Manecklal,

Mr. Nenuram.

& others

Master Nissar, who noted an GULFAM in Madan's Film, will play the part of Gulfam on the stage.

This Drama needs no introduction

INDRA SABHA Means

Songs and Dances

IMAGINE you are in *Indra Sabha* How will you enjoy

So we have arranged

INDRA SABHA

Please come and enjoy

MASTER NISSAR

Special Purdah arrangement for Ladies

Daily at 9-30 p. m. Sundays at 6-30 p. m.

RATES 5 10 0, 3 6 0, 2-4-0, 1-2-0, 0-7-11, 0-3-11

LADIES 3 6 0, 2 4 0, 1 2 0, 0-12 0

The Youngman Press, Dialpot Cross, It City.

2.2. Handbill announcing 1938 performance of the *Indar Sabha* by the New Parsi Coronation Theatrical Company of Calcutta. Reproduced with permission from the Natya Shodh Sansthan.

together with other influences, into a new style of musical theatre called *bangsawan* (Tan 1993: 16–18). Professional troupes invoked the popularity of the IS by echoing its name. The Pushi Indera Bangsawan of Penang was established in 1885; the Comedy Pusi Indra Bangsawan was active in northern Sumatra in 1895. An advertisement for the play *Lakuan Inder Sabah in* 1905 lured the audience with transformation scenes:

> Come and see our splendid scenes.
> The breaking of Clouds and the appearance of the Sun
> The appearance of a Gigantic Lotus from the clouds
> The breaking of the flower . . .
> Come and see the wonderful lotus and birds from it
> Every petal opens, when you will see a flock of birds
> The stem of the flower breaks and there comes out an
> Elephant and seated amidst grandeur is King Indra.[20]

The widespread impact of the IS can be judged in a different manner by the negative opinion registered against it by the literati. It is not surprising that although Muhammad Husain Azad includes Amanat the lyric poet in *Ab-i hayat*, Amanat the dramatist and the IS find no place in this seminal work of modern Urdu criticism, dated 1880 (Rosen 1892: 8). Bharatendu Harishchandra, known to Hindi literary historians as the 'father' of Hindi drama, attempted to create an alternative to popular theatrical spectacles like the IS in Banaras in the 1880s. Mentioning specifically 'the Bhand, Indrasabha, Ras, Yatra, Lila, Jhanki, etc.' as premodern genres 'corrupt, that is, there is no theatricality left in them' (Anand 1978: 51). Although it is not known whether he actually saw a production of the IS, he certainly saw a number of Parsi plays. While his amateur stage was simpler and more restrained, Bharatendu nevertheless absorbed the influence of the popular style in his plays *Bharat durdasha, Chandravali,* and *Nildevi,* where the characters introduce themselves, praise their own beauty, and sing *thumris* and *ghazals* in the dialogues (Tivari 1959: 115–20).

Circulation in Print Culture

Meanwhile, the IS in another medium was also being widely consumed. Print technology and vernacular printing in particular came into their own in this period. The colonial regime, recognizing the political threat posed by the new medium and concerned to tighten its control, passed the Press and Registration of Books Act in 1867 and established a repository at the India Office Library, which today contains many editions of the IS and other nineteenth-century dramatic texts. As catalogued by J.F. Blumhardt, the India Office and British Museum, now both incorporated into the British Library, hold 28 Urdu editions of Amanat's play published between 1853 and 1890, 15 editions in Devanagari (1862–89), six in Gujarati script (1867–96), and one in Gurumukhi (1878).[21] Additional editions include both Amanat's IS and Madari Lal's *Indar Sabha*, a drama written in imitation of it (11 Urdu editions, 1 Devanagari, 1869–89), and separate editions of Madari Lal's IS also exist (3 in Urdu).[22] (See Appendix.)

The British Library information undoubtedly contains gaps, and other sources such as Rizvi and Rosen list additional editions, especially for the years between 1853 and 1867 when systematic government collection was not yet under way. Nonetheless, the data are sufficient to indicate that, beginning shortly after its appearance in print, the IS quickly became an unprecedented bestseller. If the statistics are definitive, its publishing peak was reached in the 1870s; during that decade forty-five editions were published from Agra, Kanpur, Delhi, Lahore, Patna, Bombay, Calcutta, and Madras.

Beyond these catalogues, an even wider sphere is indicated by the record of translations of the IS into other Indian languages. The library of the School of Oriental and African Studies at the University of London contains a Sindhi version published in 1902.[23] In south India, translations or adaptations were made into Tamil, Telugu, and Kannada. A.N. Perumal lists no less than ten versions of the play *Intira capa* in Tamil, the first published in 1886.[24] Some of these have fanciful names, e.g. *Fire IS, Lotus IS, Mountain IS* (Perumal 1981: 182–254). Further research is required to establish the context for these dramas and the meaning of their distinctive sobriquets. For Kannada, two references have been located: *Indrasabha natakavu*, by V.P. Guru Siddappa (1893) (Das 1991: 668) and *Indracapa*, translated by Tateri Ranga Rav (1915) (Kesavan 2, 1962: 333). In Telugu, several versions of plays entitled *Indracapam(u)* are extant, published in the mid-twentieth century (Kesavan 4, 1962: 304).[25]

The British Library contains an edition of a Sinhala IS dated 1893, published at Colombo by B.J. Preravana. It is described on the cover as one of the most interesting of the dramatic stories performed in Colombo by a group called the Lanka Drama Society, composed of men from Kollupiti (a neighbourhood within the current city limits).[26] Several other Sinhala dramas published in the 1880s include *Sattiangini nattyaya*, described in the bibliographical records as an 'Indian love story versified in "Hindustani" metre for the Sinhalese stage' and *Nattal peraliya*, 'A farcical play in five acts: "Christmas brawls" in "Hindustani" metre.' The composition of these dramas and their publication as books appear to follow visits by popular theatre troupes from India, which in turn spurred the formation of local theatrical companies.

Yet more interesting is the Malay translation, entitled *Syair indra sebaha*, by Mohammad Hassan bin Nasaruddin, published in Singapore in 1891. Two editions of the lithographed text are found in the British Library, both published by Haji Muhammad Siraj, a prolific nineteenth-century Malay publisher. A modern edition was prepared by Khalid M. Hussain and published together with introductory notes and a facsimile of the original by Dewan Bahasa dan Pustaka, Kuala Lumpur, in 1992. The illustrations to the 1891 text are very well done and show interesting cultural adaptations. In one picture, women wear knee-length skirts, short-sleeved blouses with buttons, and high heels. In several, the characters exhibit Chinese features of dress and hairstyle. Some pictures also show western military costumes. One wonders about the kind of music that accompanied the performances, for in one picture we see a violin being played in the western style, while several illustrations of the Emerald Fairy as a *yogini* show her holding the dual-gourd veena upside down.

In the German translation and scholarly essay by Friedrich Rosen, published in Leipzig in 1892, we note a somewhat different consumption pattern, that associated with nineteenth-century orientalism. Rosen provides a detailed genealogy, philological analysis, and literary approximation of the original for an erudite audience. As such, the IS was one of the few pieces of Urdu literature available in German translation at the time. Even in Germany, however, the drama could not leave behind its close links with popular performance. Rosen's translation was transformed into a libretto for *Im Reich des Indra*, composed by Paul Lincke, which according to Annemarie Schimmel became an 'oft-played' operetta (Schimmel 1975: 214).

The publishing record becomes somewhat fuzzy after 1900, but there is little question that the play's life as a printed text continued late into the twentieth century. This is established by my own purchase of a cheap Devanagari edition published by Agrawal Book Depot in Delhi, from a footpath in Jaipur in 1983. The recently acquired Nami Collection at the Library of Congress in Delhi may help to fill in the gap. According to Mohammad Burney, five dated and six undated editions of the IS are held in this body of theatre texts and ephemera collected by the late Dr Abdul Alim Nami, author of the four-volume series *Urdu thetar* and the *Bibliografia Urdu drama*.[27] Two of the dated editions are published by popular houses in the first half of the twentieth century, two are later scholarly editions, and many of the undated editions appear to belong to the early twentieth century.

Theatre as Spectacle, Text as Artefact

It is now possible to summarize some of the characteristics of nineteenth-century popular consumption that can be drawn from this discussion. As a multimedia, hybrid performance work, the IS was consumed by its theatre audience at many levels. Its various languages, song genres, verse forms, and dance items were probably placed mentally by connoisseurs of these arts into micro-environments within which the compositions were judged with reference to other *ustads'* creations. This, to a large extent, is how the IS as 'Urdu drama' has been treated by Urdu's literary critics, who judge Amanat's plot in relation to well-known *masnavis*, or measure his *ghazals* against those of Ghalib and Mir. Even to these consumers, as well as those less well versed in its constituent artistic traditions, the IS was still something greater than the sum of its parts.

The added ingredient, the hidden quality that cannot be located in the text, was the element of surprise or wonderment, generated by the use of visual illusions and stage devices to an unprecedented degree. When the early Parsi companies moved into the English-style playhouses erected in Bombay and Calcutta, they took over the technology of European theatre: the proscenium arch with its painted backdrop and curtains, western furniture for the audience (sofas, chairs, benches) and props for the stage, elaborate costumes, and a variety of mechanical devices for mounting special effects. The latest in 'elaborate applicances' were regularly ordered from England, so as to achieve 'the wonderful stage effects of storms, seas or rivers in commotion, castles, sieges, steamers, aerial movements and the like' (Yajnik 1933: 113).

In the case of the IS, the magical character of the story allowed for a full realization of what traditional Sanskrit aesthetics termed *adbhuta rasa* (the sentiment of wonder), what the nineteenth-century Hindi dramaturge Bharatendu called *kautuk* (surprise), and what a contemporary American cultural historian has labelled the 'technological sublime'.[28] Fairies appear out of nowhere at the clap of hands or shot of a pistol. Flying cots descend magically onto the stage. Trap doors make visible a scene like Gulfam's confinement in the well. Painted curtains bring the jagged perspective of European painting and baroque details of Mughal architecture within the proscenium arch. All of these added to the spectacle already manifest in the monarchical *mise en scène*.

As Anuradha Kapur suggests, stage technology functions as a modernizing element, enabling the audience to feel contemporary, up-to-date. It is an instrument in the translation of older, familiar narrative material into something new and strange (Kapur 1995: 418). The promise of novelty, even as imitation replaced imitation, drew audiences back to repeat performances. At the same time that they enjoyed a well-known tale, their encounters with stage technology allowed them the pleasure of partaking of modernity. The drama's songs, too, circulating independently of the play, acquired their own life just as film songs do today and remained a consistent source of audience pleasure. At a deeper level, the central preoccupations of the drama—romance, feudal luxury, and exotic fairies and djinns—were consumed within a post-feudal sensibility that although deemed escapist by nationalists nonetheless possessed a kind of cultural authenticity.

Along with these modes of reception and consumption, let us now turn to another aspect of this work, namely its status as an artefact. Whereas all Urdu manuscripts and early printed books bear an artful aspect based on their calligraphy, the IS's artistic interest is greater because pictures often illustrate the text. Beginning with its early published versions, the printed page was enhanced by penned drawings representing scenes from the play. Cover drawings were standard fare for nineteenth-century popular texts, enclosed by borders on four sides featuring floral motifs. Two scenes illustrate the cover of the 1853 Kanpur edition: one of Raja Indar (named by a tag) seated on his throne, watching a *pari* dance while two *devs* provide music on sarangi and tabla; the other of Gulfam Shahzada and Sabz Pari (tagged) sitting on the ground with two other fairies; the Emerald Fairy offers the prince a morsel to eat from a *thali* (platter). Subsequent editions contain a number of illustrations within the text, many of key scenes that are repeated with regularity. A detailed comparison of these drawings and their variations in style and content would be interesting as a study in its own right. It would additionally serve as a gauge of changes and continuities in consumption as the text and performance migrated from place to place.

While the IS's illustrated editions have neither been systematically catalogued nor analysed, a fascinating find at the India Office Library clearly establishes that in at least one instance, illustrated texts of popular plays were prepared not for ordinary readers but as objects of artistic value for elite consumers. This is exemplified by the discovery of a unique illuminated manuscript of the IS in Hebrew characters, dated March 1887 (Illus. 2.3).[29] Conforming to the evidence already provided of the Urdu IS published in Devanagari, Gujarati, and Gurumukhi scripts, the manuscript in question is not a translation into Hebrew but a transcription of the original Urdu in Hebrew characters. It belongs to a minute body of texts available from the late nineteenth century of Indian Jewish literature in Urdu. The only other such texts are an illustrated lithograph of the IS, published in or before

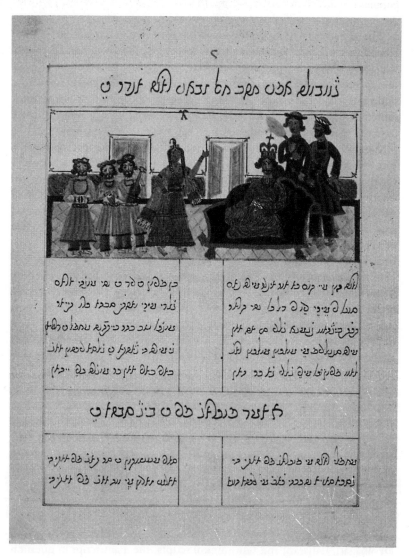

2.3. A hand-illuminated plate depicting the Topaz Fairy dancing before
Raja Indar, from the Hebrew-character edition of the
Indar Sabha, Calcutta 1887.
Reproduced with permission from the British Library.

1880, held privately by the Sassoon family in Jerusalem; and a version of the popular *Laila Majnu*, another Urdu play in Hebrew characters, housed in the Jewish National and University Library in Jerusalem.

The manuscript, lavishly illustrated in colour, was acquired by the British Museum from an antiquarian book dealer in London in 1970. The work was apparently produced by a scribe for a patron within the Baghdadi Jewish community of Calcutta, one of the three historical Jewish communities settled in India. This is surmised both from its provenance and from the difficult Iraqi cursive in which the manuscript is written. The scribe may have transliterated the text upon visual examination of a printed copy of the play, or lacking literacy in Urdu, he may have received it via oral transmission. The illustrations, which follow a style consistent with the Urdu editions of the play, must have been prepared by an artist outside of the Jewish community.

This manuscript, although an oddity within the textual history of the IS, suggests a point of intersection between Urdu's widening circle of literary production in the nineteenth century and a Hebrew-identified Jewish diaspora. One can speculate upon the consumption practices that brought the Hebrew IS into existence. Performed in Calcutta in 1874 by the Victoria Theatrical Company, the IS had achieved fame in the cultural market place of the city. Quite possibly, the Jewish community's leaders had attended performances, and they may have patronized the play or sponsored benefit performances. It is likely that its widely reprinted text was available either in the form of one of the migrating copies published in Delhi, Lucknow, or Kanpur, or in a Calcutta edition such as that of 1878 held in the India Office Library. The Baghdadi Jewish community was accustomed to writing Arabic in Hebrew characters. From there it was not an unthinkable invention to attempt to write Hindustani, the lingua franca used in everyday life and commerce, in Hebrew as well.[30] Cultural, religious, and historical traditions similarly inclined wealthy Baghdadi Jews toward appreciation of manuscripts and books as works of art. The conjoining of these factors prompted the commissioning of an artefact that is hybrid in language, concept, and design.

Recordings and Films

By way of epilogue, it will suffice to mention briefly the transmutation of the IS into the mass media of the twentieth century, namely gramophone recordings and cinema. F.W. Gaisberg, the original recording engineer of The Gramophone Company, London, came to India in 1902 seeking performing artists to provide recordings of popular songs. Two managers from the Calcutta theatre world, Amarendu Dutt of the Classic Theatre and Jamshedji Framji Madan of the Corinthian, closely collaborated with Gaisberg, as a result of which almost all of the 550 recordings made during the tour of November–December 1902 were by singers and musicians associated with these two theatres. According to Michael Kinnear, the Corinthian Theatre continued to be utilized as the main source for recordings in Hindi, Urdu, and Gujarati over the next few decades (Kinnear 1994: 18–19). Songs from the IS are listed on seventeen recordings (7- and 10-inch formats) in Kinnear's discography. The artists include Miss Mohatal (Corinthian Theatre), Miss Acheria (Corinthian, Classic), Miss Subashi, Miss Mahtab, Miss Gafooran, Master Takul (or Tikol), Mr Pestonji, and Sohrabji R. Dhondi, and all of the recordings were made between 1902 and 1907. In the circular pattern of consumption that characterizes the IS phenomenon, Kinnear notes: 'The artists of the Alfred Natak Mandali had also been recorded by several recording companies, including the Gramophone and Typewriter, Ltd., and the success of the recordings of these artists, no doubt contributed to the continuing popularity of the Alfred Natak Mandali' (Kinnear 1994: 19–20).

The availability of recordings of the IS's songs independent of live performances ushers in yet another mode of consumption, whereby the public voices of professional theatre personalities could be brought into and contained within the private salons and drawing rooms of those who had the means to purchase gramophones. A step along the path of commodification and distanciation between performer and consumer, the technology of sound recording, it must be remembered, was in the beginning received with the same reactions of wonderment and surprise as flying machines and trap doors. It is perhaps no coincidence that a new type of publication, the IS song book, also makes its appearance in the first decades of the twentieth century. These song books, three of which are contained in the Nami Collection of theatre ephemera at the Library of Congress in New Delhi, reproduce the lyrics of the most popular songs from the drama, detached from the narrative.[31] Although lacking the visual component that has made the Chitrahar television series such a success, song books and sound recordings made possible the exclusion of unwanted speeches, plot complications, and whatever moral dilemmas a story might pose, giving the consumer free rein to recombine the songs in a different order and create his/her own medley.

By 1918, J.F. Madan had turned his entrepreneurial skills towards film production and investing in cinema houses. The Madan chain of theatres and cinemas grew by the 1930s into an empire numbering more than 170,

spread across India, Burma, and Ceylon. Many of the motion pictures produced by Madan Theatres, Ltd., were filmed versions of popular dramas,
and they often featured the recording artists associated with the Corinthian
and Alfred theatres. The first filmed version of the IS was produced at Kohi-
noor Studios in Bombay by Manilal Joshi, a major silent director, in 1925
(Rajadhyaksha and Willemen 1994: 108). Although little is known about
this film, it is worth mentioning that silent films commonly employed tri-
lingual subtitles and were accompanied by live music supplied by theatre
artists. As popular entertainment, these shows were a direct continuation of
the travelling bioscope shows that popularized scenes and songs from the
Calcutta theatres in the first decade of the century; here too J.F. Madan's
enterprise played a major role.

One of the first motion pictures made with sound was *Indra Sabha*
(1932), directed by J.F. Madan's third son, J.J. Madan (Illus. 2.4). Running
to 211 minutes, this epic production boasted a total of seventy-one songs,
many of which were already familiar from stage shows and gramophone recordings (Rangoonwala 1979: 40). The cinematography was directed by
T. Marconi, an Italian who had earlier worked with Madan Theatres and
an Italian cast in *Savitri* (1923). Madan asked Marconi to model the choral
mise en scène after the Italian epics, and he ensured the film's popularity with
the Indian audience by casting the popular singing duo, Nissar and Kajjan
(Rajadhyaksha and Willemen 1994: 237–8). A Tamil version of the *Indra
Sabha* was directed by A. Narayanan and R.S. Prakash in 1936. In 1956,
Nanubhai Vakil, known for his remakes of silent films based on Parsi
theatre plays and considered a defining force for 'B-movie production in
post-WW2 period', directed a Hindi film entitled *Indrasabha* (Rajadhyaksha
and Willemen 1994: 211–12). None of the film versions of the IS is preserved in the National Film Archive of India in Pune.

In conclusion, just as the IS returned to its viewers a spectacular,
romanticized vision of its collective past, it facilitated the very production
of spectatorship within the new environment of the public commercial
theatre. Even in the modern trappings of the proscenium arch, the figure
of Indar surrounded by his court of admiring beauties constructed a
visual icon that synthesized religious, erotic, and political modes of self-
identification. The performance of kingly spectatorship within the diegesis
of the drama, moreover, established a set of patron/performer correspon-
dences linking the internal and the external audiences. The relevance of this
particular paradigm of desire faded in the later twentieth century, yet the
implantation of performative song and dance sequences before a pictorialized

audience remained a defining feature of the narrative structure of Indian cinema.[32] The IS was surely not the first dramatized composition to structure this mobile movement among texts, but it was certainly one which achieved long-lasting pan-Indian popularity. Despite its seeming archaism,

2.4. A still from the 1932 film of the *Indar Sabha* directed by J.J. Madan.
Reproduced with permission from B.D. Garga.

it continues to shed light on the construction of the visual vocabulary of modern India, even as it provides an illuminating example of the erotic, playful preoccupations of late premodern culture.

NOTES

1. An earlier version of this essay was published as 'The Migration of a Text: The *Indar Sabha* in Print and Performance', in *Sangeet natak*, nos 127–8 (1998: 3–34).

2. Patronage of Hindi–Urdu theatre in Nepal was to attain new levels in the late nineteenth century with Rana sponsorship of visits by the Parsi theatrical companies. See Onta (1997).

3. In my translations I have used the convention of italics to represent words that appear in English in the original Indian-language passage.

4. Translation is mine.

5. Oman (1908: 190–1). Although the citation is from the 1908 version entitled *Cults, Customs and Superstitions of India*, rather than the original, published as *Indian Life, Religious and Social*, a playbill dated 1881 and other details of performance mentioned by Oman suggest that his theatre section reflects the climate prior to 1889.

6. All citations are from the Urdu text edited by Rizvi (2, 1957). For a Devanagari version of Rizvi's edition, see Husain (1990). The translations are mine.

7. The idea of differentiating the beloveds by assigning them separate colours appears to be common in the *masnavi* tradition and is found in works such as Nizami's *Haft paykar*.

8. Ibrahim Yusuf (1980: 57). Translation is mine.

9. According to Frances Pritchett, 'The association of *dastan* narration with opium is mentioned in so many contemporary accounts that it should not be overlooked. If both *dastan-go* and audience were slightly under the influence of opium, they might well enjoy the long catalogs and other stylized descriptive devices, which slowed down the narrative so that it could expand into the realms of personal fantasy' (Pritchett 1991: 17).

10. As Shanta Gokhale has suggested in the context of Bombay and the nineteenth-century Marathi stage, what distinguished the emerging urban theatre from the traditional plays staged for the lower classes was the desire to be seen by others. 'Theatre-going to this class was a badge of class, a ritual for which you dressed and behaved in certain ways' (Gokhale 1995: 197).

11. Although the popularity of Parsi theatre decreased after the coming of the talkies, it was not completely displaced. Even in the 1960s, the Moonlight Theatre in Calcutta offered patrons a double bill—a film followed by a live drama—for the price of a single ticket (Agraval 1986: 56).

12. Masihuzzaman, cited in Ibrahim Yusuf (1980: 57).

13. Translation mine.
14. Maharaja Ram Singh of Jaipur was a great aficionado of drama. He had a play-house constructed at the present site of the Ram Prakash Cinema. Dadabhai Thunthi and several Parsi lads were retained to instruct Jaipur's professional musicians (including courtesans) in dramatic arts. In Patiala, the maharaja built an auditorium in 1891, for the use of the Parsi theatre companies.
15. Translated with aid from Carla R. Petievich.
16. Local companies (loosely called Parsi theatre, although not necessarily containing Parsis) were formed in a number of cities: the Albert Natak Company in Madras, the Nizami Company and Mahbub Shahi Natak Company in Hydera-bad, the Ripon Indian Club in Peshawar, the Oriental Opera and Dramatic Company in Lahore, the Victoria Theatrical Company in Amritsar (Gupta 1981: 239–43). For Parsi theatre in Dacca and East Bengal, see Ahmad (1990: 25–35) and Rehmani (1968: 209–19).
17. Gora Singh, a former resident of Queens, New York, remembered seeing the IS performed in Guyana in his youth. Peter Manuel acquired this information in the course of his fieldwork on Indo-Caribbean musical traditions and kindly relayed it to me (e-mail communication of 6 July 1995). (Gora Singh died in 1997).
18. I am indebted to Mary Des Chene for drawing this passage to my attention and translating it from the Nepali.
19. A draft translation of the Bahasa introduction to the Malay version of the IS was prepared with the help of Ninie Syarikin of the Voice of America in Washington, DC.
20. *Straits Echo* (11 February 1905), cited in Tan (1993: 41).
21. Although it remains to be proven by examination of the texts, my assumption is that the Devanagari, Gujarati, and Gurumukhi editions all are transcriptions of the original hybrid Urdu, not translations into 'purified' (i.e. Sanskritized) Hindi, Gujarati, and Punjabi.
22. A consideration of the large number of imitations of the IS is beyond the scope of this chapter. These dramas are designated as *sabhai natak* in Urdu literary histories and have received ample treatment by Gupta (1981: 227–36), Husain (1990: 71–9), Rizvi 2 (1957: 121–32), and Ibrahim Yusuf (1980: 52–71, 307–9). Most of the imitations appear to fall into one of three categories: 1) Stage adaptations in which new material is added and/or rearrangements are made. Among these *tarmim-shuda* ('improved') versions are the ISs of Madari Lal, Hafiz Abdullah, and Lala Kedarnath 'Surat'. 2) Freer variations on the general theme of fairy-mortal romance, using a different cast of characters but many of the same plot elements, e.g. *Pariyon ki havai majlis, Farrukh sabha, Khurshed sabha*. Several scholars mistakenly include in this category dramas based on other *masnavis* like *Benazir badre munir* and *Gul bakavali*. 3) Parodies, such as

Bharatendu Harishchandra's *Bandar sabha* and Habab Inayat Ali Beg's *Nechur [Nature] sabha*, a spoof on Sir Saiyid Ahmad Khan's Aligarh movement.

23. The full citation is *Indra sabha Amanat*, ed., Nevand Mal, 48 pp. lith. Sukkur, Lahore, 1902. S.XII. Hindi 10610/2. Christopher Shackle generously shared this reference with me.

24. Stuart Blackburn's help in locating references to Tamil versions is gratefully acknowledged.

25. Kesavan lists *Nelavanka, Indracapamu*. Venkataran-garavu, Avantsu (1904–). Vijayanagaram: Sahiti Samiti, 1949, 51 p. 21 cm. The Library of Congress contains a work *Indracapam*, by Rudrasri. (1970) ix, 20 p. 23 cm. PL4780.9.R77.15 (Orien Tel). As this work has not been examined, it is not known whether it is a translation of Amanat's IS.

26. My thanks to Ariya Diwullewe for providing an on-the-spot translation at the IOL in August 1994.

27. I am grateful to Mohammad Z.A. Burney, Urdu Cataloguing Officer, and Lygia Maria Ballantyne, Field Director of the U.S. Library of Congress Office in New Delhi, for special access to the Nami Collection prior to its being catalogued and preserved on microfilm. To Allen Thrasher goes the credit for alerting me to its treasures.

28. William Irwin writes, 'Throughout nineteenth-century America . . . the technological sublime, which invested canals, bridges, railroads, and other human constructions with transcendent significance, played a central role in forming American social and cultural identity.' *The New Niagara: Tourism, Technology, and the Landscape of Niagara Falls*, reviewed in the *New York Review of Books*, 9 January 1997.

29. For most of the details that follow, I am indebted to Brad Sabin Hill, former head of the Hebrew section at the British Library, who shared his research and gave me the opportunity to examine the manuscript. I am also extremely grateful to Rabbi Ezekiel Musleah, of Calcutta and Philadelphia, who painstakingly read portions of the manuscript with me.

30. According to Hill, the Baghdadis' spoken vernacular became influenced by Hindustani in this period, and the matriarch of the Sassoon family, Lady Flora (born in 1859), was fluent in Hindustani (Hill n.d.: 3–4).

31. The song books in the Nami Collection are as follows: *Indar sabha ke gane* (Lahore: Istim Press, 1905); *Indar sabha natak ke gane* (Bombay: Matba-i Murtazvi, 1917), 16 p.; *Indar sabha natak ke gane* (Bombay: Matba-i Gulzar Ahmadi, 1918), 16 p.

32. As Ravi Vasudevan has perceptively noted, the para-narrative of song and dance 'inserts the film and the spectator into a larger field of coherence', one that comprises a complex series of intertextual references to practices that exist independently of the film (Vasudevan 1989: 45).

References

Agraval, P., 1986, *Mastar Fida Husain: Parsi thiyetar men pachas varsh* [Master Fida Husain: Fifty Years in the Parsi Theatre], Calcutta: Natya Shodh Sansthan.

Ahmad, M., 1990, *Bangal men Urdu drama* [Urdu Drama in Bengal], Calcutta: Maghribi Bangal Urdu Akademi.

Anand, M., 1978, 'Bharatenduyugin rangmanch' [The stage in the time of Bharatendu], in N.C. Jain (ed.), *Adhunik Hindi natak aur rangmanch* [Modern Hindi drama and stage, Delhi: Macmillan: 51–64.

Das, S.K., 1991, *A History of Indian Literature, 1800–1910*, Delhi: Sahitya Akademi.

Gokhale, S., 1995, 'Rich Theatre, Poor Theatre', in S. Patel and A. Thorner (eds), *Bombay: Mosaic of Modern Culture*, Bombay: Oxford University Press, 1981: 194–209.

Gupta, S., 1981, *Parsi thiyetar: Udbhav aur vikas* [Parsi Theatre: Origin and Development], Allahabad: Lokbharati Prakashan.

Hansen, K., 1989, 'The Birth of Hindi Drama in Banaras, 1868–85', in S.B. Freitag (ed.), *Culture and Power in Banaras: Community, Performance and Environment, 1800–1980*, Berkeley: University of California Press: 62–92.

————, 1992, *Grounds for Play: The Nautanki Theatre of North India*, Berkeley: University of California Press.

Hill, B.S., n.d., 'Indra Sabha: An Urdu Fairy Tale in Hebrew-character Transcription', unpublished paper.

Husain, M.S., 1990, *Indar-sabha ki parampara* [The *Indar Sabha* tradition], Delhi: Simant Prakashan.

Hussain, K.M. (ed.), 1992, *Syair Indra sebaha*, Kuala Lumpur: Dewan Bahasa dan Pustaka.

Ibrahim Yusuf, 1980, *Indar sabha aur Indar sabha'en* [The *Indar Sabha* and Its Imitations], Lucknow: Nasim Book Depot.

Ilahi, N. and M. Umar, 1982, orig. 1924, *Natak sagar* [Ocean of drama], Lucknow: Uttar Pradesh Urdu Akademi.

Kapur, A. 1995, 'The Representation of Gods and Heroes in the Parsi Mythological Drama of the Early Twentieth Century', in V. Dalmia and H. von Stietencron (eds), *Representing Hinduism: The Construction of Religious Traditions and National Identity*, Delhi: Sage Publications: 401–19.

Kesavan, B.S. (ed.), 1962–90, *The National Bibliography of Indian Literature, 1901–1953*, 5 vols, New Delhi: Sahitya Akademi.

Kinnear, M.S., 1994, *The Gramophone Company's First Indian Recordings, 1899–1908*, Bombay: Popular Prakashan.

Leonard, K., 1996, 'Hyderabadis Abroad', unpublished paper presented at the University of Chicago South Asia Seminar.

Nami, A.A., 1975, *Urdu thetar* [Urdu Theatre], vol. 4, Karachi: Anjuman Taraqqi Urdu Pakistan.

Namra, V.L., 1972, *Hindi rangmanch aur pandit Narayanprasad Betab* [The Hindi stage and Pandit Narayanprasad Betab], Varanasi: Vishvavidyalay Prakashan.

Nasir, S.A.K., 1970, *Tazkirah khush ma'arika-i ziba* [An Elegant Encounter: An Anecdotal Literary Biography], Lahore: Majlis-i Taraqqi-i Adab.

Oman, J.C., 1908, *Cults, Customs and Superstitions of India*, London: T. Fisher Unwin.

Onta, P., 1997, 'Activities in a 'Fossil State': Balkrishna Sama and the Improvisation of Nepali Identity', *Studies in Nepali History and Society*, 2 (1): 69–102.

Perumal, A.N., 1981, *Tamil Drama, Origin and Development*, Madras: International Institute of Tamil Studies.

Pradhan, P.M., 1980, *Balakrishna Sama*, Kalimpong: Bhagyalaxmi Prakashan.

Pritchett, F.W. (ed. and trans. 1991), *The Romance Tradition in Urdu: Adventures from the Dastan of Amir Hamzah*, New York: Columbia University Press.

Rajadhyaksha, A. and P. Willemen, 1994, *Encyclopaedia of Indian Cinema*, Delhi: Oxford University Press.

Rangoonwalla, F., 1979, *A Pictorial History of Indian Cinema*, London: Hamlyn.

Rehmani, I., 1968, *Urdu drama ka Irtiqa* [The evolution of Urdu drama], Lahore: Shaikh Ghulam Ali and Sons Publishers.

Rizvi, M.H., 1957, *Urdu drama aur istej* [Urdu Drama and Stage], pt 2, *Lakhnau ka awami istej: Amanat aur Indarsabha.* [The People's Stage of Lucknow: Amanat and the *Indar Sabha*], Lucknow: Kitab Ghar.

Rosen, F., 1892, *Die Indarsabha des Amanat*, Leipzig: F.A. Brockhaus.

Sadiq, M., 1984, *A History of Urdu Literature*, 2nd edn, Delhi: Oxford University Press.

Saksena, R.B., 1940, *A History of Urdu Literature*, 2nd edn, Allahabad: Ram Narain Lal.

Sama, B.,1972, *Mero kavitako aradhan* [My dedication to poetry], 2nd edn, Kathmandu: Sajha Prakashan.

Schimmel, A., 1975, *Classical Urdu Literature from the Beginning to Iqbal*, Wiesbaden: Otto Harrassowitz.

Sharar, A.H., 1976, *Lucknow: The Last Phase of an Oriental Culture [Guzashta Lakhnau]*, ed. and trans. E.S. Harcourt and Fakhir Hussain, Boulder: Westview Press.

Singh, R., 1990, *Parsi thiyetar* [Parsi Theatre], Jodhpur: Rajasthan Sangit Natak Akademi.

Tan, S.B., 1993, *Bangsawan: A Social and Stylistic History of Popular Malay Opera*, Singapore: Oxford University Press.

Tivari, G., 1959, *Bharatenduyugin natak sahitya* [Dramatic Literature in the Time of Bharatendu], Jalandhar: Hindi Bhavan.

Vasudevan, R., 1989, 'The Melodramatic Mode and the Commercial Hindi Cinema: Notes on Film History, Narrative and Performance in the 1950s', *Screen*, 30(3): 29–50.

Yajnik, Y.K., 1933, *The Indian Theatre*, London: George Allen and Unwin.

Yusuf Ali, A., 1917, 'The Modern Hindustani Drama', *Transactions of the Royal Society of Literature*, 2nd s., 35, 79–99.

Appendix

Indar Sabha Editions in the British Library[1]

Urdu Script

Kanpur, 1853, 28 pp.	IS Amanat
Kanpur, 1853, 32 pp.	IS Madari Lal
Agra, 1860, 31 pp.	IS Madari Lal
Kanpur, 1863, 28 pp.	IS Amanat
Gorakhpur, 1865, 30 pp.	IS Amanat
Delhi, 1867, 28 pp.	IS Amanat
Delhi, 1869, 27 pp.	IS Amanat
Lucknow, 1869, 48 pp.	IS Amanat & Madari Lal
Kanpur, 1870, 23 pp.	IS Amanat
Delhi, 1870, 28 pp.	IS Amanat
Bombay, 1870, 64 pp.	IS Amanat & Madari Lal
Lucknow, 1870, 48 pp.	IS Amanat & Madari Lal
Lucknow, 1871, 23 pp.	IS Amanat
Patna, 1871, 28 pp.	IS Amanat
Delhi, 1872, 36 pp.	IS Amanat
Lucknow, 1873, 24 pp.	IS Amanat
Delhi, 1873, 32 pp.	IS Amanat & Madari Lal
Lucknow, 1874, 24 pp.	IS Amanat
Lucknow, 1874, 48 pp.	IS Amanat & Madari Lal
Lucknow, 1875, 24 pp.	IS Amanat
Delhi, 1876, 28 pp.	IS Amanat
Delhi, 1876, 28 pp.	IS Amanat
Lucknow, 1876, 16 pp.	IS Amanat
Lucknow, 1876, 32 pp.	IS Madari Lal
Madras, 1876, 28 pp.	IS Amanat
Amritsar, 1877, 36 pp.	IS Amanat
Delhi, 1877, 20 pp.	IS Amanat
Madras, 1877, 32 pp.	IS Amanat
Kanpur, 1877, 48 pp.	IS Amanat
Kanpur, 1877, 48 pp.	IS Amanat & Madari Lal
Lucknow, 1877, 48 pp.	IS Amanat & Madari Lal
Calcutta, 1878, 48 pp.	IS Amanat
Delhi, 1878, 28 pp	IS Amanat

Lahore, 1878, 28 pp.	IS Amanat
Lahore, 1879, 39 pp.	IS Amanat
Kanpur, 1882, 48 pp.	IS Amanat
Kanpur, 1882, 48 pp.	IS Amanat & Madari Lal
Kanpur, 1888, 48 pp.	IS Amanat & Madari Lal
Kanpur, 1889, 48 pp.	IS Amanat & Madari Lal
Lahore, 1889, 48 pp.	IS Amanat & Madari Lal
Lucknow, 1890, 24 pp.	IS Amanat
Lucknow, 1890, 32 pp.	IS Amanat
Amritsar, 1914, 24 pp.	IS Amanat

Devanagari Script

Agra, 1862, 40 pp.	IS Amanat
Agra, 1863, 40 pp.	IS Amanat
Agra, 1870, 40 pp.	IS Amanat
Agra, 1871, 40 pp.	IS Amanat
Lucknow, 1874, 40 pp.	IS Amanat
Meerut, 1874. 40 pp.	IS Amanat
Lucknow, 1875, 40 pp.	IS Amanat
Delhi, 1876, 40 pp.	IS Amanat
Bombay, 1876, 56 pp.	IS Amanat
Bombay, 1876, 96 pp.	IS Amanat
Bombay, 1876, 89 pp.	IS Amanat
Lucknow, 1876, 80 pp.	IS Amanat & Madari Lal
Delhi, 1877, 40 pp.	IS Amanat
Delhi, 1877, 40 pp.	IS Amanat
Delhi, 1879, 40 pp.	IS Amanat
Lahore, 1889, 39 pp.	IS Amanat

Gujarati Script

Bombay, 1867, 96 pp.
Bombay, 1874, 86 pp.
Bombay, 1874, 96 pp.
Bombay, 1876, 101 pp.
Bombay, 1880, 40 pp.
Bombay, 1896, 26 pp.

Gujarati Language

Ahmedabad, 1875, 114 pp. A translation by Kunvarji Hathisang with Muhammad Arif.

Gurumukhi

Lahore, 1878, 40 pp.

Sinhala
Colombo, 1893.

Malay
Singapore, 1891, 79 pp.
Singapore, 1901, 96 pp.

Hebrew Script
Calcutta, 1887, 54 pp.

Imitations
Bandar-sabha. (Guj. char.) Adamji Mulla Nurudin, Bombay, 1877, 24 pp.
Bazm-i suleman. No author, Lucknow, 1876, 12 pp.
Hawa'i majlis. Maqsud Ali, Delhi, 1879, 24 pp.
Jalsah-i paristan, urf Bazm-i Sulaiman. Muhammad 'Abd al-Wahid 'Qais', Fatehpur, 1892, 46 pp.
Mohana-sabha. Shaikh Khuda Bakhsh, Lucknow, 1877, 36 pp.
Pariyon ki hawa'i majlis. Daulat Ram and Lalchand, Lahore, 1878, 16 pp.
Tohfah-i dilkosha, urf nai indar sabha. (Guj. char.) Saiyid Muhammad 'Harif', Bombay, 1885, 57 pp.

---

[1] These editions are listed in the following catalogues:

Blumhardt, J(ames) F(uller), *Catalogue of Hindustani Printed Books in the Library of the British Museum*, London, 1889.

Blumhardt, J(ames) F(uller), *Catalogues of the Hindi, Panjabi, Sindhi, and Pushtu Printed Books in the Library of the British Museum*, London, 1893.

Blumhardt, J(ames) F(uller), *Catalogue of the Library of the India Office*, vol. 2, pt 2, *Hindustani Books*, London, 1900.

Blumhardt, J(ames) F(uller), *Catalogue of the Library of the India Office*, vol. 2, pt 3, *Hindi, Panjabi, Pushtu and Sindhi Books*, London, 1902.

Blumhardt, J(ames) F(uller), *Supplementary Catalogue of Hindustani Books in the Library of the British Museum*, London, 1909.

Haq, Qazi Mahmudul, *Handlist of Urdu and Panjabi Manuscripts Acquired by Oriental Collections since 1899*, London, 1993.

Quraishi, Salim Al-Din, *Catalogue of Urdu Books in the India Office Library 1800–1920 (Supplementary to James Fuller Blumhardt's Catalogue of 1900)*, 2nd edn, London, 1991.

Wickremasinghe, Don Martino de Zilva, *Catalogue of the Sinhalese Printed Books in the Library of the British Museum*, London, 1901.

The Tale of the Book
Storytelling and Print
in Nineteenth-century Tamil

STUART BLACKBURN

Folklore and Popular Culture

BOTH THE STUDY of folklore and the study of popular culture are blessed by a lack of fixed boundaries ('who are the folk?'; 'what is popular?'). One reason for this shared ambiguity is a common conceptual history: both fields of study arose in contradistinction to an emphasis on elite culture, official norms, and orthodoxy; both developed (primarily) in England and Germany, one in the nineteenth century as a romantic critique of industrialization, the other in the twentieth as an inquiry into post-industrial cultural change. This difference between an early nineteenth-century and a mid-twentieth-century reaction to the changes of modern life separates folkloristics and the study of popular culture, since although each field is defined by the relations between culture makers and users, or tellers and audiences, those relations are not the same.

It is often said that the principal difference between folklore and popular culture is media of production and distribution, that is primarily oral and manual versus mechanical and electronic technologies. These differences in technology or technique, however, are important because they lead to other differences in contexts of production, relations between makers and users, and, finally, cultural forms. Oral and manual methods ensure that folklore is produced locally, usually in a face-to-face interaction, while the technologies of popular culture make possible a much greater separation between producers and consumers in time, space, and personal relations. The important point is that mass production and distribution requires fixity and uniformity, whereas folklore is as variable as the tongue and the hand. Folklore tends to be anonymous, without labels or copyright lawsuits. Of course, some verbal folklore is fixed, but even quoting a proverb is conditioned by the wit of the speaker and its reception by listeners.[1]

Today folklore is also reproduced and consumed as popular culture (and elite culture) all over the world, and India is no exception, with TV and film adaptations of folk narratives, folk songs on audio cassette, and *pat* paintings produced as lithographs, to name only a few hybrid forms.[2] Is this folklore or popular culture? Does technology control content? Such questions are less useful than those which enquire into the histories of hybrid cultural re-productions, into their motives and receptions. Print, which more than any other technology, has taken folklore into popular culture is the focus of this chapter. I begin with a question: What were the early uses of print and its effects on oral tradition and storytelling in nineteenth-century Tamil?

The story begins in 1835, not with Macaulay's infamous 'minute on education' but with the legislation that relaxed restrictions on the Indian press. No matter that the primary aim of this law was to remove differences in controls over the press in the three Presidencies, or that it was directed at the seditious foreign-owned English press, its immediate effect was that Indians began to own and operate more printing presses, to publish books and pamphlets and newspapers, in English and in regional languages. This new technology of print created new forms of communication, as well as tra-ditional forms recirculated to traditional audiences, that would play a criti-cal role in the creation of a new social elite and new political structures. Was this India's print revolution?

In certain objective terms, nineteenth-century India did undergo a 'print revolution' comparable to that of sixteenth-century Europe. The Jesuits in India had printed books from the late sixteenth century, but government and private foreign presses began to print substantial numbers of books only at the beginning of the nineteenth century, as did a few presses in princely states, such as Tanjore.[3] Printing by private Indian-owned presses began largely, as mentioned, only after 1835. Printing in Europe also began before the 'revolution' of the sixteenth century and was primarily religious, but it became widespread and secular only after 1500. In addition, in both Europe and India the emergence of commercial, popular printing as a medium of communication was concurrent with an expanding market economy, reli-gious upheavals, and political realignments. A third and more specific simi-larity is the chapbook, cheaply printed on poor quality paper, often with wood block illustrations, which played a major role in both sixteenth-century Europe and nineteenth-century India. In other respects, of course, the coming of the book was very different in the two centuries and areas. For one thing, printing developed gradually over three hundred years in Europe, whereas those technological innovations collapsed India's 'print revolution' into less than a century. The novel, for instance, which might be considered the end-point of a print revolution, developed over two or three centuries in European literatures but only at the close of the nineteenth century in India. The comparison also breaks down in the face of colonialism in India, especially the valorization of English language and education. Nevertheless, the sheer force of change attributed to the advent of print in these two continents makes comparison difficult to resist.

In particular, an outline of nineteenth-century Tamil presents a compelling case for a print revolution that transformed the oral tale into the printed book. When the century opened, the earliest (non-missionary) printed books included not just grammars but many collections of folktales. At mid-century, Indian-owned presses were printing hundreds of Tamil texts, including ancient poetry, schoolbooks, translations from Shakespeare, and folk dramas. By the end of the century, Tamil was established in newspapers, journals, the university curriculum, and eventually prose fiction. The century-long transition from oral tale to printed book drew near when a folklorist published collections of Tamil folktales (in both English and Tamil) during the 1880s and 1890s, and the final seal was set when this same man published a Tamil novel, very conveniently, in 1900 (Natesa Sastri 1884–93; 1900).

Print Revolution and Its Effects

Print, like the rise of the middle class, has been held responsible for a good many things; as a sign of its influence, the noun has become an adjective which generates its own scholar-speak ('print culture', 'print capitalism'). Perhaps the most definitive statement on the print revolution in Europe is Elizabeth Eisenstein's two-volume study, which emphasizes technological and economic changes, giving rise to the term 'print capitalism'. Other writers have followed her lead in arguing that the emergence of printing led to a fundamental shift in social and economic relations, to a print culture in which knowledge is produced more efficiently and more quickly, and is transmitted not by personal experience but mediated through manuals, digests, and almanacs. This new, mechanized means of cultural production reputedly brought forth our modern concepts of copyright, plagiarism, and censorship, and redefined our ideas of authorship and creativity. Even nationalism, according to Benedict Anderson, is the consequence of print culture, especially its standardization of language and its visual fixity, which create and demonstrate a simultaneity and a collective belonging upon which a national identity rests (Anderson 1991). Print, apparently, was also one of the weapons wielded by the West in its conquest of the Islamic world (Lewis 1995: 23–4).

Beneath these various formulations, there is also consensus on a fundamental point: print disrupted a prior oral culture. As Wlad Godzich recently wrote, 'Disjunctions . . . occurred between the new mode of production and the old modes of consumption. The traditional sense of community, which entailed gatherings to receive a message, was undercut by the new technology, which made possible the fragmentation of directions' (Goldzich 1995: 83). In other words, the primary consequence of print was a disruption in the relation between tellers and listeners, the separation between makers and users mentioned in my introductory comments about folklore and popular culture. To some writers, this change is creative since splitting-off narrators from direct contact with audiences produced a new heterogenous, unconnected readership for mass-produced and widely distributed print. For Anderson, this fragmentation across time and space led to a new audience: the nation. Similarly, for Bakhtin, this disruption of traditional storytelling led to a new genre: the novel. Or, consider this triumphant conclusion to a study of the coming of the book in Europe: 'Unified Latin culture of Europe was finally dissolved by the rise of vernacular languages which was consolidated by the printing press' (Febvre and Martin 1976: 332). For other writers, however, the fragmentation let loose by the advent of print spells loss. Godzich is not nostalgic, but his statement, quoted above speaks in a language of loss ('undercut', 'fragmentation') favoured by many who view the disruption of pre-industrial culture with dismay; Anderson, too, claims that the nation was possible only after 'cultural concepts of great antiquity lost their axiomatic grip' (Anderson 1991: 36). We have no thorough study of orality and literacy in India, but the following description for Tamil may serve as a check-list for the perceived sins of the print revolution in other Indian languages:[4]

> Unlike in most western societies, the dimension of primary (genuine) orality is still alive on various levels in India . . . However, in Tamil culture, the second half of the nineteenth century witnessed a decisive break with this tradition: the introduction of large-scale printing and of periodical journalism; the decline and demise of village 'veranda schools' . . .; the first printed editions of classical literary heritage, until then taught and explained in oral transmission; the early chapbooks fixing in print folk-ballads, folk-plays, folk-narratives, etc. and, last but not least, the origin and development of

indigenous, standardized 'high' fiction appearing in print [Zvelebil 1990: 157–8].

Although he does not name it, in his last phrase Zvelebil refers to the novel, a fitting end to any print revolution since its detached narration is seen as the final step in severing listeners from tellers; people no longer communicated by speech or even handwriting but by typefaces.[5] In the end the word was made metal.

Misconceptions and Reappraisals

This picture of a print revolution, in Tamil at least, is misleading. I now identify three mistaken assumptions (which derive in part from earlier scholarship about orality and writing) and discuss reappraisals of the relations between orality, writing, and print.

1. The first misconception is the notion of a pure oral culture later polluted by print. Many writers, from Herder to Ong, perhaps because they have had no contact with oral tradition, are free to idolize it as a repository of rustic simplicity, primal communality, and social egalitarianism. At the heart of this touching scene stands the village storyteller, whose edifying tales that once reached eager ears are now etched in metal type, owned by publishers, and read by solitary individuals. This picture flies in the face of what we have learned about tale telling in India: it is rarely innocent of writing, and even print; it is not entirely free of notions of individuality; and its audiences are not always active. Storytellers may not be readers, but written and printed texts are often consulted for details or for authenticity, while texts are sometimes read aloud in performance. Professional tellers performing in temples and open streets take a proprietorial view of their art; authors are ascribed to traditional stories (legends rather than tales). Legal copyright probably did begin when the Company began to seek rights to print old books, but indigenous ideas of ownership and authorship are older.[6] Finally, the relationship between teller and audience is not so interactive and immediate as the notion of pure orality presumes. In some ritual contexts, for example, no audience is necessary or present; if print distances audiences, these performances eliminate them.

2. The second misconception in the literature on 'print revolution' is that this precious oral culture disappears at the first sight of the enemy, the printed book. In short, print not only disrupts but replaces orality. The replacement of orality by printing is an extension (and contradiction) of the earlier argument that it was killed off by writing; orality miraculously survived the first

revolution only to be declared extinct after the second. Goody and Watt's influential essay (1968)[7] on the 'consequences of literacy' comes to mind, as well as Albert Lord's brilliant book *The Singer of Tales* (1960), which claimed that oral tradition does not survive the onslaught of writing, let alone print. That oral culture should disappear is not an unexpected conclusion from scholars for whom oral tradition had always been flawed; it not only will but should die off. Goody and Watt, for instance, claimed that oral tradition was 'homeostatic' in that it prevented change by a 'structural amnesia' which enabled it to adjust to the demands of each new generation (Goody and Watt 1968: 31). Writing, on the other hand, fixed words and left a visible record that exposed the deceptions of fluid speech, paving the way for logic, history, and scepticism. Oral genealogists in West Africa could cheat, whereas written cultures like ours courageously separate myth from history. In sum, scholarship on the print revolution is not altogether free of a certain 'cult of literacy', practised not only in classrooms, where it is still taught that civilization is impossible without writing, but also in public policy in which literacy is next to cleanliness.

Fortunately, a counter-revolution to this early scholarship has taught us that print and writing do not replace but supplement orality. Writing about ancient Greece, Rosalind Thomas provides a broad critique of the literature and demonstrates that orality and writing cohabited quite nicely not only in Athens but in medieval Europe as well (Thomas 1992). For South Asia, A.K. Ramanujan frequently made the point that no one in India ever reads the epic stories 'for the first time' because they have already heard them. Again, for India, V. Narayana Rao has coined the term 'oral-literate' to refer to the large number of tellers, singers, and intellectuals who live simultaneously in oral and written worlds (see Narayan Rao 1993).[8] What sort of hybrid literature is produced by these overlapping worlds is sketched by Godzich's essay on chapbooks in sixteenth-century Spain. Beginning with the fateful disruption between teller and audience, Godzich describes a transitional literature, popular tales in chapbooks, lodged between 'pure oral culture' and print culture. This intermediate literature/culture he calls 'auditive, where . . . even the written is received for the most part in an aural form' (Godzich 1995: 79). Storytelling no longer proceeds by a traditional repertoire of images, episodes, and formulas, but at the same time it is not produced for silent, individualistic readers. Godzich's auditive literature 'valorized novelty in contrast to the attachment to the traditional found in oral cultures, and it strives for emotional impact as opposed to the more deliberative mode of more purely written culture' (Godzich 1995: 79). Godzich does at times romanticize the oral ('concepts of plagiarism and copyright did not exist in the communal culture of the minstrel'), but his portrait of print literature in sixteenth-century Spanish bears a resemblance to that of nineteenth-century Tamil (Godzich 1995: 82).

3. Print and orality form hybrid literatures precisely because they are not equivalent phenomena, and the belief that they are equivalent opposites is the third common misconception about the print revolution. If they were equivalent, then one would cancel, replace, step in for the other, but this is patently not the case. Rather than proclaiming premature deaths, we would do better to look into the varieties of their coexistence, which ironically requires that we first draw more sharply the distinctions between them. Godzich (1995: 78) points out that oral and print literatures are not functional equivalents, they and I would add that both these and writing refer to different processes of storytelling and that these aspects may overlap but are not interchangeable. Those three processes and their respective media are indicated in the chart below:

Composition: oral, (hand) written
Transmission: oral, (hand) written, print
Reception: oral (aural), (hand) written, print

As this chart indicates, stories may be composed, transmitted, and received orally or by writing, or in any combination of the oral and written. Print, however, is not a mode of composition but of transmission and therefore reception; singers may compose as they perform, but no one composes as he typesets. Typing the original form of this essay on my computer is not printing or typesetting; it is still a form of composition, albeit electronic (and we could add 'electronic' to each of the lists in the chart). For this reason printed stories do not necessarily replace oral or written stories, and herein lies one cause of what I will conclude is only a limited 'print revolution' in nineteenth-century Tamil.

The overlapping differences shown in the chart are not only more accurate than the symmetry of rustic orality in opposition to destructive print, they also encourage us to consider the 'uses' of both orality and print. As Thomas points out in her critique, a focus on uses avoids the 'technological determinism' that assumes print or writing have universal effects in all cultures (Thomas 1992: 24). How we might approach such a study in South Asia is suggested by Natalie Zemon Davis' essay on the uses of print by literate peasants and urban dwellers in sixteenth-century France (Davis 1991). She found that print generated change (women as authors, for example) as well as considerable continuity. Specifically, she notes what I found for Tamil in the nineteenth century—that the pre-print favourites continued to be popular in print; *Reynard the Fox, Aesop's Fables, Shepherd's Calendar, Book of Hours, the Golden Legend* (saints' lives), for example, are matched by the *Pañcatantra*, collections of Tamil maxims, and didactic poetry. 'On the whole', she concludes, 'the first 125 years of printing in France, which brought little change in the countryside, strengthened rather than sapped the vitality of the culture of the *menu peuple* in the cities [because] they were active users and interpreters of the printed books they heard and read' (Davis 1991: 85–6). For Davis, however, use does not simply mean reading; she distinguishes two audiences for early books—readers and those to whom the books were addressed—and insists that books are 'a carrier of relationships' (Davis 1991: 66).

These reappraisals of the print revolution in Europe inform my analysis of the effects of print in nineteenth-century Tamil. In the early decades, print did not replace but popularized oral literature by spreading well-known tales to new audiences. As Davis demonstrates for sixteenth-century France and Eisenstein (1983: 114) for Europe generally, the main difference in the first half of the century was not new books but more (old) books. Heeding Thomas' advice to look for 'uses', I will also argue that although print did produce change by disseminating ideas and information to new audiences and despite the substantial numbers of tales published after 1850, the primary mode of storytelling remained oral. Early printed tales and later novels did serve new public purposes, but print did not significantly alter traditional storytelling in Tamil.[9] The revolution, if any occurred, was not narrative.

Printing in Nineteenth-century Tamil

Even before the printing press, Tamil writing was affected by another technological innovation. Around AD 1500, when paper was fast replacing palm-leaf as writing material in north India, a new kind of palm-leaf was introduced into south India; the broad, soft, round leaves of the talipot palm gave way to the narrower, finer-grained palmyra, which remained in use right up until the early part of the twentieth century.[10]

But Tamil printing began long before 1800. Called Malabari, or Tamoul or Tamel by early Europeans, it was the first South Asian language to be printed (in Roman script, in Lisbon in 1554) and the first South Asian script to be printed (in Goa in 1577).[11] These early missionary efforts, however, are not the main story to be told here. Rather it is the nineteenth century when printing in Tamil, as in other languages in colonial India, including

English, entered into the social life of ordinary people. I divide the discussion into two parts, roughly the two halves of the century.

Part 1: 1800–1850 'Edifying Tales'

One of the first printed books in Tamil, not from a missionary press, appeared in 1811. *Tamiḻ Viḷakkam* ('Tamil Expositor') by Soobroya Modelliar was printed at Madras, with the express permission of the Governor of Madras (Soobroya Modelliar 1811: Preface). Tamil translations of Manu's *Dharmaśāstras, The 1001 Nights, Aesop's Fables,* the *Pañcatantra,* a portion of Valmiki's *Rāmāyaṇa,* a Tamil folktale collection, a Telugu dictionary, and other books soon rolled off the government press. As this partial list indicates, most of these early books were traditional tales, but their intended purpose was not primarily to narrate. The government's stated purpose for printing them was to gain 'knowledge of the general grammar and connexion of the several languages of Southern India and . . . the sources whence they sprung'.[12] Like a modern academic press, the Government of Madras (through the College of Fort St. George) solicited manuscripts, paid for original works and translations, some of which they rejected as too 'stiff' (Srinivasachari 1927). A second use of these early books commissioned by the government was teaching the language to foreigners. But why not print the extensive Tamil literature available in palm-leaf manuscripts? After all, Ziegenbalg's handlist from the early eighteenth century contained more than a hundred such manuscripts (Gaur 1967). Why pay for original works and translations, from Sanskrit or Marathi? The answer is that the Company's civil servants, who were required by law to learn one if not two local languages, could not penetrate the poetry in which existing Tamil grammars and poetry were composed.

Verse was the villain. As Viswanathan points out in her study of English literature and the Raj, this distaste for poetry in British India derives from a suspicion, among influential religious groups in England, of literary affectations (Viswanathan 1989: 47). In fact, poetry was adequate for none of the new intentions of print; tales might be useful specimens of 'pure' and relatively simple language (this, too, was naive, as we shall see), but poetry served no good purpose and was even singled out as a cause of moral deficiency in Indians (Viswanathan 1989: 82–3). Prose, on the other hand, was not only efficient; it was soteriological.

The blessings of prose were nowhere more evident than in the field of education, which has dominated Tamil publishing since its inception. As the school system grew from the 1820s onward, a public debate ensued about the lack of proper books. The government and some Tamil- and Telugu- speaking residents of Madras began to feel acutely the 'want of a treatise in the Vernaculars of India professing to be a systematic collection of morals in easy prose suited to the capacities of young minds, and calculated to lead them into a virtuous path' (Theroovengada Pillay 1853: i). This pursuit of public morality led to numerous early publications of the *Tirukkuṟaḷ* (a collection of moral aphorisms dating from about AD 500) whose ecumenical tone charmed the missionaries and the government, and has never since fallen from grace.[13] Another popular choice was another, later and Jain-influenced book of maxims, the *Nalaṭiyār*. The runaway favourite for stories of public morality, however, was the celebrated *Pañcatantra*. It was assumed that these traditional tales could be told to edifying ends, but it was soon apparent they did not always match the intentions of their new users.

We know that a Tamil *Pañcatantiram* 'in an easy verse-form and frequently taught in the schools' existed from at least the early eighteenth century.[14] However, in order to rescue this valuable book from indulgent Oriental verse, the government commissioned a prose version from Tantavarayar Mutaliyar, an influential Tamil pundit at the College of Fort St. George and later Head Pundit at the Government High School (which later became the University of Madras). His perception of the necessity of the task is expressed in his preface to the first edition of 1826: 'Learned people [in Tamil] who attempt the study of such *Pañcatantra* texts as exist in Tamil are like those who wish to bathe but find themselves smeared with mud' (Tantavarayar Mudaliyar 1826: Preface). Although the pundit's work was admired, enjoyed many reprints, and secured a place in the curriculum at Madras University, the conversion to prose did not entirely remove the mud. Even the scholarly missionary, John Murdoch, for instance, worried over the subversive quality of these folktales:

> Another most injurious influence exerted by some Hindu tales is, that they virtually inculcate INFLUENCE BY DECEIT. The lesson has been taught to apt scholars. As a nation the Hindus glory in the fox-like cunning, with which they so often outwit their bovine European rulers. The conscience of the people will never be right until it is felt that all trickery is bad and despicable. The *Pañcatantra* contains many stories of the objectionable character now mentioned. They should be carefully weeded out of any selection used in schools [Murdoch 1865: 203–4).

When one recalls these tales, in which predatory crocodiles are outwitted by crafty monkeys, one appreciates why British observers viewed them with suspicion. These animal allegories are the only genre in which the characters regularly consume each other, and in the colonial context, their potential for political satire was not far below the surface.

Later Murdoch was pleased to note that many objectionable passages had been cut from later editions of the *Pañcatantra*, but he still opposed its use in schools because it 'is so saturated throughout with a tricky morality' (Murdoch 1901: viii). Englishmen love 'manly straightforwardness', he wrote, and 'few things will more militate against the formation of such a character than the study of a book abounding in examples of *successful trickery*. . . . It is an exceedingly clever book but one which tends to lower than to raise the tone of the morality prevalent in the country'.[15] Although the *Pañcatantra* was and continues to be taught in schools throughout the Tamil area, it remained controversial. In 1921, a Tamil editor added a scholarly Introduction in which he explained the foreigners' lack of appreciation of these tales in this way:

> Each fable in this book is intended to teach some particular precept for human conduct, and in some cases the lesson taught is not of the highest ethical standard. To the eastern mind this is not so perceptible as to the western mind and consequently the work is underestimated [Rajaruthnam Pillay 1921: Introduction].

These prose *Pañcatantras* give us a first glimpse of the pitfalls in supposing that storytelling in Tamil was revolutionized by print. Oral tales did not convert easily to new public purposes, and the reason was not that tellers were separated from listeners; since these widely known stories were probably read aloud in schools, the infamous disjunction between authors and audiences, which apparently defines a print revolution, was mitigated. Rather the tension arose because the irreverence of these folktales was nothing like the public morality which their new users wished them to express. Closer to the ambiguous poetry which they were meant to replace, even in print these tales resisted reduction to a single intention.

Part 2: 1850–1900 'Creating a New Vernacular'

Nevertheless, oral tales in Tamil did fulfil one of the demands of printed prose during the first half of the nineteenth century: foreigners and schoolchildren would use these books to learn the language, if not the approved morality. Crib books for the Tamil examination at Madras University, for instance, now consisted of prose summaries, in dramatic dialogue, of major texts (*Kamparāmāyaṇam, Nalaṭiyār,* and *Viḷḷipāratam*). Prose thus saved the

Tamil curriculum from poetry in the early decades of print, but entirely new demands were placed on it in the second half of the century (Rajagopal Pillay 1876). Not just prose tales but a new language was required, a language able to articulate new concepts, to debate in newspapers and pamphlets the serious social and political issues of the day. As this new prose eventually developed and print was used to inform and reform, speakers would finally be separated from their audiences. However, when this campaign for a new language expanded to include a new literature, further incompatibilities between the new technology and storytelling emerged.

The new demands on print arose as part of the rapid changes that swept over colonial India from mid-century—not only English education but also railways, widening markets, increasing trade, and the growing participation by Indians in politics and public life (Rajagopal Pillay 1876). C. Baker, however, concludes his study of the rural economy in Tamil Nadu between 1880 and 1955 with an emphasis on continuity (Baker 1984: 522), and a similar continuity in storytelling during the nineteenth century will be shown in this chapter. As others have shown in detail for Madras, the new elite consisted of Tamil and Telugu speakers with an English education from the University of Madras (Suntharalingam 1974: esp. p. 10 ff; McGuire 1983). Although this institution was established as a university (like those at Calcutta and Bombay, modelled on the University of London) in the watershed year of 1857, it developed out of Madras University High School (1841), which itself had evolved from the College of Fort St. George. Thus the Tamil pundits who had prepared the first Tamil books were the same pundits who taught in the high school and trained those who later taught in the university. By 1881, Madras university had expanded to include twenty-five colleges spread all over the Presidency (Suntharalingam 1974: 110). These new elites were not numerous; by 1894, a little over 3000 had BA degrees from Madras University, but they formed the core of Indians in print-oriented professions: law, education, medicine, engineering, government, and journalism (Suntharalingam 1974: 112; Sadasivan 1974).

Indians in Madras had formed public groups earlier in the century, but not until after mid-century did they use print to voice their opinions on political and social questions. At first, English was the language of communication, especially when the addressee was the government. Although most English-language newspapers were published by Europeans, a half-dozen Indian-owned papers appeared and died quickly around mid-century; the still-running *Hindu* appeared weekly from 1878 (and daily from 1889) as the mouthpiece of a particular section of English-educated Tamils and eventually for the Congress Party in the region. A good example of this new political use of print is the publication of a speech by George Norton, President of the Board of Madras University. On 20 March 1850, Norton spoke on the subject of 'native' education at Pachaiyappa's College (founded in 1842 by a Hindu charity to support English education for Indians) (Norton 1850). Following his talk, 720 men sent him a letter urging him to publish his speech and to have it translated into Tamil. When the requested pamphlet duly appeared in the same year, English speech had been converted to Tamil print and distributed to a wider audience.[16]

Even more important is the message that this printed pamphlet spread. Although Norton did not use the term, what he supported was known as the 'filtration theory' because it advocated the use of English-educated Indians as filters to popularize modern reforms (Viswanathan 1989: 113–14). Since the vernaculars were hopelessly mired in poetry and paganism, only the English language and its literature could serve as instruments of moral uplift and modernization. But these new ideas would only reach the masses when filtered through English-educated Indians who would convey them 'in native dress' (*The Hindu*, 13 April 1894). Not much clothing was required to translate Norton's own speech, or the laws regulating the office of Village Munsif, or the innumerable, popular compendia of legal information.[17] Translation, however, would not satisfy reformers, and eventually Tamil entered the public world of print communication on its own terms. The first (non-missionary) Tamil newspaper, for instance, *Swadesamitran*, appeared in 1880 and played a major role in the politics of the next few decades. According to one estimate, sixty Tamil periodicals were published between 1869 and 1900 (Bayly 1989); most led brief lives. Tamil journals dedicated to literary and social issues also appeared and were even admired for their use of the latest technology.[18]

Still, something more would be needed to modernize Tamil so that it could take its place alongside the prestigious language of the rulers. 'A new Vernacular literature has to be created', Norton declaimed in 1848, since the vanguard of English-educated Tamils would be able to spread new ideas only if Tamil was itself first equipped to communicate them (Norton 1848). Filtration was not enough; the filter, too, had to change. But reform would not be easy for if the first deadly sin of Tamil literature had been its self-indulgent poetry, the second was its lack of originality. Prose had driven out the first, but something stronger was needed to overcome the second and infuse Tamil with the initiative and individuality of English. An 1854 report on Tamil instruction at the University of Madras put it this way:

Boys who take no interest in the sententious and dogmatic propositions of poetical works . . . may . . . acquire a useful knowledge of Tamil by reading smaller works of a nature to excite their interest and to afford real information. I think I may say that no prose works exist in Tamil that meet the above requirements; they are generally silly, or at least uninstructive Tales and Fables, answering well enough for European learners, of more mature years, whose object is to obtain the common idiom of the language and not to obtain information from Tamil books, but they are not suited to instruct the youthful native [Bayley 1854].

As usual, George Norton was more succinct: The 'bulk of all Native writing (which are poetical) contain little else than legendary and superstitious nonsense' (Norton 1848: 54). The campaign for a modern vernacular, to culminate in the *fin de siècle* Tamil novel, had begun.

That Tamil literature was enslaved by the past was an accepted truth of the day. A Government of Madras report on books published and registered in 1883 was typical in its complaint that Tamil books were not originals but abridgements from the epics and the *Puranas*: 'It is the usual tale of compilations, or reproductions or imitations . . . [we] looked in vain for even one work by a native author which can be called a genuine original literary or scientific production' (*The Hindu*, 1 October 1884). A week later *The Hindu* printed a letter, signed by an 'Educated Hindu', who blamed the lack of originality on a faulty education system; others asserted different causes, but there was no disagreement that Tamil literature lacked originality. Some years later the editor of the newspaper, G. Subramania Iyer, urged more attention to writing good Tamil books for schools. Today, he wrote in 1893, the university graduate is 'unable to read with pleasure or profit a well-written paper or magazine in the Vernacular. He despises his Vernacular and has no desire to enrich the Vernacular literature by translations or original works' (*The Hindu*, 3 February 1893). The editor also noted that Bengali had the richest literature in India, Marathi was second, and Tamil a poor third. In the following year, the editor criticized The Society for the Improvement of Vernacular Language and its Secretary, Mr V. Krishnama Chariar who was also the long-serving Registrar of Books in Madras, for not developing Tamil literature. He should select the best books that pass his desk and encourage their authors, argued the editor, since '[w]e cannot believe that our countrymen are so downtrodden as to have evinced no spark of intellectual capacity or literary philanthropy (*The Hindu*, 13 April 1894). Only the Tamil novel, it seemed, would provide proof of that capacity.

Early Tamil Novels

By 1880 Tamil was broadly and irretrievably in print; 900 Tamil books were published in 1892 (and 82 in English) (*The Hindu*, 15 October 1894).[19] A public school Tamil and a publicly political Tamil, however, would not satisfy the emerging nationalist culture which demanded a Tamil literature capable of expressing modern humanistic ideas. Similar movements arose in Calcutta and Bombay, but the Tamil case was complicated by the concurrent discovery and printing of its ancient and medieval literature. Publication of these traditional texts not only elevated Tamil, which had lost prestige as Sanskrit, Telugu, Marathi, Urdu, and then English received royal patronage, but it also valorized the poetry that the reformers thought they had put behind them. However, printing classical literature served the cause for reform in an unexpected way. Partha Chatterjee has argued that Bengali literature in the late nineteenth century carved out a private sphere of national culture, protected from the depredations of colonialism (Chatterjee 1993: 7–9, *passim*). This need for a cultural safe-haven and separate linguistic identity in Tamil, however, was satisfied by publishing these ancient and medieval texts. Freed from the task of national identity, the novel in Tamil could express a less politicized modernity, but it was also cast adrift at the same time.

But where was the Tamil novel? After Bengali and Marathi had achieved this ultimate prize of literary modernity, Tamils began to worry more and more about their linguistic inadequacy.[20] Eventually, a Tamil novel did appear in 1879 and others followed in the 1890s. Like the early novels in other Indian languages, these Tamil experiments were largely dedicated to social themes, especially the twin evils of child marriage and the ban on widow remarriage. Here at last was the 'new vernacular', sought after since 1850—a new genre, written and printed in Tamil, but were these novels read? Limited evidence suggests that they were not and that the new vernacular failed to achieve any revolution in storytelling.

Judging by advertisements in Madras newspapers during the last two decades of the century, English novels were avidly read. Adverts for English novels often covered nearly the whole front page of newspapers in the 1890s, leaving little space for the other popular items: inducements to buy special creams to prevent baldness or impotence. These advertisements for 'New Novels' in English sat next to ones for Tamil classics. One advert that regularly appeared in the issues of *The Hindu* contained over a hundred Tamil books but not a single Tamil novel, whereas notices for traditional

Tamil poetic works (such as *Civañāṉapōtam, Cīvakacintāmaṇi*) and modern poems (such as *Maṉōnmaṇiyam*) were common. *The Hindu* published its own Excelsior Series of inexpensive books 'devoted exclusively to the cause of Hindu moral and religious progress' (*The Hindu*, 23 February 1894), but these were mostly translations from Sanskrit or English into Tamil, or from Sanskrit into English. The more commercial presses published few English novels in Tamil, whose readership was fed a delicate mixture of Sanskrit and Shakespeare. If reading habits among English-educated elite in Madras were anything like those in late nineteenth-century Calcutta, the public preferred sensational novelists like GWM Reynolds to the high-brow Scott or Thackeray (Joshi 1998). Despite frequent advertisements for 'Some Excellent Novels', editorials deplored the tendency of many to read sensational novels in English. Concerning the new vernacular in Tamil, one writer lamented that no one took any notice when novels were published.[21] As for reading habits in Tamil, the editor of *The Hindu* wrote that 'the reading of the general public is confined to the *Ramayana* and the *Bharata*, or fanciful stories such as those of the *Arabian Nights*. Purely literary works have comparatively few admirers (*The Hindu*, 1 September 1894).

Between 1879 and 1900, approximately (depending on one's definition of the genre) a dozen Tamil novels were published. They failed, however, to produce the sensational effects of a print revolution. One reason is that these novels appeared when the new vernacular was expected to inform and reform but before the habit of reading print had developed among anything more than a tiny slice of the Tamil public. Male literacy in Tamil at the turn of the century was about 10 per cent (and about 1 per cent in English), and female literacy much lower. However, as mentioned above, numbers of literates and books are less revealing than the uses of print (see Irschick 1969: 16–17). The new novels did extend Tamil from newspapers into fiction, but only in the hands of the most talented writers are social arguments successful as stories. A further, and I believe the primary, reason that these early Tamil novels failed is their misapplication of a technique of oral storytelling to print technology.

This takes us back to the misconceptions concerning orality discussed earlier. A corollary of the failure to distinguish modes of composition from modes of distribution is the assumption that oral tales are told to a private audience and the novel to a public audience: the tale is local and limited, spoken to village folk gathered under the banyan tree, whereas the novel addresses the urban masses. If we distinguish composition and distribution, however, we can argue that the reverse is true. It is the tale which is public because its speech is heard by anyone present and its themes portray the common experiences of a culture. The novel, on the other hand, although publicly distributed, is privately produced and read, and its focus is the experience of individuals. As evidence of the 'new vernacular', the novel was expected to convey useful ideas to the public, but, as with the earlier example of the *Pañcatantra*, intention and vehicle were mismatched.

Let me illustrate this discrepancy with a brief description of *Kamalāmbāḷ Carittiram*, a Tamil novel serialized from 1893 to 1895 and published as a book in 1896.[22] Rajam Aiyar's work is certainly not the first but it is the first good novel in Tamil. The young Brahmin author (he was only 22 when he began to write the novel) graduated from Madras Christian College, wrote this novel, met Swami Vivekananda, became editor of *Prabuddha Bharata* ('Awakened India'), wrote a good deal about Vedanta philosophy and died at the young age of 28. Unlike other early novels in Tamil and other Indian languages, *Kamalāmbāḷ* is not a social novel attacking child marriage and the ban on widow remarriage. At one point in narration, the author intervenes to declare that 'nowadays some young people think that women can live happily with their husband only if they marry after the age of twenty. Knowing well the love of Srinivasan and Laksmi [the young hero and heroine], it doesn't appear that way to me (Rajam Aiyar 1930: 193).

The novel begins brilliantly with a domestic repartee between a Brahmin husband and wife in a small village. As the story unfolds, we hear local dialect, meet some eccentric characters, and watch scenes of rural life, all presented with wit and little moralizing. The burden of the narration is delivered by direct dialogue, which is the legacy of oral storytelling; however, without the live audience the author did not know how to sustain such dialogue.[23] In the second half of the novel, Rajam Aiyar abandons his successful use of conversation and drifts into impersonal description and narration, especially Vedanta-inspired discourse. Here the novel would appear to function as the print revolution predicts and the campaign for a new vernacular demanded: as a vehicle for expressing ideas to a large number of spatially dispersed readers. Presumably the author's philosophy of life was the 'useful' knowledge that the publisher wished to convey to the public.[24] The result, however, was a collision of genres, intentions, and uses; relying on the oral storytelling method of public dialogue, but without a public audience to hear it, this and the other novels collapsed into moralizing. Early novelists were not successful because they had not yet learned to adapt an oral technique to tell a story to a private audience through publicly distributed print.

Conclusion

By the end of the nineteenth century, Tamil was printed in every imaginable form. Newspapers, journals, books, pamphlets, and novels indicate an ever-widening sphere of public debate made possible by print. Just how these new physical objects, for instance the fabulously popular personal diaries, affected social thinking is far from clear at this stage of research into print culture in nineteenth-century Tamil. What we can say, however, is that no print revolution occurred in the realm of storytelling and that oral storytelling continued, without severe disjunction between teller and audience. Further, no catchphrase such as from 'tale to book' or from 'teller to author' will suffice since printed stories did not replace but were added to spoken stories. The curious Natesa Sastri, for example, famous folklorist and novelist, was not a tale-teller; he collected, rewrote, and published volumes of south Indian folktales in both English and Tamil for audiences other than those who would normally hear them. Print also provided public audiences with information and debate on social and political questions, as demonstrated by the printing of Norton's speech on education, but it did not dislodge orality as the primary medium of storytelling.

The printed tale and novel did, however, introduce a new public dimension to storytelling. As we saw in the case of the *Pañcatantra* printed for schools, the public use of tales stirred controversy; as Davis pointed out for sixteenth-century France, the newly printed tale reached a new audience beyond the reader/listener, and part of that public found some tales offensive. Similarly, Tamil novels were printed within a public debate about social ills and a campaign for a new vernacular. As stories, they were not widely read or influential, but as cultural artefacts they carried a social significance beyond any oral tale. In the last decades of the century, during the debate over 'originality' and the campaign for a modern Tamil literature, novels supplied evidence of the parity with English culture that South Asians were beginning to assert as the grounds for their wider participation in the political system. Poetry, superstitious legends, and myths of the Hindu gods would not advance their claims, nor would the edifying but ambiguous tales; only the novel, the genre popularized by print and emblematic of contemporary urban culture, would suffice. Almost without exception, early Tamil novels did not announce themselves as 'tales' (*katai*) but as 'histories' (*carittiram*), perhaps because the latter had greater truth-value.

Print in nineteenth-century Tamil may have produced an information revolution but not a narrative one. One reason for this is that print and orality are not equivalent; an oral technique of composition does not easily transfer to the print technology of distribution; authors in print were not the tellers of tales. Even at the turn of the century, when the novel failed as a narrative medium, another form of oral storytelling, the drama, held more of the popular imagination than did print. Movies and political speechmaking would also soon succeed where printed stories failed not because they are public but because they are oral.[25]

NOTES

1. The boundaries between folklore and popular culture are discussed for verbal folklore by Bauman (1989: 180) and for folk art by Glassie (1972: 258).
2. For a detailed discussion of changing technology and audiences in contemporary India, see Manuel (1993).
3. On books printed in Sanskrit and Marathi in the first two decades of the century in Tanjore, see Shaw (1978).
4. For the effects of print on South Asian Islam, see Robinson (1993).
5. Some early Indian books were also printed with wooden fonts or produced by lithography.
6. About this time Mutthusami Pillai, a Tamil pundit at the College of Fort St. George, was apparently sent into the countryside to collect Tamil manuscripts written by the missionary Beschi and to negotiate permission to publish them (Srinivasachari 1927: 5).
7. Note, however, that the authors explicitly state that writing was an 'addition not an alternative' to orality (p. 68).
8. See Narayana Rao (1993). For analysis of reading practices in early twentieth-century Tamil, see Venkatachalapathy (1994).
9. This time-frame could be advanced a hundred years: although Tamil novels and short fiction have exploded since 1950, the primary medium of narration for the majority of the population, even in the late twentieth century, remains oral.
10. For details on this technological change, see Hoernle (1901); Losty (1982).
11. Details on these early Tamil books are found in Shaw (1993).
12. Srinivasachari (1927: 5), quoting Public Consultations 1 and 5 May 1812, Madras Record Office.
13. The *Tirukkural* is composed in a metre suitable for didactic works, which did not prove difficult for foreigners to penetrate.
14. Such is the comment (translated from German) of the Protestant missionary Ziegenbalg, working in Tranquebar in the early eighteenth century (Gaur 1967: 74).
15. Caldwell, as quoted in Murdoch (1872: 16–17).
16. Of the 720 signatories, the majority were non-Brahmin, most were Tamils,

several were from Andhra, and a few Marathas; many signed in English, two in Persian.

17. For the Munsif's manual to laws, see Iramasvami Ayyar (1867).
18. *Vivēkacinatāmaṇi*, a leading Tamil journal at the end of the century, was admired for its use of electrotype engravings (*The Hindu*, 30 September 1895).
19. If the 1891 Census is to be believed, 15,710 people worked in the book and printing trade in the Madras Presidency (*Census of India 1891*, p. 432).
20. On early novels in all Indian languages, see Das (1991); in Tamil, see Asher (1970); Kandaswami (1984); Zvelebil (1990).
21. Subbiramaniya Ayyar's (1895) (review of Guruswami Sarma's *Pirēmakalāva-tyam*).
22. For a full translation and analysis of this novel, see Rajam Aiyar (1998).
23. The first Hindi novel also suffered from an overemphasis on dialogue as a result of an unsuccessful transfer of this technique from a more traditional genre (drama) to the new genre (Kalsi 1992: 787).
24. The novel was first serialized in a Tamil journal, *Vivēkacintāmaṇi*, begun in 1892 and sponsored by 'Knowledge Diffusion Agency' whose goals were to 'spread general information on useful subjects among the masses'.
25. The first Tamil talkie, 'Kalidas', was screened in 1931 (personal communication, Rachel Dwyer).

REFERENCES

Abrahams, Roger, 1972, 'Proverbs and Proverbial Expressions', in Richard Dorson (ed.), *Folklore and Folklife*, Chicago: University of Chicago Press: 117–28.
Anderson, Benedict, 1991 (1983), *Imagined Communities* (revised edn), London: Verso.
Asher, R.E., 1970, 'The Tamil Renaissance and the Beginnings of the Tamil Novel', in T.W. Clark (ed.), *The Novel in India: Its Birth and Development*, Berkeley: University of California Press: 179–204.
Baker, Christopher J., 1984, *An Indian Rural Economy: 1880–1955: The Tamilnad Countryside*, Delhi: Oxford University Press.
Balfour, Edward, 1850, 'Remarks on the Amount of Education in Madras', *Madras Journal of Literature and Science* 16: 380–400.
Baskaran, S. Theodore, 1981, *The Message Bearers: Nationalist Politics and Entertainment Media in South India, 1880–1945*, Madras: Cre-A.
Bauman, Richard, 1989, 'Folklore', in E. Barrow (ed.), *International Encyclopedia of Communication*, vol. 2, New York: Oxford University Press: 177–81.
Bayley, W.H., 1854, 'Report on Tamil', in *13th Annual Report from the Governors of the Madras University, for 1853–54*, Madras: Christian Knowledge Society: 100–3.

Bayly, Christopher, 1989, 'Introduction', in S. Theodore Baskaran, *The Message Bearers: Nationalist Politics and Entertainment Media in South India, 1880–1945*, Madras: Cre-A.

Campantan, Ma. Cu., 1980, *Accum Patippum*, Madras, np.

Census of India, 1891, vol. 14, 1893, Madras: Madras Government Press.

Chatterjee, Partha, 1993, *The Nation and Its Fragments: Colonial and Postcolonial Histories*, Princeton: Princeton University Press.

Clark, T.W. (ed.), 1970, *The Novel in India: Its Birth and Development*, Berkeley: University of California Press.

Classified Catalogue of the Public Reference Library (Attached to the Office of the Registrar of Books, Old College, Madras), Consisting of Books Registered from 1867–1889, 1894, Madras: Government Press.

Das, Sisir Kumar, 1991, *A History of Indian Literature*, vol. VIII, *1800–1910: Western Impact and Indian Response*, New Delhi: Sahitya Akademi.

Davis, Natalie Zemon, 1991 (1975), 'Printing and the People', in Chandra Mukerji and Michael Schudson (eds), *Rethinking Popular Culture*, Berkeley: University of California Press: 65–95.

Diehl, Katherine Smith, 1964, *Early Indian Imprints*, London: Scarecrow Press.

———, 1981, 'Early Madras-printed Tamil Books', in *Aintām Ulaka Tamiḻ Maṉaṭu Viḻa Malar*, xxxi–xxxv, Madurai: Government of Tamil Nadu.

Eisenstein, Elizabeth, 1983, *The Printing Revolution in Early Modern Europe*, 2 vols, Cambridge: Cambridge University Press.

Febvre, L. and Henri-Jean Martin, 1976 (1958), *The Coming of the Book: The Impact of Printing 1400–1800*, trans. David Gerard, London: NLB.

Ganesan, S., 1992, *Indian Publishing Industry, An Analytical Study with Special Reference to Publishing in Regional Languages*, New Delhi: Sterling.

Gaur, Albertine, 1967, 'Bartholomaus Ziegenbalg's *Verzeichnis Der Malabarischen Bucher*', *Journal of the Royal Asiatic Society*, 63–95.

Glassie, Henry, 1972, 'Folk Art', in Richard Dorson (ed.), *Folklore and Folklife*, Chicago: University of Chicago Press: 253–80.

Godzich, Wlad, 1995, *The Culture of Literacy*, Cambridge: Harvard University Press.

Goody, J. (ed.), 1968, *Literacy in Traditional Societies*, Cambridge: Cambridge University Press.

Goody J. and I. Watt, 1968, 'The Consequences of Literacy', in Goody, 27–68.

Hoernle, A.F.R., 1901, 'Epigraphical Notes on Palm-leaf, etc', *Journal of the Royal Asiatic Society of Bengal* 69(1): 93–134.

Iramasvami Ayyar, 1867, *Kirāma Mūncippu Caṭṭam*, Madras: Hindu Press.

Irschick, Eugene, 1969, *Politics and Social Conflict in South India: The Non-Brahman Movement and Tamil Separatism, 1916–1929*, Berkeley: University of California Press.

Joshi, P., 1998, 'Culture and Consumption: Fiction, the Reading Public, and the British Novel in Colonial India', *Book History* 1: 196–220.

Kalsi, A.S., 1992, '*Parīkṣāguru* (1882): The First Hindi Novel and the Hindu Elite', *Modern Asian Studies* 26(4): 763–90.

Kandaswami, S., 1984, 'Tamil', in K.M. George (ed.), *Comparative Indian Literature*, Trichur: Kerala Sahitya Akademi: 693–702.

Kesavan, B.S., 1985, *History of Printing and Publishing in India: A Story of Cultural Re-awakening*, vol. 1, *South Indian Origins of Printing and Its Efflorescence in Bengal*, New Delhi: National Book Trust of India.

Lewis, B., 1995, *Cultures in Conflict*, New York: Oxford University Press.

Losty, Jeremiah P., 1982, *The Art of the Book in India*, London: The British Museum.

Madras Hindu Reading Room, 1856, *3rd Annual Report, 1855*, Madras: Hindu Press.

Madras Tract and Book Society, 1853, *34th Annual Report, 1852*, Madras.

———, 1862, *Annual Report, 1861*, Madras.

Manuel, Peter, 1993, *Cassette Culture: Popular Music and Technology in North India*, Chicago: University of Chicago Press.

McGuire, John, 1983, *The Making of a Colonial Mind: A Quantitative Study of the Bhadralok in Calcutta, 1857–85*, Canberra: Australian National University Press.

Mukherji, Chandra and Michael Schudson (eds) 1991, *Rethinking Popular Culture*, Berkeley: University of California Press.

Murdoch, John, 1865, *Classified Catalogue of Tamil Printed Books*, Madras: Christian Vernacular Education Society.

———, 1872, *Idolatrous and Immoral Teaching of Some Government and University Textbooks in India*, Madras: Caleb Foster.

———, 1901a (1870), *Classified Catalogue of Tamil Christian Literature at the Close of the Nineteenth Century*, Madras: Christian Literature Society for India.

———, 1901b, 'Introduction', in Rev. S. Winfred (ed.), *Pancha-Tantra, translated from the Tamil*, Madras: Christian Literature Society.

Nambi Arooran, K., 1980, *Tamil Renaissance and Dravidian Nationalism, 1905–1944*, Madurai: Koodal.

Narayana Rao, Velcheru, 1993, 'Purana as Brahminic Ideology', in Wendy Doniger (ed.), *Purana Perennis, Reciprocity and Transformation in Hindu and Jaina Texts*, Albany, NY: State University of New York Press: 85–110.

Natesa Sastri, S.M., 1884–93, *Folklore in South India*, 4 vols, Bombay: Education Society's Press.

———, 1900, *Tiṉatāyalu*, Madras: Lawrence Asylum Steam Press.

Norton, George, 1848, *Native Education in India; Comprising a Review of Its State and Progress within the Presidency of Madras*, Madras: Pharoah and Co.

————, 1850, *Speech on Education, Delivered at the Opening of Pacheappah's Hall, in Madras, on 20th March 1840*, Madras: Pharoah and Co.

Raghava Menon, K.P., 1941, 'History of the Madras Government Press', in K.V. Krishnaswami (ed.), *Madras Library Association, Memoirs*, Madras: Madras Library: 104–8.

Rajagopala Pillay, 1875, *Tamil Text Book for the First Examination of Arts, 1876*, Madras: Commercial Press.

Rajam Aiyar, B.R., 1930 (1896), *Kamalāmbaḷ Cariṭṭiram*, 5th edn, Madras: S. Natarajan.

————, 1998, *The Fatal Rumour: A Nineteenth Century Indian Novel*, translated from the Tamil and with an Afterword by Stuart Blackburn, Delhi: Oxford University Press.

Rajaruthnam Pillay, C.H., 1921, *Panchatantram, Pañcatantiram*, Madras: Christian Literature Society for India.

Robinson, Francis, 1993, 'Technology and Religious Change: Islam and the Impact of Print', *Modern Asian Studies* 27: 229–51.

Sadasivan. D., 1974, *The Growth of Public Opinion in the Madras Presidency (1858–1909)*, Madras: University of Madras.

Shaw, Graham, 1978, 'The Tanjore "Aesop" in the Context of Early Marathi Printing', *The Library*, 5th ser., xxxiii: 207–14.

————, 1981, *Printing in Calcutta to 1800*, London: The Bibliographical Society.

————, 1993, 'The Copenhagen Copy of Henriques', *Flos Sanctorum. Fund Og Forskning*, 32: 39–50.

Soobroya Modelliar, Teroovercaudoo, 1811, *Tamiḻ Viḷakkam*, Madras: College of Fort St. George.

Srinivasachari, C.S., 1927, 'Dravidian Linguistic Studies in the Company's Days', *Indian Antiquary* 66: 1–9.

Subbiramaniya Ayyar, B.S. 1895, 'Pirēmakalāvatyam', *Vivēkacintamaṇi*, 3(8): 269–75.

Suntharalingam, R., 1974, *Politics and Nationalist Awakening in South India, 1852–1891*, Tucson: The University of Arizona Press.

Tantavarayar, Mudaliyar, 1820, *Katāmañcari*, Madras: College of Fort St. George.

————, 1826, *Pañcatantira Katai*, Madras: College of Fort St. George.

Theroovengada Pillay, A., 1853, *Aesop's Fables, Containing Instructive Morals*, Madras, n.p.

Thomas, Rosalind, 1992, *Literacy and Orality in Ancient Greece*, Cambridge: Cambridge University Press.

Venkatachalapathy, A.R., 1994, 'Reading Practices and Modes of Reading in Colonial Tamil Nadu', *Studies in History*, 10(2), 273–90.

Viraraghavachari, Mr, 1941, 'Tamil Newspapers', in K.V. Krishnaswami (ed.), *Madras Library Association, Memoirs*, Madras: Madras Library: 95–103.

Viswanathan, Gauri, 1989, *Masks of Conquest: Literary Study and British Rule in India*, London: Faber and Faber.

Warren, H.W., 1941, 'Early Tamil Printing', in K.V. Krishnaswami (ed.), *Madras Library Association, Memoirs*, Madras: Madras Library: 39–43.

Zvelebil, Kamil, 1990, 'The Dimension of Orality in Tamil Literature', in Mariola Offredi (ed.), *Language versus Dialect*, New Delhi: Manohar: 127–69.

Invitation to an Antique Death

The Journey of Pramathesh Barua as the Origin of the Terribly Effeminate, Maudlin, Self-destructive Heroes of Indian Cinema[1]

ASHIS NANDY

THE PERSON WHO most dramatically symbolized the capacity of new forms of popular culture to express some of the changing concerns of Indian society that could no longer be handled within the traditional, more enduring art forms was Pramathesh Chandra Barua (1903–51). He was certainly not the greatest among the early generation of film directors, but he was one of the larger-than-life figures that Indians learnt to associate with these new modes of self-expression. Barua paved the way for and represented the final triumph of the worldview of Saratchandra Chattopadhyay and the special meaning that the novelist gave to the new journey from the village to the city and, sometimes, the tragic attempts to return to the village from the city. So authoritative was the presence of this mythic journey that all other modes of creativity had to define themselves in opposition to it and, to that extent, had to remain captive to it.

Thus Satyajit Ray was dismissive about the films and the directorial skills of Barua, whom Ray saw as the most respected mascot of popular cinema in India and as the ultimate measure of public taste in cinema. Ray considered Barua's cinema stylized, unrealistic, imitative, dependent on heavy make-up and stilted dialogue. Ray believed that he had learnt nothing from this part of his ancestry. In contrast, Ritwik Ghatak once said: 'To my mind P.C. Barua is the greatest director till this day. I have heard modern day directors have made very good use of "subjective camera". But they have a long way to go and could have learnt a lot from Barua.'[2]

Why this strange anomaly in the evaluation of a film-maker by the two greatest names in Indian art cinema? At first the answer may seem obvious. Ray defined himself in defiance of and in opposition to the worldview Barua and Saratchandra consecrated. Ray's self-definition had to include an element of aggressive negation of Barua. Ghatak, on the other hand, belonged to a generation that had seen the beginning of the decline of Saratchandra and Barua in the aesthetic sensibility of the urban middle class. In this brief biographical note, I shall give the same answer in a roundabout fashion, in the hope that the attempt will tell us something about the core fantasies and the mythic life Indian popular cinema copes with, particularly the changing poetics of the hero that links such cinema to its audience.

I

Pramathesh Barua was the first son of the ruler of a tiny native state, Gauripur, in eastern India. Though called a princely family, the Baruas were basically owners of a large estate. They were Kayasthas and connected with the better-known ruling family of Coochbehar. Gauripur was at the margins of Bengal and Assam, both geographically and culturally. It even had its own dialect, Gauripuri, which appeared to bridge Bengali and Assamese. This marginality—actually a form of biculturality—was reflected in the family culture of the Baruas. Despite the name Barua, usually an Assamese surname though also found in East Bengal, the family was deeply immersed in Bengali traditions and Pramathesh himself wrote and sang elegantly in Bengali. His scripts and letters, though often unbearably maudlin and purple, are a testimony to his mastery over the Bengali language and it is said that the legendary singer Kundanlal Saigal, after listening to Barua sing some Bengali songs at a party, felt that Barua was a better singer than he was (Basu 1976). Satyajit Ray's suggestion that Barua 'naturally' escaped overacting in his films because of his inadequate command over Bengali is obviously uncharitable and an attempt to rationalize his deeper discomfort with Barua (Ray 1982: 40). Chidananda Dasgupta, distinguished film critic and Ray's friend and biographer, is more perspicacious in this respect. While sharing some of Ray's antipathy towards Barua, Dasgupta suggests that Barua deliberately opted for understatement and an intelligent use of his voice.

Young Pramathesh was close to his mother, a devout Vaishnava in a Shakto household, and an excellent singer. It may be of some interest to the psychologically minded that, after being weaned, he lived entirely on milk for eight years. He had his first solid food at the age of nine when the customary ritual of *annaprashan* was celebrated. Whether as a consequence or not, he remained a spartan eater all his life. His food habits were to pose a problem later in this life, when he contracted tuberculosis. There also persisted in Barua a strange but identifiable sense of exile from a maternal utopia, and he attempted to regain it through fleeting relationships with women and through fantasies of women at the margins of social morality (providing absolute, unconditional nurture to substitute for lost love objects). Later, these associations and imageries were to get intertwined with what many consider the central motif of his work, the sense of exile that came from his ambivalence towards the village and the city and the journey from one to the other. Evidently Barua's relationship with his mother, though described by many as idyllic, probably had more to it than meets the eye. It is certainly not insignificant that the two events involving the mother most friends and relatives recount were both sources of acute frustration for the son—his arranged marriage and his inability to go to England for higher studies. More about that later.

Throughout life, Pramathesh admired his father Prabhatchandra, a learned man with excellent knowledge of literature and classical music, a social reformer, patron of education and music, and a builder. Prabhatchandra was fond and proud of his eldest son and heir, almost blindly so. He granted Pramathesh enormous freedom from an early age and, even afterwards, though often shocked by the son's chaotic marital life and financial problems, Prabhatchandra continued to have faith in his unconventional but brilliant son. However, the father–son relationship, too, had its underside. For Pramathesh pushed his father's faith in him to the brink at every opportunity. At the same time, he followed up some of his major transgressions, the ones he knew would hurt his father, by writing self-abnegating, guilt-ridden letters to Prabhatchandra.

Though his parents had, apart from Pramathesh, two other sons and two daughters, they doted on their eldest son. There were reasons for that. Pramathesh was born to them after years of childlessness, reportedly after they received the blessings of a Himalayan sadhu visiting Agra. Another version of the story goes that the couple had a child eight years earlier, who died soon after birth; Pramathesh was born only after the sadhu intervened.

Pramathesh lost his mother when he was 22 and it was a traumatic loss for him. His father lived till 1945 and saw his son acquire immense fame.

But after the mid-1930s, he probably did not see much of his son, whose visits to Gauripur became infrequent after his scandalous second marriage.

Barua's early education began at home under a private tutor. As the scion of a princely family, however, he had learnt to fire a gun even before learning to read and write. By the time he was 12, he had already bagged his first tiger, at the time viewed as a sure sign of a great sportsman. He also played billiards superbly and tennis and badminton reasonably well. Later he was to become an expert rider and, still later, owner of a number of race horses.

From an early age, Barua fitted middle-class India, especially Bengal's idea of a romantic hero. Remarkably handsome, with a poetic and fragile look and a pronounced touch of the androgynous, his appearance and style were thrown into relief by his paradoxical fascination with big-game hunting and philandering, as if he were constantly trying to reaffirm his masculinity. Barua's life, however, was a bundle of paradoxes. This interest in hunting went with a lifelong distaste for meat, fish, and egg (which he probably picked up from his Vaishnava mother) and his conspicuously pacifist, almost ascetic style. After bagging a large number of heads, in later life, he gave up hunting.

When young, Pramathesh wanted to be a doctor—so as to be able to serve the people of his state. His father even modernized the local hospital at his behest. Later he went to Calcutta's Hare School and, for a while, to Shantiniketan. At the end of his schooling, at the age of 14, he got married to Madhurilata, the 11-year-old daughter of one Birendranath Ganguly of Calcutta. The initiative in the matter was taken by his mother. Her precocious son was already in love with the daughter of a doctor at Dhubri but had to comply with his mother's wishes.

In 1918, at the age of 15, Barua joined Calcutta's Presidency College to study science. The college still attracted the cream of eastern India's youth and boasted one of India's premier experimental laboratories for testing out new ideas from the West. Its products were still a conspicuous presence in India's public life. But Calcutta had a greater impact on young Pramathesh than his college. He quickly developed an active interest in theatre and organized a company in his native Gauripur to stage plays that had proved successful in Calcutta's commercial theatre. His style of acting then bore the stamp of the famous actor Sisir Kumar Bhaduri. However, that was obviously not the whole story, for he also successfully played a number of female roles. Satyajit Ray's other proposition—that Barua, probably despite trying, could not overact or be stagy because he had had no exposure to theatre—seems as unconvincing as the one about Barua's skill in Bengali (Ray 1982: 40).

In 1924, Barua graduated and wanted to go abroad for higher studies, but his mother objected. Perhaps she did not want her favourite son to go that far, but it is also possible that she shared the widespread old belief that crossing seas was polluting. He finally managed to go to England for the first time in 1926, after his mother's death in 1925. While there, in 1926, he was nominated and elected unopposed to the state legislature of Assam. Prabhatchandra was friendly with the Viceroy who nominated Pramathesh and probably expected his friend's son to be loyal to the Raj in the assembly. Pramathesh turned out to be a nationalist. He even became chief whip of the Swarajya Party launched by freedom-fighter Chittaranjan Das. Later he was reportedly invited to join the Assam ministry, but by then he was already obsessed with the idea of making films.

Barua's association with India's nascent film industry began accidentally. He knew Dhirendra Ganguli from his days at Shantiniketan. Once, while visiting a filmset at the invitation of Ganguli in a Calcutta suburb, he found an actor in a scene handling a gun incorrectly. That was one thing Barua knew well; he intervened. The director of the film, Devaki Bose, now requested him to play a small role in the film, which he did after initial reluctance.

During his visit to England in 1930, while recovering from an operation to remove kidney stones, Barua went to Paris armed with a recommendation from Rabindranath Tagore, and got his training in cinematography. He also briefly studied film lighting at Fox Studios during the visit. He came back the same year to found a new film company at Calcutta, Barua Film Unit. Its first film, *Aparadh* (1931), was directed by Devaki Bose. It was the first film in India to be shot in artificial light.

When Barua joined films, the film world constituted an uncertain marginal culture, ill-defined both in terms of social norms and artistic creativity. He in fact joined a group of pioneering film-makers—directors, artists, writers, musicians, technocrats, actors, and actresses—of Calcutta who were then trying to adapt the new media to Indian conditions and taste. They included persons like Dhirendra Ganguli, Devaki Bose, and Dineshranjan Das. Thanks to such pioneers, films were becoming an important form of mass entertainment in the country and the various aspects of filmmaking were opening up new careers for the more daring.[3] But the filmwallahs themselves composed a liminal group at the periphery of society. Barua seemed to like that ambience. Cultural liminality was not unknown to him and that gave him a certain confidence in that atmosphere of uncertainty, self-experimentation, and openness. In 1929, he joined the Board of Directors of the British Dominion Films. He first acted in a series of silent films during 1931–2 and, once sound was introduced into movies, directed the film *Bangla 1983,* a futuristic fantasy. It was released in a new cinema hall, christened Rupabani by Tagore, but did not do well at the box-office.

Though by the end of his life, Barua made a large number of movies as an actor-director, for the older generation of Indians, his name is associated mainly with eight films: *Devdas* (New Theatres, 1935*), Adhikar* (New Theatres, 1936), *Mukti* (New Theatres, 1937), *Rajat Jayanti* (New Theatres, 1939), *Shapmukti* (Krison Movietone, 1940), *Mayer Pran* (M.P. Productions, 1941), *Uttarayan* (M.P. Productions, 1941) and *Shesh Uttar* (M.P. Productions, 1942). All of them had their Hindi versions and reached a pan-Indian audience. Like Ray, Barua was also a total director; his cameramen and editors were usually a secondary presence in his unit. He wrote his own screenplays and sometimes even the stories. Frequently he was his own editor and, in one or two cases, cameraman.

II

A new world opened up for Barua in 1933 when he joined the New Theatres, one of India's most respected film studios. It was also a studio that 'adopted' Saratchandra Chattopadhyay as its principal literary inspiration and patron saint. Certainly no other studio was to get so closely identified with movies that were, even when not based on Saratchandra's works, so obviously coloured by his worldview.

Barua's first film under the new banner was *Ruplekha* (1934). The following year he made *Grihadaha,* based on the famous novel of Saratchandra Chattopadhyay. Both were moderate successes. He really arrived as a major public figure after making *Devdas* (1935) and *Mukti* (1937).

Devdas particularly was a spectacular success and, after its release, its hero and its director quickly became a part of India's film folklore and landmarks in the country's cultural history. In addition to directing the film, Barua played the hero in the Bengali version.[4] The film was made when Barua was under much emotional strain. His tempestuous second wife Amaladevi, better known as Khiti had just died, and her death was associated not merely with a sense of immense loss but also guilt.[5] Barua could not meet Khiti before she died; he was returning from one of his usual trips to England and his ship reached India a few days after her death. Khiti left behind a small child (who was later on brought up by Madhurilata). His letter to his father after the death of Khiti, written on 31 May 1934 (Basu 1976: 229–30) is revealing:

> You want me to come to Gauripur. I shall not probably come to Gauripur again. I am ashamed. . . .

I once told you—and I say so again—life is a gamble. I gambled and lost. Now there is no life; there is only existence.

Diwanji [the Prime Minister of Gauripur] must have mentioned the matter of my marriage to Khiti. I lost the trust of others when I did not marry her before she bore me a son. That is why I have fallen so low. I have vowed to ruin myself as a penance for that sin.

The same year Barua came to know that he had contracted tuberculosis, then an incurable disease. Presumably he caught it from Khiti, who had died of the same disease. The contagion must have carried special meaning for a person living in a world of sin, expiation, and repentance.

This sombre mood was reflected in *Devdas*. Its emotional tone was sharpened by the music of Timir Baran, particularly the haunting songs that Saigal sang for it. They took India by storm. For some reason, most viewers saw it as a personal testimony and confessional. Chidananda Dasgupta (1991: 29) says:

He came into his own in the solemn tragedy of *Devdas* (1935). Saratchandra Chattopadhyay had written the novel at the age of 17. It is surprising that this immature piece of fiction should have created such an archetypal hero, a romantic, self-indulgent weakling, who finds solace in drink and the bosom of a golden-hearted prostitute. The character of Devdas has been reincarnated a hundred times in Indian cinema under many guises; its ghost refuses to die. Perhaps . . . the dream of surrendering life's troubles to the solace of drink and the arms of a lover-mother is too attractive an escape to be banished altogether from our secret selves.

Barua was not only the creator of Devdas, he *was* Devdas. That is why the Hindi version looks too drab to anyone who has seen the Bengali version. Apart from being handsome . . . Barua had a tragic, if rather solemn intensity. His voice had depth, and he spoke in a low, understated manner.

Bengalis have never drawn a sharp line between cinema and literature. The term for a film in Bengali is *boi*, a book; a film is supposed to narrate a novel, play, or *purana* faithfully. This has spawned, some like Dasgupta believe, a cinematic language that is never entirely independent of literature. (The language was to face its first serious challenge from Ray.) One suspects that to Bengalis at least, *Devdas* was Barua's book of life, perhaps even his autobiography written uncannily before his times by a gifted novelist.

A detailed discussion of *Devdas*—as a novel, film, new mythopoetics of the hero—is beyond the scope of this chapter. But is its protagonist only a weakling who finds solace in drink? Or is he one who defies tradition for the sake of romantic love to lose both and then, when he turns to the city as an escape, finds modern urban life a disloyal ally, as heartless as the norms he has disowned? Is the golden-hearted prostitute only a counter-factual rationalization of unacceptable sexuality or is her maternal care an attempt to humanize the seemingly dehumanized, deadening impersonality of civic life? Is the divide between Parvati or Paro (the village girl Devdas loves and loses) and Chandramukhi (the urban prostitute) a divide between the past and the present, between two ways of defining Devdas, between an increasingly distant village and the 'tinsel glitter' of India's now-burgeoning cities offering their versions of community life? Could Devdas have been something more than the teenage hero created by a famous novelist in his teens? I shall argue later that Indian cinema still grapples with these questions. The final answers to them are yet to be given.

Devdas must have been many things to many people, but he was above all the first successful hero in Indian cinema who seemed to seriously negotiate the anguish of the first generation of rural élite entering the pre-War colonial city. His self-destruction bears the imprint of both his ambivalent defiance of the village—to which he tries to return before his death in one last, doomed effort to reconnect with a lost past and to escape anonymous death in a soulless city—and his final rejection of the urbane charms of a seductive new lifestyle. The city looses Devdas and probably does not even notice it; the village cannot own him, even in death. He is mourned, privately and in loneliness, only by two women who serve as the coordinates of his torn life—by Parvati, to whom he is the lovable rebel who defies norms only to affirm his higher-order conformity to them, and by Chandramukhi, for whom he symbolizes the squandering generosity of a pastoral prince self-destructively opposing and, thus, revalidating her personal knowledge of the calculative rationality of a bourgeois culture. Both coordinates must have made immense sense to an audience facing the problem of refashioning their selves in response to the changing demands of Indian modernization. Both invoke in Devdas nostalgia mixed with ambivalence. Not merely his conservative society but he, too, is unable to acknowledge either of them fully.

The making of *Devdas* brought another woman in Barua's life. For playing the role of the heroine, he chose Jamuna, a woman who had lived at the margins of respectability and with whom he had fallen in love. They got married in 1934 itself, when *Devdas* was being made.

In 1937 Barua's other great success, *Mukti* was released. It was produced, directed and scripted by him. The name of the film was suggested by Tagore who had heard the story from the film's music director Pankaj

Kumar Mallik and liked it. Though finicky in such matters, Tagore also permitted Mallik to set to music one of his poems for the film, an unheard-of privilege. The poet also specifically recommended the use of two of his songs for the film.

Mukti was mostly shot outdoors, in Gauripur. A major role in the film was played by Jang Bahadur, Barua's personal elephant. Both were major innovations in Indian cinema. Once again there is, in the main protagonist of the film, the same mix of unrequited love, betrayal, transition from village to city and a doomed attempt to return from the city to wilderness, loneliness born of the inability to handle the impersonal heartlessness of the city, and self-destructiveness. This time the journey from village to city is implicit and has already taken place when the story begins. The narrative and the hero's search for freedom begins in the city and ends tragically, as it had to do for Barua, in the sylvan surroundings of his childhood—in the magical, adventure-infested rainforests of Assam. The hero returns there to seek in nature a solace and a respite that earlier he sought from the women in his life. But nature betrays him as decisively as the city and his well-bred, urbane lover; at his moment of death he is left only with the tribal youth he has befriended. As in *Devdas*, even in death he is separated from his estranged lover, but the separation is sharpened this time by his belief that it means freedom for her, for she had felt burdened by his private ghosts. *Mukti*'s hero, too, is the scion of a rural aristocracy, but he is so in the sense in which Barua was one; there is a clear touch of class in him, despite what Dasgupta calls Barua's 'execrable taste' reflected in the paintings and sculptures of the artist-hero.

Mukti's hero too caught the imagination of India's middle classes. He looked like a more modern variation of Devdas and even more like Barua himself. *Mukti* is not merely a story of a self-pitying, rejected lover. It invokes memories of a number of other heroes of Saratchandra, and it does so in a particular way. Its hero spans the spectrum that defined Bengal's middle-brow ideal of a hero—in epics, contemporary literature, art, theatre, and politics—to give that ideal a more urbane content, without disturbing its psychological moorings. As if Barua was determined to take over and embellish, with the help of Saratchandra, what was lurking in the hearts of the Bengalis and important sections of India's urban, semi-westernized middle classes, the fantasy of an archetypal mother's son perpetually trying to find a touch of uterine warmth and oceanic feeling in his encounters with women and the world, and to recreate situations of grand defeat and personal tragedy that would allow the ultimate woman to enter his life to reinstate a lost, maternal utopia.

Whatever else this myth did or did not do, it consolidated cinema as a form of self-expression in Indian society. It also made Barua a rage. Not only was he the most conspicuous symbol of that new art form, he was the one who was living out the myth of the new hero, breaking down the barriers between cinema and life, myth and reality, past and present. Even his sartorial style was now copied. People wore Barua jackets, shirts, and collars. Dasgupta (1994: 24, 40)describes the bonding between Barua and the Indian, particularly the Bengali, middle classes in the following words:

> No personality in the cinema had established more identity between his private life and the films he created, the roles he played. His films were not objective records or interpretations of the work of others, they were intensely personal. He did not merely make Devdas. He was Devdas.
>
> Rarely has a film-maker been as much of a legendary hero as Pramathesh Barua, Prince of Gauripur, Assam. Aristocrat, horseman, marksman, dancer, tennis player, hunter, music lover, foreign travelled actor and director, his image was of an irresistible prince charming descended upon common folk, honouring them by his very presence in their midst.

Between them, *Devdas* and *Mukti* sum up the legend Barua was, on screen and in life. Both are paradigmatic journeys, from the village to the city and from the city to the village. But the psychological geography of these journeys also includes less territorial voyages—from maternity to conjugality to maternity, and from the past to the present to the past. All heroes are defined by their voyages, and Barua too is etched forever in public memory as the first one in Indian cinema who could never return home, who in the final moments of his journey, when he seemed to have made it, was tragically felled by his own character flaws and fate. That his journeys exteriorized the inner journeys of millions in his audience only added to the poignancy of his failures.

Soon after making *Mukti*, Barua left New Theatres, without any obvious provocation. Many of his friends and well-wishers were aghast; others were perplexed, shocked, or anxious about his future. Their apprehensions proved justified. Though he made a series of commercially successful movies afterwards, none came anywhere close to capturing the magical effect of *Devdas* and, for that matter, *Mukti*. Till the end, his association with New Theatres remained his most rewarding phase of life. Though obviously not a non-partisan observer, his one-time mentor Birendranath Sarkar, who headed New Theatres, expresses what many of Barua's friends were to feel about the vicissitudes of his career. While affirming that Barua was a 'true artist', Sarkar (Barua 1994) says:

However, he was extremely sentimental and egoistic. He left N.T. at the prime of his career. The reason is not known for sure. Perhaps we had unwittingly hurt his feelings. . . . A certain dissatisfaction and melancholy, a secret revolt against society lay buried deep within him. Despite his multiple talents and capabilities, he failed to attain complete fulfilment in his lifetime. This was the greatest tragedy of his life.

Barua's career as film-maker was interrupted by his fragile health. This meant frequent visits to England for treatment—a time-consuming affair in those days. Interruptions also resulted from his frequent changes in producers, financial crises, and affairs of the heart. It was a minor miracle that by the end of his career, he had made so many films and so many of them were such resounding hits.

True to his popular image and the life cycle of some of his favourite heroes, Barua died of tuberculosis. As in nineteenth- and early twentieth-century England, the disease carried rich cultural meanings for urban, modernizing India. Especially among the Bengali élite, tuberculosis was as much a personal statement as a medical diagnosis. Often associated with a delicate, poetic temperament, it also conveyed waste, self-imposed suffering, reckless surrender to the seductive charms of urban life, and doomed or unrequited love. In Barua's case, these associations were strengthened by his suicidal carelessness about his health and the half-heartedness with which he got himself treated in Europe, even when he went there ostensibly for reasons of health. (He used these trips abroad mainly as excuses for travel.) As if he had accepted his disease as a gift of Khiti and was determined to die with it as a penance for his past transgressions. Even in death, no one could accuse the lost prince, haunted by his inner demons, of deviating from his chosen way of life.

Illness, however, was only a part of Barua's problem in his later years. He had earned and spent money like a gambler prince. Now his recklessness was taking its toll. Even more painful was his loneliness. That, too, Jamuna says, he took in his stride, as the deserved fate of all artistes negotiating and surviving on popular taste (Sen 1967).[6] But he did begrudge his 'routine existence', despite being fatalistic about it:

> I could not imagine living a mundane and routine existence. Yet now I have been compelled to lead such a lifestyle. This is the irony of fate. I have no regrets about this. . . . I have been defeated in the battle of life and I accept my defeat.[7]

Barua died in 1951 at the age of 48. He used to say that no one had the right to live beyond the age of 50. Even in death he had conformed to Saratchandra's—and his own—standards of a tragic, romantic hero.

When he died, Independence had already come, along with massive communal riots, the partition of India and an exodus of millions. Bengal itself was now divided between two brand new nation states, with the film studios, professional skills, and producers concentrated in Calcutta, and a majority of the consumers in another country, Pakistan. It was obvious, even to the most obtuse, that Bengali cultural life and Bengali cinema would never be the same again. Whether they admitted it or not, the Bengali middle classes knew that Barua's death symbolized the end of an era. Describing his last journey to the cremation grounds, distinguished writer Sailajananda Mukhopadhyay says,

> To see him for the last time, every house on the roadside had become a jungle of people; there was not an inch of space anywhere. Behind his flower-adorned dead body were his innumerable, grieving friends. . . . It seemed that everybody in the huge metropolis, old and young, was running out to pay his or her last respect to their beloved 'Devdas'.
>
> I had not guessed that he was so popular, perhaps because I was so near to him.[8]

Mukhopadhyay underestimates not so much Barua's popularity as the extent to which he had come to represent the defeat and demise of Bengal's first innocent affair with the urban-industrial vision. Mourning the death of Barua so spectacularly was only one way of expressing the inability to mourn that other death. Barua had lived as if death defined a person in a manner that life by itself could never do; he never knew that his death in turn was defined by a larger, unacknowledged loss of innocence and the demise of a way of life.

III

Barua was already a legend when he died. Yet his immense success as an actor-director failed to camouflage the story of dissipation, disorganization, and injudicious emotional investments that his life had become. He *did* give the impression of being a vulnerable, overprotected mother's boy who never grew out of what sometimes goes in India with such vulnerability and protection—a certain non-calculative, self-pitying, adolescent romanticism and self-subversion. Few public figures epitomized so neatly in their personalities the transition from the relatively self-contained world of the traditional landed gentry to the world of modern, monetized, mass entertainment and the demands of urban, impersonal, cosmopolitan living.

Nothing revealed that ability to symbolize the transition more dramatically than Barua's attitude to two major components of that new urban-industrial world he had entered—money and sexuality. He was always uneasy with money; he just could not handle it. In addition to being an expensive producer-director, his style of film-making often involved costly retakes and budget overruns. In a nascent, highly disorganized industry where financial management was a vital skill, Barua always maintained the touch of a gullible amateur. From an early age he had lived in style. The monthly stipend his family sent him when he was a student at Calcutta was higher than the revenues of many smaller princely states and in adulthood he earned enormous sums of money as an actor-director. But much of it had gone down the drain. Though he never lived in conspicuous luxury—he never used a guard and never had a proper secretary—he was often out of pocket and had to draw upon his family wealth to cope with financial crises. Even that sometimes did not work. Towards the end of his life, his personal finances were in a mess.

What was true of Barua's attitude to money was also true of his sexual exploits. In all, he married four times. (One of the marriages still remains a secret. The details of the marriage, from which he had a son, are not known except reportedly to one biographer who refuses to divulge them.) It is said that only his first marriage to Madhuri was a well-considered step and that too because she had been chosen by his mother after a long search. Madhuri remained steadfastly loyal to him and tolerant of all his aberrations from the conventional idea of an Indian husband. In fact one suspects that she gradually became for her wayward husband a maternal presence, tolerant of his escapades but also firm and protective about her own dignity and individuality. In his other three marriages, he wanted to give social status and financial security to his lovers who bore him children. In addition, there were his countless extramarital affairs, including visits to prostitutes which he converted into flamboyant, demonstrative affairs of the heart *a la* Saratchandra Chattopadhyay.[9] But he was never comfortable about them either; all of them were sources of misery, especially intense feelings of guilt, and most ended painfully. As he wrote to Madhuri on 16 September 1934 (Basu 1976: 232) after marrying Khiti, 'I had expected not happiness but escape from the hand of my conscience'.

Reading Barua's letters and the reminiscences of those who knew him, one begins to suspect that he was no Don Juan or Casanova. Women were not so much objects of conquest for him as lumps of clay waiting to be moulded into something beautiful—physically, socially, aesthetically, and intellectually. As if he sought mastery not over inner doubts about his own masculinity, as philanderers usually do, but over a powerful, uncontrollable, natural force that could be shaped into more creative forms. Jamuna relates how reluctant she was as a plain-looking, non-Bengali-speaking woman to enter films, and adds, 'He [Barua] was a creator who experimented with my life. He wanted to know whether he could trace two different entities in the same woman. His experiment was successful. He could find Devdas' Paro and his wife Jamuna in one and the same woman' (Barua 1994: 38).[10] This search went with pathetic attempts to get nurture and demonstrative love from all his wives and mistresses. Patently in the case of the tempestuous Khiti, and less directly in the case of Jamuna. But the attempt was, strangely enough, most sustained in the case of his 'abandoned' first wife who emerges from his correspondence and the fading memories of contemporaries as an emotional refuge, source of sympathy and acceptance, and perhaps also the final judge and arbiter in his battles with himself. When Khiti left him and took with her their son, it was to Madhuri that he turned for solace and understanding.[11] One is tempted to guess that, in additional to being a nurtural but strong maternal authority, she also became over the years, in a peculiar reversal of roles, the reincarnated mother with reference to whom his other lovers had to play out their roles as the Paros of his life. He seemed more willing to face social censure than Madhuri's rejection; yet he had to defy her to come back to her. One thing, however, is certain. Despite a clear narcissistic strain in his personality, Barua was never calculative about his affairs. This was bound to be a self-destructive enterprise in the end.

Barua was ever ready to fall in love, but never knew how to fall out of it. A shy, romantic moralist with a sense of *noblesse oblige*, he had internalized middle-class values and he shared the fantasies that he played with on screen. What this ultimate hero of the world created by Saratchandra had once said about Devdas remains a vital clue to his own life: 'Because the love of Devdas could not transcend the physical, it took him towards destruction.'[12]

As it turned out, it was not so much an impersonal appraisal as a self-fulfilling prophecy. And such was Barua's mythic stature in middle-class India's fantasy life that that prophecy seemed to set the norms for an entire generation of great actor-directors of commercial cinema who followed him. Particularly the ones who, like Barua, had the kind of looks and personality that conveyed the image of an innocent, artistic dreamer lost in an overly realistic world and waiting to be protected or mothered (the kind of image actor-director Guru Dutt and, less directly, Raj Kapoor, both brought up in the ambience of New Theatres, cultivated, built upon, and died with).

To adapt Ramchandra Gandhi's (1992) comment on the theatre, cinema can be subversive in a society where identities have become fixed, for it challenges the rigid boundaries of the self by owning up, temporarily, other identities. In South Asia, where the plurality of the self is culturally given and even celebrated in both folk and classical traditions, cinema's role in society should therefore be more modest. Yet, for those partly uprooted from their traditions and entering the more impersonal urban-industrial culture in South Asia today, the fluidity or play of identities Gandhi talks of might have acquired some radical potentialities.

Every revolution, however, throws up its own versions of triumphalism, self-certain millennialism, and tragic dead-ends. If in colonial India mythological films showed that Indians could be gods and defy their subjecthood, Barua and his contemporaries, when they broke out of the tradition of mythological films, showed that the new world India was entering with such innocent enthusiasm could turn, with cannibalistic pleasure, on anyone who did not read all traditional norms and pieties as fatal liabilities.

Looking back, one recognizes that Barua not merely broke the barriers between his personal life and the characters he portrayed on screen, but also those between the idea of the hero he had internalized from the literary and cultural life around him, and the parabola of his personal life. Living out his life as an urbane Devdas—whose tragedy he captured for the screen with such moving, if maudlin and self-indulgent elegance—Barua took to a logical conclusion his created persona. His social location only sharpened his ability to deploy the self-definition thrown up by the entire gamut of heroes Saratchandra Chattopadhyay had created. Though Barua once claimed that the characters on screen he had created were inspired by the life around him, the inspiration came filtered through the novelist's imagination.[13] Saratchandra was the one who combined for his protégé aristocratic 'decadence', nineteenth-century romanticism, the pathos of exile from a protective village life, defensive aestheticism and self-destructiveness, and, as a psychoanalyst might add, narcissism tinged with oral dependency needs. As an archetypal hero of Saratchandra, in life and in art, Barua *had* to be in constant search for maternal nurture, unconditional love, and firm handling. The women who entered his life seemed eager to meet these needs and the women in his audience were also probably as willing to offer him that mix of nurture and authority. His fans identified with him not merely because they saw in him their ideal selves, but also perhaps because their needs coincided.

When the well-known director Bimal Roy remade *Devdas* (1955) in Hindi, with the gifted thespian Dilip Kumar as hero, despite the director's efforts, he produced, many hard-hearted viewers believed, only a polished, new version of Barua's classic. Roy had been Barua's cameraman and admirer. He knew the power of Saratchandra's myth, which neither the novelist when he wrote *Devdas* in his teens nor literary critics took seriously. In the 1950s, as an independent, famous producer at India's new film capital, Bombay, Roy wanted to make full use of that awareness. In its third incarnation, too, *Devdas* was a huge success.

Anyone who had seen the three films knew that Roy's version was cinematically more polished than the two earlier ones made by Barua. Dilip Kumar, who had for years specialized in tragedies, put in an excellent performance as Devdas. But almost no one thought so. Certainly no Bengali film critic seemed happy; they praised Roy and could find no major flaw in his *Devdas*, but felt that it had not met the standards set by Barua. As for Dilip Kumar, one critic in a major journal, perhaps not finding any good reason to dislike the new Devdas, claimed that the actor's overly mature looks and acting were no match for Barua's slender innocence (*'chipchipe saralya'*).

For these critics, not only had Barua's life and cinema overlapped, once he had portrayed and personalized Saratchandra's hero, it was impossible to outperform him. For Barua had taken over, deepened, and enriched the Devdas myth; he had lived and died as only Saratchandra and his readers could have imagined. 'Perhaps the whole purpose of your advent in the world of cinema,' the novelist himself had said, was 'to give life to my brain-child Devdas' (Barua 1994: 19). It is not surprising that when the famous Bengali actor Uttam Kumar was invited to play the title role in a new version of *Devdas* in the 1970s, he refused. He said that he would not be able to equal Barua's performance. Perhaps he sensed that even if he matched Barua's acting, there was little chance of his breaking into the myth Barua had left behind. Perhaps as the other great personification of Saratchandra's hero, who had made the archetypal journey from village city, Uttam Kumar felt duty-bound not to poach in an area marked out as the domain of Barua in public memory.

IV

Let us now return to our original question. Satyajit Ray and Ritwik Ghatak looked differently at Barua because they coped differently with that archetypal hero and the shared fantasies that gave him substance. Ray would have hated to admit this, but many of his own heroes—from the *Apu Trilogy* to *Mahanagar*—can also be read as variations on an archetypal mother's son banished from a flawed pastoral bliss and lost in an urban, impersonal, commercial jungle. Sometimes even when they look very different, as for instance in *Jalsaghar* or *Seemabaddha*, the tensions in their personalities—and the inner contents of their tragedy—either replicate Barua and Devdas or rebel against that stereotype. Even Ray's first story for a film, *Kanchenjunga*, can be read as a story of the same archetypal hero trying to transcend his self, painfully and with immense effort. The protagonists in some of his later works, especially in his highly popular science fiction and crime thrillers, do not follow that model, but Ray himself suspected them to be his lesser creations (Nandy 1995: 237–66). Not only are they written for children, their heroes live in a virtually all-male world. The protagonists in these works have no opportunity to sweep their heroines off their feet the way Barua might have done in the case of some of Ray's more consequential heroines. After all Barua did turn many of Ray's own cultural heroes—from Rabindranath Tagore to Bibhutibhushan Bandopadhyay—into his unqualified fans.

Ray's contempt for Barua *was* a defensive manoeuvre, an attempt to cope with the fear of a liminal film-maker who unwittingly spanned traditional commercial cinema and serious art films by negotiating the common core fantasies of both. Barua was too deeply into Saratchandra and looked too compromised and yet, at the same time, too close to be a comfortable presence. He had taken the first step on the road Ray was to walk but the step was unsure and ungainly. The contempt was sharpened by two other factors. First, there were Ray's self-conscious attempts to defy the established conventions of popular Bengali and Hindi cinema. His realism, his avoidance of the maudlin, his refusal to view cinema as merely a means of visually portraying a novel, and his austerity did not come so much from the masters of world cinema as from attempts to produce works which would flout the conventions of popular films made in Calcutta and Bombay. Few represented these conventions more arrogantly than did Barua.

Second, there was the distance between Ray's middle-class, almost puritanical morality (informed with a social realism that supplied the basis of his concept of good cinema as an art meant for the discerning film-viewer and having its own form of classicism) and Barua's amateurish concept of commercial cinema as a popular art form that made its point mainly by touching the hearts of millions. Barua was nothing if not blatantly high-brow in his lifestyle and middle-brow in his artistic tastes. His tiger shoots, domestic elephants, tennis, expensive cars and wines, and haremful of mistresses proclaimed social status; his 'execrable taste' in the matter of contemporary art, to some extent even his total immersion in Saratchandra, proclaimed his middle-brow taste. Ray was middle-brow in life and high-brow in artistic taste. To him the belief that cinema was a popular art form was itself an indicator of an earlier, more primitive phase in the history of cinema (Ray 1982: 38).

To put it another way, Barua was an indirect product of the world created by Saratchandra Chattopadhyay. That world constituted the mythic underground of middle-class consciousness not merely in Bengal but, at least in the inter-War years, the whole of undivided India. Even this chapter, ostensibly written as a biographical note on Barua, can be read as a counter-factual obituary on or an enquiry into the real-life fate of a hero of Saratchandra. Barua's strengths and limitations were largely those of the novelist; so were the contours of his moral universe. Ray, on the other hand, was a direct product of the world of Rabindranath Tagore. To him Barua, as indeed Saratchandra, was not merely a popular artist with insufficient sensitivity to the classical, Barua's was the model that had to be defied to create a space for art cinema in Indian public life. Cinema, Ray recognized, was a medium that could not be as disdainful of public taste as some other forms of art.

Finally, there was in Barua the same touch of marginality that, unknown to his admirers, Ray had to live with. Born in a naturalized Bengali family known for its enormous contributions to Bengali literary and cultural life, on that half-forgotten, only theoretically significant marginality Ray added his acquired liminality. He started life as a person who had poor acquaintance with Bengali literature and Indian music and none whatsoever with Indian village life, later so closely identified in world cinema with his films. His familiarity with western literary classics and music, on the other hand, was deep and abiding. He had not even read Bhibhutibhushan Bandopadhyay's masterpiece *Pather Panchali* when he illustrated a children's version of the novel for Calcutta's Signet Press and got the idea of making a film based on the novel (Gangopadhyay 1986). If anything, Ray was, despite being a part of Calcutta's gentry, in some ways culturally more marginal than Barua. He had reasons to see in Barua a distorted projection of his own marginality.

Ghatak's response was more mixed. Well-exposed to world cinema, he rejected the conventions of popular cinema. Yet, always undersocialized by the global trends, he also celebrated these conventions by working for commercial film directors like Bimal Roy and Hrishikesh Mukherjee, often writing highly successful scripts with which the likes of Barua would have been perfectly at home.[14] Ghatak also was loyal to the first identifier of the practitioners of popular arts: he yearned for a large audience. (He once reportedly thought of shifting to television, thinking that the new medium might give him an even larger audience.) Above all, as a maker of art films and as one who had followed in the footsteps of Ray, he had to defy Ray himself. A part of that defiance was the absence of any overdone denial of middle-class taste in films. Ghatak sometimes used, much less self-consciously than Ray, variations on the model of the hero that Barua projected. But that was not the only model he had. There were others that defied Saratchandra. While the hero of *Bari Theke Paliye* (1959), even though only a child, is Saratchandra through and through, the hero of *Ajantrik* (1957) or *Jukti, Takko aar Gappo* (1974) is not in Barua's mould, though in the latter he is probably too obviously a defiance of Saratchandra to qualify as 'free' of Saratchandra. However, in neither case was Ghatak burdened by the 'pasts' of his heroes in popular consciousness. Both kinds informed his self-definition as a creative film director and he moved between them with ease. He was never unduly defensive about the immensely popular, middlebrow novelist's influence; already an entire generation separated the two. Ghatak could, therefore, admit Barua as a part of his cultural heritage.

One final comment. It was by jettisoning Barua's model of the hero that a new generation of commercial Hindi films, from *Zanjeer* (1973) onwards, supposedly made their presence felt in the mid-1970s. Amitabh Bachchan, actor-turned-politician-turned-actor, was to typify that genre for millions of Indians. That negation of Barua, though it went along entirely different lines, was as spirited as that of Satyajit Ray. Much has been written on the subject, and one needs only draw the readers' attention to the available works in the area.[15] Yet, despite much talk about a virile industrial man supplanting a chocolate-pie, effeminate hero, in this transition from the earlier romantic heroes on the Indian screen to the present breed of tough, modern killing machines,[16] Barua, Saratchandra, and *Devdas* have not been truly superseded. As I have argued elsewhere, in one block-bluster after another starring Amitabh Bachchan, the hero starts with a personality that is not very different from Barua and Devdas, and he is pushed, against his inclinations and will, into becoming a tough, hard-hearted industrialist of violence operating at the margin of law (Nandy 1998a). Circumstances and a new set of villains bring about this change and the audience is left wondering if, once the ungodly are defeated and handed out their just desserts, the hero would have preferred to return to the old self he had reluctantly shed, a self with which only occasionally the heroine, his double, and, of course, always his mother maintain a link. Hence the nature of tragedy in these films, when it comes, is so different. It is not self-destruction and passive resignation to fate as in *Devdas* and *Mukti*. It is a form of active intervention in fate that turns physical, hyper-masculine violence into a new form of self-destructive alcoholism and sexual engagement, and makes the conjugal presence of woman mostly a passive, ornamental appearance in a film. It is the self-sacrifice of a person who has been forced into a life of violence and who, while defeating the villains in a paroxysm of violence, dies with the dream of returning to his 'normal' self unfulfilled. From *Deewaar* (1975) to *Sholay* (1975) to *Mukaddar ka Sikandar* (1978), *Kaliya* (1981), *Shakti* (1982)and *Agneepath* (1990), it is the same story.

Notes

1. This chapter was written for 'The Comsumption as Popular Indian Culture in India', organized by Chris Pinney and Rachel Dwyer at the School of Oriental and African Studies, University of London, 19–21 June 1995. The present version owes much to the criticisms and comments of the participants. Mrinal Dutta Chaudhuri was the first to suggest that I do a cultural and 'psychological autopsy' of Pramathesh Barua; he also put me in touch with Debolina Barua, without whose help this chapter just could not have been written. I have also gained much from the detailed responses of Rachel Dwyer and D.R. Nagaraj to an earlier draft. A few of the quotes used in this chapter are taken secondhand from popular cinema magazines not known for careful annotations and are incomplete.

2. Ritwik Ghatak, 'Film', 1966, quoted in Barua (1994). *Elsewhere Ghatak (1987: 22–3) says: 'Even in the olden days, there were some exceptions to formula film-making. The name P.C. Barua comes to mind. Here was a man who, in the late thirties, sometimes explored the potentialities of this plastic medium. His *Grihadaha* marks some of the earliest successful and significant transitions in films. In his *Uttarayan*, he utilized the subjective camera to telling effect. Surrounded by mediocrity, he sometimes gave off sparks of pure cinema. Though, in the ultimate analysis, he remained a product of his milieu.'

3. For a charming exploration, in cinema, of the creation of the new profession,

see Shyam Benegal's *Bhumika*, 1977, based on the autobiography of Marathi stage and film actress, Hansa Wadekar.

4. He played the role of the heroine's stepson in the Hindi version; Kundanlal Saigal played the hero. The Hindi version was also a superhit. However, those who have seen both versions will immediately admit that the presence of the hero in the two versions is entirely different. The Hindi version seeks to compensate, with the help of the magic of Saigal's voice and Timir Baran's music, for the absence of the fragile vulnerability of Barua.

5. Khiti had run away from her home to come and stay with him in utter poverty for a while. She belonged to a landed family that owned the Lakshmipur estate and were close to the Baruas of Gauripur; Prabhatchandra had reason to be embarrassed and angered by his son's elopement.

6. Barua's acceptance of the fickleness of public taste might have been less than total. A friend remembers how, on finding out that a very handsome, very old, starving woman begging at the entrance of his studio was a once-famous actress, Barua gave her his entire month's salary, a princely sum, which he was carrying at the time. But he also warned her: 'If I ever see you here again, I shall shoot you to death.' (Prabhat Mukhopadhyay, 'Madhuparka', *Galpabharati*, Puja Number, 1977.)

7. Pramathesh Barua, quoted in Barua (1994: 40).

8. Sailajananda Mukhopadhyay, quoted in *Chalacchitralok* (October 1963).

9. Pramatheshchandra Barua, Letter to friend Prafulla Dasgupta, 16 April 1933. Also the letter to sister Niharbala, 10 April 1933, on his visits to a prostitute and on his romantic, deeply emotional relationship with the latter (Basu 1976: 221–2).

10. Was this search for a woman who would be her own double a perennial Indian quest? Why have generations of mythmakers in South Asia grappled with this issue? For a brief discussion of the two aspects of the mythic woman, see Nandy (1980: 32–46).

11. E.g., Pramathesh Barua's letters to Madhurilata of 5 April 1933, 14 August 1933, and 8 May 1934 in Basu (1976: 220, 224, 227).

12. Barua, cited in Mukhopadhyay (1977).

13. Pramathesh Barua, quoted in Barua (1994: 18).

14. For example Ghatak wrote the script for Bimal Roy's commercially highly successful *Madhumati* (1958), a typical romantic fantasy, using reincarnation as a leitmotif.

15. For a succinct statement, see Kazmi (1998). For an excellent, if somewhat uncritical and frothy, treatment of the Amitabh Bachchan genre, see Dasgupta (1993).

16. Vallicha (1979) was probably the first to identify, in the persona Bachchan acquired in the middle of the 1970s, the emergence of the urban-industrial man in the fantasy life of the Indians. See also Kazmi (1998).

REFERENCES

Barua, Debolina, 1994, 'Pramathesh Barua', unpublished paper.

Basu, Rabi, 1976, 'Rajar Kumar', *Desh*, Vinodon, no. (1383: 194–235).

Dasgupta, Chidananda, 1991, *The Painted Face: Studies in Indian Popular Cinema*, New Delhi: Roli Books.

Dasgupta, Susmita, 1993, unpublished Ph.D. dissertation, Jawaharlal Nehru University.

Gandhi, Ramchandra, 1992, Presentation at the Seminar on Bhartrihari, Organized by the Lalit Kala Akademi at Rabindra Bhavan, New Delhi.

Gangopadhyay, Sunil, 1986, 'Priya Lekhak Satyajit Ray', in Shyamalkanti Das (ed.), *Lekhak Satyajit Ray*, Calcutta: Shivarani: 17–20.

Ghatak, Ritwik, 1987, 'Bengali Cinema: Literary Influence', in *Cinema and I*, Calcutta: Ritwik Memorial Trust: 21–5.

Kazmi, Fareeduddin, 1998, 'How Angry is the Angry Young Man: "Rebellion" in Conventional Hindi Cinema', in Nandy, 1998b.

Mukhopadhyay, Prabhat, 1977, 'Madhuparka', *Galpabharati*, Puja Number.

Nandy, Ashis, 1980, 'Woman versus Womanliness: An Essay in Cultural and Political Psychology', *At the Edge of Psychology: Essays in Politics and Culture*, New Delhi: Oxford University Press: 32–46.

———, 1995, 'Satyajit Ray's Secret Guide to Exquisite Murders: Creativity, Authenticity and Partitioning of the Self', in *The Savage Freud and Other Essays on Possible and Retrievable Selves*, New Delhi: Oxford University Press and Princeton, N.J.: Princeton University Press: 237–66.

———, 1998a, 'Introduction: Popular Cinema as a Slum's Eye View of Indian Politics', in Nandy 1998b.

———, (ed.), 1998b, *The Secret Politics of Our Desires: Innocence, Culpability and Popular Cinema*, New Delhi: Oxford University Press and London: Zed Press.

Ray, Satyajit, 1982, *Vishaya Chalacchitra*, 2nd edn, Calcutta: Ananda Publishers.

Vallicha, Kishor, 1979, *The Times of India*, 9 September.

The Home and the Nation
Consuming Culture and Politics in *Roja*[1]

NICHOLAS B. DIRKS

THERE IS ONE scene that is indelibly set in the memory of all those who have watched or read about Mani Ratnam's blockbuster film *Roja*, one of the most popular Indian films of 1992–3. Rishi Kumar, the hero who is held captive by Kashmiri separatist terrorists, leaps upon an Indian tricolour that has been set ablaze by the terrorists, angered by news that the Indian government will not negotiate a prisoner exchange. Rishi Kumar writhes in pain, but converts his pain into patriotism, moving his body in a valiant effort to contain and control the flames that threaten the ultimate modern symbol of the nation. He saves the flag, and rises, still on fire, to avenge the perpetrators of symbolic violence, with the soundtrack building in momentum to a song by Subramania Bharati that evokes the geographical unity and integrity of the Indian nation. The scene is framed, in a manner that seems clearly to set Islam against the principles of Indian nationalism, by shots of the main terrorist calmly praying to Allah. Various reports from viewers around India suggest that audiences are typically most demonstrative during this scene of patriotic self-sacrifice apotheosized into the visual pleasure of the nationalist spectator. But for a Tamil film made in 1992, the pleasures, and the associations, are in fact rather complicated.

Major moments in Tamil politics have for years been accompanied by self-immolations, though frequently around issues and figures that have set the Tamil polity against, or at least aside from, the Indian nation. Perhaps more significant for 1992, we must recall that the film was made shortly after the political horror of the assassination of Rajiv Gandhi in 1991, not by fire but by suicide bomber, an act of terrorism performed by Sri Lankan Tamil terrorists in revenge for the actions of the Indian Army against the Tamil Tigers. In this context, a Tamil hero sacrificing himself for the Indian nation in Kashmir readily displaces the guilt by association for the death of an Indian national hero on Tamil soil, even as it dramatically enacts the sudden change in Tamil political relations with the national state; after 1991, the Tamil Tigers were designated as enemies of all Indian Tamils and Jayalalitha's government associated itself more comfortably with mainline Indian nationalism than any previous DMK or AIADMK regime. But the scene of self-immolation also recalls, particularly for audiences that saw the Hindi dubbed version of *Roja* in northern India, the self-immolations of young students in Delhi and other northern cities in protest over the adoption by V.P. Singh of the Mandal Commission's recommendations to extend backward caste reservations. These fiery scenes of horror became the emboldened images of disempowerment and division, signs of the tragic cost of setting community against community (as the protest read the issue of reservations), in this case caste rather than ethnicity, nation, or religious community, though in the political turmoil of South Asia one identity bleeds into the next. In short, the dramatic apotheosis of *Roja*, and the conspicuous jingoism of its most dramatic scene, was mediated by a great many other scenes from recent Indian political life, and the visual pleasure was as immediate as it was problematically aligned with the triumphs, as well as the contradictions and tragedies, of the national project signified by Rishi Kumar's sacrifice.

Roja has attracted unprecedented attention from public intellectuals in India in part because of its popularity, because it was awarded the President's National Integration Award (which, by waiving the entertainment tax, made the film even more popular), because of the high production values that Mani Ratnam brings to popular Indian cinema (and that too via the site of Tamil cinema), and because even the film's detractors acknowledge that the music is superbly composed and integrated into the film. However, even more importantly, *Roja* has called out for commentary and debate because, in a film that was both extraordinarily popular and well-made (and thus afforded pleasure even for viewers who were made particularly uncomfortable), the melodramatic love story becomes integrally intertwined with a larger story of nationalist struggle, against both Kashmiri separatists and Pakistani aggressors, and is told/enacted through the lives of ordinary (read new middle-class) citizens of the Indian nation. Tejaswini Niranjana set the tone for critical evaluation in her article in the *Economic and Political*

Weekly (Niranjana 1994) in which she argues that *Roja* celebrates the new Indian middle class, which is shown to be decent, secular, patriotic, and ultimately able to unite sacrifice and victory, nationalism and bourgeois desire. Niranjana's concern about *Roja* is that there is no critical edge. Unlike the case for other similar films, she argues, there is no hint of social critique concerning existing inequalities: 'Maniratnam's middle-class characters are unapologetic in every way, and the films celebrate rather than criticize their life-styles and aspirations' (Niranjan 1994: 79). Even more problematic, middle-class citizenship is depicted as secular in a new Hindu way, Hindu associations and ritual practices having been emptied of specifically religious content and made into markers of modal national/cultural identity. Islam, not Hinduism, is rendered a sign of difference, a threat to secularism. The cultural nationalism of *Roja*'s India, in other words, is predicated on middle-class consumption and managerial competence, Hindu forms of everyday life, and national opposition to the benighted forces of separatism/disruption within and their inevitable affiliation to the great threat from outside (always there, though not always named, as Pakistan).

Niranjana's critical review of the film has generated considerable further debate, and despite its preliminary character, crystallizes the kinds of concerns left-wing intellectuals have felt in the face of Mani Ratnam's technical brilliance and almost technocratic neutrality. *Roja* is a text about nationalism, the power of the state, the future of secularism, the character of gendered subjectivities, the nature of city–country relations; *Roja* is a love story set in a context of separatist terrorism and international intrigue that allows for a critical interrogation of middle-class culture and its relations to changing values about both the state and community. Niranjana reads the film as a symptom of (even as she sees it working through the magic of cinematic pleasure to naturalize) a new consensus about contemporary India, in which the question of national integration has become central once again, though in a rather different register: 'As the Hindutva forces reoccupy the discourses of liberal humanism in India, an anti-colonial bourgeois nationalist project is refigured and the secular subject is reconstituted' (Niranjan 1994: 79). Gone is Nehruvian secularism, the national commitment to state socialism, the reticence to use Pakistani exceptionalism or aggression as the bait for Indian nationalism. *Roja* has thus become a window onto the modern Indian predicament, discomforting precisely because the pleasure of its text is analogous to all the other pleasures promised (and in part delivered) by the contemporary spiral of liberalization and middle-class consumption. That cinema is all about pleasure, of course, is part of the problem, and in the case of the cinema of Mani Ratnam, definitely not part of the solution. Perhaps this is why the debate that follows the suggestions of Niranjana and the problems raised by *Roja* betrays a deep unease: what do we have at our disposal to counter the pleasures of the new apart from relentless critique and the implicit exhortation to the secular nationalism of an earlier age, when post-Independence exuberance, Marxist ideology, colonial memory, and middle-class subordination generated different rhetorics of political consensus, and different affects of national sentiment? Perhaps most paradoxical of all is the sense that the critical laments about *Roja* from left-wing intellectuals reveal a sense of loss that is as evocative, and as resonant with pathos, as the dominant message of the film itself, which vividly recalls, and mourns, the failure of both the Indian nation and the Indian state. But this too is fitting, for if the cinema is all about pleasure, cinematic pleasure is all about loss.

A recent issue of the journal *Seminar* begins a special issue on the subject of secularism with an extraordinary reflection about the differences between then and now:

> Our childhood in the fifties was something beautiful. It was a period of innocence where every child was proud to be an Indian. There was something secure about a world where Gandhi was in heaven and Nehru in command. Every citizen was a craftsman, every child an apprentice in the most exciting craft of all, the process of nation-building. . . . We felt that the idea of the third world was invented for us to lead. We were both modern and uniquely civilizational. We had a copyright on both the past and the future [Visvanathan and Visvanathan 1992].

The rhetoric here is clear enough. The voice speaks from adulthood and things are no longer what they seemed. More dramatically, the present crisis goes beyond anything imagined, or from that vantage of childhood memory, imaginable. The process of nation building now seems a process of dissolution and decay, the idea of leading the Third World forgotten in the inability to lead oneself. And, even more troubling, both the modern and the civilizational have been catapulted into crisis; it is no longer clear what these categories imply, and whether in any case they are desirable or useful, let alone salvageable. The copyright on both past and future has been revoked. Small wonder perhaps that Mani Ratnam's narrative wavers so dramatically between the abstractly symbolic—the invocations of Jai Hind at the cost of being beaten senseless, the extinguishing with one's body of a burning flag—and the humanistic particularisms of the personal—the bond between terrorist and captive forged out of a recognition of mutual pain, the de-eroticized if heavily charged collaboration on the part of the terrorist's sister with Rishi Kumar refusing to be part of a political deal/exchange, in his own attempt to mask the evacuation of political logics more weighty than a calculus of relative murder and betrayal.

Mani Ratnam's ideological retreat is at one level crude and formulaic, but at another level he speaks out of the same disenchantment expressed in the quote above, which leads to the following analysis:

> But as the nation became the *nation-state*, something got bureaucratized. What was a vision, a living language, froze into a dead grammar. . . . The corset tightened as the nation-state became a *national security state*. Unity became uniformity and the celebration that was India became a dull regime. The old words *swadeshi* and *swaraj* were forgotten. The nation was no longer a cultural identity; it became a military one, suppressing differences beyond and within itself [Visvanathan and Visvanathan 1992].

Whoever is speaking (or making movies), there is a general recognition of the loss of something fundamental in India's birthright. When this loss maps itself onto an idea of the past that inscribes some nostalgic version of tradition onto the geography of subcontinental history, and then, often related, becomes the pretext for an embrace of certain opportunities in the new—whether around participation in the market or in a new politics of, say, Hindu assertiveness (the two frequently, though not always, seem to go together), the stage is set for what can only be a perilous attempt to re-enchant the nation and reconstitute the grounds of cultural (read national) identity. But despite all the trenchant criticisms of *Roja*'s political framing, the film itself argues modestly for a personal politics of humanism, personal sacrifice and loyalty, love, and recognition. Despite the overarching nationalism, the film depicts 'security' (a word used, in English, throughout the film) as the only real reason of state; at the same time security is the basis for the state's immediate failure in the narrative drama of the film. The military is ennobled by the sacrifices of its members, but is ultimately the agent of a state that has lost its capacity to control the political agenda. In the end, *Roja*'s bad politics may have less to do with its complicity in communalism and jingoistic nationalism than in the bankruptcy of old liberal ideals of individual will and goodness.

I. *Roja*: The Movie

The film opens with the sound of warfare—regimental marching, armoured vehicles, automatic weapons fire—juxtaposed with gentle sounds of nature, the singing of birds—soon revealed as the soundtrack of the second beginning of the film. The titles come to a close when we hear the call to prayer, from an Islamic *mullah*. Under Mani Ratnam's careful control, the *muezzin* signifies place—Kashmir—but also evokes, particularly since his calls are blended so well with the sounds and sights of military action, danger. What follows in the opening scene of the film is a dramatic chase in the darkness of night, the scene signified by the opening martial noises, with the Indian army in pursuit of a band of terrorists; after serious combat and mortal losses, the army apprehends one of the terrorists, an especially menacing-looking man identified as Wasim Khan.[2] The scene then shifts from the murky black and white combat of military night to the brilliant green and bucolic splendor of the south Indian countryside, the music lighthearted and set to lyrics about innocent desire. The camera shows a young woman cavorting in ponds and fields, with scenes of agricultural labour and village life, mostly populated by women. It soon becomes clear that the young woman has commandeered a local shepherd's goats in order to clog the only road into the village, with the hope of catching a glimpse of Rishi Kumar, a young executive from Madras who is driving to the village to marry her older sister. She succeeds, pronounces him very beautiful, and then runs back to the village, via the local temple (where she prays for the happy marriage of her sister), to announce the arrival of the bridegroom. Rishi Kumar enters the village, charms a number of skeptical older women who interrogate him about his intentions, and goes to meet his prospective in-laws. The village exchanges are bathed in light and humour, and centre from the start on women, young and old. If the northern forests of Kashmir are peopled with men carrying lethal weapons and fighting a stark and deadly war, the southern fields are populated by women expressing the rhythms, desires, and laughter of domesticity and agriculture, production and reproduction.

The plotted narrative is disrupted when Rishi Kumar is allowed (only because, we are told, he is a city boy) a private interview with the chosen bride in order to confirm his choice; she begs him to refuse the marriage because she has already pledged her heart to a village sweetheart, son of a man locked in a long-lived feud with her own father. Forced to defer her wishes to the agency of the bridegroom, she confounds Rishi Kumar, who hardly expected to come to a village and encounter female will in the form of refusal; to oblige her, he rejects her in public and chooses, in her place, the younger sister, Roja, who first planted her desiring gaze upon him.[3] Now, however, Roja is terribly upset since her gaze had been vicarious on behalf of her sister, and she imagines that she has been forced to be complicit in ruining her sister's chances of happiness and her family's reputation. This misunderstanding, ironically cast within the village community (between two families and two sisters) rather than between city and country folk, provides the narrative tension in the new couple's love, and is only resolved after they migrate unhappily to Madras and just before Roja is about to flee her marriage to return to the village. All the differences between city and country are collapsed in love, once Roja realizes that her new husband has chosen her at her sister's request; 'modern' and 'traditional' narratives are so promiscuously intermixed that the viewer happily accepts the unlikely premise of the story, that the most modern of men chooses happiness through what seems a random choice made because he desires a village woman from a place he finds beautiful. The love story thus (barely) conceals its own allegorical character for, it seems, Rishi Kumar is in part the embodiment of urban middle-class nostalgia for the simple, rooted, unalienated, traditional life it has left behind. The city's desire for the village is here highly aestheticized, interchangeably impersonal, predicated on a romantic fantasy that combines the full cinematic firepower of the modern cinema with an impressive anthropological imaginary of folk village life and the rural feminine ideal. Significantly, the village is marked by class but not caste; the caste identities are hidden and either implicit or unimportant.[4] Folk culture is wittily and powerfully depicted by narrating the wedding through the songs, dances, and lyrics of the older women, who anticipate the rhythmic creaking of the newlyweds' bed and the hoped for fecundity of new love with a directness and charm that evokes yet another sense of loss, in this case of sexual candour and sensual freedom on the part of the expanding, increasingly westernized, but repressive urban bourgeoisie of modern India. But in the cosmopolitan fantasy of (male) urban (middle-class) romance with (female) village (peasant) India, marriage and love, legitimate sanction and sexual passion, free choice and fated accident, all comes out fine in the end.

Well, almost. . . . Just as the young lovers reconcile, the nuclear home is disrupted by the sound of the phone, informing them that Rishi Kumar's boss, a senior cryptologist, has had a heart attack. We met the boss earlier, when Rishi Kumar took his new wife to meet him because of the stated need for her to get a security clearance. It turns out that the boss is from Roja's village, which delights him, and also makes him declare the official security clearance unnecessary, in what is partly a joke about village solidarities and partly a reassertion of the purity (and inherent national loyalty) of the village. The boss now, from his hospital bed, asks his subordinate to go in his stead to Kashmir, where he must undertake a delicate assignment. He apologizes for sending him all the way to Kashmir, to which Rishi Kumar responds by saying: 'Kashmir is in India, isn't it? To go anywhere in India is part of my job.' This line is meant to be noticed, for it is more than a statement of fact, an explicit nationalist assertion that, after the opening scene of terror, is made against the context of obvious contestation. And this context is about to become the stage for the rest of the film. Roja insists on accompanying her husband, and so the two set out for Kashmir, in a dramatic reversal of the usual conceit of a popular Indian film, where Kashmir was, until the recent political troubles, the ideal locale for romantic trysts and honeymoons. This honeymoon, however, will take place under the signs of danger and difference, established by the opening scene of the film. For politics has intruded with its nastiness and its violence into the heart of the romantic narrative of Indian (cinematic) love.

The scene of arrival is framed through a series of still photographs which represent the ominous surveillance of a man who has now entered a military domain (he is met by the military, escorted to his quarters and work site by military convoy) and a political theatre. The photographs are taken by Kashmiri terrorists, one of whom is soon clearly revealed to have been an associate of Wasim Khan, the man who was apprehended in the opening shot of the film. This initial framing makes it additionally clear that the ordinary lives of Rishi and Roja will collide with the political crisis, though peril is deferred and the first episodes in Kashmir mimic the most romantic of Bollywood honeymoons; juxtaposed against occasional scenes of the cryptologist working at his computer, the two lovers traverse the landscapes of paradise—its high mountains, snowy fields, sylvan lakes—and finally consummate their marriage. The morning after, Roja wakes first, and goes unescorted to a nearby temple, to thank God for her wonderful married happiness and attempt to convey news to the village god she had earlier abused, due to what then seemed her grave misfortune, that all is forgiven. The episode at the temple, where she addresses the deity as the God of Kashmir (in what is simultaneously a national/secular slide, a heartwarming gesture, and a metonymic mistake) takes the form of comic relief, and is carried by a local palmist/tourist guide who, as the genuine secular subject, speaks all languages and laments the replacement of tourists by terrorists. When Roja tries to break a coconut to perform puja, the sharp noise brings security guards running, and occasions her significant aside, 'In Kashmir even breaking a coconut is a crime,' obviously signifying the sense of militant Islam's repression of Hinduism (and by implication the secular capacity to tolerate all religious practices). And so we are less surprised that comedy only precedes tragedy, for when Rishi Kumar panics at the disappearance of his wife (the empty bed after the night of bliss) and runs off to find her with only a limited escort, he sets himself up to be taken hostage by the terrorists who lie in wait. Although one might speculate that this momentary challenge to the secular rationality of the public domain was the cause for retribution, or at the very least realize the cost Rishi Kumar has now to pay for having allowed his wife to enter the space of his work, the scene is also one in which the sanctity of the temple, and the marital happiness that is being celebrated there, is violently disrupted by the forces of terror, which are of course Islamic. No matter how viewers decode the overdetermined semiotics of this moment, the film suddenly changes register, and does so when, for the first time in the narrative space of Mani Ratnam's contrivance, the story of hero and heroine, male and female, collides.

Critical reviews of the film tend to focus, justifiably enough, on the way the secular message of the film is undermined by the coding of Hindu as secular and Islam as anti-secular. As Niranjana suggests, the scenes of Roja praying at temples are shown as neutral, almost privatized, in marked contrast to the displays and effects of Islam. Her observation is strengthened by the obvious association of Hindu religiosity with women, the fact that the temple is for Roja what the state seems to be for Rishi Kumar, in what at first appears to be a symmetrical relationship. But while it is appropriate to map the evident slippage between religious practice and cultural identity onto the gender politics of the film, and to interrogate as well the assumptions about how Hinduism can be modernized and generalized for the purposes of a problematic cultural nationalism, we should note that for Mani Ratnam's film the gender divide seems at some level much wider than that associated with religion. Mani Ratnam is careful to displace his sense of religious affiliation from a confessional to a national grid, with his final invocation of the betrayal of Pakistan, but he is much less concerned to complicate his depiction of gender relations. Roja may symbolize the nation for which Rishi Kumar is prepared to make the ultimate sacrifice, but Roja not only creates the opportunity for terrorist intervention, she refuses both the state's political logic and her own husband's calculus of sacrifice. Her body, which she throws in vain at the terrorists who capture her husband outside the temple, becomes the ground on which the contradictions of Mani Ratnam's narrative resist ultimate resolution.

No sooner is Rishi captured than Roja runs to the police station to demand his return. Frantic, she speaks hurriedly in Tamil to the uncomprehending officers, none of whom understand her southern tongue. Indeed, it is as if the gender division has been rendered linguistic, since even when the message of her husband's capture is translated, we now confront a fundamental incommensurability. The police, and then the military who take over the case, are moved, sympathetic as they are to the entreaties of a woman for the return of her husband. But they are forced to adopt the rationality of the state, and ultimately must respond by saying that while they devoutly wish the resolution of the crisis, they are unprepared to capitulate to the demands of the terrorists for an exchange. Wasim Khan has killed many citizens of India; his capture alone cost the Indian army the lives of a number of good men, all of whom left mothers and wives and children behind. Why should the life of Rishi Kumar, a loyal citizen among many others, be accorded such pre-eminence; how, in other words, could the logic of the state accommodate the particularism of the personal?

Roja is unconvinced and unfazed. While on the one hand she blames the tragedy on her own personal fate, she declares that the state promised them security, and is thus obligated to do whatever is necessary to guarantee the safe return of her husband, who after all is a servant of the state. She refuses to enter into the discourse of state rationality, even after a heated, and poignant, exchange with Royappa, the chief army officer. Royappa accuses her of wanting only her husband, of having no obligation to the nation. Roja replies with suspicion about the workings of the state: 'Would you say the same thing if I were a Minister's daughter? I won't leave you until you return my husband safely to me.'[5] Writing to her sister, she notes that if only the old women from the village were there, those women who represent the folk soul of India, they would immediately rescue her husband. She finally manages to secure an audience with the Union Minister, who breaks protocol to listen to Roja's plea; Roja says that she comes from a small village in Hindustan, that her people may be unimportant but that they are India's people, that as far as she is concerned, her husband is god incarnate. Obviously moved, he promises that he will speak to the appropriate authorities and request action on her behalf. When shortly afterwards Royappa breaks the news to her that the Union Minister has been successful in his entreaties, that the government will in the end entertain an exchange, he tells her the 'good' news with bitterness and rebuke: 'Everyone will be happy that the person whom we captured will now roam free; the fifteen soldiers who died in capturing him will have died in vain. God bless you.' As far as he is concerned, the special treatment on the part of the Minister undermines both the Army's national struggle and the very state rationality that Roja simultaneously rejects and critiques. Indeed, this capitulation, a major break in the narrative, sets up the possibility that Roja's personal romantic desire will altogether overtake the nationalist narrative (or, at least that put forward by the state).[6]

Meanwhile, Rishi Kumar is in the hands of Kashmiri terrorists. But his detention begins with an act of tenderness, performed by the sister of Liaqat Khan, the main terrorist. She brings him food, unties his arms so that he can eat, and is hit by one of the terrorists for her careless kindness. Rishi tells them to leave the girl alone, and, after being warned that while they mean him no personal ill he should not try to escape, asks what they want. 'We want freedom.' 'Whose freedom?' 'Our freedom, for Kashmir, for all of us here, the flowers and the trees; we want freedom from your rule.' In a subsequent exchange, Rishi Kumar is asked to speak into a tape recorder, in order to prove to the Indian government that while he is alright, they should do what the terrorists request. Rishi Kumar can only say 'Jai Hind, hail to India', over and over again, though he is beaten and bloodied for his intransigence. Later on, when being moved to another location, Rishi Kumar engages in a longer conversation. He asks Liaqat Khan how many men he has killed (the number of men killed appears repeatedly as the index of barbarism), asks whether his leaders are in this country or in 'the neighbouring country', whether, if his leaders asked, he would kill his children? To the last question, Liaqat Khan responds by saying, 'Yes, this is a *jihad* with Hindustan.' After more discussion, Liaqat Khan says in frustration: 'These issues will not be solved by talk, but by partition.' And as a Subramania Bharati song celebrating the geographical unity of India begins to build momentum on the soundtrack, Rishi Kumar says, 'India will not be partitioned a second time.' When referring to the leaders from the neighbouring country, and when mourning the wound of partition, the film is unequivocal. But the terrorists are nevertheless firmly planted within India. Not only will partition be resisted, the terrorists must learn that their interests rest with India. And in the film, they learn this when fifteen of their number (in an even exchange with the Indian army), including Liaqat's younger brother, are massacred by the Pakistani army, an event announced on the television news, in the only filmic enunciation of the actual name of the territorial enemy.

For the first time, Liaqat is shown praying in a moment that contains no threat, but instead suggests the vulnerability and sorrow of a man who has just suffered a terrible loss. Rishi Kumar says to him softly, 'I am sorry. Your brother should not have been killed.' Liaqat confesses that 'they' have betrayed him, that now his group will have to carry on by itself. But Rishi does not let the issue rest, instead asking whether all the fighting and killing is in fact acceptable to his god: 'Is it in your religion that man should kill man? Is anyone pleased at the death of these children? Save people instead; wipe their tears, let go of your guns.' Through the death of a loved one, and through the common recognition of the betrayal/crime of Pakistan, the two individuals recognize each other. In this glowing humanistic moment, Rishi Kumar offers Islam a new 'secular' version of itself, splitting off the militant associations of jihad by associating it with another nation rather than another religion. Politics, even the discourse of freedom and oppression, vanishes in the overdeterminations of national rivalry, intention, and character.

But, as if to relieve the almost unbearable burden of conversion (and to return to the conventions of a political thriller), the moment of recognition is suspended by the arrival of news that the Indian government has reversed its stance agreeing to the exchange of Rishi Kumar and Wasim Khan. The terrorists rejoice, grateful for the return of a leader whose resolve seems more than ever necessary. We then move back to Roja, and see her as she prepares to witness the exchange and recover her husband. The van that once kidnapped her husband approaches the bridge at the other side of the river, but then disgorges cloth rather than a man, and drives off furiously. Roja, who runs across the bridge, gathers up what are revealed as Rishi's blood-covered clothes. She refuses to accept defeat, and announces to Royappa, who by now has been (somewhat mysteriously, given his earlier pronouncements) converted to her cause by her dedication and love, that she will find him: 'I will go to those rebel households; there must be a woman like me there.' She is right, for it turns out that Liaqat's sister has connived with Rishi to set him free, allowing him to escape the terms of the exchange that seem to Rishi, as they seemed to Royappa (and the state) at an earlier stage (before he was 'feminized'), as a national capitulation. Once again, the role of the woman has been to challenge the political terms of the state (or counter-state); but in this instance Liaqat's sister has acted not simply in the interest of saving Rishi's life, or of reuniting him with his wife, but rather to gratify his desire. Given the Kashmiri woman's exquisite beauty, what might have constituted an alternative site of romantic possibility is suggested only by her inexplicable actions against the interests of her brother and his men, a mystery that is itself completely sublimated in Rishi's nationalist resolve. Can it be that she was seduced by Rishi, not for any love of his for her, but instead for his love for the nation? All these questions are left in abeyance as the camera shifts abruptly to the last action scene, an epic chase down glaciers and snow-covered slopes, as Rishi struggles to free himself from what he clearly sees as the logic of the state, the crime of exchange, all the while seeking to convert the sacrifice of one woman into the grounds on which the other, his beloved wife, would need neither make, nor occasion, any sacrifice at all, personal or national.

At the end of the chase, only Liaqat stands between Rishi and liberation. Rishi looks Liaqat in the eyes, and again their human connection prevails. Rishi says, 'You can't kill me; when your brother died I saw your pain.' And despite the possible implications of his actions for Wasim Khan and the movement, Liaqat tells Rishi to go indicating that in allowing his free passage he will expiate the death of his brother: 'I will wipe my tears now.' And so Rishi is finally free to join his beloved Roja, in a scene of final rejoicing and reunion.

II. *Roja*: The Debate

The couple's embrace appears to signify the resolution of the myriad conflicts in the film. Husband and wife have been reunited, but without having to relinquish the dreaded terrorist, or to engage the terms of exchange that would have obviated the call for national sacrifice and contaminated the higher reason of the state. The state could have its cake and eat it too; moved by the personal tragedies of its ordinary subjects, it could respond humanely and yet find its higher purpose rescued by the sacrifices of its ordinary subjects. The Kashmiri terrorists created the terms of an exchange that had placed them firmly on the side of Pakistan and murder; by the end of the film they have returned Rishi Kumar in exchange for the sin of Pakistan, at the same time they have encountered, through the proximity and recognition of human tragedy and desire, the common humanity of all Indian subjects, whatever their particular politics. Thus both the state, in the first instance, and the nation, in the second, have been apparently triumphant. And the triumph has been accomplished by Rishi Kumar, a skilful middle-class technocrat who, even in the new age of liberalization, works for the state rather than a private corporation, but reveals himself also as a hero who refuses to accept the sullied political terms of compromise and exchange. Liaqat's sister demonstrates that even women, when acting out of natural instinct, compassion, and love for mankind (well, for Indian men), can convert their local desire into national service (remember here Roja's suggestion that the old village women would be able to do what the state could not). And Roja herself gets her man back; the film seems to assume that her happiness will be even greater when she realizes that her husband returned of his own free will, outside the terms of exchange, inside a narrative of heroism.

Nevertheless, the triumphant though abrupt ending barely conceals the fissures and contradictions of the filmic story. First, neither the nation nor the state have remained unscathed. The nation itself is only invoked in the film through abstract symbols and slogans, personal sacrifice, and national rivalry. The nation has in fact failed to sustain the loyalties of many of its subjects, and can only hope to reclaim their loyalty once the betrayal of an opposing nation drives them back. The logic of opposition here works in part through jingoistic nationalism, in part through the memory of the primal wound, the historical tragedy of partition. But the problem with partition is that while it has produced the crisis that the state has constantly to confront and struggle to control, it also expresses the originary failure of the nation, the horrible fact that history, culture, and geography did not coalesce in the spirit of national unity. India's unity was fractured from the start.

The terms on which the nation can by hyphenated with the state have also been challenged on a number of fronts. The fact of partition has meant that the state has had to become, first and foremost, a security state; thus the loyal bureaucrat expends his dazzling cryptological skills in deadly combat with Pakistan, working for RAW rather than for India's industrial enrichment (as the real middle-class dream would have it), thus what should have been a honeymoon in India's romanticized theme park becomes a dangerous nightmare, thus the state must ask its ordinary citizens to sacrifice on a regular basis, to accept a state of constant warfare simply to maintain the quotidian borders of the polity. Perhaps it is this constant drain on state resources and resolve that occasions the undertones of corruption and favouritism that provide the basis for Roja's deep suspicion of the state's claim on her national loyalty. The state is hardly pilloried in Mani Ratnam's account; Niranjana is correct that there is no real critical edge. But Roja's refusal to negotiate her emotional demands with the state is presented as more than simple female intransigence and familial isolationism. And in the story, the state does finally bend its resolve to special pleading. Roja rebukes the chief Army officer for the state's special interest in the lives of its political elite, but then joins that circle by establishing what in effect is a personal relationship with the Union Minister. The state's interests are not in the end protected by the state, but by a rogue individual acting on his own, and against the immediate plea, and particular interest, of Roja.

That the rogue individual (and exemplary citizen) is the beloved husband of Roja seems to ameliorate this subtextual aberration. But Roja's subject-position is shown to be highly contradictory, and deeply flawed. As I suggested earlier, she created the danger that led to the kidnapping in the first place. Even granting the validity of her critique of the state, she is presented as completely unmoved by nationalist sentiment and uninterested in the sacrifices of others. Despite her capacity to move into an urban household and marry a cosmopolitan technocrat, she is ultimately a village girl incapable of seeing the big picture. As Niranjana notes, the film's title is misleading, because there is no way that Mani Ratnam can tell his story through the eyes of the heroine; her only story is a simple love story, without any of the political overlays that have brought to this film both national acclaim and academic notice. In the end, Roja gets what she wants, though not how she chooses, and without any need for her to experience an epiphany of nationalist desire. Indeed, the conclusion of the movie patronizes Roja quite literally; she must be humoured, she must be satisfied, but ultimately either ignored or circumvented.

Why, then, is Roja the supposed centrepiece of the film? The simple answer to this question is of course that the film is a standard misogynist melodrama, in which Roja is the perfect object of desire; in so far as Roja becomes a subject of desire, she does nothing but cause trouble, which for the movie becomes the narrative mechanism that propels the drama and allows the conceit that her subjectivity—both in her actions and her emotional state—is at the centre of the story. But because of Mani Ratnam's cinematic ambition, the stakes are rather higher, and Roja becomes the site of allegorical desire: for a rural life and village self that have been lost by the urban middle-class technocrat; for a religious sensibility that can be recuperated without inflaming the communalist passions of Hindu fundamentalism or coming into competition with other forms of religious commitment that seem to be linked to nationalist violence, territorial ambition, and collectivist destruction of the humane individual; for a nationalist referent that pre-exists the terrible history of partition, that self-inflicted wound of national humiliation. *Roja* is, in the end, about loss, fantasy, and failure; and thus *Roja*'s ending is necessarily so incomplete, so unsatisfactory, so vague in its ultimate allegorical message. Perhaps too this is why while on the one hand it is necessary, and easy, to write the story of *Roja*'s complicity in jingoistic nationalism and bourgeois communalism, it is also necessary to understand that, when all the shouting in the cinema halls and academic journals has stopped, the pleasures of the film are purchased with extraordinary ambivalence.

My reading of *Roja* is meant to exonerate neither the politics of the film nor of the film's reception and appropriation more generally at a time when aggressive nationalism, and associated forms of communalism, market liberalization, bourgeois social irresponsibility, and state corruption are the preferred and subsidized modalities of pleasure in Indian popular culture. Left-leaning critiques have insistently raised important questions about the character and popularity of cultural forms such as this film. I have already suggested many points of general agreement with Niranjana's brief critique, even if I think her analysis begs a number of questions, misses a great deal in assuming the mapping of the film's success straight on to a political reading of India's new pathological nationalism, and unfairly simplifies both the reading of the film and the explanation for its appeal. Tellingly, none of the film's reviewers have allowed the pleasures of the film to coexist with ideological critique; equally significantly, far too little is made of the genuinely pleasurable aspects of viewing the film, perhaps most importantly, the music, which is both catchy and, at times, sophisticated. At best, Rustom Bharucha, who is the most vigilant of *Roja*'s critics, notes that the deepest influence on Mani Ratnam is advertising, which provides him with the craft and the ideology of his filmmaking.

Bharucha's critique is situated in a larger interrogation of the rise of fascism and the associated complicities of the culture industry in contemporary India. Bharucha best summarizes what he means here when he distills another similar essay by Sumit Sarkar on 'The Fascism of the Sangh Parivar': 'The emergence of a "communal consensus" in which "a whole series of assumptions and myths have turned into common sense", and the construction of "a powerful and extendable enemy image" through the appropriation of old prejudices and the combination of new ones, which are being propagated in the media with increasing intensity' (Bharucha 1994: 1389).[7] Stated like this, it is hard to take exception, particularly since communalist discourse and assumption have shifted and been steadily naturalized in increasingly shocking and dangerous ways in recent years. The media, through the bourgeois western images and narratives beamed by transnational television companies, the popularization of religious epics in local television productions, and the blatant xenophobia and Islam-bashing of films like *Roja*, have played an important role in this process. But Bharucha's larger critique, that the culture industry has only one totalizing ideological register and meaning, seems not only to make the enterprise of cultural criticism bankrupt and boring, it confers complete epistemological power to the forces of the right.[8] He argues that 'the very perception of culture is being determined by the growing hegemony of national and global market forces, whose right to interpret the world is being propagated almost without dissent. This peremptory and fundamentally uncritical valorization of the market and the state (and their collusions) by a range of media representatives in advertising, television, journalism, commercial cinema, constitutes to my mind a form of cultural fascism—liberal and even idealistic on the surface, but dangerous in the hold it has on people's minds and votes' (Bharucha 1994).[9] Small wonder that his analysis of *Roja* lacks subtlety and eschews without reserve the critical analysis of ambivalence, complexity, and pleasure.

Bharucha reads *Roja* as if its primary purpose was to naturalize India's undisputed claim to Kashmir, and to suggest that all the trouble and dissent concerning Kashmir is illegitimate, at best the manipulated result of Pakistani intervention. There is little doubt that the film presents a perniciously simple, one-sided account of the Kashmir crisis, avoiding all issues of history, sovereignty, not to mention the atrocious evidence of human rights abuses on the part of the Indian army. And when Bharucha calls for citizen groups and public forums in India concerned with democracy to demand better knowledge about the history of the Kashmir situation, he makes an important political point, though not one that is especially helpful for either film studies or cultural critique. With reference to the film, Bharucha is particularly concerned that the much-vaunted subtlety of Mani Ratnam's presentation of the 'terrorists' (he correctly notes the choice of term, as opposed, for example, to 'militants')—displayed in the ultimate humaniza-tion of Liaqat Khan—be used to represent his film as balanced and plau-sible, and to conceal a blatant misreading of the political situation.[10] He is also particularly alarmed by readings of the film that suggest an implicit critique of and distance from the state, in relation, for example, to the em-phasis on individual 'heroic' action. He writes that it is a 'euphoric mis-reading to imagine that *Roja* is celebrating individualism above the power of the state. The fact is that Roja and Rishi Kumar are integrally a part of the state. If the fervent wife gets hysterical and places her husband above the state, that is only to be expected. Ultimately, it is the patriarchy of marriage and the benevolence of the state that protect her' (Bharucha 1994: 1394). In this rejoinder he attacks Niranjana for having suggested, in a similar vein though in fact not nearly as strongly as I have in this essay, 'the failure of the state, which cannot defeat the militants, cannot rescue its employee', and then to have linked this sense of failure to liberalization and the middle-class embrace of market enterprise. Although he elsewhere notes the complicities of market and state, he seems unwilling to accept any limitation on the modern legitimation and power of the state, in a manner that parallels his complete acceptance of totalizing discourses of state enunciatory power.

In this last point, Bharucha's concern is shared by Pandian and Chakra-varthy (1994), who argue that the 'apparent inability of the state in the film actually masks its silent and powerful ability and in that sense the ultimate victors in the film are the state and the Hindu-patriarchal culture with which the desire of Rishi Kumar, the hero, coincides'. They argue that the disavowal of state violence is what affirms rather than defeats the state. But although they make their argument in the language of film studies, using an application of the concepts of condensation and displacement to demons-trate that disavowal works to accrue both power and legitimacy to the state, their reading seems forced and unpersuasive, much like Bharucha's. Their most significant insight, similar to part of my own argument here, concerns the patriarchal character of the film, and the ultimate disempowerment of Roja herself.[11] But in the end, *Roja* has become a vehicle for a particular set of political arguments about the state, communalism, gender relations, and the family, in the midst of which the film itself seems long forgotten.

If the *EPW* debate on *Roja* is ultimately disappointing, the point is not to return *Roja*, or film criticism generally, to the happy embrace of film studies, not something I could represent in any event. Academics and public intellectuals have an obligation to attend to the meanings and politics of popular cultural forms and forces, and to write against the positive reception accorded *Roja* in the mainstream Indian press that typically worked to justify the political, social, and cultural assumptions forefronted in political critique.[12] However, the metaleptic character of many political readings has the unfortunate effect of mistaking the symptom for the cause, of ascribing to culture the very power it would seek to possess in a world of post-modern mystification and symbolic overdetermination. It is necessary to attempt to understand the multiple registers through which cinematic pleasure works, why it is that cinema is so compelling, and why it might be that cinematic reception/interpretation/interpellation operates in such circuitous ways.[13] That *Roja* is retrograde seems virtually self-evident in the circles within which we write; but that it establishes its identities, elisions, and displacements through cinematic techniques that not only call upon the market-driven character of advertising but also open up a plenitude of affective and interpretive responses is something we must both recognize and engage. Mystification may work through screens that both displace and distract[14] while they also provide languages for testimony and reflection, destabilization and slippage, catachresis and transcoding. The purpose of performing a reading of a cinematic text should never be to get it right (and for good), for that would either fail to recognize or work to suppress the multiplicities of meanings that are generated by any cultural performance or text.[15] Rather, we should link political critique to the more sympathetic (though also analytical) project of engaging the power of the cultural form itself, as well as the spectatorial subjectivities[16] that are shaped by these forms even as they occasionally refuse (or simply fail to absorb) the full implications and totalizations of fascist cultural projects. The public may, in Walter Benjamin's terms, be an absent-minded examiner (Benjamin 1982: 243), but its modes of examination are still as mysterious to modernist criticism as the originary intentions of the cultural producers themselves.

III. Desire and the Nation

Ultimately, of course, the interpretive burden placed on a film like *Roja* is far too heavy for its formulaic melodramatic frame to withstand, its technical brilliance and massive popularity notwithstanding. But in my own reading of the film, I have sought to suggest the fractures, fissures, and ambivalences within the basic text that both problematize a simple political dismissal and convey the categorial weaknesses at the core of a seemingly triumphant state/market appropriation of the filmic text, though I grant the salience of all the political dangers (and then some) suggested by critics such as Bharucha. The film in fact serves to illustrate the promises and the costs of a newly humanized, and individualized, version of secularism, as well as the contradictions and confusions in the position of the state apparatus in India today, even as it is symptomatic of the historical burden that weighs down any practical realization of the national ideal. The naiveté of the film is cloying and alarming; its confidence in individual recognition an inexorable reminder of the sad marriage between shallow sentiment and market capitalism. But it is worth attending to the dissonance and awkwardness of the narrative, in the hope at least that we might not have been the only ones to notice.

If the film does evoke, at least in its undercurrents, the failure of both the Indian nation and the state, it does so, as I suggested before, in the language of loss. Whatever may be blamed for the present impasse, the secularist self-representation of early Indian nationalism provided a post-colonial promise of progress and political utopia, amidst the pressing but practical problems of poverty and underdevelopment. The promise has now been declared empty, the premises of secular society and democratic politics attenuated and uncertain, but for reasons that go back to the beginning, that declare not only that things have changed but that they have always been that way, since the beginning of the nation. The specific reason for this in the Indian case is partition, the historical fact that India no sooner shed its colonial skin than it experienced a nationalist nightmare, not just terrible violence and dislocation, but a fundamental challenge to the claims of universality and citizenship that nationalism had used to justify itself. Partha Chatterjee has written that nationalism is in some sense inevitably caught in the chasm between utopia and irrationality: 'If nationalism expresses itself in a frenzy of irrational passion, it does so *because* it seeks to represent itself in the image of the Enlightenment and *fails* to do so. For Enlightenment itself, to assert its sovereignty as the universal ideal, needs its Other; if it could ever actualize itself in the real world as the truly universal, it would in fact destroy itself' (Chatterjee 1993: 17). For India this predicament was hardly either abstract or invisible, since Pakistan represented its failure, its threat, and its new (post-colonial) self-justification. But increasingly the justificatory rhetoric has shifted in emphasis, from asserting the exemplary ideal of universal secularism and democratic representation *vis-à-vis* the other, to reacting to the security threat and the mystificatory cultural alterity of the other. And with this xenophobic reaction has come the increasingly visible tendency to see the other within, and to use the threat of the internal other to write a script of paranoid mimesis, eschewing secularism (now called pseudo-secularism) as a western/colonial imposition, embracing a refurbished Hindu religiosity as the authentic means to re-enchant cultural and national identity.

It is within this contemporary context that one can read *Roja* both as symptom of a larger crisis and as a text that articulates the fascist presuppositions of a new consensus. However, the film also works to expose some of the lies of that consensus. As I have suggested, the nation has become almost unbearably abstract, its symbolic representations irreversibly intertwined with images of communal strife, suffering, and sacrifice. The state has become increasingly paralysed by its double mandate, its security rationale necessarily endangering the actual security of its citizens. In *Roja* this tension is mediated by the heroic sacrifice of Rishi Kumar, but it leaves Roja herself unmoved, and almost widowed (no matter which choice the state might make). And the individual is left only with the phantasmatic myth of the heroic everyman, the gestures of human recognition born out of the tragedy of the nation (as in the death of Liaqat's brother) and the maintenance of patriarchal domination (as in the exclusion of Roja from the nationalist project, as well as from the net of state protection). There may be a 'magnificence to national existence', a citizen's erotics to the utopian aspirations of the nation, to use Lauren Berlant's apt phraseology (Berlant 1991: 191), but there is blindness and despair when nothing is left to mediate the abstractly symbolic and the resolutely particular. Thus it is, perhaps, that Mani Ratnam simplifies the situation of Kashmir, eliding the political suppression of plebiscite and the military violation of rights, evoking the contemporary crisis as the inevitable outgrowth of partition, re-membering the nation as that dream forever fractured by history, and now finally recuperable only through melodrama.

Like many other melodramas, *Roja* traverses public and private spaces, love and politics, the home and the world. The film begins by mapping Rishi Kumar's aesthetic desire for the beauty and simplicity of the village— the feminine source of the nation's power and virtue—on to the person of Roja, arbitrarily as it turns out. It then maps the traditional love story of a couple who engage the mysteries of intimacy only after marriage on to the national stage, as cinematic honeymoon becomes film thriller horror, albeit with Mani Ratnam's sincere allegorical intent. And then it tacks back and forth, first enunciating the ultimate incommensurability between political reason and personal desire, then collapsing the two domains in the benevolent paternalism of the Union Minister, finally restoring the primacy of the political through the heroic sacrifice of Rishi Kumar, itself only made possible by the unexplained intervention of the personal, through the agency of Liaqat's sister's displaced desire. In the final instance, it is as if female desire can only genuinely enter the national domain if it is completely disinterested, clearly mobilized against the interests of the immediate family, in the form of generalized love for a man who could never actually materialize a narrative of romantic interest. Despite the multiple mappings, the home and the world remain intransitive, fundamentally at odds. But the melodramatic form wishes away both complexity and failure, and the expressions on the faces of the principal characters suggest the power of forgetting. Roja kneels at her husband's feet, the very image of the unquestioning traditional wife, and Rishi Kumar stands victorious, no tears in his eyes.

Perhaps melodrama has now become the unfortunate genre for narrating the post-colonial nation, a way to forget the tragic histories of colonialism in order to claim complete originality and to erase the eruptions of cultural difference that threaten to implode from within: to negotiate, in other words, the contradictory project of nationalism's universalizing primordialism. Homi Bhabha helps us understand the appeal of forgetting: 'To be obliged to forget—in the construction of the national present—is not a question of historical memory; it is the construction of a discourse on society that performs the problem of totalizing the people and unifying the national will. . . . Being obliged to forget becomes the basis for remembering the nation, peopling it anew, imagining the possibility of other contending and liberating forms of cultural identification' (Bhabha 1994). But in the case of melodrama, remembering becomes the transposition of current anxiety onto historical memory, and the basis for imagining possibility becomes linked to empty narratives of desire and misleading calls for national enmity.[17] The love story that begins with misrecognition thus ends with misrecognition, the happy conclusion a cover for the dissatisfactions of home and world, love and politics.

If these ultimately unfulfilled and incommensurable narratives thus inhabit the ambivalence of *Roja* (and by implication, of other similar cultural forms), I suspect they also line the empty shell of melodrama, providing vast and protected spaces for the writing of aggressive versions of cultural nationalism and religious fundamentalism. Cultural critique would here be incomplete if I did not give voice to my own worries that films like *Roja* both express and provide legitimations for a host of rewritings: of secularism as predicated in Hindu majoritarianism, of the protection of minority rights as the basis for constructing different grades of citizenship, of the national mission as the jingoistic maintenance of hostilities with Pakistan and other 'foreign hands', of the state as fundamentally about security on

the one hand and the conversion of agendas of social justice to the subsidiza-
tion of further inequalities in the name of the market on the other, of claims
about national identity into recuperations of modern forms of tradition
that mask communalism, retrograde gender politics, and greater state
authoritarianism, to mention just the most obvious. And if the 'humanistic'
sentiment of a film like *Roja* fails to satisfy, not only because it disinvests
political responsibility but because it distracts individuals from the political
character of their relationship to both state and nation, we must at least be
prepared to point out the myriad ways in which this kind of liberal humanism fails to be sustained within the melodramatic narratives of contemporary popular culture as well as in the compelling accountabilities of modern
political life, even as we must acknowledge, and seek to understand, the
powerful (and pleasurable) effects these narratives can have.

NOTES

1. With special thanks to Janaki Bakhle, for working through the argument of this
   chapter with me, and translating the Hindi version of the film before I was able
   to see the original Tamil film. I am also grateful to Lalitha Gopalan for several
   conversations about the films of Mani Ratnam. The chapter is still in rough
   form and not yet ready for retextualization.
2. Despite the evident danger of this menacing looking individual, V. Chakravarthy
   and M.S.S. Pandian are correct to note that the film shows the Indian army as
   the aggressor, with no originary scene or reference to establish the reason for
   army action. See Chakravarthy and Pandian (1994). Nevertheless, the film
   assumes the sense of danger that terrorism evokes, and it could be said that the
   muezzin's call stands in for any political narrative. It is noteworthy, however,
   that Rustom Bharucha simply assumes that the viewer would side with the
   Indian army in this opening salvo. See Bharucha (1994). As the reader will soon
   become aware, this journal (*EPW*), has devoted a great deal of press to critical
   reviews of the film, thus occasioning this chapter as well. Virtually all the
   critical essays referred to in this paper were published in *EPW*.
3. In my discussion here I am privileging the subject position of the urban viewer,
   male or female. In a recent unpublished paper by Madhava Prasad, it is Roja
   who becomes the site of the disciplining gaze of the state. Despite Roja's intention to continue studying rather than get married, the misunderstanding between her sister and her family on the one hand and between her and her new
   husband on the other deflects the larger issue, which is that her desires are overcome and redirected into conjugality, which she only acknowledges as a

wonderful thing because of the way she comes to see her husband as such a good man; in other words, Roja is punished rather than rewarded for her independence and free spirit. Prasad's argument is interesting but somewhat beside the point, for while Roja is tamed and domesticated by marriage, she only becomes the vantage point of the narrative after her full domestication. Until then, Mani Ratnam situates *Roja* uncomplicatedly within the fantasy village life he has constructed (and not at odds with traditional patriarchy, as Prasad contends). See Prasad (1994).

4. Even in the Tamil version of the film, which usually marks caste position (certainly between Brahmins and non-Brahmins) rather conspicuously, the question of caste identity is confusing for those without a good sense of the local cultural cues. Thus, for example, Pandian and Chakravarthy (1994) comment that Rishi Kumar is an upper-caste Tamil Pillai, while Rustom Bharucha (1994) calls him 'a nice, suitable, brahmin "boy" '.

5. The reference here is clearly to the furore that was generated over the kidnapping of Rubaiya Sayeed, the daughter of the former home minister Mufti Mohammed Sayeed. Bharucha (1994) also suggests that Mani Ratnam was partially inspired to make *Roja* after the kidnapping, and subsequent release, of the oil executive, D. Doraiswamy in the summer of 1991.

6. It is tempting to use this example to predicate some generalizations about the way desire always threatens to overtake the nationalist project, either by compromising its rationalizing rhetoric or by transforming it altogether. For an extraordinary analysis of the theoretical implications of the relation of self-recognition, desire, enjoyment, and the fascist proclivities of new democratic systems, see Zizek (1991). *Political factor*, London: Verso, 1991.

7. It might be noted that while the essay by Sarkar is indeed a powerful indictment of fascism and its relationship to the cultural normalization of critiques of modernity, Sarkar indicts subalternist historians, and post-modernism more generally, for their complicity in the rise of fascism; it seems to me that this capitulation to a particular narrative of the enlightenment and its positivist genealogies as the only alternative to fascism is both a spectacular misreading of history and an unfortunate strategy for polemical engagement.

8. I find this particularly surprising given the fact that in his book (1993), *The Question of Faith*, he takes what seems a radically different position, namely that left secularism has an obligation to take faith seriously enough to instil it with possibilities of tolerance, diversity, and self-realization (p. 91). Indeed, he even finds merit in Doordarshan's recent production of the *Ramayana*, and is insistent that religiosity should be encouraged and empowered in a newly re-thought secularist enterprise.

9. Bharucha seems to use a particular reading of Adorno's critique of the culture system to predicate and justify his sense of the totalizing appropriation of

thought in contemporary popular culture, with its emphasis on absorption into the logics and desires of modern states and market systems. While Adorno's analysis of the effects of the transformations of modern culture is devastating and depressingly accurate, his critique need not be read to justify the closing off of interpretive engagement with film (and by implication video and television). See Adorno (London: Allen Lane 1973).

10. Bharucha (1994), suggests at the end of his essay, by his own admission somewhat lamely, that he would have preferred it if Rishi Kumar and Liaqat Khan had embraced at the end of the film in addition to the embrace of Rishi and *Roja*. It is hard to imagine how this would have done anything more than further humanize the once benighted terrorist; indeed, the film does show Rishi putting his hand on Liaqat's shoulder, in what could be seen as a physical gesture of intimacy, if only of a male bonding sort.

11. The argument here is simply that the state displaces its power onto the family but by so doing masks its own power at the same time that it is sanitized.

12. I take Bharucha's word for this, since I have not yet been able to locate most of the reviews to which he refers in his essay.

13. Preoccupations with pleasure have obviously been of central importance in film studies, which has used various theoretical discussions in psychoanalysis to formulate propositions about pleasure: about the relationships among identification, imagination, scopophilic mastery, phallic loss, transgression, disavowal, condensation, displacement, and bodily incorporation, to mention just a few terms, about which there are major disagreements and debates. If there is no consensus on how to treat pleasure, there is general agreement that pleasure is fundamental to understanding cinematic experience. Within feminist film studies, there is also general dissatisfaction with Laura Mulvey's early contention that cinematic pleasure requires the hegemony of the male gaze, and a lively sense of the appropriative possibilities of feminist perspectives. See Mulvey ((1975/1981); Clover (1992); Penley (1989). But even in Marxist critical studies, for example in the work of Fredric Jameson, there is the acknowledgement that pleasure has to be taken seriously, if only in the commitment of the Marxist critic to politicize pleasure. See Jameson *(1971–86:* 73, 74).

14. I use distraction here in a Benjaminian sense: he writes: 'Reception in a state of distraction, which is increasing noticeable in all fields of art and is symptomatic of profound changes in apperception, finds in the film its true means of exercise.' Benjamin (1982: 242).

15. I write here in an anthropological vein, in the hope that it might be possible to develop a method that would engage culture both as a structure/system/habit of meaning and as the site for critical confrontation and engagement. See my recent essay, 'Ethnographic Translation: Post-colonial Criticism and the Politics of Location'.

16. For an extremely helpful account of the rise of spectatorship in relation to film, see Hansen (1991).
17. Again, for a rather more pessimistic view of the relationship of desire and nationalism, see Zizek (1991).

REFERENCES

Adorno, Theodore, 1973, 'The Culture Industry: Enlightenment as Mass Deception', in *The Dialectic of Enlightenment*, London: Allen Lane.
Benjamin, Walter, 1982, *Illuminations*, London: Jonathan Cape.
Berlant, Lauren, 1994, *The Anatomy of National Fantasy: Hawthorn, Utopia and Everyday Life*, Chicago: The University of Chicago Press.
Bhabha, Homi, 1991, *The Location of Culture*, New York: Routledge Press.
Bharucha, Rustom, 1993, *The Question of Faith*, Delhi: Orient Longman.
————, 1994, 'On the Border of Fascism: Manufacture of a Consent in *Roja*', *Economic and Political Weekly*, June.
Chakravarthy, Venkatesh and M.S.S. Pandian, 1994, 'More on *Roja*', *Economic and Political Weekly*, March.
Chatterjee, Partha, 1993 (1986), *Nationalist Thought and the Colonial World*, Minneapolis: University of Minnesota Press.
Clover, Carol, 1992, *Men, Women, and Chain Saws: Gender in the Modern Horror Film*, Princeton: Princeton University Press.
Dirks, Nicholas, 'Ethnographic Translation: Post-colonial Criticism and the Politics of Location.
Hansen, Miriam, 1991, *Babel and Babylon: Spactatorship in American Silent Film*, Cambridge: Harvard University Press.
Jameson, Frederik, *The Ideologies of Theory: Essays 1971–1986, Syntax of History*, vol. II, Minneapolis: University of Minnesota Press.
Mulvey, Laura, 1975, 1981), 'Visual Pleasure and Narrative Cinema', *Screen* 16: 6–18. Reprinted in her *Visual and Other Pleasures*, Bloonington, Indiara University Press.
Niranjana, Tejaswini, 'Integrating Whose Nation? Tourists and Terrorists in "Roja" ', *Economic and Political Weekly*, 15 January: 79–82.
Penley, Constance, 1989, *The Future of an Illusion: Film Feminism, and Psychoanalysis*, Minneapolis: University of Minnesota Press.
M. Prasad, '*Roja*: Living the State', Unpublished Paper: 1994.
Visvanathan, Susan and Shiv, 1992, 'The Problem', *Seminar*, No. 394, June: 12.
Zizek, Slavoj, 1991, *For They Know Not What They Do. Enjoyment as a Political Factor*, London: Verso.

Bombay and Its Public[1]

RAVI S. VASUDEVAN

I N THIS CHAPTER I look at Mani Ratnam's much-debated film, *Bombay*,
in its movement between cinematic address and public reception. As
a film, and as a form of popular narrative, my concern is to understand
its structural features, its generic location and its intertextual animation of
key motifs in public life. In terms of reception, my analysis is concerned
with the response of the articulate strata of 'the public', as expressed in the
outlook of mainstream politicians, journalists, and reviewers. Writers of
liberal outlook, left-wing affiliation, and the votaries of majority and minority identities have been outspoken in their evaluation of *Bombay*. They
have argued about the rules of representation that ought to govern the exploration of national crisis, in particular the place of the 'real' in this enterprise, and the way prohibitions surrounding women are central to definitions
of communal identity. I also try to understand a practice which is both a
form of production as well as one of reception, that of government censorship. The prohibitions enforced by the censor board add up to a certain
image of the state and its understanding of the impact of images on social
perception and official authority.

I have argued that the narrative construction of this film has a tendency
to discontinuity, with segments acquiring a certain autonomy from each
other. However, a pattern emerges over the time of the narrative, one of
forgetting the past within the text. These features are echoed in the way the
narrative is constructed by segments of the audience. The opinions I draw
upon make sense of the text through a selection of material, and by high-
lighting the logic of certain narrative phases. The last section of this chapter
presents my own susceptibility to vesting the film with coherent meaning.
In seeking to go beyond the existing terms of the debate, I focus on a

referearticular feature which has not attracted much attention, that of the sacrificial male body. Through this figure, I try to suggest that the particular way the text seeks coherence generates contradictory elements which offer the spectator an ambivalent viewpoint on the narrative of communal relationships and sectarian violence.

Towards a Modern Identity: The Basic Narrative Structure

In *Bombay* we have one narrative logic running through the film: how can a family be constituted across the divisions that define Indian society? These are divisions at once between families and communities, and the divisions, re-figured in the larger frame of the riot, dismember the family *generationally*. Although the children are separated from each other for a while, each generation finally retains its integrity. The film thereby sets out a symbolic temporality, a common enough past, present, future logic. The constitution of the family, its rupture with the past, and its drive to preserve its legacy for the future provide the overarching motivational structure, one which brings the nuclear family into dialogue with the representatives of state and society. This dialogue is avowedly one which the 'innocents' of the film conduct with those who wield power. 'Innocents' is a term regularly employed by the reporter Shekhar in his discussions with Hindu and Muslim leaders, as well as with the police; 'Are they not disturbed by the death of innocents?' Ultimately, the innocents are condensed in the image of dead children, and the notion feeds back into the narrative structure which sees the parents struggling to recover their children and the social future, torn from them by the upheavals. The discourse of the family meets with that of state and civil society when the protagonist moves beyond his own concerns into a wider frame of action and restitution. Thus from the logic of recovering his family the hero is thrust into the logic of protecting society. The achievement of the one enables the other, as the children suddenly emerge in the wake of Shekhar's successful bid to diffuse an angry mob, and the nuclear family is reunited.

The commutation of spaces is a key device in the unravelling of this narrative logic. Bombay must replace the village in order for the marriage to take place under the sign of modernity, the film's ultimate goal and resource. Shekhar Mishra's home in Bombay now becomes the iconic space in which all the significant kinship relations can regroup on the basis of a twofold fantasy. The first is revealed in the names of the twin grandchildren, Kabir Narayan and Kamal Bashir. The mix in which they reincarnate their grandfathers' names is the idyll of reconciliation. In this fantasy Shekhar and Shaila give birth to their parents to reconcile their differences with them, or more pertinently, to exercise authority over them and refashion them in terms of their ideals. The second fantasy is the wish expressed by the newly arrived grandparents to recover the family unit from the catastrophe of the riots by reclaiming it for a reconstituted village. With this comes the now 'comic' contest over who will oversee the religious upbringing of the children. That which was a source of tension earlier can now be comic because it is deferred to a future condition of utopian revival. Simply put, these are fantasies generated out of an opposition between modernity and tradition, and the fantasy of modernity ultimately supplants that of tradition. That one fantasy is organized to deal with the other is indicated in a significant instance of narrative amnesia. This is when the hero and heroine, caught in the vortex of the riots and in the trauma of losing their children, forget that they have lost their parents (whom we, the audience, know are dead). This lacuna could be attributed to weak and hurried scripting but it is consistent with an obsessive narrative logic, in that the protagonists have already introjected their parents in their children. Not only are the children two, they are twins, so that Shekhar and Shailabano have in effect recreated, in their children, their parents without difference, without conflict. This is therefore an ideal image generated by modernity, one which incorporates the past gesturally. The full logic of this substitution emerges when the iconic family space which has seen the dispersal of the family, the death of the grandparents, the desperate search of parents for children, finally sees the reunion of the twins. In a classical Hollywood shot-reverse-shot arrangement, Kamal Bashir looks, and sees Kabir Narayan, who returns the look (or is it the other way around?); there is no differences between their images. Where the grandparents were pitted Hindu against Muslim, here the children are drained not only of the signs of religious difference but of any marks of difference at all.

We can say that the film is a reflection on the transformation from one structure of authority (a traditional patriarchy) into another which denies that it is authority. It claims instead that it is an identity and a point of view predicated on mutuality with the beloved and freedom of choice. However, if we penetrate below the structure of sentiments we find that Shekhar generates Shailabano through an anticipatory (and therefore markedly fantasy) point of view.[2] As he is walking along the jetty, he comes to a halt, distracted, it would appear, by something off-screen. The next shot shows the woman in a burqa, but the burqa only lifts in the wind now, suggesting that Shekhar's look exposes Shailabano to his, and our, gaze. It is also Shekhar, largely, who generates the momentum for the romance, in terms of meetings, ultimata to parents, the blood bonding with Shailabano, denial of parental authority, the mastery over movement by his sending of rail tickets to his beloved, the privileged view of Shailabano at Victoria Terminus, the setting-up of the registered marriage. . . . Perhaps most significant of all: it is his non-religiosity which defines the non-identity of the children. Whatever we may imagine of the practical problems posed by the marriage of the communally differentiated couple for the identity of the children, in effect the children follow the father in not practising religion.

Cultural Difference

Apparently contrary to the orientation of the narrative to the modern, in its basic understanding of cultural difference the film lies squarely within the dominant representations of communal relations in Indian cinema and popular narrative. While the traditional society of both communities is caught within a conservative outlook, the Muslim is lower in the social hierarchy. More sparse in its dwelling, associated with fishing and brick-making, Bashir Ahmed's family stands in contrast to Narayan Mishra's. In Mishra's upper-caste dwelling, clearly based on landed wealth and community standing, labour is not mentioned or seen at all. That the Muslim is also affected by modernity is reflected in the education of his daughter. However, these attributes make narratives sense only in her being aligned with the beloved. She knows English which, while not the everyday language of the lovers, comes to be symbolically central. For Shekhar uses it to write to Shailabano, enabling her move to the city and into modernity. These sociological imaginings are complemented by a familiar iconography of community. When the Muslim father is confronted with perceived slights and open insults, his response is composed of a gestural aggression. Bashir takes immediate recourse to sharp-edged implements, knives, swords, cleavers; Narayan, on the other hand, is given to verbal anger and noticeably backs down in certain exchanges, urging moderation. Again, as a parent he much more readily succumbs to sentimental appeals than the Muslim, even accepting the important distinction that he is dealing with a son already expressing autonomy and Bashir's authority relates to a dependent daughter.

While this stereotypical image reproduces a characteristic othering of the Muslim, it should be noted that the film institutes another logic of difference which seeks to disavow the first, that between city and village. The film portrays inter communal conflict in the village reaching a certain point and no further. Thus the particular frozen iconicity to even the most precipitate of encounters, the Muslim father, brandishing knife, but allowing himself to be held back by his womenfolk and community fellows. One is reminded here of Anuradha Kapur's references to conventions of representation in which iconic figures rest in autonomous space, not quite engaging/referring to other iconic figures juxtaposed to them in the frame (Kapur 1993). It is in the city that we are given a representational mode for intercommunal relationships which is more goal oriented in its construction. The menacing features held in balance by the codes and emotions of social acquaintance in the village now surface in bloody conflict.

The film covers its traces here. For the very structure of representations already has this conclusion built into its premises, the knife-wielding Muslim already given within the iconography of village life. Characteristics do not change or emerge within a community or scatter amongst communities; they are already inscribed in the community, awaiting particular circumstances to bring them to the surface.

The Pattern of Public Events

The apparent evenhandedness in the representation of communal violence is then undercut at the outset, in terms of the basic digits of community representation. What happens subsequently allows us both to be aware of that premise, but also to be forgetful, and even to become confused. I suggest how this happens through the way the film represents the communal violence of that period as taking place in three phases.

(i) The Hindus assume the aggressive stance—the *rathyatra*, the collecting of funds; the destruction of the Babri Masjid on 6 December. The muslims react in attacks against police and property: unidentifiable assailants threaten the life of the twins.

(ii) 5 January : two *mathadi* workers, load carriers, are killed; 'Bombay burns'; the *maha arti* and the *namaaz*; Muslims threaten the Hindu grandfather, Narayan Mishra, but move away on Bashir Ahmed's intervention; the burning of the Hindu house; the parents' death; the loss of the children.

(iii) Intercommunal rioting, interspersed with the search for the twins; the twins receive succour from the *hijra* and the child 'Shailabano'; Shekhar upbraids his communalized friends. In the climax, Shekhar, two Muslims, and the *hijra*, defuse the rioting; the twins are reunited with their parents.

One of the features of the public debate on the film has been the degree to which Muslim aggression has been visibly more evident, especially through the film's tendency to fetishize their image in the white filigreed cap.[3] I believe that this is largely correct, and indicates the premise of a mainstream, and therefore necessarily *Hindu* secularist narrative dealing with cultural difference as its central theme: in its reconstruction of events, and its bid for intercommunal reconciliation, the narrative cannot neutralize constructions of the Muslim as other. What is missed in this observation is the amnesiac propensities of popular narrative, as it states certain premises only to skirt them, a process centred on more than one elision.

In this connection, we may consider the film's introduction of a specifically Hindu aggression, both in the city and in the countryside, around the agitation at Ayodhya. This fearsome image of the Hindu is a most extraordinary one, a landmark perhaps in the history of popular film narrative in India. The image is shown to us through Shailabano's point of view, in a context where her somewhat uneasy position in the Hindu locality has been established. Already vulnerable, she sees the emergence of the *rathyatra* as a fearful sight, an ominous soundtrack coding the moment in this way for us as well. A ragbag of *sadhus* conjure up an image of unruly force, followed by the *rath* bearing a figure aloft who resembles the BJP leader Advani. Our alienation from this vision of Hinduism is further solicited when members of the 'Shakti Samaj', standing in for the Shiv Sena, approach the couple for a donation to build the temple. In a lesser key is the village encounter in which Narayan Mishra in a calculated insult orders a truckload of bricks for the Ayodhya temple from Bashir Ahmed.

There is, as I have suggested, an extraordinary unprecedentedness to this accumulation of anxiety-inducing images of a Hindu communal consciousness as far as popular cinema is concerned. Following again upon the image of the anxious Shailabano, this segment concludes with the newspaper headlines announcing the demolition of the Babri Masjid. The atmosphere of foreboding generated in the opening stages of communal mobilization would have concluded with documentary footage of the demolition but the censor board had these images deleted. The representation of communal violence in the second phase focuses almost entirely on Muslim activity in the riots of December 1992, though it depicts it as aimed at property and state rather than against civilians. It also allow for the representation of Muslim deaths under police firing. The overall lopsidedness of the narrative continues into the depiction of another turn in the riots. Here the attack on the *mathadi* workers (loaders), the murderous advance on Narayan Mishra, and the burning of a Hindu household in a slum relentlessly focus our attention on anti-Hindu actions. Indeed, the only point of relief in the representation up to this moment is one which remains ambiguous. When the children are attacked, the identity of their assailants is obscured by the scarves that swathe their faces.

However, in the last phase of the film, there is a noticeable shift in the treatment, as the film shows both communities involved in an alternating pattern of blood-letting. It is this impression that liberal and left-wing public opinion has taken away from the film, despite the fact that the earlier episodes contradict such a clear-cut picture. However, the reasons for this impression vary considerably with left-wing and civil rights activists on the one side and liberal humanist votaries on the other. The former argue that the apparent 'evenhandedness' of the film is a terrible misrepresentation of the riots which were in reality an anti-Muslim pogrom.

> Did someone say it's a balanced view because the director has shown one *maha arti* for *every namaz*? But what of the sleight of hand by which what was an effective pogrom engineered by state forces against one community became a riot between sections of two communities [Padmanabhan 1995]?[4]

Liberal opinion, on the other hand, does not recognize that there is a misrepresentation. One such writer concedes that the film did not draw out the complexities of the riots in terms of police and criminal involvement, but 'the juxtaposition of street corner *artis* and congregations at mosque is powerful enough' (Sethi 1995). A particularly strident version of this view berates the Muslim lobby for not appreciating the evenness of the treatment:

> Offence was taken we are told, because a Hindu family was shown being burned alive. A Muslim family is also shown being similarly murdered, because this also happened in the terrible riots of 1992, but our Muslim objectors are selective in their opinion [Singh 1995].[5]

Here the 'equality' in the treatment of communities is understood as truthful 'because this . . . happened'. I think it is part of the liberal argument that instead of being critical, the Muslim lobby should be grateful for

> *Bombay* is one of the first films to portray the Muslim victims of the Bombay riots sympathetically. And yet it is somehow typical of the pathetic leadership of the Muslim community that the objections should have come from Muslims [*Sunday*, 28 April 1995: 84].

These liberal views are based on an acceptance of the film's misrepresentation of the riots as finally centring on the equal guilt of the two communities. More remarkable though is the fact that observers who are ideologically opposed are susceptible to a common miscognition, that the film holds

Muslim and Hindus as culpable in a similar manner. Can it be because the moment of the figuration of equal culpability is also that of the coherence, reparation, and renewed legitimation of Indian society in the film? This is the moment that engages both critics and apologists, making the film an essentially coherent object to engage with, rather than an inchoate and dissonant one. Or is it a miscognition that the narrative process successfully generates, containing/disavowing earlier figurations of identity and conflict?

In an article by S.S.A. Aiyar the liberal apologia abandons its references to the real and demands an investment in the *myth* of equal culpability. Referring to criticisms that the film had failed to represent the violence for what it was, a pogrom, Aiyar (1995) writes:

> This objection cannot stand scrutiny. No film can or should claim to represent the absolute truth (there is probably no such thing). Besides the whole point of the film—and indeed of secularism—is that violence is wrong in principle, not because one community suffers more casualties than another. Numbers are not irrelevant—they add another dimension to the injustice of violence. But the fundamental issue is the inhumanity of all slaughter, and it is unwise to get diverted from this by looking at riot statistics. Had 'Bombay' been a documentary film, a mention of numbers would have been appropriate. But as a film trying to show that there are no winners in the inhumanity of communal strife, it would have lost its message by going into who did how much to whom.

This is active advocacy for the suppression of facts except, rather contradictorily, in the format of the documentary. Is this because the documentary is generically and ethically oriented to representing facts? Or is it because it is a minority medium which does not have the communicative possibilities of the mainstream fiction film? I sense it is the latter. The detail that *Bombay* knowingly draws upon documentary conventions, and therefore might be expected to observe the ethics of the documentary, is beside the point in Aiyar's position. For what matters is that the film is a vehicle for the mass communication of myths, and these must be rendered as consensually as possible.

In writing about that which *should* be addressed by the film (and on 'secularist' principles), Aiyar unwittingly raises a genuine problem. While the working premise of social representation in mainstream cinema is the stereotype, we must understand that Bombay cinema has always tended to reserve a notion of normalcy for the Hindu hero, the apex figure in the composite nationalism of its fictions. Exaggeration in cultural behaviour is attributed to other social groups, especially Muslims, Christians, and Parsis.

If this is the conventional mode of representation, should we castigate *Bombay* for reproducing it? As a mainstream film engaged in purveying myths for the nation, we need to look at the popular film in terms of what it can represent within the limits historically and institutionally set for this form. However, even within these limits, one may ask whether *Bombay* is not part of a larger regressive move. While the attributes of social backwardness, cultural conservatism, and deep religiosity are common enough to the stereotype of the plebeian Muslim in popular cinema, popular cinema does not usually cite *aggressiveness* as a defining quality. This characteristic may recur in popular cultural stereotypes of the Muslim (Pandey 1990), but cinema has been much more careful in this context. In the recent past Bombay cinema has redefined these conventions by showing Muslims as villainous characters in films such as *Tezaab* (N. Chandra 1988), *Gardish* (Priyadarshan 1993) and *Angaar* (Shashilal Nayar 1993) (Doraiswamy 1994). But Muslims in these narratives come from Bombay's criminal groups. Mani Ratnam's *Bombay* participates in this shift (as did his *Roja* in a sense), but it also makes a distinct intervention by figuring aggression as residing within the community rather than as characterizing its criminal offshoots. In this sense the film may have brought about an alignment between mainstream cinematic fiction and the popular Hindu imagining of the communal other.

While *Bombay* has made these contributions to popular cinematic modes, it has other features which significantly distinguish it from mainstream convention: its proximity to the events it depicts, and the invocation of documentary methods, the use of dates, newspaper headlines, and place names to situate the violence. These features place the film in the arc of recent public memory and make it an intervention in the construction of that memory. Indeed, where reviews actually claim that the film is objective and balanced in its account of what took place in Bombay, it could be said to be a substitute for memory.[6] It is here, in the historical proximity and the truth claims of the fiction that we need to apply a different register of reception than that accorded to the mainstream consensual form. In *Bombay*, the inbuilt cultural politics of the mainstream, its constituent units of representation, are harnessed via documentary simulation to the politics of the immediate, the justification, condemnation, or disavowal of Hindu actions, depending upon the particular narrative segment highlighted. Thus it is remarkable that Thackeray, the Shiv Sena leader, concentrates on the *facts* which the film draws upon, and how it organizes these facts, not on the myth of equal culpability around which left and liberal critics orient their positions:

We didn't start the violence. If you look carefully at the film, you will find that it is all there. The murder of the *mathadi* workers. The burning of the house in Jogeshwari. We had no choice but to retaliate (in *Sunday*).

It is no coincidence that the 'Muslim lobby' also highlighted these references to identifiable incidents as 'giv[ing] the impression that the Muslims are the aggressors'.[7] While the liberal and left-wing critics dwell only upon the narrative's process of equalizing responsibility, it is the communal lobbies on either side which point to how significant documentary strategies construct a tale of Muslim aggression as a central component of the riots. Of course, these constructions also exclude a great deal which goes on in the film in their own particular bids for narrative coherence.

The discourse around censorship and the bid to ban the film draw out the political implications of its representation of Bombay's communal violence for the state and a certain image of the Muslim community. It would seem that the censors operated through a mixture of considerations regarding the film's portrayal of the state and its impact on diplomatic relations and on the sentiments of the Muslim community.[8] Thus the cutting of references to Pakistan, Afghanistan, and 'Islamic state' must be related to diplomatic prohibitions. Sensitivity to reminding Muslims of the campaign against them appears to underlie the censor board's deletion of the following: visuals of the *rathyatra* along with dialogue '*Babri masjid todenge, Ram mandir banayenge*'; dialogue relating to a door-to-door collection of funds from Hindu households; visuals of the Babri Masjid and its demolition; and, amongst other dialogue cuts, '5000 years ago there was a temple here. Who destroyed it?'

The suggestion is that the depiction of certain incendiary anti-Muslim rhetoric and actions might inflame passions, presumably of the Muslims rather than of the Hindus. This means that these events are isolated from their treatment within the narrative process. The presumption is that even if a director employs a method which alienates the spectator from such scenes of anti-Muslim aggression, this would nevertheless involve the re-experiencing of the affront with possible political repercussions. What the censors particularly feared, I would think, was the rekindling of anti-government sentiment among the Muslims, on the assumption that the demolition of the mosque was a failure of the government to represent their interests. The censor board's cutting of references to the high incidence of Muslim deaths in the December violence, and of visuals showing police firing on Muslim crowds conforms to this imperative. There is also another anxiety: not only that the government should not be shown to be ineffective or opposed to the community, but that it must not appear vulnerable to popular assault. Thus an episode showing the death of a policeman was also removed. Anxiety about the government image amongst Hindus, on the other hand, is hardly in evidence. Perhaps the excision of the dialogue, 'Go and ask the government which is cheating you in the name of secularism', is the solitary instance, suggesting a concern for the impact of Hindu communalist propaganda on public perceptions that the government was guilty of 'minority appeasement'.

Despite such anxieties, the censor board still displayed a respect for realist representation for it did not demand a complete excision of any reference to the demolition of the Babri Masjid. But, within this 'reality orientation' they made a distinction: only newspaper clippings could be shown, implying that documentary footage had the capacity to stir passions in a way that the photograph did not. Indeed, we can say that the censors reflected a general concern to contain movement, whether of people's emotions, or of the image, in keeping with the motivations of order.[9]

If the censor board allowed for a muted representation of reality, it made excisions which were significantly opposed to the clear articulation of a *causal* logic. This is especially indicated by two cuts. The first is the response of a policeman to the Muslim actions of December: 'These people have started the riots against the demolition of the masjid in Ayodhya'. The second is the deletion of visuals and dialogues spoken by Tinnu Anand while distributing bangles. Apparently the Thackeray stand-in was shown giving his followers the bangles in the wake of the killing of the *mathadi* workers. While these cuts follow the logic of blocking the recreation of injured sentiment and of the rhetoric used to justify violence, they contribute to critical gaps in narrative causality. To a large extent the film's organization of images around the demolition provides an explanation of the Muslim response despite the cut. But the particular location of Tinnu Anand's dialogue suggests that the film offers an explanation for Hindu violence in the last phase which now stands obscured. At least one of the discontinuities of the film's present structure derives not from the peculiarities of its organization but from censorship cuts.

The official Muslim lobby, on the other hand, objected to representations of Hindu mobilization and the image of the demolition even after the censor's excisions.[10] We must assume that the demand derived from the sensitivity of the spokesmen to the re-enactment of a humiliation. But, at another level, their outlook amounts to an ironic intensification of Chidananda Das Gupta's thesis that, in the case of the Indian audience, seeing is believing (Das Gupta 1992). Das Gupta of course sought to conjure up a cognitive mindset here, the gullible spectator for whom the 'impression of reality' achieved by the cinema makes the unreal real. In this case of course the image refers to reality, and the lobby fears that to see it will make it, shall we say, more real or hyper-real. Whereas Eco uses that term to describe a striving for reality effects by cultures lacking history (Eco 1987), such as America, here I would suggest that we are presented with a very distinct viewpoint. The images in contention suggest that the sacred is fallible and can be violated. I am not suggesting that the Babri Masjid had an uncomplicated sacred status. Rather, I think what is important here is a process of displacement, where politics causes the sacred to re-surface in particular locations which then come to stand not for the sacred but for the socio-political community constructed in its name. The hyper-reality effect then speaks of a particular imaginary public sphere in which images are impacted with affect, a cluster of emotive political intensities which become the object of psychic and public defence. Such an imaginary investment is not necessarily shared by the community as a whole. The trauma suffered by the mass of Muslim people over the destruction of the masjid is not under question here, but their hypostasization as a community in the representational claims of both government and Muslim spokesmen is. The government displayed an intention to contain images which conjured a reality in which it was culpable. And the drive of Muslim leaders to erase the trajectory of loss may reveal a need to maintain the imaginary of the socio-political community in which they as a limited interest group have a particular stake.[11]

Each of these components in the public response to *Bombay* is characterized by indifference to particular representations in favour of others. These investigations suggest that amnesia is a procedure more generally observable in the reception of popular narrative forms and goes against the grain of discontinuity which characterizes these forms. In the case of *Bombay*, we have seen how censorship has contributed to certain discontinuities, but this does not explain all of them. The explanations of communal violence implicit in various parts of the film can be considered as comprising both discontinuity, and as organized in such a way that earlier events are systematically contained by later ones. The description of cultural difference through popular stereotype, the gesture to the documentary mode, the fictive reconstruction in its various hues, these modes of representation amount to a certain layering, iconically and temporally, of the narrative's construction of Indian identity. A deep structure of cultural difference provides the bedrock of perceptions, one coloured by Hindu, and more broadly modern modes of 'othering'. While this never actually undergoes any change in the film, the figuration of the dangerous Hindu must cause us to reflect that the film's mode of address is a rather complicated one. These images need to be held on to even as we consider the operation of ideological coherence at work in the film.

Community and Sexuality

The Hindu right has been relatively quiet in the discussion around censorship. It was given a privileged position over Muslim groups when Amitabh Bachchan organized a meeting between Mani Ratnam and Bal Thackeray, providing the film's initial image with a slanted sense of political negotiation. Despite liberal disclaimers, the film has not been able to discount this image in terms of the emphases of its own narrative structure. The discussion was a minimal but significant one. Apart from Thackeray's argument that the film should be renamed 'Mumbai', something he did not persist with, the Shiv Sena leader demanded the deletion of a scene showing his stand-in (Tinnu Anand) repenting the riots. This demand fed into the terms on which Thackeray would admit the film's narrative of the riots, as a Hindu retaliation against Muslim aggression. In other words, there was nothing to repent about (*Sunday*, 2–8 April 1995: 81). The Shiv Sena's relationship to the film has subsequently acquired the aura of a liberal defence of free speech; Thackeray stridently asserted that he would ensure the release of the film against the drive of Muslim groups to have it banned.[12] This pattern of response indicates that the fiction does not, overall, *directly* assail the Hindu right or their understanding of what happened. In fact, Thackeray called it 'a damned good film'.[13]

The Hindu right also had not objection to the film's romantic scenario; the official Muslim position, on the other hand, argued that the implication of Muslim tradition and identity in the heroine's moving out of the community (the association of the Koran with her flight to her lover, the throwing off of the *burqa*) was anti-Islamic (*Times of India*, 9 April 1995). Characteristic to both positions, however, is the significance attributed to women in the definition of wider group identities. That communal spokesmen mirror each other in this premise is clear from the following statements:

Love knows no barriers and can blossom even under a rain of fire and brimstone. No one can therefore object to a Muslim man falling in love with a Hindu woman and vice versa [Syed Shahabuddin in *Hindustan Times*, 7 May 1995].

It was a fact that there were marriages between Hindu boys and Muslim girls, but no one created a fuss [Interview with Bal Thackeray in *Pioneer*, 9 April 1995].[14]

We may observe that both spokesmen assume the masculine position for their community when they speculate about intercommunal marriages. While *Bombay* constitutes a departure in referring to such marriages, it does so within the rules of the Hindu nationalist hegemony that popular cinema has by and large reproduced. The hero must come from the majority community, thereby exercising a symbolic patriarchal-communal authority over the constitution of the nation.[15] Once again, Thackeray obviously has no problems on this account.

I want to reflect on how this order of symbolic narrative is worked out in the domain of romance, sexuality and of domestic life, and what tensions surface within a narrative of the subordination or assimilation of community identity through marriage. As with the larger narrative of public events, amnesia is important here too, and centres on the codes of deportment of the woman, and the signs through which she is represented. The first half of the film clearly codes Shailabano as a Muslim, perhaps most emphatically in her springing free from her burqa to meet her beloved. From the time of her arrival in Bombay onwards, her identity is marked not through clothes and the burqa, but by her name. Though she does not apply *sindoor* or the *bindi*, she now wears the *sari*. The subtle neutralization of her identity is only seriously disturbed in the fleeting but significant glimpse of her going through the *namaaz*, during a song montage. The persistent signs of her Muslim identity derive from a narrative strategy which cannot afford to forget it entirely. To recall secures a position not only for Shailabano the Muslim but also for a secular position which is provided with an assimilable rather than an intractable other (the one who bears the sword). The power-laden terms of the assimilation are indicated in Shailabano's vulnerability, not only to larger public forces, but also, in her perception, to the whims of Hindu patriarchy. Thus Shailabano anxiously enquires whether Narayan Mishra seeks to take her children away from her. The particular resonances of this scene are one of subtle masquerade, the Muslim woman pleading her case by adopting the demeanour and submissive idiom of the dutiful Hindu *bahu*.

But the fragments of her Muslim identity are not easily dismissed. The instance of her prayer is assimilable because it fits the film's sociological imagination: the jeans and T-shirt clad ex-Hindu male stands discreetly in the background, overseeing his wife's immersion in prayer, the moment iconizing a benevolent (Hindu-derived) modernity indulging a private and unobtrusive Muslim religiosity.[16] However, a more conflictual note is sounded when Shailabano first enters Shekhar's landlord's house. In a film which obscures and hypostasizes the Muslim community, or frames it as otherwise assimilable, these circumstances force an assertion of identity from the heroine. Encircled by a shocked and pollution-fearing household, she firmly announces that she is a Muslim.

However, beyond the fragment, which I take to be the transient surfacing of a silenced subjectivity, there is a *mise-en-abîme* effect which derives from the observation of a structure of taboo, the repetitive tracing of a ritually coded mark of difference. The burqa as veil, as material which conceals, separates, but also allows a constrained intimacy, resurfaces when Shekhar grapples with Shailabano through the *saris* on a washing line, and when Shailabano's *pallu* covers her face when Shekhar kisses her. The sign of the taboo weaves into the narrative of assimilation, tracking back over it by maintaining a symbolic division even at the moment of consummation.

The film's complicity with community prohibition is woven into a larger narrative of the place of romance and sexuality in public and private spaces. Some of *Bombay's* critics have suggested that, from the beginning, the romance between Shekhar and Shailabano is defined by a Hindu male gaze motivated by a curiosity to penetrate the exoticism of the other (Menon 1995). This interpretation fails to note that this gaze is an infringement of a prohibition with a much wider currency. This is the public monitoring and containment of sexuality, and its corrolary, the difficulty of carving out a private sphere for the register of the intimate and the erotic.[17] The infringement of public regulation is common to popular film romance. As Khalid Mohamed (1995) and Iqbal Masud (1995)[18] have pointed out, *Bombay* draws upon the tradition of the romantic Muslim social whose narrative is generated by a fleeting glimpse of the woman. *Bombay* inaugurates its romantic scenario around a fantasy of the look roaming in public space, unbounded by public scrutiny. In the song sequence *Kehna Hi Kya*, Shekhar's free movement through the Muslim wedding yokes this fantasy to the tale of intercommunal love. Shailabano is constantly repositioned for Shekhar's view as well as ours within the characteristic discontinuities of the song sequence. The swish pan affords an accelerated pace for recentring the woman in different spaces and bodily dispositions. But its usage in the later riot scenes is anticipated here when Shailabano, in a kaleidoscopic sweep, turns her look in search of Shekhar, whose look she has hitherto evaded. Centred on female performance for a male spectator, this turnaround in the last stages may be said to set the scene for Shailabano's own desiring look at Shekhar in his family house and the subsequent centring of the man as a vulnerable, emotional figure in the *Tu hi re* song sequence.

The larger problems of the representation of romance and sexuality emerge only after the couple is married. Here the film defers the consummation of the marriage by denying privacy to the couple, children of visiting relatives being quartered in the tenant's dwelling. This amounts to the institution of a public gaze *within* the fiction, mirroring the prohibitions of the censor-ship code. Does this articulation of the symbolic then negotiate a second-level prohibition with the imaginary, not only upholding the primacy of patriarchal-communal norms but their extended observation in the marking out of a space between communities?

We may turn to the position of the Hindu matriarch of the hosuehold for an elaboration of this problem of the public and the private. In opposition to the street mother who flirts with Shekhar, this one highlights in her person the repressiveness which Narayan Mishra and her own husband transcend (she also balances an absence: a Hindu matriarchal presence in the absence of Narayan Mishra's wife). This return of a repressive attitude serves to point up the question of boundaries, the playing out of those everyday taboos through the vehicle of women as prime repository of the virtues and rituals of the household. The Muslim woman has to be made acceptable in everyday Hindu life, so the Hindu landlady as the domestic image of a communal ethos has to be humanized. She is shown to relent at the sight of heady youthful love. When Shekhar mistakenly embraces her in his pursuit of Shailabano, she is taken aback and is then *made* to smile. Put plainly, this is an instance of bad acting. A glitch in the performance of a minor character suggests a problem for representation; how to employ marginal characters in such a way that the transformation of attributes, their main function, does not appear imposed on the material. If such minor systems of representation fail, an interesting gap opens up in the relations between the pro-filmic and the filmic, where the former becomes a kind of unnarrativized dead weight in the texture of the narration. Put into the structure of the film's regime of affect, the failure of performance suggests a difficulty in superceding an earlier representation. The transformation of this character that follows is still inflected with an anxiety: the young couple, walking through the proximate red-light area are shooed into the domestic interior by the matriarch, anxious that their flirtation is not the object of public scrutiny.

Why is this Hindu domestic space composed in such tight narrative proximity to the red-light area? Shekhar and Shailabano's walk is cast against the backdrop of his rueful exchange with the prostitutes; perhaps the narrative invites us to speculate about a bachelor's familiarity with these women. But the point is that the couple, on the threshhold of sexual relations now that the children have left their apartment, communicate the taint of sexuality from one space into the other, eliciting the matriarch's anxious plea that they go inside. The red-light area then becomes a meta-phor for the sexuality of the couple, one which the matriarch must conceal in the household. We can see a slippage here between the general prohibitions operating around the companionate couple, and their particular refraction through the prohibitions of a Hindu–Muslim romance.

In contrast to the amnesiac propensities of the narrative, whose problems and uncertain features are periodically suppressed, a performative register is drawn upon to invest the surplus arising from the deferment of the couple's sexuality. In the song sequence *Hamma Hamma* identity is trans-formed arbitrarily, relayed now in the way the lovers are projected through their bodies and to the rhythms of disco-sensuality. Instead of a careful development of expressive attributes through narration, these are abruptly rendered through gesture and performance. Indeed, this is a performative coding of the access to sexuality, one displaced onto the *Hamma Hamma* performance, where the figure in white from the *Kahna hi kya* song se-quence returns as a ramp artist (Sonali Bendre). The problems of identity addressed in the narrative are fleetingly transcended. Skirting the require-ments of character development, modernity defines itself here as composed of the pleasures of performative surfaces rather than 'authentically' evolved psychologies. And with disposition of the body now integral to the cultural refashioning of the character, there is a foregrounding of the vivacity of the star personality, Koirala's impishness surfacing from the constraints of the shy and timid Shailabano. However, there is still a trace of the problem that sexuality poses for the narrative in the strangely ornate and sleazy environs of the performance; here couples are glimpsed in intimate poses as they take pleasure in the dance. While the sexuality of the couple is secured in the domestic interior, a peculiar undertow of the illicit and disreputable suf-fuses the scene.

Reconciliation

Performance, contrived out of generic resources such as the romantic Mus-lim social and the fashion show, allows for a release from the constraints of social representation. As a result, the film generates a certain spectrum of personality traits rather than a tightly coded pattern of identity. Something of these effects of dispersal characterize the climactic sequence, in which a multi-communal agency (now forgotten in the more characteristic narrative of the mainstream cinema), an agency of aggression but now of reparation becomes the configuration through which the nation can finally be imagined.

However, this configuration too is hierarchically coded, and finally clusters around the offer of sacrifice from the position of a modern Hindu identity. This particular organization is clearly highlighted in the film's climax.

The actions are systematically developed along a particular axis. Shekhar's defence of a Muslim family from a Hindu mob provides the centre to the others, and has the phenomenal form of an epicentre, the travelling camera describing an arc around his space. A generation and repetition of the new spaces in which communal antagonism is neutralized takes place around this centre, segments getting shorter, with a greater frequency to the recurrence of the original scene, on which, of course, the sequence concludes.

If this master space generates the narrative rhythm of the sequence, it also provides rules for the construction of decommunalized space. Pacification is undertaken by figures who make appeals to aggressors of their own denomination. There is an important implication to this. As they are amongst their co-religionists, they can draw upon the safety of a common identity; they are not victims pleading for their lives, they are not the other, but an alienated figuration of the self. While these figures perform at the boundary of identity, an active claiming of the other as the self, as in the case of the Muslim woman who claims those she protects as her child and her sister, is not a common strategy.

It could be said then that the hero generates a model, an exemplary instance which is echoed in a number of actions of a similar kind. But this model of decommunalization has a certain discreteness of community address built into it. There is a suggestion here that the film's vision of the bringing to an end of antagonism nevertheless entails the reproduction of difference. However, there are two, possibly three, instances in which the rule of community self-address does not operate. The first instance is that of the policeman who intervenes between communities, gesturing here to the highly ideological image of a transcendant state. The second is the *hijra*, whose self-image is *beechwala*, one who stands in between. This ironical self-image alludes of course to gender identity as well as community identity, suggesting that there is a relationship between a clear-cut communal identity and a clear-cut sexual one. The idiom here would conjure up a certain distance from the gendered terms through which hierarchies of authority and submission, oppressor and victim, are played out across the masculine–feminine opposition. But the *hijra* is shown to be protecting a Muslim from a Hindu mob, rather than mediating 'in between' communities. The placement of this character therefore establishes a homology with others similarly placed, and pre-eminently with the hero. For the *hijra*, like the hero, invites the mob to kill the dissenter first. This 'doubling' must not obscure an earlier identity that the 'hermaphrodite' conjures up, that of the mother who protects the lost child; after all, the first, fleeting image we have of the *hijra* is as a figure in a *sari*. . . . But perhaps we are doing a disservice to this figure by constraining him/her within this grid of parallels; for the main parallel, the hero, proceeds through a process of negating identity to the avowal of an Indian identity, something the *hijra* never does.

Identification

Let me go back now to the set of problems which have emerged in the course of this analysis. How does the film's project of a transcendent secular modernity and national identity square with its reproduction of the minority as other? At one level it can do this because it figures modernity as evolving from the trajectory of Hindu subjectivity. To that extent it remains within the conventions of the popular Indian cinema. It is this authoritative structure which generates a number of apparently dissonant elements: from the invocation of popular stereotypes of the Muslim and the film's skewed rendering of their role in the riots, to the position of assimilation (through marriage) and multi-community integration on the model of the Hindu hero at the climax. We an see that the apex Hindu position identifies the particular position the minority is to occupy in various situations.

However, against the drive to coherence in the text and its various public constructions, I suggest that we need to locate the sources of discontinuity, and to capture its timbre. The key issue here is how the narrative places the spectator; how does it seek to persuade us of its particular project of modernity? It does this, I suggest, by inviting us to assume a melodramatic subjection, where notations of victimhood and powerlessness bind us to the film's vision. It is clear enough that in the case of the Muslim woman, the terrified children and ultimately even the grandparents, we are immersed in a melodramatic subjecthood, the situation of the disempowered. But how does the film work out a relationship between the hero's authoritative position and such a melodramatic subjection? Is a position of narrative authority, defined by a culturally confident voicing of a rational-humane viewpoint automatically a position with which we can identify? Or does some other process, or repositioning, have to take place? For there is no automatic process by which we should empathize with the hero's attributes. Indeed, Shekhar's passion for Shailabano is attractive not because it is controlled but because it is out of control, tumultous, culminating in the remarkable agony of the song *Tu hi re*, where the hero's face crumples in a helpless weeping. There are notations here of hysteria, of an outpouring that will not be contained by the confidence of his oppositional rhetoric. It is such an aspect of melodramatic excess that the film uses to structure an identity, a strategy through which the rational modern both creates affect by a focus on the powerless and then increasingly thematizes itself as ultimate locus of the marginal and the dispossessed (a patriarch without his children). This is an unusual narrative strategy, for it is much more common that innocence and victimization, and in terms of narrative tropes, silence, are favoured to elicit feelings of pathos (Brooks 1985). Here it is the clearly articulated voice of rationality that is put on the margins, bearing a truth-claiming rhetoric, but a powerless one.

This rationality on the margins ironically displaces the feminine figure who would be the conventional locus of such a disempowerment, appropriating to its person those 'feminine' features of emotionality and most interestingly, a making vulnerable of the body. There is a working out here of a logic stated early in the film where Shekhar cuts his hand to indicate the depth of his passion for Shailabano.[19] The culmination of this repositioning of the body as object of a self-inflicted wound occurs when Shekhar douses himself with petrol and invites the rampaging Hindu mob to burn him alive.

This invitation to harm the body follows upon two premises: the hero's negation of his given identity and his making that negation visible. In negating his given religious identity in the first instance he embraces sheer negativity: *hum koi nahin hain*; but then he claims a name: *hum sirf* Indian *hain*. In the second move, the hero, safe from aggression, desires, *demands*, that he be like the other, and that the threat of the self he denies be visited upon him. The hero's invitation that the mob immolate him is a direct visual and rhetorical throwback to Rishi Kumar's throwing himself on the burning Indian flag in *Roja*, except that act was not preceded by a step of negation; there was a repulsive fullness to the protagonist's affirmation of an identity. In contrast, it is the negativity of *Bombay* which puts natioinalistic rhetoric into perspective as predicated not on a fullness but on an absence of identity. The rhetoric distinguishes the hero and makes him visible amongst a body of other Hindus, the distinction of marginality proving to be the yardstick of differences. The narrative effects a displacement of authority where the hero's confidence, his control over his destiny at the microcosmic level, at the level of decisions concerning family and career, is rendered ineffectual when the wider universe consorts to negate that logic of freedom. Melodramatic subjection here enforces an evacuation of positions of power and authority in a nightmare articulation of the desire to negate oneself publicly, to exonerate oneself of the taint of identity.

The hero's offer of sacrifice requires us to reflect on certain practices of male self-immolation. The Tamil instance—and after all, this is also a Tamil film[20]—has been associated with the cult of MGR and also with Tamil separatism in Sri Lanka. The Tamil experience offers a negation/sublimation of the self into the large image of the leader, an image which is indeed confirmed and constituted by such acts. The second instance is that of the anti-Mandal agitation which dramatized the despair of an identity grounded in perceptions of fallen status, but also reflected the sense of closure amongst isolated lower middle-class youth.[21] The Mandal context did not provide the act with a positive or purposive name such as leader or nation. However, the image of the immolation was appropriated to a discourse of merit generated by the privileged and mobile sections of the middle class who linked it to a dynamic of national reconstruction. One could speculate that these acts emerge out of a sense of marginality, an experience obscured by the discourses surrounding them. Rishi Kumar's act in *Roja* reproduces the discourse of appropriation by sublimating individual, class, and in this case, regional identity, into that of the nation. *Bombay*, on the other hand, echoes much more strongly the negativity which underlies discourses of sacrifice. While speaking in the name of humanity and nationhood, Shekhar Mishra simultaneously speaks the language of alienation, indeed of revulsion.

Although *Roja* and *Bombay* solicit quite different sentiments, both arise from a similar subjectivity; that of a modern nationalist view, with the modern hero bearing the characteristic attributes of professional identity, cosmopolitanism, ideological humanism, rationalism, and the marginalization of religion. In *Roja*, the hero's religion is at best a desire for a lifestyle which is simple, unadorned, and therefore gesturally fulfils that need of the modern to secure its roots, to specify an identity. Otherwise the significance of Hindu identity derives not from its reference to religiosity, but its capacity to adapt to modern social and cultural processes, and is cast in opposition to the intractable Muslim fanaticism of the Kashmiri separatists.[22] In contrast, in *Bombay*, the hero finds himself stranded on the margins of a social space inundated with genocidal identity conflicts in which he is ultimately pitted against Hindus. Alienation from the Muslim other is here subordinated to self-alienation.

The desired identity is always above other identities, and this transcendental situation has a name: 'Indian'. It is against this resolution that Sadanand Menon expresses his unease, indeed abhorrence, urging that a resolution of conflicts cannot be founded on transcendental denial but on an admission of difference and an acceptance of it (Menon 1995). Important (and difficult) as this argument is, it perhaps fails to consider that whatever the cultural 'thinness' of the modern-universal, its will to negativity exercises pressure on the notion of a single dominant identity.

It is through such a negativity that it is possible to conceive of the aspects of discontinuity which characterize the film. The dangerous Hindu, perhaps the most startling image the film has generated, emerges from the negative reflections of a protagonist whose modernity must at once derive from his Hinduness and deny it of any significance. It is thus a peculiarly inward discourse of the self, an inwardness which allows for the peculiar self-alienation which abides in the film alongside the firm tracing of the communal order. The modern ponders on its national unease, performs versions of itself that abruptly and pleasurably depart from troubled scenarios of antagonistic identity, and generates spaces in which the other may be assimilated only to surface in a less congenial disposition. That discontinuity at the level of form and narrative statement can be integrated within the conflicts of a unique subjectivity must lead to skepticism. I can only suggest, in conclusion, that this is indeed my own surmise, and leaves me to conjure with the disconcertingly calm reflections of a subjectivity which should have no room in this narrative discourse:

> We know hundreds of people fall in love with persons of another religious community, caste, and marry the person they love. A film cannot be rejected on that ground. And it is for the people themselves to judge whether a film is worth watching or not. In the case of *Bombay* also, the Muslim masses did not respond to the Muslim leaders initiative [Engineer 1995: 6].

We can only wait upon the moment of the popular to disabuse us of the impertinence of analysis.

Plot Synopsis

Shekhar Mishra, a journalist working in Bombay, visits his village home in Andhra, where he sees and falls in love with Shaila, daughter of the brick-maker, Bashir Ahmed. Both Shekhar's father, the village notable Narayan Mishra, and Bashir are incensed at the idea of the match, but Shekhar arranges for Shaila to flee the village and join him in Bombay, where they are joined in civil marriage. Twins, Kamal Bashir and Kabir Narayan, are born to the couple, and they are visited by parents anxious at news of communal rioting in the city. The reconciliation is blighted by a renewed spate of rioting, leading to the death of the elders and the loss of the children. As

Shekhar and Shaila search the strife-torn city for their sons, Hindus and Muslims are locked in unrelenting slaughter. At the climax we see Shekhar and several others pleading with the rampaging mobs to stop the killing; Shekhar douses himself with kerosene, urging Hindu rioters to kill him. The appeal quietens the crowd, and amidst the dispersal of the riot, the twins emerge and the family is reunited. Hindus and Muslims clasp hands in a gesture of social renewal at the conclusion.

NOTES

1. I thank Radhika Singha, Mukul Mangalik, and Ravi Sundaram for helpful discussions, and Sunil Khilnani for his comments at the seminar, 'The Consumption of Popular Culture in India', School of Oriental and African Studies, London, 19–21 June 1995.
2. A classic instance of such a narrative move is when Guru Dutt's look generates Mala Sinha in *Pyaasa* (Guru Dutt 1957).
3. The first show of the riots is a Muslim picking up the sword in aggression. The number of white caps is always foregrounded and framed well, in tasteful colours, while the Hindu mobs are more indistinct, it is difficult to make out faces' (Padmanabhan 1995).
4. Cf. also Joshi (1995). 'Mani Ratnam has virtually re-invented the Bombay "riots" in a grotesque expression of what it "ought" to have been—universally played and, ultimately, amenable to cessation in the face of sentimental, moralistic rhetoric. A version even Bal Thackeray approves. . . . His "reality" is a communal "riot"—shot much in the style of a ding-dong *kabaddi* match. . . . It is a contest between equals, with points being scored by either side with a pendulum like regularity—and fairness. . . . Though the theme of communal conflict engulfs the film for nearly three fourths of its duration, there is no hint of the possibility of the entire episode in Bombay in 1993, having been an organized and planned pogrom against a minority, the scars of which are yet to heal.'
5. In Tavleen Singh's writing, there is a slippage between official Muslim opinion, or the views of the Muslim leadership, and Muslims as a whole. e.g., 'Emboldened by their success in stopping *Bombay*, Maharashtra's Muslims notched up another little fundamentalist victory last week'.
6. 'The film maker has taken great pains to structure his objective and impartial documentation of the communal riots in Bombay two years ago'. 'Battle over *Bombay*', editorial, *Screen*, 14 April 1995.
7. 'Muslims Object to "Bombay" Scenes', *Times of India*, 9 April 1995.

8. For details of censorship, *Times of India*, 12 March 1995 and *Frontline*, 16 June 1995.

9. Thus, too, the much publicized induction of Bombay police officers to evaluate the impact of the film on public emotions.

10. According to the Muslim League corporator, Yusuf Abrahani, 'who has emerged as a spokesman of the protestors', the following scenes are anti-Islamic: 'In a shot showing a procession of Hindus, a placard demands "Tala Kholo". . . . This is an obvious reference to the removal of locks on the Babri Masjid. . . . The hero's father who is a Hindu flings money at the heroine's father, who is a brick manufacturer, and asks him to make bricks with Ram inscribed on them. . . . There is a shot of the Babri Masjid. Even though its demolition is not shown, newspaper clippings carrying news about the demolition are shown while the sound track makes it clear that the structure is being demolished.' *Times of India*, 9 April 1995.

11. Cf. for example, Rashmee Z. Ahmad's (1995) analysis of the protest by Sahahuddin Owaisi's Majlis Ittehadul Muslimeen in Hyderabad.

12. He said efforts to give a communal tinge to the film's release would not be tolerated. 'Thackeray warns Muslims on *Bombay*', *Pioneer*, 9 April 1995.

13. 'I have never called Muslims traitors, says Bal Thackeray', *Times of India*, 31 March 1995.

14. Thackeray also noted that actors like Meena Kumari, Dilip Kumar, and Madhubala were Muslims and no one had objected when they took Hindu names. This again fits the rules of a Hindu nationalists hegemony, in which it is perfectly acceptable that minorities negate their identities and assume the majority one.

15. Cf. Javed Akhtar's eolquent elaboration of the problem of popular cinema's inability to represent Hindu–Muslim romance: 'This is actually part of a larger taboo area in popular cinema. . . . The real taboo is that a high-caste Hindu girl will never be shown marrying an outcaste boy. Never. If at all the great caste divide has to be bridged, it will be done via a highcaste boy falling in love with an outcaste girl as in *Achoot Kanya, Sujaata*, or *Parineeta*. Similarly, the one who rebels against the Hindu–Muslim divide will never be the Hindu woman, it will be the Hindu man. Ratnam's *Bombay* bears this out' (Akthar 1995).

16. The other side of this indulgence is the hero's offer to give up his religion to compensate for his father's attitude. The offer is a gesture rather than a belief, and so does not compromise the modern transcendence of religious identity.

17. For a suggestive consideration of the problems surrounding the distinction between public and private in the constitution of the Indian cinema, see the work of Madhava Prasad, e.g., 'Cinema and the Desire for Modernity', *Journal of Arts and Ideas*, nos 25–6, 1994.

18. Masud castigates Mani Ratnam for not being able to understand and represent

Muslim culture; one wonders if this is not to mistake the project of the film. Strangely, he advises viewers to see Nana Patekar in *Krantiveer* (1994) for a better representation of the riots. To my mind this is a film which underwrites Hindu male authority much more brutally than *Bombay*.

19. This is of course followed by the much more ambiguous and for me repulsive act of Shekhar cutting Shailabano's arm for a blood-bonding.

20. But, unlike *Roja*, it is not primarily a Tamil film. In its conception from the outset as a multiple version film, it is a new type of film which is also an old one, harking back to the 1930s practices. A more considered analysis of this feature is necessary to situate the film market as a critical component in Mani Ratnam's 'nation'.

21. Cf., for example, Mohan (1991) and Sethi (1991).

22. Significantly, the Muslim is a modern too, one who has denied rationality but can be recovered into it; the hero and the extremist leader can speak the same language, not only Tamil, but intellectually, too.

References

Ahmad, Rashme Z., 1995, '*Bombay*: Competitive Communalism', *Times of India*, 21 March.

Aiyar, S.S.A., 1995, in *Times of India*, 15 April 1995.

Akhtar, Javed, 1995, 'The Great Evasion', *Times of India*, Sunday Review, 23 April.

Brooks, Peter, *The Melodramatic Inauguration: Balzac, Henry James, Melodrama and the Mode of Excess*, New York.

Das Gupta, Chidananda, 1992, *The Painted Face: Studies in India's Popular Cinema*, New Delhi: Roly Books.

Doraiswamy, Rashmi, 1994, 'Narrative Strategies in Popular Indian Cinema', *Cinemaya*.

Eco, Umberto, 1987, 'Travels in *Hyper-reality*', London: Picador.

Engineer, Asghar Ali, 1995, 'A Controversial Film on Bombay Riots', *Mainstream*, May.

Joshi, Namrata, 1995, 'The Film Represent Reality!', *Economic Times*, 16 April.

Kapur, Anuradha, 1993, 'Deity to Crusader: The Hindutva Movement in Ayodhya', in Gyanendre Pandey (ed.), *Hindus and Others: The Question of Identity in India Today*, Delhi: Viking.

Masud, Iqbal, 1995, 'A Damp Squib', *Indian Express*, 14 May.

Menon, Sadanand, 1995, 'Bombay is Political Cinema at Its Best', *Economic Times*, 16 April.

Mohammed, Khalid, 1995, Lenseye, 'Truth or Dare', *Times of India*, Sunday Review, 2 April.

Mohan, Dinesh, 1991, 'Imitative Suicides?', *Manuchi*, 63–4, March–June: 31–3.

Padmanabhan, Chitra, 1995, ' "Money" Ratnam Walks the Razor's Edge to Self in a Communal Market', *Economic Times*, 16 April.

Pandey, Gyanendre, 1990, 'The Bigoted Julaha', in Gyanendre Pandey, *The Construction of Communalism in Colonial North India*, Delhi: Oxford University Press.

Sethi, Harsh, 1991, 'Many Unexplained Issues: The Anti-Mandal "Suicides" Spate', *Manuchi*, 63–4, March–June: 69–72.

Sethi, Sunil, 1995, 'Much Ado about Nothing', *Pioneer*, 16 April.

Singh, Tavleen, 1995, 'Pampering the Minority Ego', *Indian Express*, 16 April.

Opposing Faces
Film Star Fan Clubs and the Construction of Class Identities in South India[1]

SARA DICKEY

O N CERTAIN EVENINGS in a Madurai neighbourhood, crowds of young men cluster on the streets under brightly painted signboards. Each board shows a movie star in a characteristic pose— dancing, giving new books to schoolchildren, or simply reclining in a tracksuit and sunglasses, inviting the adoration of his fans. These signs bear names like 'Disco King Rajni Fan Club,' 'Prince Kamal Social Welfare Club,' or 'Heroic Leader of the People MGR Fan Club'. The animated young men discuss the star, his movies, the club's plans. These men are lower-class fans talking about glamourous idols whose own lives and movies are in the most obvious sense very distant from the fans'; and what these fans say and do reveals much about their images of the poor and the wealthy. This chapter focuses on the images that fan club members construct of the stars and on the social service activities that operationalize those images, in order to examine what fan club involvement in south India tells us about lower-class male fans' images of themselves, of the lower class and the upper class, and of the class system in general.

As I have argued previously (Dickey 1993a), much of the meaning derived from Tamil cinema has to do with the socially, culturally, and economically subordinate position of the urban poor, who form the great majority of its audiences; and issues of class, power, and dominance are central to understanding the relationship of viewers to the medium. This is as true of fan clubs as it is of film watching. Class is a critical component of identity, rank, and political power in contemporary India, especially in urban areas (Dickey 1993a, 1993b; Kapadia 1995; Fernandes 1997; Manor 1989: 333; Kumar 1988). When Madurai residents talk about 'people like us', they are much more likely to be identifying themselves with a socioeconomic category such as 'poor people' than with forms of identity that have historically received more frequent consideration by analysts, such as caste or religion. Yet while recent scholars have taken to task what many see as a prevalent academic fixation on caste and purity-pollution scales of hierarchy (e.g. Appadurai 1986; Dirks 1987; Raheja 1988; Ram 1991), and others have begun to demand attention to the 'modern sites' of Indian daily life (e.g. Breckenridge 1995, Marriott 1990; Freitag 1989), little direct attention has been focused on class structures and relations. As a result, although consensus now suggests that the categories of class analysis commonly applied to western societies have little 'empirical fit' in Indian societies (Kohli 1987; Caplan 1987; Sharma 1978; Béteille 1974; Washbrook 1989), we have an insufficiently positive grasp of the nature of class in India or its relation to culture.[2]

The young men who join fan clubs are sharply aware of their social and cultural distance from the upper class, and use their club membership to address and redress that distance. In its relation to a class system, film star fandom in south India shares a striking number of attributes with fandom in Europe and North America. Fiske argues that 'fandom is typically associated with cultural forms that the dominant value system denigrates. . . . It is thus associated with the cultural tastes of subordinated formations of the people, particularly with those disempowered by any combination of gender, age, class and race' (1992: 30). In southern India, mainstream film is particularly derogated as an entertainment medium, and any strong attachment to cinema is mocked, even by lower-class viewers, as 'cinema madness'. In Bourdieu's terms, then, specialized knowledge of and participation in film culture should not provide positive 'cultural capital.' In other words, in a model correlating aesthetic taste and economic achievement with class difference, it does not produce class 'distinction' (Bourdieu 1984). Fiske argues, however, that Bourdieu's model ignores the heterogeneity of proletarian culture and underestimates 'the creativity of popular culture and its role in distinguishing between different social formations within the subordinated'. Instead, he contends, fans 'create a fan culture with its own systems of production and distribution', through which they construct an alternative cultural capital that is parallel to that produced by the dominant cultural systems, and that differentiates fans from other members of the subordinate group who lack this distinguishing capital (1992: 32–3). Fiske's ideas remind us not only of the class differentiations involved in the creation and consumption of popular culture, but also of the active cultural production that is part of fandom.[3] In producing images of their heroes and carrying out social service activities, film star fans in Madurai also produce class images; and just as they distinguish their heroes from the rest of the upper class, so through their fandom they distinguish themselves from the poor as a whole.

The Fan Clubs

Literature on membership in voluntary associations in India suggests that membership in such organizations is quite low among the urban poor, especially when religious activities and trade union membership are excluded (Dotson 1951: 690; Babchuk and Gordon 1962: 116; Driver and Driver 1987: 102–8). In a study of formal organizational participation in Madras, Driver and Driver also concluded that a far smaller percentage of lower-class respondents' memberships were in national or international organizations than were those of the middle and upper classes, and that the lower class did not participate in 'social welfare associations' (1987: 105–6).[4] Film fan clubs appear to be unusual among lower-class organizations, then, in that they are extensive—most of them organized on a national level— and specifically concerned with social welfare.

Fan clubs (*racikar manrams*) are active and popular organizations in Madurai. They possess a certain visibility in the city, though not nearly so much as the cinema industry as a whole (whose posters and billboards line all the main streets). In addition to signs on the main streets of lower-class neighbourhoods and in the midst of college dormitories, announcements of club events pasted at bus stops and other public places remind city residents of the clubs' presence. Like the movie stars they celebrate, some clubs come and go overnight; others have lasted for over twenty years, and their members have become influential in local social and political circles. They are male institutions: virtually all members are men, and almost all are devoted to male stars, although a few of the most successful actresses have organized clubs, including Jayalalitha Jayaram, the chief minister of Tamil Nadu from 1991–6.

I first met fan club members in the course of doing research on film watching in Madurai in 1985–7. I wanted to learn about the clubs as institutions, and about the connections that some of them had to politics and to individual political leaders. Since almost all organized fans are young men, the strong gender segregation of Tamil society makes it difficult for them to speak freely with an unrelated young woman (and vice versa), and thus getting to know club members required persistence. I began by talking with members with whom I already had a 'safe' connection; this strategy was especially successful where I knew the young men's mothers well, which enabled me to establish a comfortable informal relationship with the men themselves. Later these club members introduced me to other members and officers, and my contacts continued to spread. The 'familial' tie to the original club members mitigated some of the tensions of our gender differences and, to some extent, those of class and nationality as well. In addition, during formal interviews with club members I was often accompanied by a male research assistant who was similar in caste and class status to most members, and his presence made the men I interviewed more comfortable since they were not 'alone' with an unknown young woman; bringing a female companion would not have accomplished this end.[5] I continued to meet with many of these men when I returned to Madurai in 1990 and in 1991–2, and over the years they have shared their changing feelings about their stars and their clubs. Finally, in addition to casual conversations and interviews with club members, officers and their families, I also attended public club functions (though rarely regular meetings, since my presence as a woman and an outsider was often inappropriate and unproductive), and also spoke with some of the movie stars who have fan clubs.

Most of my conversations took place with members of M.G. Rama-chandran (MGR), Kamalhasan, and Rajnikanth clubs, the three largest fan club organizations in Tamil Nadu in the 1980s.[6] I spoke with members of clubs in several neighbourhoods in different parts of Madurai, all of them predominantly lower-class residential areas but with a mix of castes and religions. Each of these clubs has thirty to forty members. Of the six branch clubs from which I draw most heavily, one of the Rajnikanth clubs was established in 1984 and one in 1989, the two MGR clubs and one of the Kamalhasan clubs in 1985, and another Kamalhasan club in 1990. I also met with officers and members of ward, city, and district 'head' clubs for all three organizations. Most of the latter were one-time meetings. City and district leaders proved difficult to contact but very willing to discuss their stars' merits at length once we met, and much more knowledgeable about the administrative aspects of their respective organizations than were branch members. In this chapter, I draw from conversations with the Rajnikanth and Kamalhasan district head clubs, and the MGR head club of one Madu-rai ward. Rajnikanth's district club began in 1976 and was claimed to be the very first Rajni club in India. Likewise, the Kamalhasan district leaders said that theirs was established in 1978 as one of the first clubs for their star, beginning as the main Madurai club north of the Vaigai River (covering approximately half the city) and becoming the head club for the entire city and district two years later. The MGR ward club is the oldest of the clubs that appear here, established in 1972 when MGR created his own political party.

There are many different fan club organizations in Tamil Nadu, with vast variations in size, activities, and administration. Estimating their numbers is difficult, since the only individuals with accurate information are district and state leaders who tend to believe that it is in the interests of their star's reputation to claim as many clubs as possible, and often make contradictory statements at any rate. In 1986, the district Rajnikanth president claimed that there were 1300 Rajni clubs in Madurai city and 2600 in the district—a number that, based on my observations, was far too high. The Kamalhasan district club leaders estimated a more likely figure of 350 clubs in the city. A ward leader of the MGR organization put the figure at almost 1000 MGR clubs in Madurai. *The Hindu* had reported more than 800 MGR fan clubs in the DMK in 1972, but MGR himself claimed 20,000 when he split from the party that year (see Barnett 1976: 312n), Hardgrave reported claims of 4000–5000 for all of south India in 1969 (1975: 18), and Pandian has cited an unattributed figure of 'about 10,000 branches' in Tamil Nadu (1992: 30). Shivaji Productions boasted of more than 3000 Shivaji clubs in 1969, but one club leader estimated that there were only 700 in the state (Hardgrave 1975: 18). My own very rough estimate in 1986 was 500 or more MGR clubs in the Madurai area, and approximately 300 Rajnikanth and Kamalhasan clubs respectively. Based on the less than definitive evidence of talks with fan club leaders and observations of new club signboards, I suspect that the number of MGR clubs has declined slightly and of the others increased somewhat in recent years. I have too little information concerning Shivaji fan clubs to estimate their numbers.[7]

Most club members are young men in their late teens to late 20s. Women, on the other hand, rarely join, mindful that involvement in activities so public and unrestrained as those of fan clubs would harm their reputations and thus their chances of marriage. After marriage, most women are too busy with household work to be involved in outside organized activities. The vaguely licentious reputation of cinema also keeps them away. I knew of only two instances of women's membership, the first in an MGR Women's Association (*makila anni*) club in 1986, which appeared to be devoted entirely to political service rather than to the more typical fan-oriented activities of most clubs, and the second in an MGR club whose male members had decided in 1991 to draft six women members for the sole purpose of choosing social service beneficiaries among neighbourhood residents.[8]

Unlike women, young men tend to have the time, the lack of family responsibilities, and the freedom of movement to permit participation in fan club work. Among the members I knew best, club membership was often a primary element of the person that they presented to the public. This could be done in a number of ways. One of the most frequent means of displaying membership is through styles of dress, either by using the star's party 'colours', as in MGR's case, or by wearing t-shirts with the star's picture emblazoned on the front. Some workers paint the star's picture on tools such as sewing machines and rickshaws. Fans may also demonstrate their affiliation through public adherence to the codes of conduct that stars promote (both in their films and through the club organs), including tenets such as defending the poor and revering one's mother. Fan identity may even be demonstrated through styles of speech. This was especially typical of MGR's followers, many of whom tried to avoid words deriving from Sanskrit and attempted to speak only literary Tamil in public.[9]

Though fans construct a specialist knowledge and cultural production that may bring them public approbation, fan clubs' public reputations are not entirely positive. Fan clubs are routinely viewed by outsiders as noisy, somewhat volatile groups of young men often characterized as 'rowdies' by non-members. (These criticisms are especially strongly expressed by the upper-class public, however.)[10] Club members' devotion to film stars is criticized as 'cinema madness'. Many people believe that some clubs demand protection money from merchants. However, fans are rarely bothered by such criticism; they are more concerned with demonstrating their devotion to the star, promoting his success by their support, and gaining a notable identity that gives them a demarcated place among the urban poor.

Most fan club members come from lower to middle Hindu castes (especially Mudaliyar, Thevar, and Nadar) and the lower or lower middle classes, and are not highly educated. Typical occupations among these (often underemployed) men include masonry, rickshaw driving, whitewashing, tailoring, tea-stall work, vegetable vending, and, among some of the older leaders, construction contracting; most household incomes in 1985-7 ranged from Rs 80 to Rs 200 per month. (There were about 12 rupees to the US dollar at this time; and the official Indian poverty figure—based on rural economies, and even less adequate in the cities—was Rs 90 per person per month in 1988 [Heston 1990: 103].) The clubs also include Muslims and Christians in what appear to be rough proportions to their numbers in the general population. Class and communal make-up vary according to the organization, however, and within it according to individual clubs. Hardgrave noted these differences between Shivaji and MGR groups in his research in 1969–70. Shivaji members, he said, were 'primarily from the lower middle class . . . the majority [having] at least some education'; most clubs included some college students (1975: 18, 19). MGR's fans, on the other hand, were 'primarily lower class, with education, status, and income a notch below the Shivaji clubs' (1975: 22). These generalizations still appeared to be valid in Madurai fifteen to twenty years later (see also Pandian 1992: 19–20), and from what I gathered, Shivaji club members also tended to belong to higher castes. Kamalhasan and Rajnikanth club members are demographically fairly similar to those of MGR's organization, although their average age appears to be lower (unlike MGR or Shivaji, these stars' appeal inside and outside of fan clubs in the 1980s was largely limited to people under 30).

Individual clubs are neighbourhood based. Their membership reflects the distribution of religions, castes, and occupations of the neighbourhood. Interestingly, leaders of upper-level fan clubs vehemently denied any suggestion of caste or religious distinctions in their organizations. I had only to ask them which castes were most frequently represented to receive the response, 'There is no caste in the club'—i.e. no attention paid to caste differences, and therefore a dissolution not only of their significance but of their existence. Leaders and members of branch clubs, on the other hand, answered the question without hesitation, suggesting that they were less concerned with maintaining the appearance of egalitarianism—and probably not aware that it should be maintained. But their deviance from the official view should not necessarily be read to mean that communal distinctions were important within individual clubs; the diversity of communal groups within clubs, outside activities among members of different castes, and the frequent diversity of caste origins among the leaders of each club suggested that communal distinctions were of less significance among fan club members than in much of Tamil society.

Each branch club has several officers, usually either the founders of the club or others elected from the general membership. All major actors' fan clubs are also part of a larger organizational structure, the intricacy and significance of which vary greatly. In the most highly organized groups, such as MGR's, there will be 'head' (talaimai) clubs at village or city ward[11] level that are responsible for helping and advising new and smaller 'branch' (*kilai*) clubs. Above these are city-, district-, state-, and even national- (or international-) level clubs and officials. State offices are all in Madras, where most filming takes place, and the leader of the state-level head club is usually the president of the entire fan club. The organizations' topmost leaders generally appear to be chosen by the star himself. Fan organizations' hierarchical structures are used to provide aid to local clubs, spread news about upcoming films and release dates, and disseminate information about the star's position on important issues.

Because they often cross caste and religious lines and are extensively organized, clubs can also provide an unusual network for finding employment and other opportunities. I knew several young men who had gotten short- and long-term work through the help of a fellow club member or an officer higher up in the organization, including masons, tailors' assistants, a construction contractor, and a videographer. One friend's son had met his sister's eventual husband while organizing his club, and was instrumental in arranging their marriage. A number of political contacts are made through the clubs as well. And head club members, who are usually older than branch club members and therefore have better contacts, may pull strings to help the younger men get bank loans or government funds for club or even personal projects.

Clubs can have anywhere from 10 to 100 members, but usually range between 15 and 30. Most clubs meet weekly or monthly. Different clubs' activities vary widely, both from organization to organization and within a single organization. In addition to club meetings, most activities are, not surprisingly, focused on films. Fan groups are also active in other ways, including staging occasional celebratory 'functions,' carrying out various activities that come under the title of 'social services', and sometimes engaging in political activities.

Film-related activities are intended to honour the star, and include pasting film posters,[12] attending a film's premiere showing, and buying up tickets to bolster a film's lagging run. At the theatre, especially during the first week or two of a movie, fans throw confetti, cheer, and recite dialogues (memorized beforehand from scripts distributed by the head clubs) along with their hero or heroine. Attending a film on its release day, when tickets are expensive and crowds huge, is seen as a sign of devotion to the star (cf. Hardgrave 1975: 16). Occasionally, some of the clubs in the city will also mark the day by decorating the theatre with garlands and even distributing sweets to waiting viewers. Clubs will also stage a celebration at the theatre when their star's film reaches the hundredth day of its run, the mark of a successful film.

Clubs also put on other public events referred to as 'functions' (using the

English term). Most are celebrations, such as those for a club's inauguration or anniversary or for its star's birthday; occasionally clubs will also put on a public meeting (*kuuttam*) to address a pressing social or political issue. A few clubs—most of them, in the past, MGR groups—put on up to six or eight large events during the year. These public events require the construction of a decorated stage and canopy, from which club officials and perhaps local politicians make speeches enumerating the film star's good deeds. Sometimes clubs will supplement the speeches with film-style dance performances. Whatever other content they may include, these functions always involve the broadcast of movie music and dialogues at full blast from numerous speakers placed in strategic locations (often from 2 or 3 a.m. one morning until 2 or 3 a.m. the next).

All of these group activities strengthen members' solidarity and renew their commitment to the group. They give the clubs public exposure, and sometimes—particularly when gifts are distributed to neighbours—promote a positive image within the neighbourhood. Positive images—of both club and star—are of greatest focus in social service activities. Social services or 'good works' are among the most idealized of all club activities, and will be dealt with in detail later.

The Stars' Images

Stars are the most crucial factor in the financial success of most Indian films, a primacy they have maintained since the 1950s (Gandhy and Thomas 1991: 107–8; Mishra *et al.* 1989: 53–4; Dickey 1993a: 61). Stories about their lives off-screen were apparently widely circulated by the 1940s and 1950s. In the 1950s, publications aimed at 'constructing star images for fans' began to feed the audience's hunger for information, and within the next decade a huge industry began selling 'a veritable torrent of salacious gossip' in dozens of languages (Gandhy and Thomas 1991: 116, 199). Today each major actor in Tamil cinema has a distinctive image, crafted through his film roles, formal publicity networks that include official fan club propaganda as well as movie magazines, and informal gossip networks. The information that circulates about stars is now substantial enough to constitute a 'parallel text,' one that audiences bring to and read in tandem with individual film texts (Mishra *et al.* 1989; Gandhy and Thomas 1991; Thomas in this volume).

Fans' descriptions of the stars, which both draw upon and contribute to this 'parallel text,' suggest the qualities that they find attractive in film heroes. All of the primary features of their depictions, I will argue, share a connection with either the attributes or the desires of the urban poor. They also reveal a picture of the contemporary, complexly masculine hero in south India. The characteristics praised most often include generosity and charity, compassion and nurturing, humility, the 'heart of a child,' virility and strength, and talent in the dramatic arts. Other notable features of the fans' descriptions are the emphasis on stars' roots in and triumph over poverty, and on their status as *guru*, teacher, elder brother, or god. The portraits that fan club members draw of their stars reveal their perceptions of ideal and actual upper-class members (male ones in particular), and tell us something about the images that members wish to project of themselves as well. Before I move on to these, I offer brief sketches of MGR, Shivaji Ganesan, Rajnikanth, and Kamalhasan, the four stars mentioned most often in this chapter. As these sketches will suggest, individual actors cultivate distinct images. Yet there is a striking amount of overlap in the characteristics that fan club members praised as they shaped those images to their own interests, and it is the cumulative realm of their images that interests me here.

M.G. Ramachandran began acting in films in the 1930s. Along with Shivaji Ganesan, he was one of the most popular stars for the last thirty-five years of his life, including his final decade, during which he became the chief minister of Tamil Nadu and stopped making films. Even after his death in 1987, his films continued to draw sizeable crowds. MGR played swashbuckling heroes and victorious underdogs, and was closely identified with the poor. He was portrayed as the saviour of the downtrodden and of the victimized heroine, and is the most renowned of all Tamil stars for his screen fights. MGR was said to be 70 years old when he died (although unofficially estimated to be five years older) and had ardent fans of all ages, both men and women.

Shivaji Ganesan is about ten years younger than MGR. In his youth, he was associated with the DMK party and played a number of 'revolutionary' roles. He soon switched to the Congress party, however (and later to the Janata Dal), and is identified by fans today as a 'family man.' His acting is somewhat stylized and overdone by current standards, but less so than MGR's was, and Shivaji is generally acknowledged to be the finer actor of the two. He too appeals to people of all ages, but this appeal tends to be stronger among the middle class than the poor. Nonetheless, he had many fans among the people I knew, especially women. Health problems have significantly reduced his film work in recent years.

Rajnikanth is from the southern state of Karnataka, but has been starring in Tamil films since the mid-1970s. He has also worked as a producer and director. His characters are usually forceful men and sometimes portray the degradations suffered by the downtrodden. By now in his 40s, he is famous for his talents in dancing and fighting, and his appeal has been strongest among young men. His image is in many ways comparable to Kamalhasan's. Both men are about the same age. Like Rajnikanth, Kamalhasan is celebrated among fans for his dancing and fighting abilities—although he is seen as a slightly more romantic hero than Rajnikanth—and has also been very popular among young men. He too is a director and producer. Kamalhasan is considered to be more of an 'artist' than most Tamil actors because he acts in non-stereotypical roles, an impression that has become increasingly pronounced over the years. In 1986, he and Rajnikanth were comparably popular (and commanded the same amount of money per movie), but by 1990 Rajnikanth was a more popular hero, though fans admitted his characters rarely varied; meanwhile Kamalhasan had lost some of his popular following but was renowned as a highly talented, sensitive, and resourceful artist. Both men have a less stylized, more 'natural' way of acting than those who preceded them. Today younger stars occasionally produce bigger box office returns, but through the 1990s Kamalhasan and Rajnikanth continued to command the greatest number of fan clubs.

Fans spoke readily with me and with each other about their star's attributes. They were eager to talk about his *kunam*, or personal character (a term that can be further glossed as disposition, nature, and inherent qualities), and the acts that demonstrated it. They build their impressions through a variety of means, including their own gossip networks, fan club publications and movie magazines, and personal contact with the star. Some fans, especially club officers, make occasional trips to Madras to meet the star,[13] but most fans get their first real-life glimpses when the star comes to town.

The predominant attribute cited for all these heroes was a spirit of generosity: a willingness to help anyone without reservation, and especially to aid the poor. Similarly, the stars were frequently portrayed as compassionate and even nurturing. Rajnikanth's fans, for example, often pointed out that the actor was a bus conductor before he got his film break, and that this helped explain his compassion for the lower class. The president of one Rajnikanth club reported that his club's main function was to promote the star by explaining to people, 'Rajni is a good actor. He is a great man. He suffered when he was young. He was a conductor and lived like an ordinary man, but now he has come up.' A fellow club member stated:

If you ask any actor or actress in the cinema industry about Rajni, they say that he is a good man. That's what we've heard. He has the heart of a child. If you go to any other actor's house you'll see a sign saying 'Beware of Dogs.' But if anyone goes to Rajni's house to get help from him at any time of the day or night, there will be people there to greet them. At any other actor's house there is the sign, 'Beware of Dogs,' but in Rajni's house there are people who will let us in.

Another young man, president of the Rajnikanth district club, spent most of an hour's interview telling me how Rajnikanth had risen from poverty, and had remained hardworking and concerned with the problems of 'the people' despite his current fame. Rajnikanth is 'like a machine [*macciin maatiri*]', he said. 'He shoots Tamil films 200 days a year, Hindi films 165 days a year. And anyone who needs help, he helps.' Perhaps defending against recent charges of discontent in the Rajnikanth fan organization,[14] he continued, 'As long as we believe in him, the organization will function well. Rajni is our god and elder brother. As long as we are alive, we must believe in Rajni.'

Kamalhasan received similar praise. He was often portrayed as goodnatured and concerned about his fans. One ardent fan, a club officer who had been to meet Kamalhasan in Madras, explained, 'He is good. He treats people with love, and makes them laugh. He does not yell angrily at them. I have never seen him talking to people in an angry mood; I've only seen him with a smiling face. He is happy, and makes others happy.' The slight suggestion of guilelessness appears in Kamal's image in other ways as well. Madurai's district club secretary, who had made several trips to meet with the actor, said that Kamal has 'the heart of a two-and-a-half year old child.' When I asked him to explain, he answered,

If some director is with him asking for his call sheets and a family friend or the fans come and want to meet him, he stops everything and comes out to meet them. He keeps the influential people waiting in order to meet the fans. . . . He does not gossip. He does not interfere in matters that are not his concern. If we ask about his personal problems, he says, 'It is my personal matter and if you interfere, we will lose our friendship.' If anyone says something that he doesn't like—well, that is, if you give a two-and-a-half year old child something that it doesn't want, then the child throws it down and starts to cry. But if you give the child something it needs then it stops crying and grows quiet. In the same way, if anyone says something he doesn't like—for example, when we tell him that Rajnikanth has just visited Madurai and that he should come too, he answers, 'I do not need fans who clap and whistle when they see me. They can function without me there. I need fans who feel that Kamalhasan is in their hearts.' That is Kamalhasan the two-and-a-half year old child.

The child-like elements that appear in this depiction—love, spontaneity, play, capriciousness and mischievousness, and rejection of socially condoned hierarchies—are strikingly reminiscent of child deities, especially the young Krishna. As a child and adolescent, Krishna demonstrates the illusoriness of proprieties by breaking a variety of boundaries and mores (stealing butter, playing sexually with women), transgressions for which he is forgiven because of his beauty and, ultimately, his divinity. Both images manipulate a tension between desire for social propriety and an affection that ultimately overcomes hierarchies (see Hawley 1983: 16–17). The effect of the image in either case is to create intimacy and closeness, as the child is forgiven and distancing hierarchies are reduced or erased.

Some of these qualities were also found in MGR's image, which included characteristics of compassion and unstinting generosity, but also gave equal emphasis to physical strength. During my research in 1985–7, MGR's generosity and his power both received the most persistently glowing praise of any star. Fans frequently pointed out that MGR had grown up poor, and therefore understood and wished to alleviate the problems of the poor. They claimed repeatedly that MGR welcomed all his fans into his home. He was both greatly loved and greatly respected; one of the titles he was known by was *vaattiyaar*, 'teacher,' a position of great reverence among Tamils. Unlike other stars, MGR had the advantage of added publicity as the head of the state government. Thus his fans frequently cited the government welfare programmes MGR had established or expanded as examples of his commitment to the poor. I asked the president of a ward head club, a man in his 40s, what MGR's *kunam* was. He answered, 'He has a thoroughly good character. This is important. He helps the poor people, and gives liberally to them, without reserve. He has been like this from the beginning. That is why we like him.' When I asked this man what he thought of Shivaji, he compared him with MGR:

When Shivaji gives things away, he is 'economical' about it. But MGR has always been liberal and uncalculating about giving—that is why there is a difference in their behaviour. Where MGR gives Rs 10,000, Shivaji gives Rs 5000. MGR runs a school for poor children in Madras in his own name. Some 2000 students study at his expense—it is a free private school. He gives them clothing and books. There are two or three places like this. At Madurai Meenakshi Women's College, he supports two students. He has helped people like that from the beginning. Not just now—even in his early film days. [He has] a mother's heart [*oru taay ullam*]—that's what we say.

Not surprisingly, Shivaji's fans said the opposite. Once again, generosity has been a primary element of the actor's image. According to Hardgrave:

His contribution of 1 lakh[15] rupees to the mid-day meal programme for children was repeatedly mentioned by survey respondents, as was [*sic*] his contributions of food and money for the relief of Madras flood victims in 1962. Although most of his contributions have been through government agencies, one fan, echoing the words of a Shivaji publicity release, said, 'He has never refused to give money to anyone who asks him for it.' Another fan was sure that Shivaji had donated at least 85 lakhs to the public cause (1975: 5).

Thus generosity, compassion, and even humility are the primary attributes these men portrayed as a star's *kunam*. Fans frequently stressed the uncalculating nature of this generosity; their heroes are not 'economical,' they do not stop to calculate either the amount of what is given or the merit that might accrue from the gift. The star is believed to feel concern for his (lower-class) fans, who depict themselves as the deserving but less influential and thus lower-status persons who are welcomed into the star's own home—an act connoting roughly equivalent status between host and guest—perhaps even in preference to prestigious individuals such as film producers.

A secondary but crucial aspect of this contemporary heroism is a set of masculine features focusing on strength and virility.[16] Tamil films, like other mainstream Indian cinema, include a number of fight sequences, choreographed as tightly as the song and dance elements of the films. Fighting and other violent action, which Sharma has termed an especially crucial 'signifier of masculinity' in Bombay cinema (Sharma 1993: 177), is one essential element of the masculine ideal in Tamil films, with other elements of forcefulness contributing as well. Rajnikanth, for example, was praised for his fighting talents and his machine-like capacity for hard work. And while fans stressed Kamalhasan's sensitivity, the film that most club members said they had attended more than once was *Vikram* (1986), in which the actor played a tough secret agent. By far the strongest claims were made, however, on behalf of MGR, whose physical potency easily elided into political terms. Members of his fan clubs boasted about his courage, enduring physical strength, amorous triumphs,[17] and political victories in almost the same breath. One MGR club member stated that MGR was the most significant figure of the Dravidian movement, and 'of all actors today, the only one who cares about the Tamils'.[18] The treasurer of another club, who volunteered a detailed (if somewhat erroneous) history of MGR's political rise, told me in 1986 that 'MGR is the centre of the Dravidian parties: Jayalalitha, Karunanidhi, even Annadurai achieved success only by MGR.'[19]

But it was the actor-politician's physical prowess that received the greatest tributes. The fight scenes in MGR's films figured heavily in such praise. In 1986 a young branch club officer gave me an extended taxonomy of the types of fights MGR waged in his films (based on the weapons used), and claimed that no current actors display the grace and skill of MGR in their fights. He continued: 'No one has his majesty. Even a coward would become brave after seeing our leader in the movies.' This young man vehemently denied that his hero, then at least 70-years old, lost physical or mental strength as he grew older. 'We expect him to live not to 100 years of age but higher, and for every year he grows older he becomes even more vigorous. He will be just like a twenty-year-old man.'

Violence is not a requisite element of Indian masculine ideals, including those ideals that focus on strength and virility (see, e.g., Alter 1992). It appears frequently in cinema, however, where it is a multivalent feature of actors' lives on- and off-screen. In films especially, violence can be used either to support social norms or to break them. Amitabh Bachchan, whose roles as the anomic anti-hero made him the quintessential 'angry young man' of Hindi cinema in the 1970s and 1980s, has arguably provided the dominant image of masculinity in that industry (Sharma 1993: 171), but I would contend that the period's dominant male models have been more diverse in Tamil cinema. Kamalhasan frequently played much gentler characters. And while MGR may have challenged the control of evil landlords and kings, he did so to uphold cherished social norms, and acted either within legal bounds or toward the end of a more just social system. Of the actors discussed here, Rajnikanth's film roles have been the closest to Bachchan's, but are not consistently of this type. In the world outside of films, however, where actors (and actresses) are frequently reported to violate laws and norms, violence is more clearly constructed as anti-social. Newspapers and movie magazines contain frequent enough reports of public brawls, divorces, affairs and multiple wives, and there are occasional charges of murder or drug and arms smuggling. There is certainly a public perception of actors as pugnacious, disorderly men. On the other hand, the same men are publicized doing charitable acts. Thus the violence, as well as the image as a whole, contains a mix of ideal and transgressive elements, a complexity I will examine further.

Finally, histrionic talent was brought up by a number of fans, though it

received notably less mention than other attributes. MGR's exceptional acting talents were praised repeatedly, and in his case at least, these overlapped
with physical strength by signifying extraordinary abilities. Likewise, Kamalhasan was frequently honoured for his acting and dancing skills. Some
called him their *guru*, a respected teacher, especially in dancing. Fans seemed to appreciate Kamalhasan's propensity for playing vulnerable and tragic
characters, and praised these roles most often. For example, a club leader
who had visited Kamalhasan in Madras described his acting and his role in
Cippikkul Muttu—in which Kamal played a young simple-minded man
who marries a widow by grabbing a *thali*[20] from a temple offering plate and
tying it around her neck—in this way:

> In that film, he gives life to a widow. By giving life to a widow he acts as an
> innocent, immature person. It is very difficult to play that kind of role. Disco
> dancing or glamourous roles—anyone can do those. But not everyone can
> act like an innocent child. His acting is terrific.[21]

Thus fans produce images that combine a variety of attributes, including
generosity and compassion, ingenuousness and intimacy, bravery and
virility, and extraordinary talent. Their praises suggest a mix of passionate
affection and respect. 'Devotion' best characterizes the club members' feelings for the stars. The ways in which the film stars are referred to in the
descriptions above—as *guru*, *vaattiyaar*, elder brother, or a god—all imply
devotion in Tamil culture. Fans' commitment to the star grows out of their
devotion; actions are intended to demonstrate such feelings. Sacrifices of
time, money, physical comfort and safety made in order to see an important
film showing or the star himself indicate a fan's love and loyalty; there is
even a sense that individual sacrifices are appreciated by the star and will
eventually be rewarded by him, in an undefined manner, as acts of merit.[22]
Similarly, the other characteristic shared by these roles ascribed to film stars
is protectiveness on the part of the star—the one who guides and protects
the fan.

What is the significance of the different elements of the heroic image?
How is it that these elements, which may appear divergent, in fact cohere
in fans' minds? These attributes, and the devotion and reverence they ins-
pire, form a constellation of related features that can be explained in part by
their congruence with traditional images of heroes and leaders. South
Indian folk heroes are portrayed in oral and written accounts as strong and
valiant in battle as well as wise, generous, compassionate, and revered (Srinivasan 1964; Kulkarni 1965; Kailasapathy 1968; Blackburn 1978). *Viiran*,
the most frequent Tamil term for 'hero' (a Sanskrit borrowing), shares the

same root as the English 'virility'. Charity and gift-giving (*taanam* or *tarumam*) carry a deep-seated cultural and political significance in Tamil Nadu. The bestowal and acceptance of gifts have long formed a definitive feature of formal leader–follower relationships in south India. The sovereignty of Tamil kings was traditionally dependent on their ability to give gifts of land, titles or honours to certain subjects, and the acceptance of such gifts denoted loyalty and service to the sovereign (Dirks 1986: 311–12, Price 1989: 563; see also Mines and Gourishankar 1990: 764, Shulman 1985: 22–3, 368). Elements of this model for authority persist today. Contemporary leaders are seen to have a 'duty to care for the material interests of [their] followers' (Brass 1990: 96). The acts of beneficence in present-day political patronage occur in stark contrast to the corruption and bureaucratic unresponsiveness met with by the poor in their attempts to acquire even those material improvements accorded them by government laws or programmes.[23] Film stars' reputations for liberal giving strengthen the leader–follower relationship, inspiring devotion and reverence, and binding the fan more tightly in his commitment to follow and honour the star. (As the preceding statement begins to suggest, however, constructing film heroes as charitable givers also separates them from the rest of the upper class, as I discuss later in the chapter.) Although not all folk heroes and not all political leaders have shared all these features (see especially Blackburn 1978), together such features form a recognizable set of attributes associated with heroes and with leaders more generally.

While many of the features praised in film stars thus construct them in the images of heroic figures, other aspects ascribed to these stars' *kunam*s are notably divergent from these images, and we must look outside the traditional models to understand the full significance of fans' constructions. Let me begin with the characteristic that is most at odds with past heroic images. This side of these heroes, which is best captured in the fans' phrase, 'a heart like that of a child,' was used most frequently in reference to younger actors. It becomes particularly notable when we compare it with MGR's image, which, with its focus on extreme physical and political potency, most closely fits that of standard south Indian folk heroes. MGR was seen as compassionate and giving, but also exceedingly powerful and forceful. While the fight scenes in Rajnikanth's and Kamalhasan's films are renowned, physical prowess never entered a fan club member's description of the *personal* nature of either actor.

As fans' explanations suggest, to have the 'heart of a child' implies not only unguarded generosity, but more precisely a loving rather than guileful or calculating nature, spontaneity, playfulness, and openness—all portrayed as a refreshing ingenuousness, placed in the service of reducing hierarchy. The child breaks adult/social rules. Similarly, all of these heroes are described (with pride) as humble: they want their fan clubs to act as instruments of service to the poor rather than as mouthpieces of praise. Ingenuousness and humility, particularly when combined with generosity, imply a personality and an approach to the poor that are starkly in contrast to those of most powerful people known to urban lower-class residents. To have the heart of a child is to interact with others based on intimacy and immediacy of feeling rather than calculation of gain. To be humble is to reject sophistication and arrogance, and to be identified with the poor—although when humility is adopted by choice, it also paradoxically imputes strength and status by demonstrating that the protection of arrogance is unnecessary (cf. Trawick 1990: 107–8). Similarly, childishness can be read as a sign of strength and maturity, when it implies that individuals find the security of adult social structures unnecessary.

In signifying a kind of power, these attributes merge into the more conventionally forceful heroic features. In this sense it is not necessary to pose a dichotomy between the specifically masculine attributes of physical power and forcefulness and the relatively non-gendered attributes of charity and ingenuousness.[24] At the same time, the stars' heroism does appear to combine sets of features that in the past have been kept distinct. Blackburn and Flueckiger, for example, have discerned a three-part typology of oral epics and heroes in India: the martial, the sacrificial, and the romantic (Blackburn and Flueckiger 1989; Blackburn 1989); others, beginning with Barth (1972), have perceived Indian leaders typically to be divided between saints and chiefs. And the stars' *public* personae, if not their screen roles, do include elements commonly perceived as contradictory. The dichotomy that cinema fans and detractors alike note most often is that between upholding and transgressing dominant values—the contrast between the hardworking altruist and the violent anti-hero. As Gandhy and Thomas have argued, 'stars are represented as finely balancing their transgressions with personifications of ideal behaviour especially in the domains of kinship and sexuality' (1991: 108). To Gandhy and Thomas, this polarity enables stars' images to deploy 'debates around morality,' particularly around the tropes of tradition versus modernity (1991). In these fan clubs' constructions, morality is indeed at issue, but the discussion is slanted rather differently around class and class relations.

All of the attributes that fans recount serve to associate the stars with the poor and explicitly dissociate them from the wealthy people with whom the poor are most familiar. Movie stars' closeness to the poor comes about either from an identity of attributes, such as humility, or from their nurturing of the poor, such as through charity and hospitality. The stars are also bound to the poor through their own histories of poverty. Fans recount the romanticized poverty that the stars were subjected to 'before,' either in childhood (MGR) or into adulthood (Rajnikanth), and the hard labour they continue to endure. The combination of past and present is crucial: the stars have triumphed over the poverty they were born into, but unlike most wealthy people they continue to share the hard work of the poor and to mark their shared roots by nurturing and honouring their lower-class fans. Thus the image of the traditional hero has been re-crafted to emphasize a special solicitousness of and closeness to the poor.

Much like the prevalent film themes that invert social hierarchies (see Dickey 1993a), fans' descriptions of the stars imply respect for the lower class despite their poverty, chide the rich for their scornful and miserly attitudes, and portray the poor as ultimately more moral and (therefore) more worthy than the rich. We can see that the rich are viewed as all that the heroes are not: they are contemptuous, selfish, cruel, proud, weak, conniving, and calculating. Heroes, on the other hand, are posed not only as ideal members of the upper class, but also as ideal *men*, men whom fans would like to be like. Interestingly, the image of heroes is not identical to the image fans construct of the poor. The glorified poor are humble (though not by choice) and uncalculating and good-hearted, but they cannot be charitable in the heroic fashion, and they are not idealized as strong and potent. Fans make it clear which image they emulate: they would rather be like the ideal wealthy than the glorified poor. Fan club membership gives them access to their ideal image in two ways—both through the closeness to the star, and through the chance to make themselves more like heroes by carrying out good works.

Social Service Activities

Like the stars they promote, fan clubs have a dual image in the public mind. They are known for fighting in the streets, demolishing movie theatres, and causing other disturbances. But they are also recognized in some circles for civic-mindedness. Almost all clubs profess an interest in carrying out 'good deeds' or 'social services' (*narpani, nalla kaariyam*). In fact, most claim service as a primary reason for their club's existence, an emphasis that I have found is essential to understanding the meaning of fan club membership. The label 'social services' actually subsumes a wide range of deeds carrying varying social significance and requiring varying amounts of exertion by club members. As I describe below, service projects include the distribution of goods at club 'functions'; various civic services; the acquisition of material capital for neighbourhood labourers; disaster relief; and wide-ranging projects such as blood drives and the establishment of eye banks. Clearly these cover different levels of service, and members may have any or all of them in mind when referring to their clubs' philanthropic deeds. All of these forms of aid work have two effects: they operationalize the movie star's reputation for charity and compassion, and they transform club members into men more like their stars.

Contrary to the public impression of fan clubs as groups of 'rowdies' who gather together simply to waste time and boast about their star, all the club officers I met claimed that the main purpose of their organization was to do good work to aid the poor. (MGR club officers also stressed the importance of their clubs' political work, which for them was often inseparable from social welfare projects.) Some of them even stated that their members were not supposed to have 'fun', only to do good work in the star's name. The president of the Rajnikanth club in a scheduled-caste slum neighbourhood, for example, told me:

We have opened this club to do good and to work hard. We don't like to play around. We must do services for the public—we must help people—that is what our purpose is. We don't enjoy putting up stages and dancing, either. As for Rajnikanth, we cannot spoil his name. If we visit him, he will receive us warmly and solicitously and [say], 'You should do only good works. Do not put up stages and dance or sing. You should help the poor. This is the way you must run the organization—if not, there is no reason to have the clubs.'

Similarly, the secretary of the same neighbourhood's Kamalhasan club said that when he and his companions went to register their new club, they were told by district leaders how a club should be run:

We must not just have a club. It must not be started for the purpose of whistling, singing, dancing, and performing. If we start the club, we should work continuously to do good. We must not spoil Kamalhasan's name. Kamalhasan's own goal is for the club [to work] this way.

These club officers wished their activities to strengthen the reputation of

their star, and believed that a failure to do laudable deeds or an involvement
in disorderly acts might instead hurt his reputation.

Like the branch club officers, the leaders of district-level clubs stressed
the importance of social welfare activities and the star's own mandate to
carry out such activities. The secretary of the Kamalhasan district club
reported that when he and a few others approached Kamalhasan to start one
of the first clubs in Madurai, the film hero told them that clubs could be
established on the condition that they 'not be like normal fan clubs'.
According to the secretary, Kamal admonished them, 'The clubs established in my name must not be for the mere passing of time. They must aid
the people; they must be a social service organization.'

In this case, the impetus for an ethos of social service does indeed start
at the top. When I interviewed Kamalhasan in September 1986, he too told
me that he had allowed his clubs to be formed only because they would be
'unusual':

> We are trying to do things different from what existing fan clubs do. So it
> becomes very difficult because they [members] cite examples [of other clubs'
> more leisurely activities], and they feel that we're making life more difficult
> for them, because instead of just being fans they are given hard work, they
> don't simply whistle . . .
>
> Slowly, it's a *very* big task, because either usually they've been trained to
> become political, or a personal army who'll help them [the star] out in times
> of stress and need. So these people have not been trained in it so it becomes
> more difficult when we're trying to accomplish [something unusual].

The president of the Madurai district Rajnikanth club explained the
need for a social service orientation because 'our brother Rajni has given us
a rich life; in this same way, we must try to enrich the people's lives and
satisfy their needs.' He recited an ambitious list of services to be provided,
including aid to people with physical disabilities; improvement of public
hygiene, drinking water availability, and ration shops; road development in
rural areas; free schooling by educated members for poor children; provision of eyeglasses and medical 'eye camps' for poor people with vision problems; and donations to poor couples on the occasion of their marriages.

Most clubs made more modest claims, although almost all stated that
such services are one of their major aims. Even those who admitted that they
had not *yet* carried out any service project held on to the belief that these
services were one of their main functions and intended to carry them out as
soon as possible. Indeed, only a small percentage of any branch club's time

and energy is spent on social services. Nonetheless, the ethos of service is crucial to members—as demonstrated by their insistence on listing service as the clubs' primary purpose—and the intention to carry out welfare projects and the belief that these remain the clubs' main objective are as important to members as the actual accomplishment of such projects. Members and officers alike appeared to have a genuine desire to carry out aid projects, and their faith that they and fellow club members would give aid whenever possible assured them that they were in fact helping to change the circumstances of the poor.

Indeed, I saw evidence that various aid was accomplished, and heard reports of many more incidents. Some of the 'services' described to me are civic-minded responses to ongoing neighbourhood problems, and include notifying authorities of emergencies, such as fires or accidents, and providing emergency aid when possible; arbitrating fights among residents ('or,' one MGR club member added, 'If we can't calm them down, we beat them and tie them up and hand them over at the police station'); and reporting problems with utilities, such as an electricity shortage or a failure in the water supply, and bringing the authorities to the site to investigate. Clubs also help provide disaster relief, such as during floods. The most frequently reported social welfare activity, however, is the donation of goods to the poor. This category can range from the distribution of sweets, textbooks, or clothing to neighbourhood children at the star's birthday celebration, to the charitable donation of much more costly and significant items, particularly tools and equipment for nearby workers.

The donation of these major gifts, which can include tools such as sewing machines, irons, and rickshaws, requires a substantial presentation ceremony. A canopied and decorated stage must be constructed outdoors, and as many club officials and members as possible sit or stand on it during the ceremony. The club's district leader and, if possible, a state political minister deliver elaborate speeches extolling the good that the star has done for the people. Finally, the chosen recipients come forward to receive their gifts directly from the minister or high club official, and perhaps make appropriate remarks of gratitude.

From what I could gather, acquisition of the articles donated by MGR's clubs was financed almost without exception by government funds. (This has not been true of other stars' clubs' donations.) However, the audiences at these ceremonies and club members themselves often believed that the goods had been provided out of the star's own resources. The president of an MGR branch club told me about his club's attempt to acquire tools for nearby residents. He and other members had approached the district club president about obtaining rickshaws for the rickshaw drivers and irons for the *dhobis* (washerpeople) of their area.

> We asked him to help us assist them in any way possible. He mentioned it to Our Golden One, Toiler for our Homeland, Honourable Chief Minister of Tamil Nadu Dr MGR, and shortly thereafter Chief Minister Dr MGR came to Madurai and with his own money bought rickshaws, irons, sewing machines, and so on and distributed them to the people.[25]

The 10th ward head club followed a similar process when it staged one of these ceremonies in 1985. According to the club's president, neighbourhood residents who make their living by pressing clothing had asked club members to procure 'iron boxes' from government welfare programmes for which the labourers were qualified. The fan club members then petitioned the Collector (the top government official of the district), who reportedly came to the neighbourhood to determine the legitimacy of the request. Once the 'donation' was agreed to, arrangements were made for the presentation ceremony. As always at such functions, the occasion involved a great number of speeches praising MGR The social welfare minister played a prominent role, eager as political officials always are to make a personal appearance, to be associated with a popular leader, and to gain credit for providing charity. Once the speeches had been made, the chosen recipients came forward as they were called, presented their cards, and received their new irons. 'Afterward,' the club president said, 'these forty people each gave us ten rupees and said, "Take these 400 rupees and conduct meetings and do something for the poor." ' (It was explained that this money helped to meet the club's basic operating expenses.) Presentations such as this one allow the fan clubs, attending political officials, and the star himself to receive credit for giving—even though, in this case, the irons actually came from public government programmes and money. (It should be noted, however, that fan clubs do in fact provide a service in such instances, since it is usually very difficult for the poor to take advantage of the welfare programmes directed toward them.)

Because it takes time to build up the substantial financial and/or political capital that these donations require, they occur only infrequently.[26] In contrast to these largely one-time activities are the ongoing social service projects operated by one or two organizations. The best example of these is Kamalhasan's campaign to set up blood and eye 'banks'. Kamalhasan described the projects and explained the need for them in this way:

[The Kamalhasan fan club members] have gone into something which is very different from [what] other people have done. They've gone into a blood donation campaign, they've started donating their eyes. And now slowly from next year, we're trying to reach a mark of 35,000 blood donors, free blood donors, throughout Tamil Nadu, which will take care of the blood shortage in Tamil Nadu according to the census. . . . Probably it's not a big problem in a country like America, but here you must have come to understand that there are professional blood donors. They are drunk, syphilitic, sometimes; we don't know what they carry. Probably even AIDS, sometimes. So we need healthy people to do that and that's what we're trying to promote. Right now a few of them have gathered somebody appreciative of their work, who has donated a 2-acre land near Salem [a city in northern Tamil Nadu]. They're trying to build a hospital. . . . I go every six months to inaugurate a blood campaign. I think it's a nice way of shedding blood [interview, September 1986].

All of the varieties of activities I have described and the reports that fan club members had heard and read of them were crucial to creating a conviction among members that their clubs were doing good work for the poor. While most club activities are in fact recreational rather than service-oriented, members were sincere when claiming that their clubs' main purpose was social welfare. And while the opportunity to serve the poor is not the main reason that most fans join clubs—rather, they would say, they join to promote and support the star—service is nonetheless what they believe to be the 'ultimate' purpose of their clubs, and in fact essential to promoting the star. Moreover, the lack of time actually spent on service activities relative to recreation need not imply that these clubs are less service-oriented than other voluntary welfare organizations, since this relative time apportionment is also characteristic of some other organizations that cite social services as their primary objective (see Caplan 1985: 159–61). I would argue that the service orientation of these clubs is not to be measured by the amount of time spent on service relative to recreation, since the *perception* of making a social contribution is as significant to members as are the acts of service themselves.

An informative comparison can be made between the aid provided by fan clubs and by other social welfare groups in south India, most of which comprise relatively wealthy people, described in the literature as upper-middle and upper-class members (see Caplan 1985; Driver and Driver 1987: 106). Fan club members differ from wealthier aid donors in a number of ways, including their knowledge of and relationship to the recipients, their methods of choosing beneficiaries, and perhaps most notably, the services they provide. Because fan clubs usually carry out social service projects in their own neighbourhoods, they know many of their beneficiaries personally, and if members are not already aware of their fellow residents' greatest needs, they can ask them directly. Members also possess the networks necessary to determine who is most in need of aid (though of course need may not be the only criterion for selecting recipients).[27] Upper-class aid organizations (such as the Lions' Club, Rotary International, or a variety of women's social welfare organizations), on the other hand, most often choose a village or poor city neighbourhood unfamiliar to most of their members, and work through a local official. They have much less familiarity with the area, and little opportunity for follow up once the aid has been donated.

But the most instructive differences lie in the types of aid given. Most upper-class social service associations call for remedies of '*uplift, reform, rehabilitation, guidance*, and *enlightenment*' for recipients whom they characterize as '*poor, suffering, helpless, backward*, and *ignorant*' (Caplan 1985: 202, emphasis in original). This terminology and depiction are also strikingly similar to those expressed by middle- and upper-class Tamil film directors about their lower-class audiences. While both these groups would offer 'guidance' and 'enlightenment'—consonant with a middle- and upper-class ideology of self-help (cf. Thompson 1963: 423)—the examples above demonstrate that fan clubs attempt to provide material aid, addressing what they see as the true cause of hardship in working-class lives. Rather than accept an upper-class model that insists on moral betterment, lower-class fans, who believe themselves to be morally superior to the judgmental and exploitative rich (cf. Trawick 1990: 110), suggest that what the poor need to escape their problems is financial assistance. They construct an image of the poor that portrays them as honest and hard-working individuals who are separated from wealth not due to depravity or fecklessness but thanks only to their lack of material resources.

Thus, to the extent that fan clubs stand as *mutual* aid societies, participation strengthens members' identification with the lower class and their intentions to assist that class. While more good is claimed than accomplished, most clubs give at least token assistance by distributing small amounts of food and other goods at their anniversary celebrations. Since the great majority of members of the clubs described in this chapter would depict themselves as well as their beneficiaries as 'poor' or 'suffering' people, it is clear that they are helping a group of people that they identify themselves with. This equation is underscored by the location of most acts of service in the members' own neighbourhoods, among the people with whom they reside.

It must also be noted, however, that the 'collective' aspect of this aid has its limits. While the identity of class standing between fan club members and the recipients of their charity can be made indirectly, as I have just done ('I am poor' and 'I help the poor' suggest 'I help people like me'), it is never stated in words by fan club members, and the consistency of this omission is striking. Rather than being expressed, for example, as, 'We help ourselves' or, 'We help people who are poor like us,' statements of aid never associate the speaker with the group to be aided. Instead, beneficiaries are always categorized as 'the poor,' 'the people', or 'the labourers.' Club members who told me that 'our organization exists to do service to the poor and suffering people' sound, in such moments, virtually identical to the members of the upper-class Madras women's organizations Patricia Caplan has studied that work 'for the "uplift of the poor and downtrodden in society"' (Caplan 1985: 202). In portraying themselves as helpers and even leaders of the poor, fan club members thereby set themselves apart from the rest of the poor, superior to them; in aiming to improve their lives, they often patronize them. Perhaps the proper characterization of members' relationship with their own 'class' is that they are members of the poor classes but also stand above them. In carrying out social services, they become the embodiment of their heroes' ideals.

Conclusion

In their words and their actions, fans construct moralizing images of three types of people: the poor, the wealthy, and the male hero. They also portray—and simultaneously produce—their own ambiguous place among these images. To be a member of a fan club is to generate a cultural capital that produces social distinction, separating the fan from the rest of the urban poor, giving him access to wealth and glamour that he would otherwise not possess, and narrowing the distance between him and the wealthy—but all of this done to remake the fan in the image of the hero rather than the typical upper-class person.

In all of this we can see that fan club activities reveal ambivalence about urban poor identity. Club members are fiercely protective of 'the poor,' and would like to be just like those movie stars who have transcended poverty but maintain loyalty to the poor. They protest the subordination of the poor by supporting heroes who, while rich and famous, nonetheless act in great contrast to the wealthy, treating and portraying the poor as the poor would have them do. They take on the cachet of violence—a violence that can be threatening, perhaps especially to the wealthy, but retains the potential of use in the name of justice. Heroes respect their fans and help them. In return, fans support them and embellish the heroes' reputations by doing good work, work that involves material aid to the poor. They insist that the poor deserve respect and assistance as morally upright people. They argue that the poor need material support to escape their degraded position in the social hierarchy, and they imply that the wealthy should be better people.

They do not, however, critique the existence of class itself. This lack of critique is emphasized by club members' attempts to distance themselves from the poor, by choosing to interpret their own social service work (which makes them patrons and helpers of the poor) as indication of higher status. Just as they distinguish their heroes from the rest of the upper class, they also distinguish themselves from the poor as a whole. Thus, in addition to delineating the opposed poles of the rich and poor, fans construct two other categories that blend what they see as the best of both, one for themselves and one for their heroes. They and their heroes are both *of* the poor and *above* them (cf. Bailey 1988: 119); and while fans lack the fame and wealth that could put them in their idols' category, fan club membership distinguishes them from the ranks of the poor and brings them a small step closer to the men they would like to be. While other lower-class residents of Madurai express the same ambivalence about their class status and evaluate class differences in the same moral terms that these fans do, fan club members possess the intangible and (often) tangible resources to enact both their critiques and their desires.

NOTES

1. I am grateful for the substantial contributions of others toward the ideas presented in this chapter. F.G. Bailey, Michael H. Fisher, and Douglas Haynes provided extensive comments on early versions. Susan Bell, Rachel Dwyer, Christopher Fuller, David Rudner, and Celeste Goodridge read and responded generously to the current chapter. A number of participants at the SOAS conference also provided helpful comments, especially Stuart Blackburn, Nicholas Dirks, Kathryn Hansen, Ronald Inden, Daniel Miller, Rosie Thomas, Patricia Uberoi, Peter van der Veer, and Pnina Werblen. My thanks to them all.

   Portions of this work have appeared in similar form in Dickey (1993a and 1993b).

2. In referring to people as members of the 'lower class' and the 'upper class' in this

chapter, or as 'poor' and 'wealthy,' I am conforming to the binary categories utilized by most poor residents of Madurai. The 'poor' or the 'lower class' corresponds to the category of people that Tamils lump at the bottom of the socioeconomic hierarchy, and to the self-ascribed identity of people in this position. Such people refer to themselves as 'poor people,' *eezhai makkal* (or 'labourers', *tozhilaalikal*; 'people who suffer', *kashtappattavarkal*; or 'people who have nothing', *illaatavarkal*), and are referred to as 'the lower class' or 'the mass' (usually in English) by members of higher classes. The poor lump all more privileged people together as 'rich people', *panakkaararkal,* or 'big people', *periyavarkal.* These wealthier people, on the other hand, tend to identify themselves (in English) as 'middle-class' or 'upper-class' people.

Lionel Caplan notes the use of similar terms for people located at the bottom of an indigenous socio-economic model in Madras, including the 'poor', *eezhaikal,* and 'those who don't have', *illaatappatta vanaka* (Caplan 1987: 11). The model his informants constructed was three-part, and most informants placed themselves in the middle category (and are identified by Caplan as middle class). My informants, however, always placed themselves at the bottom.

For a more detailed examination of the composition of the urban poor, of the application of class labels, and of the class system in Madurai, see Dickey (1993a: 7–11) and Dickey (2000).

3. Such production includes but exceeds what Hardgrave refers to as the folk culture of cinema (1975: 2), and ranges from fan magazines to film star decals and t-shirts to social service ceremonies in the streets to insider gossip about movie stars and films.

4. Fan clubs do not appear on the list of respondents' organizational memberships. Since Driver and Driver's survey on voluntary association membership was open-ended, the lack of mention of fan clubs cannot be attributed to the researchers' oversight. Their interviews were, however, restricted to heads of households and their spouses. My observations in Madurai suggested that club membership drops off after marriage, and this plus the relatively higher age of household heads partially explains the absence of fan clubs among these lower-class men's affiliations. Moreover, the Drivers' sample size was fairly small, including 55 'young' (i.e. under the age of 40) lower-class men.

The only other study I am aware of to identify the sample's lower-class members' organizational affiliations (Hardgrave and Neidhart 1975) did elicit fan club membership as a response. Four per cent of lower income (Rs 500 per month or less in 1969) urban respondents and about 3 per cent of respondents of middle- or upper-income levels reported membership in film fan clubs. Twenty-four per cent of lower-income urban respondents reported membership in some kind of association, compared to 47 per cent of higher-income urban respondents (from Hardgrave and Neidhart 1975: 19, 50). While the amount of fan club participation I observed in Madurai was similar to what Hardgrave and Neidhart report, I would be surprised if more than 15 per cent of lower-income residents belonged to voluntary associations in 1985–7.

5. Of course, it is also likely to have raised questions about my relationship with my research assistant, but I was never privy to such questions.

6. I was unable to make the proper connections to speak with local members of Shivaji Ganesan's clubs, the other large fan organization, whose members tend to have higher incomes and educations than the members of these three clubs. There were almost no Shivaji club members in the three neighbourhoods where my research was based, whereas numerous young men belonged to the other three organizations.

   The number of fan club members in a neighbourhood is not necessarily an accurate reflection of the star's popularity in that area, however. Shivaji was very popular among married women of all three neighbourhoods, none of whom could belong to fan clubs.

7. Unfortunately, these are the most helpful statistics to be found. To my knowledge there are no reliable quantitative data about any aspects of fan clubs, and my contacts did not provide a sizeable enough sample from which to project such data.

8. I am grateful to Delwin Wilson for bringing the second instance to my attention.

9. Speaking 'pure' Tamil—meaning Tamil purged of words derived from Sanskrit, a language associated with Brahmins and north Indians, although the term is sometimes conflated with literary Tamil—became an important political symbol during the rise of the anti-Brahmin, Tamil chauvinist Dravida Munnetra Kazhagam (DMK) party in the 1960s and 1970s.

10. Complaints occasionally appear in the editorial pages of the area's Tamil and English newspapers. In the 'Citizens' Voice' column of the *Indian Express* (18 August 1986), a college professor deplored the conditions of movie theatres and complained that 'the various racikar manrams (fans associations) play havoc in the sale of black market tickets and in spoiling the upkeep of the theatres'. In another *Indian Express* column of the same day, it was charged that fan clubs with political associations lent their names to 'encroachments' (buildings or other structures illegally intruding onto a sidewalk or roadway). According to the writer, the structures associated with fan clubs would be allowed to stand when other encroachments would not, and while the fan clubs would let them to businesses in the day, the shelters 'become veritable "casinos" with gambling and other unlawful activities when night falls. They also become nerve-centres of anti-social elements causing nuisance to the neighbourhood'.

11. The boundaries of these wards correspond closely to the city's political wards.

12. In Madurai, fan club members do not usually paste up the official distributors' posters advertising a film. Distributors and exhibitors pay others to do this. The

clubs print and post less glossy announcements, which include the star's picture and a proclamation extolling the star (often including the works he has done for the poor) and the new film.

13. These trips are usually made for an organized event such as a birthday celebration. Typically, many fans gather together for such events and few if any have a chance for individual contact with the star. The event generally begins with a group meal, followed by a speech in which the star thanks the followers and exhorts them to carry on the good work, and afterward the fans file past and shake their hero's hand. One Madurai club officer made his first trip to see his star when he attended Kamalhasan's 31st birthday celebration in Madras. He and his companions had planned on talking to Kamal there, he said, but 'that time it was very crowded, so we couldn't get in a good talk. We just shook his hands and came back [to Madurai]. Next time we go, we expect to be able to talk freely with him'.

Stars use such appearances to reinforce and intensify their fans' support. For example, the head of the district Kamalhasan club reported that when Kamal came to Madurai to celebrate the 150th day of his film *Kaakki Cattai* (Khaki Shirt), he proclaimed in a speech to the fans, 'Recently I received the President's Award. Even that did not make me happy. But today the sight of you all gives me the happiness that I could not gain that day: this honour is all because of you.' MGR had a similar talent for making his fans feel appreciated. The president of the 10th ward head club told me that MGR's thanks were the only reward they needed. 'When MGR comes to Madurai,' he said, 'he will thank us for doing the fan club work. He will say, "*Rattattin rattamaana utan pirappu*" [roughly, We are born blood of the same blood], and that's all we want to hear.' Most stars recognize that their fan organizations are potentially capable of independent action. Arguing that he could not force decisions on his fan organization, Kamalhasan explained, 'They are an independent unit. Tomorrow, if they decide, I'll have to move out' (interview, September 1986). And sometimes there can be real discord between a star and his fan clubs, especially when they disagree on the image to be produced.

14. Rajnikanth has some history of uneasy relations with his clubs. In June 1986, for example, *Aside* magazine reported that Rajni's fans became upset when the actor hit a photographer in a film studio. 'Shortly after this', according to the magazine:

> Pookadai Natarajan, the [state-level] president of one of Rajini's fans associations, announced to the press that all Rajini fans associations were disbanding, following the star's unhelpful attitude towards them and his lack of concern for issues of importance to the Tamils—his refusal of donation to help Sri Lankan refugees was cited as an example. The star, however, gave a counter-statement to the press the next day, saying that not all, but only the one fans association operating under Pookadai Natarajan, whom Rajini

had suspended because of it coming to his notice that Natarajan was mis-using the association's funds, had been disbanded. 'I am not a person who will kick off the ladder upon which I have climbed to success,' Rajini said emotionally. 'Although I am an all-India star now, I can never forget that it was Tamil films and Tamil audiences that have brought me where I am today' [*Aside* 10 (3: 46–7)].

15. A lakh is 100,000.

16. Whether this set of features is actually secondary in club members' minds is not certain. It was mentioned less often than generosity and compassion, but might have been emphasized more if fans were speaking to a male researcher.

17. This was a delicate subject, however, for two reasons. First, in his later films MGR took care to be pursued rather than to court; and second, many people in Tamil Nadu believed Jayalalitha to be MGR's 'secret' or second wife.

18. This statement, like the one about Rajnikanth's donation to Sri Lankan Tamils in n. 14 here, was made in 1986, a time when Tamil Nadu's and India's governments were involved in various ways with the treatment of Tamils in Sri Lanka. Like the one that follows, it is also clearly intended to link MGR to the roots of the Dravidian parties in south India.

19. C.N. Annadurai was the extremely popular founder of the DMK party, and drafted MGR into its ranks. He was succeeded by Mu. Karunanidhi—the present party leader and in 1996, for the third time, chief minister of Tamil Nadu—who ejected MGR from the DMK in 1972. Karunanidhi and Annadurai wrote film scripts for MGR in the 1950s and 1960s. Jayalalitha Jayaram was MGR's last major co-star and was drafted by him into his Annadurai-Dravida Munnetra Kazhagam (ADMK) party in the early 1980s, where she served off and on as Propaganda Minister, and after his death emerged as leader of the party; between 1991 and 1996 she was chief minister of the state. At the time that the club member made this statement in 1986, Jayalalitha led one of the two main factions in the ADMK.

20. A *thali* is the pendant tied by a groom around the bride's neck at the wedding. The tying is a central act of the ceremony, and is generally considered irreversible.

21. Kamalhasan himself described the film and the character in the following way:

    It is about a village boy. You cannot call him a moron, you cannot call him a fool, nor retarded, but he's somewhere in between a retarded man and a *maharishi* [great sage]. You cannot define him as a fool, nor can you say that he's a maharishi. Those qualities—there's a thin line dividing a prophet and a fool. . . . He makes them think with simple works [interview, September 1986].

22. The intensity of this devotion resembles that felt toward deities worshipped in *bhakti* relationships. It is also interesting to note that the fan organizations

themselves bear some resemblance to religious sects. In addition to devotion for the idolized leader (who may be credited with god-like and miraculous powers), shared features include a promise of proximate salvation for the poor, and a strong social ideology and related behavioural ideal. Of the fan clubs discussed here, MGR's bore these features most strongly.

23. For a discussion of the importance of cinema in creating contemporary political patronage relationships, see Dickey (1993b).

24. And violence has become less strictly a masculine domain in cinema with the recent rise of films portraying women as violent avengers, a trend that began in Tamil cinema with *Puu Onru Puyalaanatu* (A Blossom Became a Gale) in 1987. Also note that there is a much earlier precedent for brave and forceful women in Indian cinema: 'Fearless Nadia', an adventurous and avenging stunt woman, was a highly popular star of Hindi cinema in the 1930s and 1940s (see Gandhy and Thomas 1991; Barnouw and Krishnaswamy 1980).

25. Leaders and other respected individuals are often referred to with honorific titles. In MGR's case, this can include the title 'Doctor', since MGR has been awarded an honorary doctorate (his official biography credits him with reaching the third grade).

26. These events are quite costly; the expense reported by the officers of the Madurai district Kamalhasan head club for their 1983 ceremony was Rs 12,000. The lavish production appeared in the local newspaper *Maalai Malar* (6 November 1983 and 7 November 1983).

27. In research in Madurai in 1991, Delwin Wilson found that fan clubs determined a family's need by looking at the number of children, number of meals eaten per day, number of family members employed, type of housing, occupations, quality of clothing, types of possessions in the home, and health of family members (since, they said, the latter affects the ability to work). Club members also told him that 'you wouldn't know' who was poor 'if you went to an area where you didn't grow up' (Wilson n.d.).

REFERENCES

Alter, J.S., 1992, *The Wrestler's Body: Identity and Ideology in North India*, Berkeley: University of California Press.

Appadurai, A., 1986, 'Is Homo Hierarchicus?', *American Ethnologist*, 13(4): 745–61.

Babchuk, N. and C.W. Gordon, 1962, *The Voluntary Association in the Slum*, Lincoln: University of Nebraska Studies, New Series, no. 27.

Bailey, F.G., 1988, *Humbuggery and Manipulation*, Ithaca, NY: Cornell University Press.

Barnett, M.R., 1976, *The Politics of Cultural Nationalism in South India*, Princeton: Princeton University Press.

Barnouw, E. and S. Krisnaswamy, 1980, *Indian Film,* 2nd edn, New York: Oxford University Press.

Barth, F., 1972, *Political Leadership among Swat Pathans,* London: The Athlone Press.

Béteille, A., 1974, *Studies in Agrarian Social Structure,* Delhi: Oxford University Press.

Blackburn, S.H., 1978, 'The Folk Hero and Class Interests in Tamil Heroic Ballads', *Asian Folklore Studies,* 1978, 131–49.

———, 1989, 'Patterns of Development for Indian Oral Epics', in S.H. Blackburn, P.J. Claus, J.B. Flueckiger, and S. Wadley (eds), *Oral Epics in India,* Berkeley: University of California Press.

Blackburn, S.H. and J.B. Flueckiger, 1989, 'Introduction', in S.H. Blackburn, P.J. Claus, J.B. Flueckiger, and S. Wadley (eds), *Oral Epics in India,* Berkeley: University of California Press.

Bourdieu, P., 1984, *Distinction,* trans. R. Nice, Cambridge, MA: Harvard University Press.

Brass, P.R., 1990, *The Politics of India since Independence,* Cambridge: Cambridge University Press.

Breckenridge, C.A. (ed.), 1995, *Consuming Modernity: Public Culture in a South Asian World,* Minneapolis: University of Minnesota Press.

Caplan, L., 1987, *Class and Culture in Urban India: Fundamentalism in a Christian Community,* Oxford: Clarendon Press.

Caplan, P., 1985, *Class and Gender in India: Women and Their Organizations in a South Indian City,* London: Tavistock Publications.

Dickey, S., 1993a, *Cinema and the Urban Poor in South India,* Cambridge: Cambridge University Press.

———, 1993b, 'The Politics of Adulation: Cinema and the Production of Politicians in South India', *The Journal of Asian Studies,* 52 (2): 340–72.

———, 2000, 'Permeable Homes: Domestic Service, Household Space and the Vulnerability of Class Boundaries in Urban India', *American Ethnologist,* 27 (2): 462–89.

Dirks, N., 1986, 'From Little King to Landlord: Property, Law, and the Gift under the Madras Permanent Settlement', *Comparative Studies in Society and History,* 28 (2): 307–33.

———, 1987, *The Hollow Crown: Ethnohistory of an Indian Kingdom,* Cambridge: Cambridge University Press.

Dotson, F., 1951, 'Patterns of Voluntary Associations among Working-class Families', *American Sociological Review,* 16: 687–93.

Driver, E.D. and A.E. Driver, 1987, *Social Class in Urban India: Essays on Cognitions and Structures,* Leiden: E.J. Brill.

Fernandes, L., 1997, *Producing Workers: The Politics of Gender, Class, and Culture in the Calcutta Jute Mills,* Philadelphia: University of Pennsylvania Press.

Fiske, J., 1992, 'The Cultural Economy of Fandom', in Lisa A. Lewis (ed.), *The Adoring Audience: Fan Culture and Popular Media*, London: Routledge.

Freitag, S. (ed.), 1989, *Culture and Power in Banaras: Community, Performances and Environment, 1800–1980*, Berkeley: University of California Press.

Gandhy, B. and R. Thomas, 1991, 'Three Indian Film Stars', in C. Gledhill (ed.), *Stardom: Industry of Desire*, London: Routledge.

Hardgrave, R.L., Jr., 1975, 'When Stars Displace the Gods: The Folk Culture of Cinema in Tamil Nadu', Occasional Paper Series, no. 3, Center for Asian Studies, The University of Texas, Arlington.

Hardgrave, R.L., Jr. and Anthony C. Neidhart, 1975, 'Film and Political Consciousness in Tamil Nadu', *Economic and Political Weekly*, 10 (1/2): 27–35.

Hawley, J.S., 1983, *Krishna: The Butter Thief*, Princeton: Princeton University Press.

Heston, A., 1990, 'Poverty in India: Some Recent Policies', in M.M. Bouton and P. Oldenburg (eds), *India Briefing, 1990*, Boulder, CO: Westview Press.

Kailasapathy, L., 1968, *Tamil Heroic Poetry*, Oxford: Oxford University Press.

Kapadia, Karin, 1995, *Siva and her Sisters: Gender Caste and Class in Rural South India*, Boulder, Co.: Westview Press.

Kohli, A., 1987, *The State and Poverty in India: The Politics of Reform*, Cambridge: Cambridge University Press.

Kulkarni, V.B., 1965, *Heroes Who Made History*, Bombay: Bharatiya Vidya Bhavan.

Kumar, N., 1988, *The Artisans of Banaras: Popular Culture and Identity, 1880–1986*, Princeton: Princeton University Press.

Manor, J., 1989, 'Karnataka: Caste, Class, Dominance and Politics in a Cohesive Society', in F.R. Frankel and M.S.A. Rao (eds), *Dominance and State Power in Modern India: Decline of a Social Order*, Delhi: Oxford University Press.

Marriott, M. (ed.), 1990, *India through Hindu Categories*, Newbury Park, CA: Sage Publications.

Mines, M. and V. Gourishankar, 1990, 'Leadership and Individuality in South Asia: The Case of the South Indian Big-Man', *Journal of Asian Studies*, 49 (4): 761–86.

Mishra, V., P. Jeffery, and B. Shoesmith, 1989, 'The Actor as Parallel Text in Bombay Cinema', *Quarterly Review of Film and Video*, 11: 49–67.

Pandian, M.S.S., 1992, *The Image Trap: M.G. Ramachandran in Film and Politics*, New Delhi: Sage Publications.

Price, P.G., 1989, 'Kingly Models in Indian Political Behaviour: Culture as a Medium for History', *Asian Survey*, 29 (6): 559–72.

Raheja, G.G., 1988, *The Poison in the Gift: Ritual, Prestation, and the Dominant Caste in a North Indian Village*, Chicago: University of Chicago Press.

Ram, K., 1991, *Mukkuvar Women: Gender, Hegemony and Capitalist Transformation in a South Indian Fishing Community*, London: Zed Press.

Sharma, A., 1993, 'Blood Sweat and Tears: Amitabh Bachchan, Urban Demi-god', in P. Kirkham and J. Thumim (eds), *You Tarzan: Masculinity, Movies and Men*, New York: St. Martin's Press.

Sharma, M., 1978, *The Politics of Inequality: Competition and Control in an Indian Village*, Honolulu: University of Hawaii Press.

Shulman, D.D., 1985, *The King and the Clown in South Indian Myth and Poetry*, Princeton: Princeton University Press.

Srinivasan, C.M., 1964, *The Heroes of Hind*, Madras: Aiyar & Company.

Thompson, E.P., 1963, *The Making of the English Working Class*, London: Victor Gollancz.

Trawick, M., 1990, *Notes on Love in a Tamil Family*, Berkeley: University of California Press.

Washbrook, D.A., 1989, 'Caste, Class and Dominance in Modern Tamil Nadu: Non-Brahmanism, Dravidianism and Tamil Nationalism', in F.R. Frankel and M.S.A. Rao (eds), *Dominance and State Power in Modern India*, Delhi: Oxford University Press.

Wilson, D. (n.d.), 'The Impact of Class on Volunteers', unpublished manuscript in author's possession.

Shooting Stars
The Indian Film Magazine, *Stardust*[1]

RACHEL DWYER

THERE IS NO questioning the centrality of the Indian commercial cinema to Indian popular or public culture.[2] Cinema reaches into almost every area of modern Indian urban culture, across every aspect of the media, from satellite and cable television, to the video industry, the popular music business, and magazine publishing. These domains are mutually dependent and form dense networks of narratives and images which contribute to the viewing experience in the cinema hall. Since the academic study of Indian popular culture is in its early days and some of these media are so recent (satellite and cable TV appeared in India only in 1992), it is not surprising that these key spin-offs of the cinema industry have been little researched.[3] One of the arenas which have not been examined is the film magazines, which date back to the 1930s, and form a long-established central feature of this culture.[4]

Among the many types of Indian film magazines is found a group which may also be described as star magazines since their major preoccupation is verbal and visual images of stars in narratives, interviews, photos, etc. They have among the highest circulation of any Indian magazines, and some even have international editions.[5] Perhaps they have been neglected because they seem too trivial, not about film at all, but consisting instead of stories of the exciting and scandalous lifestyles of the stars of the film world presented in a manner guaranteed to titillate bored, middle-class metropolitan housewives. I argue that it is these very assumptions which make these magazines so interesting. Although I question these assumptions here, this dismissal of the metropolitan middle class needs to be addressed by scholars. I know of no study of this section of society, one which has been ignored in favour of the elites and the oppressed by Indian and western academics. It is this section of society which is fuelling India's economic growth, and playing an important role in the Hindu nationalist movement. I have argued earlier (Dwyer 1998) that there has been great intellectual hostility to this emerging middle class and to its culture. The opprobrium generated by my earlier study of one of the exponents of this culture, Shobha Dé, typifies the rejection of this class and its values.

Film magazines deserve serious study not only for their coverage of the stars, their lively stories and visual images within the wider study of Indian cinema but also because they originate from and are consumed by the new metropolitan middle classes. They have created and developed a new variety of English, the language of many of the magazines notwithstanding their exclusive concern with Hindi movies; they provide a forum for the discussion of sexuality; they link the commercial interests of this class with the semiotics and economics of advertising and its generation of lifestyle and consumption issues. These magazines are central to the history of the printed media in India, a major economic and cultural phenomenon of the 1990s.

Although cinema is a key component of an emerging 'public culture' in India (Appadurai and Breckenridge 1995), as an academic discipline it has generated very few publications. One of the many important gaps in the studies of Hindi cinema is the relative absence of any ethnographic study of cinema audiences. The only significant ethnographies are Dickey (1993a) and Pfleiderer and Lutze (1985b). The latter describe how, after a screening in a rural area, the villagers rejected the film as entertainment, saying that it depicted a modern worldview which is of little interest to them. This research was carried out when the reach of television was far more restricted than it is today. There is likely to have been a great change in viewing patterns now that there are frequent film screenings on the various TV channels. However, on a recent field visit, Chris Pinney reported little interest in TV among the rural population of Madhya Pradesh. Nevertheless, one can make certain assumptions about the composition of the audience. It is widely known that cinema is a major leisure activity in India: some 13 million people a day go to see a film in a cinema-hall. Since a pattern of wage labour and a division of work and leisure is required for there to be an audience, it is widely assumed that most cinema goers are urban, male, lower-class industrial workers. This is supported by evidence internal to the film:

Vasudevan (1989: 30) points out that the social referent of the Hindi film is generally the plebeian or the declasse; this view is supported by Dyer's (1997) model of the appeal of entertainment forms to the audience. However, there is little information available as to the precise composition of the audience or variables such as gender, age, class, and occupation.

It is clear from features such as the magazines' advertising and use of the English language that their readership does not coincide with the cinema audience as described above. Rather, it is middle class or aspiring middle class, with possibly more women than men, and likely to be drawn from a wider age group.[6] It may be closer to the audience for domestic consumption of video cassettes of films. After the boom in VCR ownership since the 1980s, many of the middle classes preferred to watch movies at home rather than in the movie halls, which are seen as suitable only for lower-class men. The composition of this video-watching audience is even less clear than that of the cinema halls but its economic status, in having enough money to afford the VCR and colour TV and in having domestic space and free time for leisure activities, suggests a middle class or at least upwardly mobile status. The middle class has returned to the cinema halls in recent years to see high budget films which are on cinema release only or 'video holdback', a practice which began with the 1994 hit *Hum aapke hain koun . . .!*,[7] these films represent only a handful of the annual releases. The change in audience can be seen in the massive hike in ticket prices: before this film the most expensive cinema ticket was Rs 25, with this it rose to Rs 100. While an analysis of the magazines in the *bhashas* or vernaculars would give greater insight into the pleasures of the cinema-going audience,[8] the study of these English magazines sheds light on the role of the middle class, in particular women and adolescents, as viewers and consumers of not only the cinema and its stars but also of a new urban lifestyle.

In this chapter I concentrate on one of the most popular of these film magazines, *Stardust*, a gossip magazine about the stars of the Bombay commercial cinema, which has been published in English in Mumbai[9] since 1971. I discuss *Stardust's* major concerns, looking at how it has constituted an 'imagined', interpretive community[10] of readers, and the activities of this social group in creating and consuming the pleasures of the magazine.

Approaches to Magazines, Popular Culture

In the western context, the few studies of women's magazines (Winship 1987, McRobbie 1991, McCracken 1993, Hermes 1995) can be seen as part of a feminist reappraisal of women's genres of popular culture. These include Radway's pioneering work on the romance (1987), Modleski's analysis of women's fantasies through romance, Gothic novel, and TV soaps (1982) and Ang's discussion of soap operas (1985).

While not adopting any of their lines of enquiry, I have found many suggestive ideas in them. I have used caution in drawing on psychoanalytic approaches, which inform many of these works, trying to use them only for a general interpretation of pleasure. Ang's study of the consumption of the soap opera *Dallas* showed that most interviewees identified the motive for watching as pleasure, but no one could define what this pleasure is. One can only identify some of the mechanisms of pleasure which she found, namely the pleasures of melodrama and of 'emotional realism'. Radway expanded the study of pleasure to include the process of reading itself; the pleasure women took in setting aside time for reading; and pleasure in the narratives themselves. Hermes built on this in her study, arguing that readers of women's magazines enjoy the fact that they can read them intermittently rather than having to set aside such long periods of time for themselves as they required for romance reading. Hermes identifies a further pleasure in the subversive 'camp' reading of magazines, often by men, which is part of the reader's repertoire of responses to the magazines

I have used a less abstract version of semiological analysis of the magazine than that of McRobbie,[11] following instead Gledhill's model of negotiation (Gledhill 1988), where meaning is constructed through the meeting of institutional and individual producers, texts, and audiences. In this model, the socio-historical constitution of audiences as well as the production process, become integral elements in the dispersion of textual meaning. My research is focused very deliberately on the magazines themselves: examining their archives, talking to magazine production teams, and to magazine readers on an informal basis. It became clear that the success of *Stardust*, whose origins are in the world of advertising,[12] lies in the close connection between the advertisers and their target audience of readers, a relationship consolidated by solid market research for commercial reasons, and those who consume the magazines.

The studies mentioned above are all primarily concerned with women's genres of popular culture and may not seem of direct concern to the study of these film, or rather, star, magazines.[13] However, a number of generic overlaps[14] becomes clear. For example, in her study of the teenage girls' magazine *Jackie*, McRobbie (1991) identifies four major codes: romance; personal and domestic life; fashion and beauty; and pop music, the last of which discusses issues relating to stars and their fans. All these codes prove useful in analysing the film magazines where they centre on the Indian star.

However, Hermes (1995) found that the reading of celebrity magazines was not very dissimilar to the reading of the more general 'women's magazine'. Nevertheless, since these magazines are one of the major media for the dissemination of narratives about Hindi film stars, I briefly consider theoretical work on the star. There are no tabloid newspapers in India equivalent to the British tabloids which narrate the lives of stars, although there is increasing coverage in the 'serious press' (*India Today* and most of the national papers) in their lifestyle columns. The gossip and rumour generated by the media in India are largely undocumented. Little has been written about the star in Indian cinema (Karanjia 1984; Kabir 1985; Mishra *et al.* 1989; Gandhy and Thomas 1911; Sharma 1993) but western film theory has proved useful in my analysis. I have drawn on Dyer's[15] work on the star, which considers stars' images in social and historical contexts, arguing that stars matter beyond their films when they come to act as the focus for dominant discourses of their time.

I begin by giving a brief history of the film magazines, their origins, and their production. I then look at *Stardust's raison d'être*, namely its adverts and the female bourgeoisie it targets, before examining narratives, theme, and language, to explore what they reveal to us about the readership and nature of the magazines.

Indian Film Magazines

The earliest film criticism in India is found in newspaper columns, but film magazines in the vernacular languages[16] and in English first appeared in the 1930s.[17] The first magazine devoted entirely to cinema coverage was the Gujarati[18] *Mauj Majah*, published in 1924. One of the major magazines in English was the monthly *Filmindia*, which was published from 1935 to 1961. This expensive magazine, containing adverts catering to an elite market, was nearly all written by one person, Baburao Patel. It published reviews, responses to readers' letters, etc. but editions from the final years contain lengthy polemics against western medicine and pages on homeopathic and other indigenous medicines.

The post-War period saw the decline of the studio system of production and the rise of the independent producer and the growth of the star system. This required new forms of information which were supplied by trade publications in English, the first being a roughly produced weekly review sheet called *Kay Tee Reports*. This was supplanted by the better produced magazine *Tradeguide* (1954–),[19] which followed *Kay Tee Reports* by producing reviews of the week's films which journalists previewed on Thursday, in time for the Friday release. This and other trade magazines are aimed at distributors and exhibitors, so their most important role is to predict the success or failure of particular films (rarely proved wrong) and to publish the box-office statistics of recent movies. They contain no information about stars other than for commercial reasons.

Another type of magazine appeared in the 1950s, published by the major newspaper houses.[20] The *Indian Express* newspaper group launched its inhouse publication, *Screen*, in 1951. Its major concerns were films under production and recent events in the film industry. *Screen* can be situated somewhere between the trade and fan magazines, containing enough hard news for the industry and interviews with people in the business; it is read by both audiences. It also discussed Hollywood films, mostly in the context of distribution in India. This weekly was in the form of a broadsheet newspaper with colour supplements but it has recently remodelled itself in a large colour magazine format and has substantial coverage of television.

The ground-breaking publication for the later wave of glossy English magazines was *Filmfare* in 1952 by Bombay's *Times of India* newspaper group. It was distributed throughout India[21] by the newspaper's good distribution networks. Its first issue contained a manifesto:

> It is from [the] dual standpoint of the industry and its patrons, whom comprise the vast audience of movie fans, that 'Filmfare' is primarily designed. This magazine represents the first serious effort in film journalism in India. It is a movie magazine—with a difference. The difference lies in our realisation that the film as a composite art medium calls for serious study and constructive criticism and appreciation from the industry as also from the public [*Filmfare*, 7 March 1952: 3].

It combined serious film journalism with coverage of glamour and had features about and interviews with the dominant figures in the industry. It was a sophisticated magazine, in keeping with the image of the *Times*, covering many cinema topics. It provided a forum for dialogue between the critics, the industry, and the audience while fulfilling the further function of being an upmarket family magazine with broad appeal to both the men's and women's markets rather on the pattern of the *Times'* political and arts paper, *The Illustrated Weekly of India*. It assured its place at the forefront of the film world in 1953 when it instituted the *Filmfare* Awards. These were modelled on the Hollywood Academy Awards with the major difference that the magazine's readers cast their votes. Regional versions in English are published with more information about local film industries. Even the Mumbai City edition caters to this regional interest; although its coverage of Marathi cinema is minimal, it carries voting pages for *Filmfare* Awards for Marathi films. *Filmfare* has evolved under various editors who have included nationally renowned journalists like Pritish Nandy and Khalid Mohammed. It was biweekly until 1988, when it ran into financial difficulties, since when it has been monthly. Itself influenced in the late 1970s by the star magazines, although remaining much less scandalous and salacious, *Filmfare* has retained its distinctive blend of film coverage and star interviews and now some of the later publications have emulated its more successful features, notably its emphasis on interviews.

An important element of the magazine market is the vernacular magazines. These are quite different from the English monthly glossies (apart from the translated versions produced by *Magna* and *Chitralekha* publications).[22] They tend to be weeklies, have low production values, and are printed on cheap paper. Photos are scarce and mostly in black and white. Their downmarket advertising suggests that they are aimed at a lower-class, male market. The majority of adverts plug dubious-sounding tonics to restore male vigour, suggesting a great anxiety about sexual performance. This poorer, predominantly male readership seems to coincide more with a large section of the cinema-going public and as such these magazines may reflect more closely the audience's concerns. Film-makers need to satisfy the demands of this readership, by covering their favourite stars from the angles in which they are interested.[23] Some of the more important titles seen in Mumbai include *Film City* (circulation 100,000); *Aar Paar* (45,000); others include *Kingstyle, Filmi Duniya* (1958– from Delhi, 118,000). *Filmfare* had a Hindi version (*Filmfare Madhuri Samahit*) from 1964 but it was not very successful and soon ceased publication. There are high circulation film magazines in all the major languages including Urdu, Malayalam, Tamil, Telugu, and Bengali.

The 1970s saw a whole new wave of magazines including the English-language glossies which are the focus of this chapter.[24] These introduced a new style of journalism in a new language, said to be invented by Shobha Rajadhyaksha (later Shobha Kilachand and subsequently Shobha Dé) (*Stardust*) and Devyani Chaubal (*Star'n'style*), although some claim that *Blitz* was the first. I shall concentrate on *Stardust*, one of the first of these magazines, which undoubtedly has been the market leader.

Stardust may well have the largest circulation[25] of any of the film magazines (in English 125,000; in Gujarati[26] 1987–, 75,000; in Hindi 1985–30,000. The international English edition 1975–,[27] sold in the UK, USA, Canada [specified on the cover] and South Africa and the Gulf, sells a further 40,000 copies;[28] no figures are available for the English-language editions, 1996–, which cover the four southern regional cinemas).[29] The only magazine with comparable sales is *Filmfare* (see above), which is said by its journalists to have recently reached 200,000 per month, although much lower figures are published for 1994.[30]

The recent *G* magazine (1989–, 15,000), edited by Bhavna Somayya, a former *Stardust* journalist, has fewer scandalous stories than *Stardust*[31] but has more chitchat and less analysis than *Filmfare*. It is distributed by the *Chitralekha* group of Gujarati magazines, and has older versions also in Gujarati (*Jee*, 1958–, 97,000) and in Marathi (*Jee* 1988–, 48,000). The other English-language magazines seem to very much on the lines of *Stardust* (*Cineblitz* 1974–, 81,000; *Movie* 1982–, 75,000; and *Tinsel Town* (1989–) which includes around ten pages of TV coverage). *Star'n'style* (1965–, 15,000), which has suffered from industrial disputes, a warehouse fire, and several changes of ownership, is now attempting a revival under Nishi Prem, another former editor of *Stardust*. Her efforts to increase the gossip content have led to her being sued for libel by Aishwarya Rai, the former Miss World.[32] Most of the above magazines now have homepages on the Internet; some pages give all the magazine stories, whereas others just provide the covers and the headlines. There were English-language magazines which seemed to be aimed at more of a men-only market, including *Film Mirror*, published by Harbhajan Singh. Its lurid reports remain legendary and unsuitable for a family readership.

Video magazines, which are mostly borrowed on rental, including *Lehren* (1988–, now on the Internet only), cover events in the film industry such as birthday parties, *muhurats* ('auspicious moment; time of the first shot'), etc. although their popularity is on the wane since the explosion of film and filmstar coverage on cable and satellite television in programmes ranging from reviews ('*Chalo* cinema') to star interview, and song sequences.

Stardust

Stardust is the flagship magazine of Magna Publications,[33] a Mumbai-based publishing company owned by Nari Hira. Hira founded *Stardust* in 1971 as a marketing opportunity for his advertising business. The only major film magazine at the time was *Filmfare* which ran film information and un-controversial stories about the lives of the stars. His idea was to publish a magazine on the lines of the American *Photoplay* with celebrity gossip journalists like Hollywood's Hedder Hopper and Louella Parsons. Twenty-three-year-old Shobha Rajadhyaksha (later Dé), who had been working for Hira for eighteen months as a trainee copywriter, was hired as the first editor. She had no interest in the movie world and had never worked as a journalist, but was given the job on the strength of an imaginary interview with Shashi Kapoor, whom she had never met. She and a paste-up man produced the first issue in October 1971 from unglamorous offices in south Mumbai.[34] Later they were joined by a production staff of three, and a team of freelance reporters collected stories which she wrote up. Dé stubbornly refused to move in the film world, only meeting the stars if they came into the office. The style of the magazine was established during her time as editor and has been maintained under the succession of editors who followed.

The first issue of *Stardust* appeared in October 1971. A statement of intent was published underlining the magazine's purpose in its 'Snippets' column:

> Very few movie magazines and gossip columns are either readable or reliable and hardly any are both. Most of them are inadequately researched and are the result of second and third hand reporting. One theory put forward has it that what often passes for news and fact is really much hearsay and gossip. Another claims that the people in the movie trade who are in a position to know are too busy to write or find it impolite to write down what they know.
>
> So, this column—largely as its reason for being—will be a reporter's column and not a mouthpiece of publicists and ballyhoos of the film trade. And here we go . . . [*Stardust*, October 1971: 39].

The magazine's manifesto is discussed throughout the issue, in particular in the Q&A and letters pages (presumably written by Dé since it was the first issue).

The production features were much less glossy than they are today. Colour was used only for the cover, in this case an unflattering picture of the top box-office star, Rajesh Khanna, and a series of photographs of the leading female star, Sharmila Tagore. The front page headlines were very suggestive: 'Is Rajesh Khanna married?' and 'Rehana Sultan: all about her nude scene' but the stories were quite innocent. The main features were uncontroversial stories about Sharmila Tagore and her husband, the Nawab of Pataudi, the international cricketer. Along with the expected combination of photos, news, and gossip, some of the staple features of *Stardust* appeared in the first issue, including 'Neeta's Natter', written by 'The Cat', the letters page, and the Q&A columns. The trademark Bombay English is not much in evidence, and there is little innuendo and few of the double entendres that become central features in later issues (the only example in the first issue was the mention of eating 'red-hot pickles' on a date). Several of the features were later dropped, including Hollywood coverage, 'A day on the sets', 'What's shooting', cartoons, and film criticism, features which brought it closer to *Filmfare*. Within a year more of the staple features were established, including 'Court Martial' (October 1972) and the special use of language is soon seen throughout the magazine.

Many of the major themes which are discussed later in the chapter begin to emerge during the early numbers including images of the body, and issues of sexuality centred around the affairs of stars and their scandalous behaviour off the sets. The magazines also have the usual self-reflexive coverage, writing about themselves, in particular about the special relationship of the magazine to the film industry, the definition of star and discussions as to whether stars have the right to privacy.

The style of *Stardust* was firmly established in the first ten years and has remained largely the same to the present, even including the use of 1970s-style graphics. The style of production has also been constant. Nari Hira, the sole owner of Magna Publications, largely delegates the editorial work but negotiates with his editors over the final version. Ashwin Varde is the overall editor of Magna group publications, while *Stardust's* current editors are Omar and Nilufer Qureshi. These editors, like most of the reporters, are college graduates from middle-class Mumbai families, without the glamourous social connections of Shobha Dé. The eight reporters and two freelancers (all under 30 years old) each have a set of stars to cover. Once the stories are collected they are cross-checked with the stars to make sure they are happy about the stories. If there is something controversial which is a good story they may run it anyway, but gossip about the star's family is taboo and they never write anything on this topic without the star's permission.

The stars usually collaborate with the magazines, but this does not always run smoothly. The first major quarrel was between *Star'n'style's* Devyani Chaubal and Dharmendra over her comment that his partner, Hema Malini, looked like a stale *idli*. Amitabh Bachchan had a long-standing dispute with *Stardust* from the mid-1970s concerning gossip about him and Zeenat Aman. He refused to give interviews and the magazine boycotted any mention of him although they were ultimately reconciled without too much damage either side. A serious dispute with the Cineartists Association in 1992 led to their boycott of six magazines (*Stardust, Cineblitz, Filmcity, Movie, Showtime, Star'n'style*). This has since been patched up by the stars who felt they needed the publicity. Yet given the gossip, why do the stars collaborate with the magazines and what is the extent of their involvement? Some stars do straightforward interviews only, while others seem to have a much more ambivalent relationship with the magazines. Many people in the industry argue that the journalists are not to blame; they are encouraged by the stars who only later regret talking to the magazines, whereas others feel that the stars are persecuted by the journalists.

The stories cover fifty or more stars, concentrating on cover girls and glamorous figures who lead exciting lives or make controversial statements, rather than the top box-office stars. For example, Aamir Khan is a big box-office star and also a pin-up but since there are no interesting stories about him, and he gives few interviews, he features rarely in the magazine. Salman Khan, another pin-up but a more variable box-office star, is a more controversial figure and the magazine publishes many stories about his off-screen activities. *Stardust* also promotes stars by putting in glamorous photos, and making romantic link-ups with other stars. This promotion was evident with the model Sonali Bendre who won a talent competition for a place on the 'Stardust Academy', an annual sponsored programme for would be starlets. While few heroines have more than minor roles in the films (even an important heroine like Kajol may take such minor roles that they have to justify their choices in the magazines: 'I did *Karan-Arjun* because I wanted to know how it feels to be an ornament. I had nothing to do in the film except look good': *Stardust*, March 1995: 112), yet great importance is given to them in the magazines, especially on the covers, since the editors believe that a woman ('cover girl') on the front generates sales. Some actresses have had magazine careers which have outshone their screen roles, notably Rekha. Although she has acted in some great roles (in 1981 *Umrao Jaan* and *Silsila*), she has remained more famous for being desirable, beautiful and unattainable, and for the scandal which has dogged her.[35]

This is part of the fairly fixed style of the magazine cover. The main picture is usually of a woman or a star couple in an amorous pose, surrounded by up to four cut-outs of stars with sensational headlines, at least one of which mentions sex. The headlines are usually far more salacious than the stories.

The magazine's regular features include the opening quasi-editorial 'Neeta's Natter', and short paragraphs of gossip, written as if by a celebrity about her social life in the film world, covering opening films jubilees,[36] weddings, parties, etc. The stories praise those who are 'in' and mock those who are 'out'. This is where the exaggerated language of the magazines is strongest, full of innuendo and puns. There is some photographic coverage of industry events but the majority of pictures are the session photos found elsewhere in the magazine. The other insider's gossip sections are 'Star Track', which covers incidents in stars' lives, mostly stories from childhood, and events on the sets; 'Snippets', which is more humorous, consisting mainly of jokes about star's gaffes in English, in etiquette, and then short puns and jokes; 'Straight talk' covers other news items about the stars.

A number of regular formats for interviews include 'Spot poll', a Q&A session with the stars; 'Court martial', where overtly hostile questions are asked of a controversial or fading star; 'Favourite things', where a star completes a cheesy questionnaire while the facing page features a signed glamour photo. Several interviews and articles about romances, quarrels, and gossip are interspersed with glamour shots of the stars. The major feature is 'Scoop of the month', which is a big, gossipy story about an affair, a break-up of a relationship, or a special interview.

Readers also have a chance to contribute to the magazine in two places: 'Rumours and rejoinders', where they address queries to stars over gossip about unprofessional behaviour or affairs and the star replies. Letters to the journalists are published in 'International Mail Call' where readers seek information about their favourite stars; the stars' addresses are given for further correspondence.

Stardust has kept very much to the style established during its first decade, apart from the increase in the number of star interviews based on letters from fans. Some of the graphics, such as those for 'Neeta's Natter' have remained unchanged and look very dated with their 'flower-power' image, but these have provided the magazine with a recognizable identity. In fact, the black cat with a jewelled necklace smoking a cigarette in a long holder, is printed on company stationery. The general consensus is that although the other glossies are of high quality and good reportage, in particular *Filmfare*, which many read in addition to *Stardust*, the latter still stands out from the other magazines because its gossip has more 'bite'.

Stardust: Adverts and the Consumer

As easy as falling in love. (Even sweeps you off your feet)
[Advert for Bajaj Sunny scooter][37]

There are no detailed surveys of *Stardust's* readership beyond the circulation figures given above. The best guide is to examine the magazine's other consumers, the advertising companies that provide the finance to produce the magazine. Market research gives advertisers an idea of who forms a significant part of the readership and hence the important places to advertise, so some connection between the adverts and the readers it to be expected. However, it is likely that there is an additional readership, namely readers with less purchasing power who aspire to the consumption of these products and the corresponding lifestyle. A large proportion of this 'wannabe' readership is likely to come from among those who rent the magazines from their local 'circulating libraries'.

Stardust is heavily subsidized by its advertising: in 1996, a colour page cost Rs 80,000. This allows the magazine to have a cover price of Rs 20 although each copy costs Rs 50 to produce. Advertisers rate it as one of the 'premium' magazines for advertising consumer goods and it has more advertisements than any magazine in India, the second being the news magazine, *India Today*. The latter's different market may be seen in the products advertised, which are mostly for male business executives, including computers, shirting, luxury housing, etc.

Of the sixty-six pages of the first edition of *Stardust*, eighteen were used for advertising in black and white, for middle-class consumer goods: household utensils, sarees, vests, creams, after-shave, furniture (mostly steel cabinets), fabrics, and a camera. The only example of star endorsement was Shashi Kapoor's promotion of Burlingtons menswear.

Products advertised in recent Indian issues of *Stardust* range from household items (tea, mosquito mats, cooking oil, cleaning fluids, tableware, cooking pots, fridges), to small luxuries (greeting cards, beauty products such as cosmetics, shampoo, soaps, deodorants, aftershave), a wide spectrum of fashion (in particular foreign clothes and formal ware), to expensive hi-fi goods, holidays, and scooters. There are also some surprising government promotions for jute and state tourist boards and more 'non-family' items such as condoms, whisky, and cigarettes. Surprisingly, almost none of them features the stars who one might expect to endorse glamour and beauty products such as soaps and shampoos.

The adverts do not show a strong gender bias towards products intended for consumption by women. While it is possible that men's products feature to a large extent because women may buy these items (such as shirts and aftershave) for their men,[38] the more likely explanation lies in the circulation of the magazine. *India Today*, a largely male executive magazine, is also circulated among the family who may be less interested in the business and political pages but who want to read its coverage of the media and the arts, features, or gossip pages.[39] *Stardust* also seems to have a similar family readership, its features do not show any particular gender divisions, apart from the gender of star, type of story, etc.

The range of advertising allows a fairly clear idea of the magazine's purported readership. It is clearly aimed at an urban middle- or upper-middle-class readership, male and female, which has the purchasing power for these products. All the products belong to the category of luxury goods; even the cleaning fluids are a good deal more expensive than the usual varieties. Although it is assumed that the cinema audience largely consists of lower-class urban males,[40] there is clearly a significant middle-class group which has a deep enough interest in the Hindi film world to buy these magazines. The class emphasis here may explain the emergence of these new magazines in the 1970s as new class formations began to crystallize in urban India (Dwyer 1998).

The only difference between the domestic and international editions is the range of products advertised. The majority of the adverts in the latter are for the UK market with several for the US and one or two for Dubai. This is one of the few places where these luxury South Asian products can be advertised overseas. The others are *India Today*, some of the Indian language press (although such glossy adverts are rare), and Asian TV and radio with occasional adverts during national TV features made for the Asian community, such as the Hindi Night film series on the UK's Channel 4. The latter has adverts on about a quarter of the pages, half in colour, half in black and white. Apart from Royal Navy recruitment, all are concerned with the South Asian economy. Some are aimed at both men and women, such as marriage bureaus, astrologers, telephone companies, cable and satellite TV stations, music recordings, concerts, clubs and films, Asian hotels and restaurants, and varieties of *paan masala*. However, the majority are clearly aimed at women only, such as perfumes, jewellery, clothes, beauty products (from plastic surgery to hair products) and some adverts for South Asian food products. These give some impression of the NRI (non-resident Indian) community reading the magazines for their 'wannabe' lifestyles, and as a way of imagining India as 'home' and a world of glamour and style where the values they brought with them overseas can be fulfilled.

Issues of consumption reach beyond the adverts, and are central to the magazines, since buying or renting the magazine is already an act of consumption. However, I wish to focus on consumption as part of the glamour of this public culture. Popular novels are often called 'sex and shopping' novels because of their emphasis on an excess of consumption of mostly luxury goods.[41] There are a whole set of overlapping perspectives on consumption presented in the magazines in the photos and in the discussions. These include health and the body, which connects to discourse on sexuality, and consumption as a way of experiencing sexuality ('Buy this and you're this kind of a woman, you live this kind of a life style, you too can belong to this kind of world'). The advertisements and their images are themselves sources of fantasies for pleasure (Winship 1987). Appeals are made to the aspirations to glamour of the target audience, with comments such as 'If it's good enough for Kim Basinger, Tina Turner and Diana Ross, it's good enough for you!' (although the model for this hair treatment seems to be Asian). Fashion is a key issue here since many women's interest in women stars is due to their display of conspicuous consumption (cosmetics, fashion, hairstyles, lifestyles) (Stacey 1993); in fact throughout the magazines, stars are presented as idols of consumption, not of production. This address to women as consumers blends discourses on femininity and consumption as do women's magazines in the West, but in India there is further emphasis on class and modernity. The necessity of money to participate in this lifestyle is unquestioned, it being required even to read these magazines. Perhaps this focus on consumption has been part of the reason for the disparaging of the magazines by intellectuals. Shopping, a necessity for urban life, is often a pleasure enjoyed by many women and as such is disparaged by many men.[42]

Stardust: Language

The fact that the most popular magazines about the Hindi cinema are written in English is initially surprising. However, cinema features in these magazines as a source of glamour and a way of locating stars rather than as the object of the discussion. The major connection of the magazine is with the world of advertising, the aim clearly being to cater only to a small section of the movie-going (or video-watching) public, the section which has the highest purchasing power. This group of people may use English as their first language or at least aspire to do so, while less educated readers regard these magazines as an important means of learning a fashionable English. The magazines use their own brand of language, a special variety of English. For example:

> Mayday darling. The heat is on again. Time for beaches, martini-on-ice, bikinis and cold-showers. Not that our cooler-than-*kakdi* stars can lose their sizzle with mere *thandai*. The higher their temperatures, the better to use their libidoes with, my dears. I'm jetting to Eskimo-land already. Phew![43]

This variety is called 'Hinglish' or 'Bombay English', a mixture of non-standard varieties of English with the odd Hindi, Marathi, or Gujarati word or phrase inserted. The English used here refers to other English texts to show an insider's knowledge ('The heat is on' is the title of a song) or to provide humour ('the higher . . . the better . . . my dears', has overtones of Red Riding Hood's wolf; 'Phew!' reminds one of comic strips, or tabloid headlines); it contains non-standard varieties (one can't *use* one's libido;

and the standard plural is libidos; note also the psychoanalytic term) and non-politically correct English (Innuit is now preferred to Eskimo). The use of Hindi is not because of a lack of ability in English; the star whose English is not up to scratch is scorned as a 'vernac', a 'vern' (user of a vernacular) or a *ghati* (a Mumbaikâr's derogatory term for someone from non-metropolitan Maharashtra, from the Ghats).[44] Although most Mumbai English-speakers use a certain proportion of Hindi words in their everyday language, the use here is deliberately humorous (cooler-than-*kakdi* is a Hinglish calque which only makes sense if one known the English—outdated—idiom 'cool as a cucumber'). Hindi is used elsewhere to add spice, to show exasperation or, more often, simply to sound 'cool'. A knowing use of *desi* terms when speaking English has become hip and is used by Mumbaikârs and widely replicated in the media, even by the hippest of all, the TV VJs. It is likely[45] to be traced to the exaggerated form (which is not used by anyone in Mumbai) invented by these magazines, a code for insiders, knowing how to use it being part of the art of being cool.[46] One has to know it to gain admission to the circle of the film world, a group imagined to speak the language. It is also a way of distancing oneself from one's everyday language with its overtones of region and social group. Being able to read, it also shows one has competence in English and in Hindi. It is a fun language for modern, fashionable people; one can write letters to the magazines in this language but any attempt to speak it out of context would result in loss of face. It also has the effect of providing a special language for the international editions. I imagine that many of the readers of these editions can understand sufficient Hindi to follow a film but are unlikely to have adequate reading skills in Hindi or other vernacular languages.

A more limited use of language is in the French phrases added for extra glamour such as 'Manisha analyses *affaire d'Nana* [sic]' (*Stardust*, August 1996: Cover). I have heard the equivalent of 'pig-French' used by Indian college girls to sound cool, with knowing irony. For example, 'Pass *le* butter and *le* milk, *s'il vous plaît*'.

This delight in language and playing with it consciously for humour and effect is seen in the use of puns and word play found throughout the magazines ('And if there's anything bigger than a Himalaya, it's actress Rambha's bulky posterior pets. Check out the circumference. I always said she had an hourglass figure. With all the sand settled at the "bottom" of course: *Stardust*, April 1996: 17). The magazines delight in the language, which Dé developed in her initial years at *Stardust* and has used to critical outcry and her amusement in her novels:

Surely there is no 'bakwas' about you. 'Abhinandan' for grinding to 'kheema' the casual remarks of stars. 'Arre bhai' what happened? I started to write in English and ended in using STARDUST'S 'apnihi pukka ghat' language [*Stardust*, December 1972: 51].

It could be argued that this language has been taken up by the Indian English novel. The Indian English used by Nissim Ezekiel in poems such as his '*From* Very Indian poems in Indian English' (Ezekiel 1989: 268)[47] is a late survival of *babu* English whereas the magazine's Hinglish has been taken up by Tharoor (1994) has been reproduced best by Dé herself[48] and by Salman Rushdie.[49]

The style of the writing is exaggerated, from the breathless style of 'Neeta's Natter', full of words of address ('pets, dahlings, darlings'), exclamations and an excess of punctuation (dashes, exclamation marks, inverted commas), to the purple prose of reports and descriptions of the stars. The stars' epithets (the 'sexy [Jackie] Shroff', the 'deadly [Sanjay] Dutt') and pet names (Dabboo, Chintu, and Chimpoo, the sons of Raj Kapoor) are used regularly and this causes confusion to the new reader. This is all part of the insider's knowledge, which has to be developed by continuous reading and accumulated knowledge.

The addresses is present in much of the writing. 'Neeta's Natter' is always addressed directly to readers (forms of address as above, sign-offs such as 'From one cat to another, meeow till next month!': *Stardust*, August 1996). This all adds to the feeling of a club, the close relationship of the fan to the magazine and the magazine to the stars. The readers have further opportunities to participate by sending in questions to the stars and writing letters for publication. The narratives provide the reader with a glimpse of a world of luxury and glamour, with events taking place in five-star hotels, de-luxe restaurants, and expensive clubs. For example, many events take place in one of India's most luxurious and famous hotels, Bombay's Taj Hotel. Readers learn of the 1900s (its nightclub whose annual subscription is Rs 25,000), its Zodiac Grill (one of the most expensive restaurants in Mumbai), and its Crystal Room (used for society weddings). The reader also learns about another favoured location, the Piano Bar nightclub, and its adjacent restaurant, the China Garden, run by India's top celebrity chef, Nelson Wang, who has featured in the magazine.

This marked style of intimacy is also seen in the narratives, which are usually written in the first person which gives a direct approach, a confessional mode, the feel of the eye witness, often seeming to be in direct speech. The interviews with the stars themselves allow them to speak in the first person, furthering the effect of intimacy and revelation. The use of innuendo requires an audience and it seems as if direct appeals are made to the reader to pass judgement on the lifestyle of the stars.

Stardust: Gossip

There are three principal modes of narrative which may be presented in the form of interviews or told as narratives by the journalists. The three major forms of gossip outlined by Spacks (1985: 4–7) (gossip as intimacy, gossip as idle talk, and gossip as malice) are found in *Stardust*.

The majority of the stories belong to the broad category of melodramas (Gledhill 1987 and 1991b), tales of heartbreak, struggle, and survival. This is the gossip of intimacy. The tales of heartbreak may be due to the ending of a relationship, but the most powerful are stories of family tragedy. For example, the details of the deaths of the mothers of Juhi Chawla and Govinda in August 1996 were written of from a personal and emotional point of view, concentrating on the grief of the bereaved stars and listing all those who supported them. The tales of struggle are usually stories of male stars who rose from ordinary backgrounds and who, through luck, hard work, and faith in their own abilities, have been able to triumph over life's difficulties. Their reliance on their moral qualities, their realization of the priority of home and family, allow them to reach self-acceptance and maturity. For example, the career of Jackie Shroff features regularly in this mode.

The backgrounds of female stars are rarely discussed; for them the central issues are those of morality and acceptability. Male stars often claim that they would not marry a girl from the industry or let their daughters go into films, and so women's backgrounds are given only when they are from star families or respectable middle-class homes. The stories are often about the star women who have reached a mid-life crisis feeling they have sacrificed their education and are missing out on home and family. While the younger can say they are biding their time and intend to retire to family life, the senior stars have less room for manoeuvre. Women's struggle is to do with the lack of friendship and support in the industry; many interviews with women focus on rivalry between stars. These can be read as stories of outer happiness, and inner sorrow, a typically melodramatic form. The moral of the women's stories is that success brings its own problems. The journalists put themselves in supporting roles here, while the reader is admitted to a world of emotion.

The second is the purely promotional treatment. This is usually reserved for newcomers, who are like you and me, but often have some 'star quality', or the recently arrived crop of models. There is no gossip about these stars, just praise, flattery, and a set of glamourous photographs. In fact, all photographic material is of this nature—scandals are not corroborated by pictures by the paparazzi, nor are emotional photographs shown (except of a real life event). All the photographs concentrate on the glamorous aspects of the stars and there are usually plenty of studio photographs of the stars in the latest fashions or in theatrical costumes to accompany them.

The third category is concerned with malicious gossip and scandal. This is the arena from which the magazines derive their fame and notoriety. The gentler form is romantic gossip which exposes hidden love affairs, often between co-stars. A more malicious variety includes incidents of broken relationships, revenge, betrayal, and jealousy. This is based on the understanding that public figures lead public lives and can have no privacy. It is a refusal to allow the stars to have too simple a life, because all their transgressions will be found out. In 'Neeta's Natter' and other snippets, the magazine makes fun of the stars who are no longer fashionable and laughs at their appearance and delusions of grandeur. Professional rivalry is a major topic and stars are offered opportunities to attack each other and to respond to attacks on themselves by other people in the industry.

These three types of gossip have two main functions, namely as a way of understanding oneself and the world, and the creation of a sense of community, a feeling of belonging (cf. Hermes 1995: 121). I discuss the third, largely type of sexual gossip, below. The second function is of vital importance to the pleasure of these magazines. The depiction of the inside world of films is the main focus, establishing the credentials of the journalists and the magazines. This has the effect of providing intimacy which stars shun in real life as they often live remote and sheltered lives, surrounded by security. The magazine allows its readers to feel that they are participating in this world. This is reinforced by highly personal forms of address, creating solidarity and connections. The effect is one of intimacy and distance: the stars are personalities like you or me, but they are different in kind, in that they have an excess or surplus of everything. The creation of intimacy with the stars makes them seem close at hand and yet remote and so can function as unthreatening figures for the projection of readers' fantasies and discussions. The melodramatic mode of the narratives is central to this phenomenon, depicting the stars as emotionally charged, quasi-family figures.[50]

In summary, there is a dynamic of consumption. The magazine has an interest in creating a community of readers for its community of advertisers.

The reader consumes these stories of the stars and the advertisements. This does not have to be in a passive manner: she can read selectively, she can reinterpret the magazine in ways which are meaningful to her and has the ultimate power of refusal: not to buy or read the magazine.

Stardust: Sexuality

The major concern of film gossip, in fact any gossip is with sexuality. This is probably due to the fact it is now regarded as one of most important and problematic areas of existence as well as one of the greatest sources of pleasure. A study of the issues raised in this context shows sources of anxiety and pleasure and, like all gossip, queries dominant values.

SEX WITHOUT STRINGS! THE INDUSTRY'S ORGY OF IMMORALITY EXPOSED!
(*Stardust*, February 1995: cover)

The central concern of *Stardust* with sex and sexuality is emblazened on every cover. The interest is not just with the sexual act itself, as is often as-sumed. It discusses ideas, notions, feelings, images, attitudes and assumptions about a whole range of topics to do with sexuality such as romance, mar-riage, feminism, masculinity, femininity, gay and lesbian issues, and the presentation of the body. This concern with sexuality is hardly surprising in Mumbai where, along with lifestyle concerns, it is the dominant topic of conversation, especially among the young, upwardly mobile middle classes. These magazines are the sphere in which these major discourses on sexuality are sited outside of state locations such as educational institutions, medical discourse, population control, and censorship.

India has a very limited and heavily-censored pornography industry.[51] There are only a few men's magazines, published in English and in the vernaculars, the most widely distributed being the soft-porn magazine *Chastity*, which has many pictures of naked women, and is entirely concerned with the discussion of sexual matters whether in narratives or 'problem pages', and *Debonair* (89,000), which belongs to the same proprietors as *Star'n'style*. However, the latter is also known for its coverage of the arts, in particular poetry. Its present editor, Randhir Khare, is also a recognized poet; formerly it has had two of India's best-known poets, Adil Jussawalla and Imtiaz Dharker, working on its reviews and poetry pages. Its up-market playboy image can be seen as part of its attempts to widen the discussion of sexuality, but the soft-porn photos have caused some controversy. Women have no equivalent, which is to be expected in view of theirw lack of interest in viewing the male body displayed in magazines. There is some discussion of sexuality in the health pages of women's magazines like *Femina* (available in English, 113,000 and in Gujarati) and *Women's Era* (English 101,000 discussed at length in Naipaul 1990) but the majority of the writing is the usual female mixture of fashion, beauty, domestic tips, and romantic stories in the numerous women's magazines such as *Grhashobha* (Hindi 315: 000). In the last few years Indian editions of international magazines have been launched, including *Cosmopolitan*. The contrast remains between women's magazines (lifestyle, fashion, beauty, romance) and men's magazines, which tend to be oriented towards sports, news or business/ financial. There has also been a rapid expansion of lifestyle magazines which can be aimed at both sexes, including *Savvy, Society,* and more recently *Society Interiors, Verve* and *India Today Plus.*

The only magazine to give cover to gay issues is *Bombay Dost*, mostly in English, with a few pages in Hindi and English. This is printed in black and white on low-grade paper and is mostly the work of one person, Ashok Row Kavi. Despite its struggle to acquire distributors and outlets, it has become an important publication for many gay activists in India. Although there are lesbian columns in *Bombay Dost*, I know of no equivalent lesbian magazine.

Apart from magazines, sexuality is discussed across a wide range of media. A discussion of the discourses on sexuality presented in film[52] lies beyond the scope of this chapter. However, while the commercial films may provide visual displays of a sexually explicit nature, they pay lipservice to a much more conservative view of sexuality than the magazines, leading to a complex and contradictory presentation of sexual desire.[53] Film songs and their picturization provide greater opportunities for sexual display than dialogue and narrative sections of the films, with their specific images of clothes, body, and body language, while the song lyrics are largely to do with sexuality, ranging from romance to suggestive and overt lyrics. A number of the latter type have caused major controversies, famously 1993's *Khalnayak's* hit song '*Choli ke peeche*' ('What's underneath my blouse?') and women's groups have demonstrated outside the home of Karishma Kapoor after her songs with Govinda, including '*Sarkailo khatiya*' ('Drag your bed over here') and her '*Sexy, sexy, sexy*'.[54] The films of the so-called parallel cinema, a term which covers films ranging from the middle-brow to the avant-garde, often deal with questions of sexuality in a more explicit way. The controversy faced by 1995's *Bandit Queen*, whose ban was subsequently lifted, was widely discussed in the press and showed the variety of problems such a film had to face from censors and women's groups, while the audience greeted scenes of rape and violence towards the heroine with the whistles and foot-stamping with which they applaud sexy dance sequences.

Television, which has been seen as a threat to the film industry, is actually largely parasitic on the film industry. Much of the TV time of the new satellite and cable channels, which now number around fifty in Mumbai, is given to film, whether screening of films, programmes about stars, music shows, or audience-participation shows. TV's own unique genre, the soap opera, which is hugely popular in India, is melodramatic family, rather than sexual romance.[55]

Women's romantic fiction, whether Indian or imported, is more concerned with fantasies of love than of sex, although Shobha Dé has introduced a new form of popular, more sexually explicit writing in English, dealing with sado-masochism and lesbianism in a way not found elsewhere. In spite of a long tradition of erotic writing in India, there has been no academic study of its recent manifestations and I know of no such writing. Indian novels written in English, while not primarily erotic, contain frequent mentions of penises, masturbation, and early sexual encounters. These tend to be highly narcissistic and are treated on the same level of fascination as lavatorial matters. Gay writing has become more widespread whether overtly as in the pioneering writing of Firdaus Kanga, and recent writers such as Raj Rao, or in more covert forms in 'mainstream' writing.

As one might expect, there is no single coherent discourse on sexuality. In the West, in particular in the USA, since the 1950s the major discourse has developed from psychoanalysis, but this has had a restricted circulation in India. However, one can identify two popular trends. One is that sexual permissiveness is seen as one of the evils of westernization the concomitant of which is that the Indian woman's major concern is her honour. The other is that there is a cover-up and deliverate obfusction, a refusal to acknowledge the high number of prostitutes in Mumbai, the AIDS problem, extramarital affairs, etc. Nevertheless the abundance of discourses on virginity, the age of consent, the life of widows, eve-teasing, etc. show the centrality of sexual discourses.

'I'M A VIRGIN AND I'M STILL AT THE TOP!' MAMTA ERUPTS!
[*Stardust*, January 1994: cover]

This declaration by one of Hindi film's top sex symbols ('the *desi* sex symbol') that she is a virgin shows the high value put on controlled female sexuality. This contrasts with the images of Kulkarni in magazines and films, where she features as the most sexy of all stars. The ideal woman as presented in the magazines, as in the films, as a virgin, but often turned on by her own body in a narcissistic manner, eager for her sexual encounter with her life partner. In other words, the woman must be sexually available but only for the one, right, man, a position which can be occupied easily by the male spectator/reader. But how does the female spectator/reader find pleasure in this position? If she is heterosexual, is she obliged to take a passive, masochistic position as suggested by Mulvey (1975)?

It seems that women readers are at least equally concerned with female stars as sources of identification as with male stars as figures of sexual fantasy. These women can be seen as providing role models for the new urban woman. I argue that one of the reasons that women enjoy reading about female stars is the opportunities these features give for questioning standard views of sexuality, by setting up opposites and negotiating new possibilities. The off-screen star is as vulnerable in her own life as the readers in hers, leading the reader to adopt attitudes of empathy and protectiveness. The star must face questions such as: Is it alright to sleep with someone without being married to him? Is it acceptable to live with someone without being married? What about having a child without being married? How should one deal with one's husband's infidelities? Are women always vulnerable?

The magazines have supported some of the female stars. For instance, it is often said that some of the major female stars began their careers as porn stars. *Stardust* (February 1985), responded to these charges on behalf of the stars by claiming that stars were tricked into acting in pornographic films, where sequences with body doubles were added later.

From its beginnings, the cinema has been seen as unsuitable for respectable women. Famously, Phalke could not persuade even prostitutes to act in his films and the first female stars were from the Anglo-Indian community. This concern with respectability remains one of the major concerns for the female star. Early issues of *Filmfare* depicted female stars in traditional saris, in their homes, engaged in domestic light chores such as flower arranging, looking after sister's children, or refined activities such as painting or embroidery. Stars had to be presented as unmarried daughters or housewives with articles on how the stars liked to relax and spend their time at home. It seemed that any reference to labour was avoided, apart from the efforts the stars, who are always busy with their work, make to cope with their private lives. There is no direct reference in these magazines to women's domestic work or even the 'servant problem'. In fact one of the major features that distinguishes these magazines from women's magazines is the silence about domestic life (except in adverts).

Nargis, who trod the line of respectability very carefully (Gandhy and Thomas 199), argued forcefully for women stars to be more highly regarded. The lack of success of this viewpoint can be seen thoughout the industry whether in the much lower pay for women, or their diminished roles. It is seen clearly in contemporary magazines where male stars claim they would never marry an industry girl or let their own daughters go into the industry. Female stars will rarely admit affairs while male stars seem to boast of their conquests whether married or single.

It may be surprising then that most female stars do not take an interest in any form of feminism. They mostly reject feminism with trite remarks such as, 'Who wants to be equal to men? We're better!' A few women (Pooja Bedi, Pooja Bhatt, Anu Agrawal) step beyond the limits of female behaviour, but this is reactive rather than suggesting meaningful alternatives to those on offer.

The stories show a lack of female bonding, emphasizing rivalry between women. Although there has been numerical dominance of women among the magazine's reporters and editors, it shows that there is either male editorial control or the women have absorbed male discourses on women's relationships in order to advance their careers.[56] The photographs of the female stars can be interpreted by the female viewer as images of the inner person, following the widely-held belief that the female body expresses the idea of female sexuality, where the inner life and sexuality are the same. Women can also enjoy the fashion, the clothes, the make-up, and the hairstyles of the stars which they may copy; they can also enjoy the pleasure of identifying with their beauty.

The photographs are always of the most glamorous women, who are not necessarily leading heroines. For example, many magazines carry photos of the actress Raveena Tandon who has not had a big box-office hit for a long time. The actresses are beautiful and elegant. The larger ideal has been marginalized, although not replaced by taller, thinner women with smaller breasts and hips like western models.[57] The actress is heavily made-up, wearing a particular type of western costume which is more high street than high fashion. These often look cheap and vulgar and are not infrequently fetishistic outfits in black PVC. The actresses rarely wear Indian clothes for these shots, which is a sharp contrast to the early editions of *Filmfare* where the women wore saris. The outfits tend to reveal rather than to conceal; camera angles are often invasive, with many cleavage shots, as well as some (depilated) groin shots. However, nudity is not even considered, *Stardust's* cover of Mamta topless, even though covering her breasts, is still discussed, and much has been made over the scene in *Bandit Queen* where Seema Biswas (Phoolan Devi) is stripped naked.

Close-ups of female stars usually fetishize 'feminine qualities', emphasizing make-up and ornaments: eyelashes, lipliner, and heavy jewellery. There are frequently staged shots of couples in passionate clinches—pre-orgasmic, orgasmic, and post-coital.

Hot! Are industry men sex-starved? [*Startudst*, November 1994: cover].

While the images of the male stars are more complicated than those of female stars, the story lines are simpler. The male star can be the subject of scandal, which he can reject or enjoy, he can utter threats to would-be rivals, he can reveal himself as a sensitive soul or a survivor. These seem to approximate quite closely to the roles that the man takes on screen, unlike the woman's which are so different.[58] Cinema provides mostly positive roles for male stars, the obvious exception being the villain. The villain is a lower category of star, even when hugely popular, for the male star is almost identical with the hero, or anti-hero.

One of the most interesting star texts is that of Akshay Kumar, a box-office and magazine idol. He is discussed as a relentless womanizer and superstud; endless stories circulate about him and Raveena Tandon who may be secretly married, may be of an unmarried relationship or may have ended their relationship, but he is also important as a gay icon.

Bombay Dost ran an interview with 'the new Eros of eroticism' (*Bombay Dost*, 1995, 4(1): 8–9), accompanied by a review of Akshay's film *Main khiladi tu anadi* (I am a player, you are innocent), finding numerous homoerotic overtones and gay codes in this two-hero film. The picture accompanying a story in *Stardust* which referred directly to the *Bombay Dost* interview, has Akshay dressed in uniform with arm around action hero Sunil Shetty. Akshay Kumar's statement in *Stardust* ('I feel nice about being a gay fantasy!')[59] was reported with delight in *Bombay Dost* (1995, 4(2): 5) showing an intertexual link between the two magazines. Akshay's status in the gay community may explain the numerous photographs of him in uniform, leather, and bondage gear.[60] Akshay himself is careful in all his interviews to offend neither his homosexual fans nor homophobes; his portrayal in film magazines is usually hypermasculine, as a body-builder and a compulsive seducer of women, which is open to gay readings.

While photographs of many other male stars suggest gay readings, this is often inherent in the subject matter, photographs of the male body, rather than necessarily saying anything about the stars' sexuality. Codes of looking (men look, women are looked at) make it difficult to eroticize the male body for the female look or to allow for the voyeuristic female.[61] Dyer (1982) argues that images of the eroticized male body appear as gay images because the active gaze is thought to be male. This requires men in photographs to avert their eyes to deny the gaze, to appear as action types, or to be hysterically male. Whether these rules apply in an Indian context is unclear. However, the direct look of the male star, the recent craze for body building, which on small men heightens the gay effect, as does the tight clothing required to display their muscles, and the use of soft textures and gentle lighting in the photographs certainly do not inhibit a gay interpretation of the images.

However, the magazines rarely speak directly about gay issues. There are infrequent suggestions that stars are gay, and, more rarely, coded references to their orientation,[62] suggestions of a gay readership,[63] and the occasional photograph such as *Stardust's* picture of two female stars, Farah and Khushboo, engaged in a passionate kiss.[64] The style of the magazines certainly lends itself to camp readings, yet camp interpretations are unpredictable. For example, the camp following of top female stars such as Sharmila Tagore and Meena Kumari, the preferred role models for drag artists, is likely to be because of the excess of femininity of the former and the tragic on- and off-screen images of the latter.[65] There seems to be little similar to the western pre-pubescent desire of girls for androgynous, non-threatening males as typified by boy-groups such as Boyzone. However, the above interpretations show a western interpretation which may not stand up to scrutiny in a serious analysis of Indian sexuality which is so far lacking.[66] The major stories are about heterosexual love and sex; the photographs of couples are almost all male and female.

The appearance of the hero indicates popular perceptions of beauty. He must be tall, and fair, usually north Indian and clean-shaven.[67] His clothes are nearly always western; a number of shots are designed to emphasize the physique; his clothes may be torn, or he may be topless; covered in sweat with his hair slicked back, or dressed as western actors (Shah Rukh Khan has been photographed dressed as Rudolph Valentino). In other words, the presentation of the male star is as hypermasculine or active.

In addition to the male practice of body-building mentioned above, two other major forms of body shaping have emerged in India in recent years. One is dieting, the other is plastic surgery. Stars are regularly criticized for putting on weight and praised for weight loss. Although this is seen in early issues of *Stardust*, it was clearly absent from early issues of *Filmfare* where many of the stars were large by today's western ideals. Anorexia and bulimia are not known as such in India and a tracing of these images of the body remains to be done.

Far more drastic is the use of plastic surgery. Several stars have talked about it in public; several have clearly gone under the knife. However, a major feature on plastic surgery in *Stardust* was the most public and controversial discussion so far (*Stardust*, May 1996: 44–52). It began by saying how common plastic surgery is in Hollywood and reported Dolly Parton's revelations about her own plastic surgery. There then follows an interview with two cosmetic surgeons, Dr Narendra Pandya and Dr Vijaya Sharma. The magazine then gives its own list of male and female stars who seem to have had work done on them. The most frequent operations are breast implants for younger female stars, who often demand excessively large breasts with prominent nipples. Across the board, the most popular operation is the nose-job and more rarely liposuction and breast upliftment, while many older stars have undergone face-lifts. The often impossible demands of the stars reflect the beauty priorities, namely to be taller and to have lighter skin. Perhaps the most surprising part of the whole piece was Sharma's advice on which stars need what sort of plastic surgery which seemed very close to British tabloid-newspaper discussion.

Despite these forms of body improvement, health trends such as reasonable exercise, healthy eating, sensible drinking, and quitting smoking are discussed less frequently and stars are even featured smoking.

The majority of the stories in the magazine are concerned with sex, love, and romance. These give different values to romance than the images portrayed on screen. On screen the focus is on the struggle with the ultimate happy ending, usually a wedding or at least the promise of one. In the magazines the emphasis is on the problems of romance, its scarcity, its lack, the failures of the marriage, the infidelities, rather than on its success. This can be interpreted as a specialized form of romance reading:

> Romance reading, in this view, is escapist, cathartic and addictive, and serves the same gender-specific functions for women as does pornography for men [Singh and Uberoi 1994: 94].

Although the terms 'escapist, cathartic and addictive' raise more problems then they answer (escape from what to where and why? etc.), this remark raises an important issue avoided by Radway (1987) in her study of romance, namely the question of whether readers find the narratives of romance sexually arousing. It seems more likely that the pleasure in *Stardust* is found in the melodramatic mode in that the stars have everything—looks, money, fame—yet they still have to worry about romance and they are still not happy. The stories of stars are more heightened versions of romance along the lines of betrayal by one's partner with another desirable person, and the public knowledge of the situation. It also allows readers among whom dating is restricted, premarital sex is taboo, and arranged marriages—however loosely we use the term—are still the norm, to fantasize about such relationships and to learn about how they would behave in certain situations. They allow readers to be able to discuss issues of romance, love, and sexuality.

Despite the prominence given to romance and sexual liaisons, there is clear emphasis on the family and on controlled sexuality, especially in the case of women. There is an underlying theme about reconciling individuality with wider duties. The stories endlessly go over problems of romance and love in heterosexual monogamy.

Marriage is a key issue in the magazine and there is no questioning the respect given to marriage. Occasional discussions on 'living in' always see it as a poor or unacceptable substitute for marriage. Marriage and a career in cinema are seen as irreconcilable for women. Women are expected to retire from the industry after marriage, partly because fans will not accept a married woman in romantic roles and also because her place is in the home. The only possibility of a return is to play mothers and character roles.

A regularly occurring feature is of the secret marriage between star couples. In 1995–6 a major story was published concerning the possible marriage of Akshay Kumar and Raveena Tandon. There were rumours of wedding photographs although these were never seen. The issue of *souten* (co-wife) is usually silently acknowledged: an article about Dharmendra's (star) children Bobby and Sunny Deol will not mention Hema Malini while an article about Dharmendra and Hema will not mention Bobby and Sunny. Divorce is seen as rather scandalous with even the divorce of star's parents reported. The issue of whether to divorce or to take a second wife is frequently raised, for example Sridevi (who was reported to be Mithun Chakraborty's second wife in 1990) has had recently a so-called second marriage with Boney Kapoor.

All melodrama highlights the importance of the family. Even if characters in a melodrama are not relatives, they take on functions and roles of relatives to assume any importance.[68] Another melodramatic feature is that the families of stars take on the star's aura. The names of star partners are well known, stories are run about how wives of unfaithful husbands are forgiving, how the star has suffered due to the ill-health of a partner, etc. Star children are a regular feature and are rarely mentioned without some reference to their parents, such as Sanjay Dutt (Nargis and Sunil Dutt), Karishma Kapoor (Babita and Randhir Kapoor, son of Raj Kapoor), Twinkle Khanna (Dimple and Rajesh Khanna). On the occasion of a marriage or the birth of children to stars, all enmities are dropped and congratulations, purple prose, and smoochy photos are in order.

Concluding Remarks

I conclude this piece by looking at the pleasure of reading these magazines provide. Following Ang (1985), I argue that although readers would accept that they read the magazines for pleasure, no one can define what these pleasures actually are. Instead, I look at some of the mechanisms of pleasure.

The most obvious pleasure is often overlooked, which is the act of reading itself. Radway's study (1987) of the reading of romance fiction found that one of the central pleasures was in designating time for oneself, refusing the demands of one's family. Hermes (1995) builds on this and finds that reading women's magazines is a secondary activity for filling time, the readers saying that they read these instead of novels because they fill gaps in the day and yet are easy to put down. This can clearly apply to the consumption of magazines in India but there is no study of domestic reading practices. These include those suggested by personal experience, such as waiting for food to cook, during the afternoon rest, or, in Mumbai, on the long commute to the office as a way of shutting out the rest of the commuters. In India, the magazine circulates among the family, some of whom may just pick it up briefly, and enjoy only the visual pleasure such as the photographs of beautiful people, clothes, consumer items, etc.

However, although Radway focused on reading in her research, she was unable to draw firm conclusions about the pleasures of reading. Most importantly, readers did not give enough information about whether they found the stories erotic or sexually exciting. The problems of eliciting such responses remain.

A second central pleasure is extra-textual, namely the pleasure of an 'imagined' community of readers (Hermes 1995), thus gaining an imaginary and temporary sense of identity and seeing the community as an extension of the family for the siting of melodramatic events. Gossip is circulated by the magazines through melodramatic stories, narratives in which the readers 'get to know' the star are addressed directly by the narratives, and share the consumption fantasies of the adverts. This is encouraged by the style of *Stardust* which invites the reader to become part of the inner world, where the stars also read the magazine. The discussions of the stars and their lives, their romances, marriages, and reconciliations become like interventions by other family members. The focus on sexuality is that the stars negotiate the concerns the readers face in their own lives (Dyer 1986). Although the concept of finding oneself through sexuality has prevailed in the West since the seventeenth century (Foucault 1981: 6–7), the strength of this growing belief in India remains unclear.

An examination of the stories raises the question: Why do the stories contradict all 'normal expectations' of behaviour and the roles associated with the star personae on screen? Clearly the audience is not passive receivers of these messages but can interpret them in a wide variety of ways. The active role of audience in folk and other performances in India has been noted by Beck (1989) and Kothari (1989) in that the audience uses texts as way of dealing with inner dramas, not as models of behaviour. This has also been noted among viewers of soap operas in the West, where the emphasis is not on 'escape' but on ways dealing with one's everyday life (Ang 1985: 3). Dyer (1986) argues that the lives of stars are places to discuss sexual morality, the role of the individual and of the family, the understanding of the body, consumer society, etc. Gandhy and Thomas (1991) apply this approach to three female stars of Hindi cinema,[69] and draw attention to the fact that the star personae off screen:

> frequently encompass behaviours that are decidedly subversive of the strict social mores of Indian society and would be considered 'scandalous' in any other context, even by many of their most dedicated fans. Of course they do not simply transgress: stars are represented as finely balancing their transgressions with personifications of ideal behaviour especially in the domains of kinship and sexuality. Both the films and the sub-text of gossip about stars are most usefully seen as debates around morality, in particular as negotiations about the role of 'tradition' in a modernising India [Gandhy and Thomas 1991: 108].

An undoubted source of pleasure lies in the creation and fulfilment of the desires of the readers, in a new urban, consumer society. The links between cinema and desire, consumerism and capitalism and desire are highly complex (Laplace 1987). While mass media and popular culture embody and communicate society's dominant ideology they also give the grounds for resisting them. The magazines must seek and create their market, but the readers also choose what they prefer. The magazines can create desires and fulfil them, but the readers can subvert them so that their own desires and needs are met. The content of the magazines must be relevant to the fantasies and anxieties which dominate the readers' concerns. Hermes (1995: 48) identifies two dominant fantasies which can be fulfilled by such magazines, namely control through understanding other people's emotions; and the control of imagining difficult scenarios and how one would cope if faced with them in real life.

We should be wary of thinking that the reader absorbs magazines passively at face value. Readers may have their own ways of reading. They can choose which stories to read and which photos to look at; they can read with a sense of irony and humour, whether a camp style as identified by Hermes, or just as part of being a cool, urban person. The magazine sends itself up, notably in 'Neeta's Natter' and the stars themselves point out they should not take it all too seriously:

> 'Stardust' proudly flaunts that it is a gossip and fun-seeking magazine, and that teaches us to have a sense of humour.[70]

The impact of the language of *Stardust* on South Asian writers in English was mentioned above, but the magazine's star stories are also appearing in the novels of Dé and Tharoor.[71] India's daily papers are now taking on star stories as features; new cable and satellite TV links are allowing more and more of this gossip to circulate to the new aspirants to this world of glamour and modernity. For example, Zee TV now offers a whole spectrum of film spin-offs in addition to the films themselves, including song shows, chart rundowns, quizzes, etc. The magazines have not stood still: *Stardust*, along with other magazines, now makes its own weekly TV show, using the language of 'Neeta's Natter', and is already available on the Internet.

Taking these magazines seriously allows us to have a closer look at the concerns and aspirations of an emerging social group. A study of the consumption of these magazines by the diaspora would provide further rewards. Almost universally condemned as trash, an analysis of the magazines reveals the creation of an 'imagined' community of readers and consumers of a new public culture. Unlike readers of women's magazines who fantasize about perfect selves, the study of film magazines shows multiple points of identification and enunciation of fantasies.

In looking at the magazines, it is clear that the central underlying themes are the issues facing these new classes, at a time when values are shifting rapidly and massive social changes are taking place in Mumbai. This can be seen in anxieties about class and respectability. For example, a recent issue of *Stardust* dealt with questions of class, money, and 'modern' views in one article (*Stardust*, May 1996: 60–6). Some film stars were hired by a diamond merchant to perform at his brother's wedding for large sums of money. In conservative terms, being hired to dance at a wedding has overtones of the *mujra* and hence associations with courtesans and prostitution. The magazine solicited the opinion of a number of stars. One admitted she had performed and taken money but claimed to feel degraded. Some stars denied any knowledge of the event, some said they had been tricked, while others said that it was shocking and degrading to the industry that any of its members should have behaved in this manner. A few of the younger female stars said that they thought a big fuss was being made over nothing and there was no problem in performing at such events. This presentation of a whole range of views allows the reader to consider this story of the breaking of a taboo from a number of perspectives. Since the magazine does not give an editorial line, the reader is allowed to draw her own conclusion on the issues raised.

Stardust does not stand apart from other cultural products, but it is a major source of pleasure among a whole range of forms. Its economy of pleasure centred around leisure, consumption, fantasy, and humour; its new language and modes of expression have reached the upwardly mobile middle classes in a national and international (diasporic) readership, tying together this class across the nation.

Notes

1. I am grateful to Shobha Dé, Maithili Rao, and Amrutlal Shah for lengthy discussions of the magazines; also Suresh Chabria and the library staff of the National Film and Television Archive, Pune; Ashok Row Kavi of *Bombay Dost*; Khalid Mohammed and the staff of *Filmfare*; and Ashwin Varde and the staff of *Stardust*, for helping to provide materials and advice on this project. Thanks also to Jerry Pinto for collecting materials and updating my information.
2. See 'Introduction' to this volume.
3. The exceptions include studies of billboards: Haggard (1988) and Srivatsan (1991); Manuel (1993) touches on concerns important to cinema in his wider discussion of the music cassette industry; and there has been some work on soap operas including Mitra (1993) and Lutgendorf (1995).
4. This reflects the wider academic neglect of the long history of Indian newspapers, magazines, and literary periodicals which began in India in the early nineteenth century, and has expanded to include film magazines, women's magazines, and lifestyle magazines. These now number 28,491 according to the *Lintas Media Guide India, 1995*.
5. See following pages.
6. See following pages for a further discussion of the readership of the magazines.
7. See Uberoi, this volume.
8. See following pages.
9. This became the official name in English of the city of Bombay in 1996. The people of the city who were called 'Bombayites', are now called 'Mumbaikârs'.
10. Hermes (1995: 121) uses Anderson's term 'imagined community' to describe the readership of women's magazines, while Radway (1991) extends Fish's term 'interpetive community' to cover non-academic reading communities.
11. McRobbie herself revised her 1980 study in 1987. Reprinted as chapters 5 and 6 in McRobbie (1991).
12. See following pages.

13. The stars who receive the most coverage in the magazines are not necessarily the biggest box-office stars. It could be said that there is a separate category of 'magazine stars'. Rajadhyaksha and Willemen (1995: 186) suggest this is true of Rekha.

14. Genres of magazines are not altogether clear-cut. There may be overlap between the various genres in formal terms and consumers may categorize the magazines differently. For example, Hermes (1995) finds what she took to be a 'feminist magazine' is seen as a 'women's magazine' by most of the readers in her survey.

15. The chapters in Glendhill (1991) a show how central Dyer (1979) and (1986) are to the study of the star. Ellis (1992) is an important contribution to the study of the star. He shows how the star is created within the films themselves as vehicles for star performances which in turn build on images in other films and in other media. He argues for a study of these performances which touches on the star's cultural meanings, acting, performance, personality, and national status and the implications of these for identity, desire, and ideology. He asks: How do stars relate to social meaning and values? How do they reconcile, mask, or expose ideological contradictions? What are their roles as utopian fantasies? Who generates and directs the images of the stars? How does the star as a cultural figure generate tension around glamour but also hard work and dedication? What is the star's role as a national icon? While such a lengthy study lies beyond the scope of this chapter, I plan to focus on such questions in a forthcoming paper.

16. Film magazines began at this time in other regional Indian cinemas but the discussion here focuses on those that are published from Mumbai unless otherwise specified.

17. Rajadhyaksha and Willemen (1995: 17–30) give details of mostly non-star magazines in their chronology of Indian cinema.

18. This was the silent period of cinema, so language issues were important only for title cards. Many of the key figures of the Bombay film industry were Gujarati speakers; at this time Gujarati was the main commercial language of Bombay so its use in the cinema industry alongside Hindi/Urdu was not surprising. However, by the 1950s it seems that English had come to replace Gujarati and was the second language of the Bombay film industry.

19. Other trade publications include *Film Information*, 1973–, *Super Box Office*, 1985– , and *Complete Cinema*, 1986–.

20. A further type of publication are journals dedicated to Indian art cinema such as the *Indian Film Quarterly*, 1957–, Deep Focus, 1987–, etc.

21. The magazine was distributed in Pakistan and the cover gave a separated PRs price, although this was the year since which Indian films have been banned in Pakistan.

22. See following pages.

23. A point made by Ashwin Varde, former editor of *Stardust*, interview, Mumbai, December 1994.

24. The social and economic reasons underlying the rapid expansion of Mumbai's advertising industry at this time are harder to discern, though international comparisons suggest that advertising only really took off in the late 1960s. The political situation is also unclear: I have found no evidence of censorship during the national Emergency (1975–7) when journalists were strictly curtailed.

25. Note that these figures are only numbers sold; most magazines are lent through 'circulating libraries' where they can be rented for around Rs 5 per night; the purchase price is Rs 20. Most copies are read by several people before they are sold and recycled at an even lower price.

26. The Gujarati version contains a page or two of information on the Gujarati film industry, but the main features are translated from the English version. The advertisements are considerably downmarket.

27. The only other magazines with international editions are *Movie* (1989–) and *Cineblitz* (1989–). They both give cover prices for the UK, USA, Canada, and Holland.

28. The major difference between the Indian and overseas versions is that the advertising caters to different markets (see discussion in following pages). The same stories may run in different months' editions of the magazine.

29. The circulation figure for the whole Magna stable is said to be approaching half a million.

30. *The Lintas Media Guide India* (1995: 42) suggests 113,000.

31. Amitabh Bachchan cited it as the only film magazine he enjoyed, interview, Mumbai (1996).

32. Devyani Chaubal, queen of gossip columnists, was the star journalist in the magazine's heyday. She wrote about herself as a star and carried stories about how the stars were in love with her. The magazine folded up in 1990 after a journalists' strike and was sold by the Somani group to a Delhi buyer along with the 'men's magazine' *Debonair*. Early copies are said to be unavailable after a fire at the offices.

33. Other Magna publications include *Showtime* (1984–) (a star magazine), *Savvy, Health and Nutrition, Parade, Society, Society Interiors, Society Fashion, Island* (a Mumbai magazine), *Family* (a Bangalore magazine) and *Citadel* (a Pune magazine). Magna also publishes romantic fiction and has recently published Mohan Deep's biography of Madhubala.

34. The Magna group now has its own seven-storey building in the inner suburb of Prabhadevi.

35. 'One of the few contemporary Indian film stars with a legendary status far outstripping her screen roles'. Rajadhyaksha and Willemen (1995: 186).

36. Celebrations of the number of weeks a film has run. Hence a silver jubilee means the film has had a twenty-five week run.

37. *Stardust*, January 1995.
38. All women's magazines have a high male consumption in the West. Hermes (1995) draws attention to the overlap in men's reading of the magazines between serious consumption and ironic or camp consumption.
39. The advertisements in these pages are not distinguishable from the others in the magazine.
40. See preceding pages.
41. This is seen in the novels of Shobha Dé (Dwyer 1998).
42. Shopping has been seen as *the* gay male activity in the West, as mocked in a gay chant of the early 1990s: 'We're here, we're queer and we're not going shopping.'
43. 'Neeta's Natter', *Stardust*, May 1996: 7.
44. Used for Mamta Kulkarni, *Stardust*, March (1995: 79).
45. The use of *deshi* images (street barbers, old women dancing) found on music videos and films by fashionable directors like Mani Ratnam may suggest a wider phenomenon.
46. This use of language is seen in Dé novels; see Dwyer (1998) for an analysis of the criticism and Dé's defence.
47. Many attempts were made in literature to produce an Indian English, notably in Raja Rao's *Kanthapura*, 1938. G.V. Dessani's unique brand of English seems to have been the role model for that of Rushdie, although no direct genealogy can be traced.
48. See Dé (1992).
49. See Rushdie (1995), in particular the passage on Nargis and Sunil Dutt (Rushdie 1995: 137–8).
50. Brooks (1976: 4) argues that characters take on essential, psychic features of family relations, including father, mother, child.
51. I know of no study of this industry in India. Imported pornographic films are said to be widely available for hire and screened in cafés, and I have heard of a series of pornographic films in Malayalam. Posters in urban streets advertise the showing of 'hot' films but these include medical films and western films appropriated as pornography. In Mumbai in 1991 a much advertised 'hot' film was Peter Greenaway's *The Cook, the Thief, the Wife and her Lover*.
52. Very little has been written about this. Uberoi (1997) gives a lively account of female desire in Guru Dutt's (1962) *Sahib, Bibi aur Ghulam*.
53. See Kasbekar (this volume).
54. From *Raja Babu* and *Khuddar* respectively.
55. Neale (1986) argues that melodrama is a fantasy of love rather than sex.
56. See a feature on women reporters in *Filmfare*, 23 April (1996: 3).
57. See following pages for a discussion of the body.
58. See following pages for a discussion of morality.
59. Akshay Kumar, in *Stardust*, June (1995: 82).

60. A recent cover of *Filmfare* showed him dressed as the 'patron saint' of gays, Saint Sebastian.

61. Theories of the gaze are mostly Eurocentric. The studies of the practice of *darshan* by Babb (1981) and Eck (1985) do not illuminate the concept of scopophilia.

62. For example a leading male star (refered to by name) is called 'mamu', which is gay slang for a gay man. *Stardust*, May (1996: 12).

63. 'It wouldn't be surprising if the mercilessly handsome Bobby Deol is someday voted "Most Likely to Guest Star in Masturbation Fantasies" by both men and women alike'. *Stardust Annual* (1996: 221).

64. No date, see 'Best of *Stardust*', III (1989–90: 16).

65. Dyer (1986) analyses the camp following of Judy Garland.

66. Kakar (1989) being the only study.

67. Although the male stars from south India usually sport moustaches the north Indian male stars rarely do. This is a marked feature since most men in north India have moustaches. This may be for a variety of reasons but in the case of the stars shows their upper class and even high caste status. See Cohen (1995).

68. See Brooks (1976: 4) and Neale (1986).

69. Fearless Nadia (1910–96), Nargis (1929–81), and Smita Patil (1955–86).

70. Rekha, in *Stardust*, August (1996: 46).

71. 'The novel parodies other genres precisely in their role as genres; it exposes the conventionality of their form and their language' Bakhtin (1981: 5).

REFERENCES

Ang, Ien, 1985, *Watching Dallas: Soap Opera and the Melodramatic Imagination*, London: Routledge.

Appadurai, Arjun and Carol A. Breckenridge, 1995, 'Public Modernity in India', in C.A. Breckenridge (ed.), *Consuming Modernity: Public Culture in a South Asian World*, London: University of Minnesota Press: 1–20.

Babb, L.A., 1981, 'Glancing: Visual Interaction in Hinduism', *Journal of Anthropological Research*, 37 (4), 387–401.

Bakhtin, Mikhail M., 1981, *The Dialogic Imagination: Four Essays by M.M. Bakhtin*, trans. C. Emerson and M. Hoequist, Austin: University of Texas Press [Essays of 1934–41, Orig. pub. 1975].

Beck, Brenda E.F., 1989, 'Core Triangles in the Folk Epics of India', in S.H. Blackburn *et al.* (eds), *Oral Epics in India*, 155–75.

Brooks, Peter, 1976, *The Melodramatic Imagination: Balzac, Henry James, Melodrama and the Mode of Excess*, New Haven: Yale University Press.

Cohen, Lawrence, 1995, 'The Pleasure of Castration: The Postoperative Status of Hijras, Jankhas and Academics', in P. Abramson and S.D. Pinkerton (eds), *Sexual Nature, Sexual Culture*, Chicago: University of Chicago Press, 276–304.

Desani, G.V., 1948, *All About H. Hatterr*, rpt. 1972, London: Penguin.

Dé, Shobha, 1992, *Starry Nights*, New Delhi: Penguin.

Dickey, Sara, 1993a, *Cinema and the Urban Poor in South India*, Cambridge: Cambridge University Press.

———, 1993b, 'The Politics of Adulation: Cinema and the Production of Politicians in South India', *The Journal of Asian Studies*, 52(2), May, 340–72.

Dwyer, Rachel, 1998, ' "Starry Nights": The Novels of Shobha Dé, in Th. D'haen (ed.), *Unwriting Empire*, in Series 'Cross/Cultures: Readings in the Post/Colonial Literatures in English', vol. 30, Amsterdam and Atlanta, Rodopi, 117–33.

Dyer, Richard, 1977, 'Entertainment and Utopia', *Movie* 24, Spring, 2–13.

———, 1979, *Stars*, London: British Film Institute.

———, 1982, 'Don't Look Now: The Male Pin-up', *Screen*, 23 (3–4), September–October, 61–73.

———, 1986, *Heavenly Bodies: Film Stars and Society*, London: British Film Institute.

———, 1993, *The Matter of Images: Essays on Representations*, London: Routledge.

Eck, Diana L., 1985, *Darsan: Seeing the Divine Image in India*, 2nd edn, Chambersburg: Anima.

Ellis, John, 1992, *Visible Fictions: Cinema, Television, Video*, London: Routledge [first edn 1982].

Ezekiel, Nissim, 1989, 'From Very Indian Poems in Indian English', in his *Collected Poems, 1952–88*. With an introduction by Gieve Patel, Delhi: Oxford University Press.

Foucault, Michel, 1981, *A History of Sexuality*, vol. I: An Introduction, trans. Robert Hurley, Harmondworth: Penguin.

Gandhy, Beroze and Rosie Thomas, 1991, 'Three Indian Film Stars', in Christine Gledhill (ed.), *Stardom: Industry of Desire*, Routledge: London: 107–31.

Gledhill, Christine (ed.), 1987, *Home is Where the Heart is: Studies in Melodrama and the Woman's Film*, London: BFI Books.

———, 1988, 'Pleasurable Negotiations', in E.D. Pribram (ed.), *Female Spectators: Looking at Film and Television*, London: Verso, 64–89.

———, (ed.), 1991a, *Stardom: Industry of Desire*, Routledge: London.

———, 1991b, 'Signs of Melodrama', in Gledhill 1991a, 207–32.

Haggard, S., 1988, 'Mass Media and the Visual Arts in Twentieth-century South Asia: Indian Film Posters, 1947-Present', *South Asia Research*, 8(2), May: 78–88.

Hermes, Joke, 1995, *Reading Women's Magazines: An Analysis of Everyday Media*, Cambridge: Polity Press.

Kabir, Nasreen (ed.), 1985. *Les stars du cinéma indien*, Paris: Centre Georges Pompidou/Centre Nationale de la Cinematographie.

Kakar, Sudhir, 1989, *Intimate Relations: Exploring Indian Sexuality*, New Delhi: Viking.

Karanjia, B.K., 1984, 'Le Star-système', in A. Vasudeva and P. Lenglet, *Les cinemas indiens*, CinémAction 30, Paris: Editions du Cerf, 150–7.

Kothari, Komal, 1989, 'Performers, Gods, and Heroes in the Oral Epics of Rajasthan'. in S.H. Blackburn *et al.* (eds), *Oral Epics in India*, 102–17.

Lintas Media Guide India, 1995.

Lutgendorf, Philip, 1995, 'All in the (Raghu) Family: A video Epic in Cultural Context', in L.A. Babb and S.S. Wadley (eds), *Media and the Transformation of Religion in South Asia*, Philadelphia: University of Pennsylvania Press, 217–53.

McCracken, Ellen, 1993, *Decoding Women's Magazines: From Mademoiselle to Ms*, New York: St. Martin's Press.

McRobbie, Angela, 1991, *Feminism and Youth Culture: From 'Jackie' to 'Just Seventeen'*, London: Macmillan.

Manuel, Peter, 1993, *Cassette Culture: Popular Music and Technology in North India*, Chicago: University of Chicago Press.

Mishra, Vijay, 1985, 'Towards a Theoretical Critique of Bombay Cinema', *Screen*, 26 (3–4): 133–46.

Mishra, Vijay, Peter Jeffery and Brian Shoesmith, 1989, 'The Actor as Parallel Text in Bombay Cinema', *Quarterly Review of Film and Video*, 11: 49–68.

Mitra, Ananda, 1993, *Television and Popular Culture in India: A Study of the Mahabharat*, New Delhi: Sage Publication.

Modleski, Tania, 1982, *Loving with a Vengeance: Mass-produced Fantasies for Women*, London: Routledge.

Mulvey, Laura, 1975, 'Visual Pleasure and Narrative Cinema', *Screen*, 16 (3): 6–18, rpt in *Screen*, 1992.

———, 1981, 'Afterthoughts on "Visual Pleasure and Narrative Cinema" Inspired by King Vidor's *Duel in the Sun* (1946)', *Framework*, 15/16/17: 12–15.

Naipaul, V.S., 1990, *A Million Mutinies Now!* London: Heinemann.

Neale, Steve, 1986, 'Melodrama and Tears', *Screen*, 27 (6): 6–22.

Pfleiderer, Beatrix and Lothar Lutze, 1985, *The Hindi Film: Agent Re-agent of Cultural Change*, New Delhi: Manohar.

Radway, Janice, 1987, *Reading the Romance: Women, Patriarchy and Popular Literature*, London: Verso.

———, 1991, 'Interpretive Communities and Variable Literacies: The Functions of Romance Reading', in C. Mukerji and M. Schudson (eds), *Rethinking Popular Culture: Contemporary Perspectives in Cultural Studies*, Berkeley: University of California Press.

Rajadhyaksha, Ashish and Paul Willemen, 1995, *An Encyclopaedia of Indian Cinema*, London: British Film Institute.

Rao, Raja, 1938, *Kanthapura*, 2nd edn 1974, Delhi: Oxford University Press.

Rushdie, Salman, 1995, *The Moor's Last Sigh*, London: Cape.

Sharma, Ashwani, 1993, 'Blood Sweat and Tears: Amitabh Bachchan, Urban

Demi-god', in P. Krikham and J. Thumim (eds), *You Tarzan: Masculinity, Movies and Men*, London: Lawrence and Wishart: 167–80.

Singh, Amita Tyagi and Patricia Uberoi, 1994, 'Learning to "Adjust": Conjugal Relations in Indian Popular Fiction', in *Indian Journal of Gender Studies*, 1(1): 91–120.

Spacks, Patricia Meyer, 1985, *Gossip*, New York, Alfred A. Knopf.

Srivatsan, R., 1991, 'Looking at Film Hoardings: Labour, Gender, Subjectivity and Everyday Life in India', *Public Culture*, 4 (1, Fall), 1–23.

Stacey, Jackie, 1993, *Star Gazing: Hollywood Cinema and Female Spectatorship*, London: Routledge.

Tharoor, Shashi, 1994, *Showbusiness*, London: Picador.

Uberoi, Patricia, 1997, 'Dharma and Desire, Freedom and Destiny', in Meenakshi Thapan (ed.), *Embodiment: Essays on Gender and Identity*, Delhi: Oxford University Press, 145–71.

Vasudevan, Ravi, 1989, 'The Melodramatic Mode and Commercial Cinema', *Screen*, 30 (3): 29–50.

Winship, Jannice, 1987, *Inside Women's Magazines*, London: Pandora.

Hidden Pleasures

Negotiating the Myth of the Female Ideal in Popular Hindi Cinema

ASHA KASBEKAR

C INEMA, AS Metz (1975) observed, is founded on scopophilia (the pleasure of looking) and therefore it constantly devises narrative strategies to solicit the 'look' and mobilize the scopic drive. In popular Hindi cinema, the film narrative is organized in such a manner that scopophilia, catered for through strategies of overt spectacle and display, takes priority over epistemophilia, (the desire to know, or to 'find out'). It has already been recognised that '. . . the Bombay film-story does not generally have an unexpected conclusion, it only has a predictable climax' (Nandy 1981: 90) and that what is important in the Hindi film is '*how* things will happen rather than *what* will happen next' (Thomas 1985: 130). Central to the pleasures of heterosexual scopophilia is the role of the woman, and, as in Hollywood films, in Hindi cinema too she functions primarily to address the erotic gaze and constitutes an indispensable ingredient in look-soliciting strategies.

The aim of this chapter is not to provide a critique of the patriachally defined female stereotypes that pervade the Hindi screen, but to examine the cultural negotiations with regimes of power that must take place in order to successfully present the woman as an erotic spectacle. It aims to show the commercial and ideological pressures that are exerted on film-makers to make a 'spectacle' of the woman, and the strategies and subterfuges that the industry must deploy in order to legitimize such erotic voyeurism without antagonizing the state, civil society, or female members of its spectating public.

The Organization of Pleasure

Popular Hindi cinema caters to a vast, heterogenous, cross-class audience which is not always entirely familiar with the Hindi language. In order to maximize its market share, it acknowledges the composite nature of its nationwide public and privileges visual and non-verbal modes of address. The frequent exhibitions of colourfully choreographed dances, daring fights, sumptuous sets, extravagant decor, dazzling costumes and iconic representations of dramatic tension[1] are examples of the industry's responses to the commercial need to prioritize spectacle over verbal address. Additionally, the complex system of film financing, whereby distributors, exhibitors, recording companies and other investors in the industry exert considerable influence on the kind of pleasures that are to be provided within a film, places further constraints on the popular Hindi film.

Ever since the establishment of its major studios, Hollywood has catered to its global audiences by organizing the production and marketing of its films around 'genres', each with its own distinctive 'system of orientations, expectations and conventions that circulate between industry, text and subject' (Neale 1980: 19). This has enabled the industry to predict audience expectations, guide their viewing, and accordingly cater to the differing needs of varied audiences (Cooke 1985: 58). Such an arrangement is commercially viable because studios calculate their profits by an averaging of total profits. In contrast, the contemporary Hindi film industry displays a conspicuous lack of generic differentiation, with most films belonging to the 'omnibus' genre characterized by a romantic plot with melodramatic renditions, enlivened by extravagant songs, dances, slapstick comedy, and innumerable sub-plots or other narrative digressions.

This was, however, not always so. Early Indian cinema too organized its production and marketing around genres, and although unlike the Hollywood genres all (bar a handful) had songs/ dance/spectacle, each genre possessed a 'recognizable repertoire of conventions running across visual imagery, plot, character, setting, modes of narrative development, music and stars' (Cooke 1985) which orientated the viewing of its spectating public. In the 1930s, each studio (or 'banner' as it was referred to in the trade), often organized around a charismatic leader, specialized in particular kinds of films with, of course, some degree of overlap among them. Bombay Talkies specialized in romances with high production values, whereas

Prabhat in Pune and New Theatres in Calcutta concentrated on devotional/ mythological films as well as 'socials' (films that proposed social reform). New Theatres' own speciality lay in screen adaptations of literary master- pieces. The Bombay-based Wadia Movietone relied on the spectacular stunts of 'fearless' Nadia to draw in the crowds, while Minerva devoted it- self to equally spectacular historicals that starred its owner/director Sohrab Modi.[2]

The rise of the independent producer in the 1940s and the overall in- crease in audience numbers brought new economic pressures to bear upon the conditions of production and marketing. Whereas studios could average out their profits over several films, for the new independent film producer every project was a 'one-off' commercial gamble, an opportunity 'for a quick sale to a territorial distributor to recoup [his] investment' (Pendakur 1990). The overriding need to secure high returns on investment in each and every film led to an increasing dependence on successfully tried-and- tested plot lines, established actors with proven box-office successes, and spectacular song-and-dance sequences. A 'formula' was thus created, which has been consolidated over subsequent decades and which has today, half a century later, become the 'mainstream' within the industry. Other genres have in the process either become defunct (such as the Muslim 'social') or have been transferred to television (such as the 'mythological' and the 'hist- orical'), or just been pushed to the periphery of the industry where they struggle to survive and maintain a foothold.

In such a formulaic structuration, the basic plot—either a love story or a tale of family break-up and reunion—whose resolution is familiar to the public, provides the framework for a narrative where affect and spectacle can alternate in ordered succession, and the spectators are offered myriad possibilities for heightened pleasure through emotional and visual spectacles located in the main narrative and the digressive sub-plots, comic interludes, choreographed fights, and dance sequences. 'Eye-catching' effects (Neale 1980) from a variety of foreign sources (mostly Hollywood and Hong Kong films) are eclectically borrowed by the film-makers and incorporated in- to the same film. The corollary of this *bricolage* of sumptuous settings and costumes (from Hollywood's 'epic' films such as *Ben-Hur* and *Spartacus*), breath-taking stunts and choreographed violence (from the Clint Eastwood 'action' films), technical wizardry and thrilling chases (from the James Bond series), and spectacular dances that keep pace with music videos on MTV and Channel [V] is that the 'parts' of the popular Hindi film become greater than its 'whole'. The resulting product, which is not always linear nor entirely logical, serves to offer a differently-structured and extravagantly spectacular aesthetic experience.

The commercial advantages of such a narrative organization are substantial. Instead of fragmenting its audiences (and thereby its revenue) by catering to varied needs through generic differentiation, the Hindi film amalgamates its socially and ethnically diverse audiences by incorporating visual pleasures from different genres within the *same* film. Particular sections of the film are then aimed at providing specific pleasures to designated constituencies (based on age, gender, caste/class, marital status, or ethnic grouping) within the amalgamated spectating public. In such a structuration of pleasures, every possibility for spectacle and visual display is avidly exploited and dedicated to the 'something for everyone' project.

For instance, proceeding on the universal assumption that women 'like to cry', Hollywood specifically created the generic 'weepie' for women viewers. However, instead of making individual films for a specifically female audience, the Hindi film industry explores opportunities for pathos and extravagant affective spectacle within the same formulaic narrative in order to solicit female interest and afford them the cathartic pleasure of tears. But these teary pleasures are situated within a wider array of other affective and visual pleasures. Many directors acknowledge such a deliberate organization. For instance, the highly successful director Manmohan Desai whose *Amar Akbar Anthony* (1977) stunned audiences by its sheer spectacularity, cheerfully admits that he deliberately incorporates the theme of physical disability into his family-oriented romantic comedies by introducing as many physically-handicapped characters as possible into his films.[3] This is undertaken, not with the intention of raising social or political consciousness among viewers, but quite simply to enhance the potential for pathos and poignant spectacle.

Male spectators, in turn, are offered the pleasures of erotic voyeurism. By manipulating the story so that it can provide as many occasions as possible for the fetishization of the woman, a film endeavours to address male desire and propose a variety of erotic visual pleasures. But, while few social constraints govern attempts to provoke cathartic tears, in order to successfully allow the erotic contemplation of the female form, a film must acknowledge and uphold the ideological and moral preoccupations of the society within which it circulates. It must contend with the directives of the state and other centres of power as well as be sensitive to the moral concerns of all its spectating public, which includes women (and men) who could find such erotic contemplations 'corrupting' or distasteful.

The role of the female spectator is a particularly complex one. As feminist critics have pointed out, in her fetishized screen portrayal, a woman is transformed into a 'commodity'. But, she is, at the same time, a paying spectator and hence a 'consumer' (Doane 1996), who must witness this commodification in the cinema halls across the nation. Consequently, in order to straddle this dual function of the woman as both 'commodity' and 'consumer', the Hindi film industry must persuade women (and men) to participate in her own exploitation as a commodity. In other words, every Hindi film in search of commercial success must not only identify the desire for different kinds of pleasures amongst its socially and ethnically diverse constituencies, but it must also accommodate sometimes incompatible desires within the same film and make them concordant with the existing cultural and moral values of the society in which it circulates. Such social and moral pressures force complex negotiations and contestations within any filmic text that wishes to successfully mediate between the state, the industry, and the audience.

The Negotiation of Pleasure

The 'corrupting' influences in entertainment are constantly monitored by the state through its formal bodies of control. Under the British colonial government, stringent guidelines were laid down by the Indian Board of Censors regarding what could or could not be shown in films. However these guidelines were primarily concerned with discouraging the nationalist movement from exploiting the power of cinema to mobilize the masses (Pendakur 1990: 236). After Indian Independence, instead of liberalizing film censorship, the new Indian Board of Censors tightened its control over the industry even further and incorporated additional directives—much to the dismay of film-makers. The most famous of these new directives was the recommended ban on kissing:

> Kissing or embracing by adults, exhibiting passion repugnant to good taste, shall not be shown. Though common in Western countries, kissing and embracing by adults in public is alien to our country. Dancing is acknowledged as an art. It should therefore be preserved beautifully, in keeping with the finer tradition of our country.[4]

The post-Independence nationalist project, seeking to create a unique 'Indian' identity, untainted by a less fortunate past sought to uphold tradition, morality, and good taste. Barnouw and Krishnaswamy (1980) write:

> Many of the new leaders of the new India were studious, ascetic men. Many were products of a rigorous education. Some had spent long years in jail, reading ceaselessly on the history of the world, pondering the rise and fall of nations, and planning the coming transformation of India. They were intent on a vast programme of change. As for the film industry, they had, like

Gandhi, 'the least interest in it'. The idea of entertainment as a necessity of life was not familiar to them. If they thought of film, they thought of it as a potential instrument of social reform that was not being used in that way. They thought of it as too much involved with romance and immature hero worship. They associated it with Western influences that needed to be purged.'

In keeping with the nationalist project, the new leaders encouraged the portrayal of the woman as 'muse' rather than erotic object, and the 'ideal' Indian woman was determined as someone who was chaste, modest, submissive, self-sacrificing, and virtuous. Such an idealized femininity sought its inspiration in Sita, the mythological prototype, and was entirely in keeping with the patriarchal ideology of Indian society, both traditional and 'modern'. As Sudhir Kakar (1981) confirms:

> For both men and women in Hindu society, the ideal woman is personified by Sita, the quintessence of wifely devotion, the heroine of the epic *Ramayana*. Her unique standing in the minds of most Hindu, regardless of region, caste, social class, age, sex, education or modernisation, testifies to the power and pervasiveness of the traditional ideal of womanhood.

Faced with ideological pressure to present the woman as muse, Hindi cinema had to develop strategies that could uphold the state directives and placate the controlling bodies, without sacrificing the erotic pleasures for its audiences. And, over the decades, some of the strategies that were devised, proved to be so successful that even when censorship recommendations were eventually liberalized in the 1980s, few in the industry were willing to change the now well-established conventions. For instance, in the case of the 'forbidden' kiss, few film directors have been eager to reinstate a practice that used to be tolerated under British colonial rule, even after the Ministry of Information deemed kissing in Hindi films to be a visually accepted practice for Indian audiences to witness now. (On grounds of cultural 'otherness', Hollywood films were allowed to keep their passionate kisses. However, the importation of foreign films was severely restricted, for economic reasons— to control the flow of foreign currency out of the country—rather than for moral ones.)

In his paper on the politics behind this seemingly irrational injunction, Madhav Prasad (1993: 79) explains that 'the prohibition of kissing is a symptomatic cultural protocol whose origins lie in the need to prevent the dissolution of pre-capitalist patriarchal enclaves'. Post-Independence India, he states, was but a formal alliance between the state (which is only formally in place and has no substance of its own) and the various pre-modern, feudal centres of power and authority. These pre-modern centres of power prohibited 'the invention of the private, the zone of intimate exchange and union where, in the Hegelian ideal, the members of the couple become as one' (Prasad 1993: 77–8). When the censor, excising the Indian screen kiss, contended that such a 'public' display of a 'private' activity was not compatible with 'Indian' values, the Censorship Committee erroneously equated 'cinematic representation with representation of the public sphere. In this account there is no recognition of the possibility that while the representation circulates *in* the public sphere, it need not be *of* the public sphere' (Prasad 1993: 75).[5] The prohibition targets the representation of the private through a meaningless ban on kissing because

> the private is a self-enclosing libidinal exchange that various forms of authority seek to oversee. Any representation of this private space and its activities in the public realm thus constitutes a transgression of the scopic privilege that the patriarchal authority of the traditional family reserves for itself. Such a representation threatens to draw a circle around the couple, thus realising its autonomy and its independence from the self-appointed sanctioning authority, while at the same time making the state the overseeing authority and the reformed public gaze the guarantor of the autonomy [Prasad 1993: 75].

Furthermore, Prasad contends, because the public spectacle of the woman does not violate any code that prohibits the 'representation of the private', and poses no threat to this informal alliance of feudal premodern powers that constitute the Indian ruling block, it is tolerated by the authorities. But the issue of female spectaclization as being politically non-threatening, and hence uncontentious, ignores a variety of concerns—such as moral values and female spectatorship. It also presents male spectators as a homogenized group without divisions of age, class, caste, and marital status, all of which play a crucial role in the moulding of desires. Indeed, the woman as spectacle is tolerated, not because it is uncontentious, but because the Hindi film takes great pains to devise ways to accommodate the moral concerns of its audiences and coax their consent. And only then does it grant them permission to enjoy.

Stratagems for Pleasure

In order to uphold the modern state's vision of the Indian woman as muse rather than erotic spectacle as well as to provide erotic pleasures to the different pockets of its vast viewership (while at the same time making the commodification of the woman acceptable to the female constituencies of its viewing public), the Hindi film industry has had to resort to a variety of strategies and subterfuges. The most important strategy has been to create an 'idealised moral universe' (Thomas 1989: 15) that upholds the 'official' definition of femininity within the main plot, and then to provide 'unofficial' erotic pleasures to its targeted audiences through the song-and-dances sequences. The paradigmatic moments of song and dance mark a shift of registers that places them well within the realm of fantasy, and frees and distances the moments of spectacle (with their displays of costumes, settings, music, dance movements) from the syntagmatic narrative. In such spectacular displays, the woman is usually the central component who solicits and intensifies the voyeuristic gaze. Her erotic display challenges the official version of femininity that has just been espoused with great rhetoric in the main narrative. These antithetical, though entirely patriarchal, functions of women thus transform the song-and-dance sequences into areas of heightened transgressive pleasure.

(i) Fetishization of Chastity

The creation of this moral universe in which idealized femininity can perform is underpinned by a festishization of chastity. Even the most cursory examination of the Hindi film narratives would reveal that of all the virtues of the idealized woman, none is more crucial than that of chastity. Indeed, Hindi cinema's intransigence on the issue of sexual purity can sometimes lead to paradoxical situations where even a prostitute remains undefiled (particularly if she is the film's protagonist) despite years of service in a bordello. To emphasize the woman's sexual purity, the Hindi film indulges in hyperbole and tumescent rhetoric on the subject of Virtue and Honour. The Indian woman is 'as pure as the waters of the river Ganges', 'as chaste as Sita', and so on. In the recent, award-winning *Dilwale Dulhaniya Le Jayenge* (Aditya Chopra, 1995), Raj (Shah Rukh Khan), having just spent a chaste night in the company of young Simran (Kajol) in a Swiss hotel, explains why he has not 'taken advantage of her virtue' by gravely declaring: 'I am an Indian, and I know what an Indian woman's honour means.'

Female chastity is even made the battleground for the frequent confrontations between the priapic villain, determined to lay waste the heroine's honour, and the hero who is determined to defend it. Fortunately, despite the villain's repeated attempts to dishonour the heroine, she rarely loses her virtue, that fate being reserved for lesser characters (such as the hero's sister or the heroine's best friend), who are then conveniently disposed off by a stray bullet during the final confrontation between hero and villain.

The Hindi film's totally uncompromising stance on the subject of female chastity is best exemplified by the resolution in *Woh Kaun Thi* (Raj

Khosla, 1964), a suspenseful thriller about a young doctor, Anand (Manoj Kumar), who is haunted by a beautiful woman. The mystery deepens when he finds that his bride, chosen by his mother, turns out to be none other than that same enigmatic woman. The hauntings persist with the woman contriving to be at different places at the same time and they gradually drive the beleagured doctor to the brink of insanity. The *denouement* involves twin sisters (both played by actress Sadhana) with the doctor's bride as the 'good' sister, ignorant of the criminal activities that have been undertaken by the 'bad' sister in the hope of inheriting the doctor's large fortune. The film ends with the accidental death of the bad sister in an encounter with the police. A compassionate police inspector then urges the good sister not to mourn the death because, her sister was, in any case, *badchalan* (an unvirtuous woman). The good sister, accepting his judgement, wipes her tears and walks away to a life of contentment with her husband.

By establishing its moral credentials and having sworn its allegiance to the official, idealized version of Indian womanhood, the Hindi film narrative then dedicates itself to soliciting the prurient gaze by offering (through mode of dress, body movements, facial expressions) the woman as an erotic object in the song-and-dance sequences. Since female nudity, as seen in Hollywood films elsewhere, is disallowed by the Indian censors, and could, in any case, be distasteful to some sections of the public, a variety of stratagems are deployed to allow for as much exposure of the female body as possible. The use of bogus ethnic costumes (scanty 'tribal' costumes, 'African grass' skirts) or of the 'wet sari' (occasioned by a sudden downpour during the song) that draw the viewers' attention to overinflated bosoms, allow for as ample a display of the female body as can be achieved, without inviting the displeasure of the nation's moral police.

Thus, the Hindi film upholds the patriarchally determined feminine idealization through inflated rhetoric on chastity within the narrative, but resists the very same feminine ideals by offering the woman as 'spectacle' in the song-and-dance numbers, both idealization and fetishization being themselves products of patriarchy. Raj Kapoor's *Ram Teri Ganga Maili* (1985), which chronicles the downfall of a pure maiden named Ganga (Mandakini), is purportedly about a metaphor for the overall moral collapse in modern India. However Raj Kapoor provides plentiful occasions for Ganga's erotic display throughout his exploration of this theme of national moral bankruptcy. Disavowing any salacious intent, he explains:

> What has inspired me in making this film is the rapidly changing values of our country, the changing morality, the decadence of moral values, the loss of our spirituality. . . . The only, real, inherent strength of our country

through our long history has been our spiritualism. This loss can be a disintegrating force, a disruptive one [Bhatt 1985: 128].

(ii) 'Performance'

A recurring feature in the song-and-dance extravaganzas where the woman's fetishized representation is central to the spectacle, is the staged dance performance (usually a 'cabaret') and almost all Hindi films include at least one such 'public' exhibition, either in a theatre, night club, bar, disco, or even the living room of a family home. Furthermore, this staged performance comes equipped with its own appreciative, diegetic audience.

Historically, the staged song-and-dance performance with the leading female star offering herself to the erotic male gaze, has been a crucial, commercially driven component of Indian cinema. Even before the advent of the talkies, the filming of women's dance performances was a well-established practice. Hiralal Sen's film work between 1901 and 1904 included dances from stage plays e.g. *A Dancing Scene from the Opera, The Flower of Persia (1898)* and *Dances from 'Alibaba'*, both taken from the repertoire of the Classic Theatre of Calcutta (Mukherjee 1985: 52; Rajadhyaksha and William 1995: 195). R.S. Choudhary's *Madhuri* (1928) was entirely silent except for a special dance performed by the celebrated Sulochana which was the only sequence in the film in sound, a strategy that proved extremely successful in the later transition to sound (Bharatah 1986: 42).

Although theatre was a privileged contributor to the cinematic institution, there are, as Christian Metz has pointed out, significant differences in the manner the two kinds of entertainment are consumed by their respective publics (Netz 1975: 2–4). Comparing the relationship between the actors and the audience in cinema with that in other performing arts such as the theatre, Metz draws attention to the visual complicity between actor and audience in the theatre (or the opera), where the spectator and performer are bound by a mutual awareness of each other's presence—an awareness that is sometimes acknowledged through the use of 'asides' or other forms of direct address to the audience. Such forms of entertainment therefore constitute a collective experience where the exhibitionism of the actors is reciprocated by the voyeurism of the spectators. But such reciprocity is ruptured in cinema because the spectator is absent when the actors perform for the camera (i.e. when the film is being shot), and the actors are absent when the spectator watches a screening of the finished product. Furthermore, the film actor disavows any relationship with his audience by never looking directly at the camera, acting instead as if he is not being looked at or even seen. Consequently, without the mutual acknowledgement between actor and spectator, the film spectator's voyeurism becomes not only an inordinately intense activity but also a 'transgressive' one.

By introducing theatrical performances, such as the cabaret, with their own diegetic audiences within the narrative, Hindi films firstly seek to overcome cinema's dislocation of the actor–performer (or the exhibitionism–voyeurism) axis. A theatrical performance within a film re-establishes reciprocity *within* the world of the film narrative to compensate for its absence in the cinema. Second, it justifies the voyeurism of the spectator because a performance is an exhibition that *demands* to be looked at. Third, any erotic voyeurism on the part of the film spectator is disavowed by the deliberate mediation of a diegetic spectator, who is determined as the true owner of the voyeuristic gaze. It is this last disavowal of voyeurism that is of interest because it reveals why and how the Hindi plot becomes unlinear, episodic and, at times, even illogical.

(iii) Disavowal of Voyeurism

Since the staged performance within a film is invariably accompanied by its own diegetic audience, the woman is presented as an erotic spectacle purportedly for the benefit of this audience. Consequently the charge of voyeurism is displaced on to the (often leering) diegetic spectator, establishing *him* as the holder of the erotic gaze instead of the actual spectator watching the film in a cinema. This happens even though after the introductory, establishing shots of mutual acknowledgement between the woman performer and her diegetic audience, the camera transfers the spectacle directly to the film spectator. And although an exchange of looks between performer and diegetic spectator(s) periodically draws attention to their reciprocal relationship, the real consumers of the erotic performance remain the actual spectators in the cinema. Such mediation by the diagetic voyeur between performer and film spectators absolves the latter of any prurient desires, and establishes them instead as dispassionate observers who are only '*looking at looking*' (Heath 1981: 120). Furthermore, such mediation and disavowal also allows the dancer to break cinema's cardinal principle and look directly into the camera (a frequent practice during 'staged performance' in Hindi films) without fear of confronting the spectators with their own voyeuristic indulgence.

This containment of any direct confrontation of the film spectator's voyeuristic desires is important if the enjoyment of woman as spectacle is to be successfully achieved, because, in addition to the political pressures that impinge on the production of cinematic texts, the status of the viewing subject himself must also be included. In addition to the three 'looks' that circulate in the cinema (i.e. the look of the camera at the pro-filmic event, the look of the viewer at the projected film, and the exchange of looks between characters within the film), Paul Willemen identifies a 'fourth look' that operates during the viewing process. This, he states, is:

> the look which 'surprises me in the act of voyeurism and occasions a feeling of shame'. It is this look which, in Sartre's *Being and Nothingness* constitutes me in relation to the Other. In the filmic process, this look can be represented as the look which constitutes the viewer as visible subject. A tangible signifier of the look (not to be confused with the look itself, which is 'imagined') could be found in the reflection of the light of the screen/projection beamed back onto the faces of the viewers . . . the presence of the imagined look in the field of the other makes itself increasingly felt, producing a sense of shame at being caught in the act of voyeurism [Willemen 1976].

This 'imagined look' that watches the viewer take delight in the projected image, must not be allowed to let him be 'caught in the act of voyeurism'. The staged performance, which, through a process of displacement determines the mediating diegetic audience as voyeurs and disavows any voyeuristic intent on the part of the spectators in the cinema, reassures this 'fourth look' thereby granting them permission to enjoy the spectacle.

A further disavowal of any voyeurism is made possible by the incorporation of an 'approving' audience. Sometimes, the diegetic audience is shown to comprise men and women of authority (metonymic representatives of the state and civil society), who not only see nothing untoward in the woman's lascivious performance, but even smile approvingly at the display. In *Mughal-e-Azam* (K. Asif 1960), an extravagant historical costume drama about a romance between Prince Salim (Dilip Kumar) and a legendary royal courtesan Anarkali (Madhubala), the latter performs a dance for the prince, in the presence of his parents Emperor Akbar (Prithviraj Kapoor) and his consort (Durga Khote). The pleasures of the highly erotic content and its lyrical *double entendre* ('*Mohe panghat pe Nandlal chhed gayo re*') are further heightened by the accompanying dance gestures and body movements. But all erotic intentions are deftly disavowed by the mediating close-ups of the devout Queen's face, shown to be smiling in appreciation, clearly innocent of its erotic content. Similarly any invitation to an erotic enjoyment of Helen's highly suggestive 'cabaret' ('*aaj ki raat, koi aane ko hai*') at a night club in the film *Anamika* (R. Jhalani 1973) is disavowed by the smiling heroine (Jaya Bhaduri), herself the embodiment of virtue, watching the show ostensibly unconscious of its erotic message. Such strategic mediation of 'approving' elders and other respectable personages, disclaims any prurience on the part of the film audiences and any intention to titillate male viewers on the part of the film-makers.

Performance also allows the leading female character to disavow, (should the narrative demand it) any moral turpitude on her part. By declaring it to be only make-believe or a pretence, the strategy of 'performance' allows the narrative to reconcile the woman's idealized, chaste Sita-image with her erotic invitations. Consequently the woman can retain her lofty moral stature while all the time satisfying the desiring male gaze. Furthermore, by frequently locating the woman's performance in a bar, night club, or some such similarly iniquitous den and directing its pleasures towards the diegetic villain and his leering underlings, the Hindi film can even denounce such erotic exhibitionism-voyeurism. In doing so, it establishes its moral credentials with the authorities, all the while offering the sexualized woman as spectacle to the film spectators in the cinema.

Motivating the Performance

Having devised the dance performance as a strategy to legitimize erotic voyeurism through the processes of disavowal and distancing, the Hindi film must then contrive socially acceptable motivations within the narrative for such erotic exhibition. Till the 1970s, the Hindi film narrative achieved this through a simple bi-polarization of women into 'good' and 'evil'. Sometimes these two women were twin-sisters played by the same actress (as seen in *Woh Kaun Thi*), but more frequently the Hindi film deployed a 'vamp', an unscrupulous adventuress, a grand seductress of men who counterbalanced the sexual modesty of the virtuous heroine.

(i) The 'Vamp'

As the overwesternized *femme fatale*, the vamp provided the antithesis to the ideal woman's embodiment of chastity, by her demonstrations of uncontrolled female lust and wantonness. With names like 'Rosie' or 'Mary', she was parodied as either an Anglo-Indian (a racial outcaste) or a member of India's Christian minority. A *demi-mondaine*, she was often a cabaret dancer operating in smoke-filled bars, night clubs, or similar 'foreign' dens of vice, usually owned by the gangster-villain, where, clad in a tight-fitting, western gown she performed audacious dances. As Rosie Thomas (1989: 11) states:

> Since it first emerged in the context of colonial India's fight for independence, Indian cinema, for a number of reasons, has been concerned with constructing a notion of Indian cultural and national identity. This has involved drawing on concepts such as 'tradition'. But a chaste and pristine

India has also been constructed by opposing it to a decadent and exotic 'other', the licentious and immoral 'West', with the films' villains invariably sporting a clutter of signifiers of 'Westernization': whiskey bottles, bikini-clad escorts, or foreign limousines.

The vamp's sexual promiscuity, her racial 'otherness' and non-Hindu identity contrasted dramatically with the heroine's own strict adherence to traditionally defined codes of behaviour required of the ideal Hindu woman. The vamp's association with clubs and bars provided the motivation for frequent 'cabarets' performed for the enjoyment of the villain and his henchmen who frequented such iniquitous dens and/or for the possible seduction of the hero. Meanwhile, the main narrative continued to eulogize the heroine's unblemished nature. Moral codes were upheld in grandiloquent and hyperbolic pronouncements on the virtues of the ideal Hindu woman, while transgressive voyeuristic enjoyment of the fetishized 'foreign' woman making a 'spectacle of herself' in a staged performance was also achieved. Once the vamp's erotic performances were successfully executed, she was usually disposed off (again by the convenient, stray bullet) as fitting punishment for her threatening sexuality (Vasudevan 1989). Such a resolution also saved the film-maker from having to relocate her in the narrative, a difficult task, given her moral depravity and unredeemable racial 'otherness'.

The use of the racial stereotype was used not only for the appointment and settling of national identity, it also allowed for the provision of transgressive pleasures. Emily Apter (1996) investigating the Sapphic theatricality in turn-of-the-century Paris, uncovers a similar use of racial stereotype where the 'acting out' in performance of the culturally exotic and caricatural 'oriental' woman became a form of 'outing' of transgressive gay/lesbian sexual identities:

> The enactment of objectification can be seen at work quite self-consciously in the way in which French feminism mobilized Orientalist stereotypes to fashion 'new' sexual identities that functioned as props on which to hang a pose. 'Monstrous superhuman figures' to borrow Mario Praz's terms, were excavated from cultural history; women such as Semiramis, Thais, and Cleopatra, whose erotic appetites were legendarily matched to their thirst for political authority. . . . What is particularly interesting . . . is the use of Orientalism as an erotic cipher, a genre of theatricality in which acting 'Oriental' becomes a form of outing, and outing is revealed to be thoroughly consonant with putting an act [Apter 1996: 19].

In Hindi cinema, transgressive desire is given access through the overwesternized stereotype, an example of which can be found in Raj Kapoor's *Shri 420*

(1954) where the corrupting Maya (Nadira), dressed in a shimmering, tight-fitting gown performs a cabaret number ('*Mudmud ke na dekh*') at a night club, to seduce Raju (Raj Kapoor) away from the simple, sari-clad, and incorruptible Vidya (Nargis). Dev Anand's *Nau Do Gyarah* (1957) too, pits the innocent Raksha (Kalpana Kartik) against the lustful night-club danseuse and seductress (Shashikala), while Guru Dutt's *Aar Paar* (1953) features an Anglo-Indian barmaid-cum-dancer who deliberately imperils the life of the beloved Nicky (Shyama). At times, the vamp was replaced by the equally stereotypical and exotic Muslim *tawaif* or courtesan who worked in a *kotha* which required her to perform several *mujras* for depraved and drunken aristocrats. However, if the courtesan was also the leading lady, as in K. Asif's *Mughal-e-Azam* (1960) and Kamal Amrohi's *Pakeezah* (1971) then not only did she have to execute several performances as required by her disreputable profession, but she also had to manage to remain unsullied throughout the film.

That it was the vamp rather than the virgin who was the object of the male interest despite the narrative's avowed concern with virtue, is confirmed by Helen, an actress who specialized in the role of the vamp. In a documentary interview, she declares:

> The public would take to a vamp more [than the heroine]. A woman is not all sugar, she has also to be spice. . . . The heroine was all goody-goody—too goody-goody for my liking! The vamp had to be seductive, a brazen hussy with a cigarette in her hand and a glass of wine. As for the poor heroine, she was just crying all the time![6]

But although Helen confirms that she enjoyed playing the grand seductress on screen, she is nevertheless anxious to assure the interviewer that she never really debased herself for her art. The 'glass of wine' was just Coca Cola and water, and despite appearances, the bare body was really enveloped in flesh-coloured body stockings—demonstrating, in the process, the power of disavowal in 'performance'.

(ii) The New Woman

The demise of the Anglo-Indian vamp coincided with Helen's retirement after 1,000 films and nearly four decades in Hindi films, and the advent of the 'new woman' in the films of the 1970s, when the political arena was dominated by Mrs Indira Gandhi. It was also the dawn of a new kind of Hindi film in which the modern state via the hero became an active player in the narrative (Prasad 1996: 31). One critique of these 1970s films concludes that the new heroines were not '. . . decorative lovers who lean(ed) on the hero's biceps' but were fiercely independent and willing 'to fight alongside their men' (Basu *et al.* 1981: 64). Equally, when required (which was quite often), these unorthodox women wore clothes that were hitherto worn only by the vamp, and were willing to execute the erotic dance performances that used to be the *raison d'être* of the seductress.

But, although the new heroines portrayed modern, independent women, they still had to uphold the prevailing patriarchal values of modesty and chastity. Accordingly, more contemporary moral justification had to be devised to provide the staged spectacle. One such contrivance was to portray the modern heroine as a campus co-ed, and the college's 'Annual Founder's Day Dance Competition' provided the justification for her erotic stage performance—a performance that was not only approvingly endorsed by her professors, colleagues and elders (e.g. Pooja Bhatt in Sachin's *Prem Diwane*, 1990) but even rewarded by a 'first prize' or an impressive trophy. At other times, the leading lady was portrayed as a working woman pursuing a career in the performing arts, either as singer in bars and discotheques (Zeenat Aman in Feroz Khan's *Qurbani* in 1980 and Parveen Babi in Ramesh Sippy's *Shaan* the same year) or as a film star (Sonam in Rajiv Rai's *Tridev* in 1989), without jeopardising her virtue.

(iii) The 'Noble Sacrifice'

The most common stratagem for erotic spectacle is the 'noble sacrifice' which pits two crucial components of the idealized female character—sexual modesty and filial (or social) duty, against each other. Typically, the villain takes hostage the heroine's beloved and/or some vulnerable member of her family and, in order to rescue them, she must agree to the villain's demands for an unabashedly erotic spectacle that only she can perform for him and the members of his gang. By agreeing, for the sake of her beloved or her family members, to the villain's demands for erotic entertainment, and thereby disregarding the threat to her own honour, the ideal woman is portrayed as someone who should be *doubly* venerated for she is in fact sacrificing her own concerns in order to fulfil a higher social duty. The 'noble sacrifice' excuse also allows the chaste heroine to offer an erotic performance without seriously jeopardizing her honour because the spectacle, delivered under duress, can always be disclaimed and contained by the make-believe nature of the staged performance.

In Ramesh Sippy's *Sholay* (1975), the villain Gabbar Singh (Amjad Khan) and his henchmen take Veeru (Dharmendra) prisoner. They then abduct his beloved, Basanti (Hema Malini) and force her to dance in the midday heat, on broken glass, threatening to kill Veeru, if she refuses. To

save his life, she reluctantly undertakes to execute the humiliating performance ('*jab tak hai jaan, jaane jahan, main nachoongi*') while the helpless
Veeru, tied and trussed, looks on in despair at the villains enjoying her erotic display, the sado-masochism of the dance being camouflaged by the
nobility of Basanti's sacrifice. Similarly in Vijay Anand's *Jewel Thief* (1967),
the heroine Shalini (Vyjayanthimala), performs for the rulers of an unnamed
Himalayan kingdom. The villain (Ashok Kumar) having abducted her
brother extracts a dance performance (*Honton pe aisi baat main daba ke
chali aayi*) from Shalini under duress, and the erotic pleasures proposed by
her body to the male spectators in the cinema are disavowed by the mediation of a leering, diegetic audience.

The 'noble sacrifice' is not restricted to rescuing just family members or
lovers from the villain. It can even extend to the safeguarding of national
security. In *Khalnayak* (Subhash Ghai, 1993) the leading lady (Madhuri
Dixit), is an exceedingly dedicated police officer, who in pursuit of a notorious terrorist (Sanjay Dutt), devotes all her talents and training towards his
entrapment. In order to infiltrate his organization, she and her female colleagues masquerade as gypsies and stage an audaciously titillating performance
(the celebrated '*choli ke peechhe kya hai*' number) for the enjoyment of the
terrorists. That the subterfuges and strategies mobilized for the disavowal of
any erotic intent can sometimes be inadequate, was proved by the 'obscenity'
charge brought against the film by Mr R.P. Chugh, a Delhi-based lawyer
who claimed that the song had a 'corrupting' influence on his young son
(Bhardwaj 1993: 74). On the other hand, the sensational success of the
seductive dance and its suggestive lyrics not only rescued the film from an
indifferent fate at the box-office it also sparked a trend for even bawdier
numbers. Even the newsmagazine *India Today* despaired that the 'choli'
song's success had fuelled 'a race for folk smut' (Katiyar 1994: 67).

In addition to the bars, night-clubs, theatres, etc. another frequent location for the performance is the 'dinner party' where the woman pretends to
get drunk and disgraces herself by an uninhibited display of passion. Such
a disgraceful spectacle undertaken by the heroine is often a poignant sacrifice, even though it may not immediately be apparent as such. The logic is
as follows: by pretending to get drunk, and then dancing and making a
spectacle of herself, the heroine embarrasses the hero (who loves her dearly)
before his family and peers. The heroine thus reveals herself as unworthy of
his love and trust. Dismayed by her disgraceful behaviour, the hero then
decides to marry the woman that his mother has arranged for him. Only
later does he understand the true nobility of her actions that were either
undertaken at the behest of his own mother so that she could secure the

more profitable marriage elsewhere, or to save his own blind sister or some other vulnerable member of his family from some blackmail or some other terrible fate at the hands of the villain, or some other equally noble reason. In *Inteqam* (R.K. Nayyar, 1969), Sadhana disgraces herself in front of an august assembly in an elaborately feigned drunken song-and-dance number ('*kaise rahun chup ki maine pi hi kya hai, hosh abhi tak hai baqi, aur zara si dede saqi, aur zara si*'). Her unabashed display is in fact a heroic act of sacrifice, undertaken to exact revenge (as the title indicates) on her beloved's family which was responsible for her father's wrongful imprisonment, even though she must sacrifice her own love in the process. In Ramesh Sippy's *Seeta Aur Geeta* (1972), Hema Malini as Geeta offers a similar example of 'disgraceful' exhibition in the song and display sequence: '*han ji han maine sharab pi hai*'. The noble cause however, does not detract in any way from the spectators' (real and diegetic) enjoyment of the erotic spectacle.

(iv) 'Private Dancer'

Sometimes the nature of the performance is destined only for the eyes of the leading man. In Raj Kapoor's *Sangam* (1964), a love triangle that treats the subject of female chastity with frequent, bombastic references to feminine virtue and Hindu mythology, the married couple (Vyjayanthimala and Raj Kapoor) are on their honeymoon in Europe. When the husband decides to go out alone and savour the nocturnal delights of Paris (such pleasures being unbecoming of the married Hindu woman), his wife decides to coax him into staying by executing her own 'cabaret' number ('*main kya karun Ram mujhe Buddha mil gaya*') within the privacy of their hotel bedroom. Similarly in *Karan Arjun* (Rakesh Roshan 1995) Bindiya (Mamta Kulkarni) attempts to arouse the taciturn Ajay's (Salman Khan) interest in her by drawing attention to her own physical desirability in a performance that is exclusively for Ajay's (and the cine-spectators) visual consumption. In *Beta* (Indra Kumar, 1992) leading man and simpleton husband, Anil Kapoor, dreams that Madhuri Dixit is dancing for him, the extreme eroticism of the number ('*dhak dhak*') being cancelled by its dream status, and became that it is destined only for him, and they are to be married. Even in *Hum Aapke Hain Koun . . .!* (Sooraj Barjatya 1994), a film about the perfect, traditional family, the performance strategem still prevails with most of the dances being performed as staged events overseen by family elders within the intimacy of the extended family instead of a public display for the debauched villain and his merry men. And, although the film was universally declared to be good, 'clean' entertainment because the revealing costumes and suggestive dance gestures and movements so characteristic of the formulaic

Hindi film are absent, the woman is nevertheless displayed as an erotic object with the watching hero and/or family members functioning as diegetic mediators to secure the processes of disavowal.

Tridev

The frequent use of the 'performance' device in popular Hindi cinema is exemplified by the highly successful *Tridev*, (Rajiv Rai, 1989) an extravagant spectacle with three leading men, each with an independent romantic life and all in pursuit of a gang of villains. In this film, five out of the seven song-and-dances are theatrical performances, and most of the strategems mentioned above can be seen in operation. The plot concerns arch-villain Bhujang, alias Bhanwar Singh (Amrish Puri), whose main business is the trafficking of arms by which he intends to foment chaos and confusion in the nation. Since the criminal activities of Bhujang have directly or indirectly affected the lives of each of the leading characters, they pool their effort and overcome the traitor.

The simple plot is then manipulated to motivate spectacular performances from the women, who are either *bona fide* entertainers—such as the film star Renu (Sonam)—or else are masquerading as entertainers—as in the case of Natasha (Sangeeta Bijlani)—who seeks to avenge her brother's death at the hands of the villain. The theme song *'oye oye'* first appears as a pro-filmic performance by Renu for the diegetic camera. Supposedly set in a 'dark' continent, the dancers wear scanty 'jungle' costumes that allow for substantial exposure of the body, and during the spectacle, the camera dwells mostly on the woman's vigorously provocative interpretation. A more pathos-filled rendition of the same song appears as another performance by the same woman (this time accompanied by her beloved) at a cocktail party held by her father to celebrate Renu's forced engagement to a man she does not love.

In the meantime, Natasha, conducting her own private vendetta against the evil Bhujang, executes two cabaret-style performances (*'gali gali mein phirta hai, tu kyun ban ke banjara'*) for the villain and his troops, and during one of them (*'raat bhar jaam se jaam takraayega'*) feigns a drunkenness that allows the intoxicated gangsters to partially disrobe her. The nobility of purpose in undertaking these erotic assignments converts these erotic spectacles into acts of supreme sacrifice that attest to the glorify and greatness of Indian womanhood.

The final confrontation between the heroes and villains is preceded by the film's most spectacular rendition of *'oye oye'* where the three leading ladies whose fathers or lovers have been imprisoned by the villain, are coerced into executing a performance for him. Furthermore, the imprisoned fathers are forced to watch this public humiliation of their daughters that is being offered as entertainment for the villain and the members of his gang.

Female Pleasures

The high morality of the Hindi film narrative and the various processes of disavowal thus serve to placate not just the agencies of the state and civil society, but also the female members of the audience. Although it is clear that some women enjoyed the cabarets of the danseuse Helen, and even sent her fan mail,[7] precisely where female pleasure resides in such erotic spectacles has not yet been established. Western film theory has so far offered only a partial understanding of the female gaze and pleasure. Mulvey (1981: 14) has proposed a 'masculinization' of the female gaze whereby the woman, assuming a masculine position, male points of view, and male identifications, enjoys the freedom and control typically available to men.

Craig Owen proposes that in performance, a subject acts an identity into existence and the 'subject becomes an object in order to become a subject' (Owen 1992: 195). In Hindi cinema, the staged performance allows the performing woman to bring a powerful and sexually-aggressive identity into existence. Temporarily discarding the self-sacrificing and idealized straitjacket imposed on her by patriarchal society, the woman assumes command of her body and defiantly acts out her own desires. Mary Ann Doane, explaining pleasure in the 'woman's film' contends that by presenting the woman as spectacle, women are offered '(m)asochistic fantasy instead of sexuality' (Doane 1987: 79). In them, women are de-sexualized, and function not as spectacle to be looked at but as protagonists in masochistic scenarios.

While the debate on feminine pleasure continues, it is clear that the song-and-dance spectacle does offer female spectators the pleasures of identification and fantasy through the female star. The song-and-dance sequences also propose other compensatory pleasures. The melody and lyrics of the songs fulfil the 'invocatory' (the desire to hear) drive. (However this is a universal pleasure, and cinema houses routinely turn up the volume during the song-and-dance numbers.) The female gaze is also solicited by the kaleidoscopic changes of extravagant sets, sumptuous costumes, fashionable jewellery, imaginative hairstyles, and daring make-up, so that 'the filmic frame is a kind of display window and spectatorship consequently a form of window-shopping' (Doane 1996: 121). The commercial success of the '*Hum Aapke Hain Koun . . .!* sari'—i.e. the sari worn during a highly seductive dance number in the film, even in such far-flung markets as Hong

Kong and Singapore, confirms the visual impact of dance performances on the female spectator/consumer.

Conclusion

The economic pressure that drives the Hindi film to propose erotic pleasure through the presentation of woman as spectacle to both its male and female spectators,[8] also requires that it take into account the ideological and moral concerns of all sections of its heterogenous spectating public. In order to reconcile the competing demands of its public, it eulogizes an ideal Indian womanhood, through grandiloquent pronouncements on the need for virtue, modesty, and honour, thus constructing a moral (and patriarchal) framework within the narrative and reassuring the state and other moral authorities as well as spectators of its 'good faith'. Then, by introducing the 'performance' as a ploy whereby the woman makes a 'spectacle' of herself, often for the sake of a greater social good, it allows erotic contemplation of the female body but simultaneously disavows any prurient intention by introducing the mediating, diegetic voyeur. Through such narrative contortions, erotic voyeurism is legitimized, and the desiring spectators in the cinema are granted permission to freely enjoy transgressive erotic pleasures. As one industry *wallah*, commenting on the need for such narrative contortions in order to legitimize erotic voyeurism, declared:

> It all depends on presentation; if you try hard enough you can please the classes as well as the masses [Bhardwaj 1993: 79].

Notes

1. See Vasudevan (1993: 51–84), for an analysis of iconic representations in popular Hindi films.
2. For an analysis of genres in early Indian cinema see Rajadhyaksha (1986).
3. 'Miracle Man: Manmohan Desai' (1987) documentary directed by Nasreen Munni Kabir and produced by Hyphen Films for Channel Four.
4. Cited in Shah (1981: 246).
5. Italics in the original.
6. 'Helen: Always in Step' (1989) directed by Nasreen Munni Kabir and produced by Hyphen Films for Channel Four.
7. 'Helen Always in Step' (1989).
8. Paul Willemen has repeatedly pointed out, and with reason, that the male figure is as much an object of male 'desire' as the female figure, thus pointing to an auto-erotic, repressed homosexual 'narcissistic identification with the

ideal ego in the diegesis'. (Paul Willemen, p. 43). While this is undoubtedly
true, and Hindi films regularly subject the male figure to the prurient gaze as
well, the question of the eroticized male is, as Stephen Neale has pointed out,
subject to a different inscription and representation (Neale 1980: 57). Also
since my concern in this chapter is limited to the strategies that popular Hindi
cinema is forced to devise in order to circumvent very specific cultural and
political pressures and present the woman as an erotic object, the problematic
of the eroticized male transcends the remit of this chapter.

REFERENCES

Apter, Emily, 1996, 'Acting Out Orientalism' in Elin Diamond (ed.), *Performance
and Cultural Politics*, London: Routledge: 15–34.
Barnouw, Eric and S. Krishnaswamy, 1980, *Indian Film*, New York: Oxford
University Press.
Basu, Siddharthi, Sanjay Kak, and Pradip Kishen, 1981, 'Cinema and Society: A
Search for Meaning in a New Genre', *India International Centre Quarterly*, 8 (1).
Bharatan, Raju, 1986, 'Showtime', *The Illustrated Weekly of India*, 22–8 June.
Bhardwaj, Praveena, 1993, 'Dirty Dancing?', *Filmfare*, September.
Bhatt, Punita, 1985, 'The Cinema of Raj Kapoor', in T.M. Ramachandran (ed.), *70
Years of Indian Cinema*, Bombay: Cinema India-International.
Cooke, Pans (ed.), 1985, 'Genre', in *The Cinema Books*, London: British Film Insti-
tute.
Doane, Mary Ann, 1996, 'The Economy of Desire: The Commodity Form in/of the
Cinema', in John Belton (ed.), *Movies and Mass Culture*, London: Athlone
Press: 119–34.
Heath, Stephen, 1981, *Questions of Cinema*, London: Macmillan.
Kakar, Sudhir, 1981, *The Inner World*, Delhi: Oxford University Press.
Katyar, Arun, 1994, 'Obscene Overtures', *India Today*, 15 January.
Metz, Christian, 1975, 'The Imaginary Signifies', *Screen*, 16 (2), Summer.
Mukherjee, Prabhat, 1985, 'Hiralal Sen', in T.M. Ramachandran (ed.), *70 Years of
Indian Cinema*, Bombay: Cinema India-International.
Mulvey, Laura, 1981, 'Afterthoughts . . . Inspired by *Duel in the Sun*', *Framework*,
Summers.
Nandy, Ashis, 1981, 'The Popular Hindi Film: Ideology and First Principles', *India
International Centre Quarterly*, 8 (1).
Neale, Stephen, 1980, *Genre*, London: British Film Institute.
Owen, Craig, 1992, 'The Medusa Effect, or, The Spectacular Ruse', in Scott Bryson
et al. (eds), *Beyond Recognition: Representation, Power and Culture*, Berkeley and
Los Angeles: University of California Press.
Pendakur, Manjunath, 1990, 'India', in John A. Lent (ed.), *The Asian Film Industry*,
Bromley: Christopher Helms.

Prasad, Madhava, 1993, 'Cinema and the Desire for Modernity', *Journal of Arts and Ideas* , 25–6 December.

———, 1996, 'Signs of Ideological Re-form in Two Recent Films', *Journal of Arts and Ideas* (29).

Rajadhyaksha, Ashis, 1986, 'Neo-Traditionalism: Film as Popular Art in India', *Framework* (32–3), London.

Rajadhyaksha, Ashis and Paul Willemen, 1995, *Encyclopaedia of Indian Cinema*, New Delhi: Oxford University Press.

Shah, Panna, 1981, *The Indian Film*, Westport, Coria: Greenwood Press.

Thomas, Rosie, 1985, 'Indian Cinema: Pleasures and Popularity', *Screen*, 26 (3–4).

———, 1989, 'Sanctity and Scandal in Mother India', *Quarterly Review of Film and Video* 11.

Vasudevan, Ravi, 1989, 'The Melodramatic Mode and the Commercial Hindi Cinema', *Screen*, 30 (3): 29–50.

———, 1993, 'Shifting Codes, Dissolving Identities: The Hindi Social Film of the 1950s as Popular Culture', *Journal of Arts and Ideas*, 23–4 January: 51–84.

Willemen, Paul, 1976, 'Voyeurism, The Look and Devoskin', *Afterimage* (6): 41–9.

Imagining the Family
An Ethnography of Viewing
Hum Aapke Hain Koun . . .![1]

PATRICIA UBEROI

I'm for the joint family system, because the joint family represents Indian culture; nowhere else in the world have they got this system still.[2]

L IVING IN DELHI, there is one way of deciding whether a movie has caught the popular imagination: a catch-phrase from the film will be found inscribed on the backside of a three-wheeler auto-rickshaw. Jostling for space and visual attention along with numerous other insignia of the owner's social and sectarian identity—salutations to gods and goddesses, expressions of gratitude to *gurus* and parents, salacious comments and naughty verses, aphorisms and proverbs, warnings to other road users and curses on the Evil Eye—these evocative phrases index both the extent of the movie's box-office appeal, and its privileged iconic status across several domains of popular culture. Even today,[3] mementos of the 1975 block-buster, *Sholay*, remind harried commuters of a larger-than-life epic contest between Good and Evil, enlivened on the sidelines by romance and sacrifice: '*Chal Basanti*'. Numerous three-wheelers still carry the expressive legend, *Maine pyar kiya* (I'd fallen in love), the title of Sooraj Barjatya's 1989 romantic hit. But the really contemporary graffito for the Delhi roads is the teasing title of Barjatya's latest blockbuster, the spectacular *Hum Aapke Hain Koun . . .!* (What am I to you!) (1994).

In a year of numerous box-office 'flops', the romantic family drama,

Hum Aapke Hain Koun . . .! (*HAHK,* as it is familiarly referred to, and as will here be termed or it henceforth), was a phenomenal commercial success, reportedly grossing more than any other film in the history of Indian cinema.[4] After more than six months, the film is still showing to packed houses in Delhi and elsewhere;[5] tickets for matinee shows continue to be sold 'in black'; and many viewers—and not only the ethnographer are returning for their third, fourth, and fifth viewings,[6] clapping, cheering, and weeping at appropriate moments, anticipating the dialogues, and strumming to the beat of its very popular songs. Delighted distributors compare the film to some of the great blockbusters of yesteryear—*Sholay* and *Mughal-e-Azam,* for instance. With opulent sets, no fewer than fourteen melodious songs,[7] a star-studded cast with Madhuri Dixit and Salman Khan in the lead roles,[8] and a canny marketing and distribution strategy,[9] this movie has enticed cinema audiences back to the theatres in unprecedented numbers, allaying industry fears that Indian commercial cinema had entered a phase of irreversible decline. In a single stroke, *HAHK* appears to have neutralized the subversive effects of the contemporary alien 'cultural invasion' and the debased cultural values of the front-benchers, bringing back nostalgic memories of a bygone golden era of Indian cinema.

This is nothing short of remarkable, for *HAHK* completely lacks the '*masala*' (spicy) ingredients of sex, sadism, and violence that are believed to the *de rigueur* for a successful 'Bollywood' production. Action, such as it is, begins only well after the interval when the film becomes, for better or worse, 'just like other movies'.[10] And though the music is undeniably catchy, it is certainly not as innovative and varied as that of some other recent films, *Roja, 1942: A love story* or *Bombay,* for instance. Besides, it is well-known that even exceedingly popular song-and-dance items cannot redeem a film otherwise destined to 'bomb' at the box-office; or rather, with the expansion of cable and satellite TV, the films and their songs increasingly follow an independent trajectory of popular appeal (Doraiswamy 1996).

It is now conceded, with a mixture of wonder and relief, that the unprecedented commercial success of *HAHK* may actually lie in the fact that it is *not* a *masala* movie. *Post facto,* film critics have been attempting to construct a genealogy for this rather unanticipated development in popular Hindi cinema. For instance, Nikhat Kazmi, the well-regarded film critic of *The Times of India,* has seen the film as indicating an emerging trend—a pendulum swing in 'low brow' taste away from 'blood and gore' and back to the uplifting themes of 'the family, the nation and love' (cf. Mayaram n.d.: 11). Postulating a sort of psychological saturation of Indian cinema audiences with themes of violence and revenge, Kazmi writes:

Clean: this is the current new word in the common man's lexicon for good cinema. In an age when cinema seems to have lost its soul to the nasty, brutish hero, both the viewers and the film makers have had their fill of the death wish. Now, they are turning from revenge, the reason for all the blood and gore in popular Bollywood cinema, to the family, the nation and love. There is a ubiquitous demand for good, clean cinema. A demand which is reflected in the stupendous success of *Hum Aapke Hain Koun*, a film which has nothing more than good, clean music, nice characters and a drama that falls soft and easy [Kazmi 1995a].[11]

As a good 'clean' movie, Kazmi puts *HAHK* in a series with the recently released patriotic melodramas, *Roja*, *Krantikshetra* and *Krantiveer*, and latterly *Param Vir Chakra*, to which she could well have added the romantic *1942: A Love Story*, a film set against the background of the freedom struggle. But the singular feature of *HAHK* in this series, which the present chapter seeks to address, is that it is quintessentially what is classed in popular parlance as a 'family' film—'family' understood in the double sense of (i) *for* a family audience; and (ii) *about* family relationships, inclusive of, but much broader, than, the true romance that provides its storyline. As one viewer is reported to have said:

The family in this film is very important. It's not a Madhuri or a Salman film [the romantic leads] but the story of a family [Mishra 1995].

Mopping her tears, she further explained to the interviewer that:

[e]verytime she watched it she cried in the same scenes, because she lived in a joint family and could relate to the happy and sad moments [Mishra 1995].

Despite the supposed authenticity of detail, on which many viewers commented, *HAHK* is not actually a work of cinematic realism (see also Section III here). As Madhuri Dixit conceded while accepting the *Filmfare* Award for Best Actress of 1994: *HAHK* presents 'a perfect utopia'—about 'simple values and guileless people'.[12] In other words, the film is not about the family as it *is*, but the family as people would like it to be: 'I would want my daughter-in-law to be as nice and sweet and domesticated' as Madhuri and Renuka, a middle-aged businessman was reported to have remarked (Mishra 1995)—suggesting, perhaps, that not all daughters-in-law match these exacting standards. Indeed, several viewers self-consciously recognized and took pleasure in the fact that this film portrayed an *ideal* of family life. Said Asha:[13]

What I liked is that everyone has good relations with each other, which is not generally found in families. . . . This is how it *should* be. It's an ideal family.

Clearly, *HAHK* is the story of the Indian family as a form of 'imagined community' (to rather stretch the meaning of Anderson's felicitous concept [1983]). Beyond this, as I seek to illustrate in this chapter, it is also about the family as an icon of the national society.

For some time now, social scientists, cinema critics, and concerned citizens have been at pains to find explanations—material, social, or psychological—for the high levels of sadism and violence in Indian popular cinema (e.g. Nandy 1995a; 1995b; 1995c). Indian feminists have recently begun to keep a vigilant eye on the stereotypes of femininity purveyed by the film industry, the commoditization of women's bodies, and the violence against women routinely displayed on the Indian screen.[14] A new generation of film critics and historians of cinema have utilized the optic of psycho-analytic film theory to speculate on the play of desire that the cinematic fantasy sets loose (Vasudevan 1995; see also Kakar 1989; Nandy 1981). And there has also been a measure of interrogation of the political agenda believed to inform the recent series of patriotic films, Mani Ratnam's *Roja* in particular, linking this to the class and communal character of the Indian state (Niranjana 1994; n.d.). But until the unexpected phenomenon of *HAHK*, romances and clean family films had not attracted the same degree of critical attention or hermeneutic effort.[15] Perhaps the general feeling is just one of enormous relief that family movies like *HAHK* can be commercially viable after all. Indeed, critiques of the politics of representation of such movies tend to be greeted with some resentment. As a middle-aged woman lecturer at a Delhi women's college asked me aggressively, after one such exercise:

That's all very well. But tell me the truth now. Didn't you *enjoy* it?[16]

And a young reporter, attempting to probe the 'anti-emancipatory' female stereotypes she found in *HAHK* was told firmly by a college girl interviewee:

Oh, come on. Don't give it a feminist angle. I would love to get married and lead such a life [Mishra 1995].

On the contrary—and here I draw sustenance from Rustom Bharucha's critique of the same film (1995)—I would insist that clean family movies are just as demanding of critical and political interpretation as the 'blood and gore' films that have attracted so much public and media attention: and that, not merely because they have proved exceedingly profitable. In this chapter, I look at some of the responses to *HAHK* of film industry personnel (directors, stars, producers, distributors), film critics, and north Indian viewers, privileging the voice of the latter and seeking to understand what exactly is meant by the universal classification of this film as a clean and morally uplifting 'family' film. I then look, as a sociologist of the family, at the ideal image of the family that the film narrative of *HAHK* seeks to construct and project, and the deliberately incomplete erasures that this process entails. Finally, I reflect on the wider social functions that such a fantasy of ideal family life might perform in the light of the sort of social science critiques referred to above.

Before embarking on the analysis, however, it would be as well to give a brief, if unsatisfactory, outline of the film plot. As already mentioned, the film barely has a storyline,[17] the excessive length of the film (almost three hours) being accounted for by the unusual number of songs, rather than by the proliferation and complexity of sub-plots. In this sense, *HAHK* lacks the 'prodigality' of narrative detail that is often regarded as a hallmark of South Asian popular cinema (see Jayamanne 1992: 147). Some viewers, and the female star herself, thought this 'simplicity' an asset,[18] though Bharucha, speaking as a connoisseur of the 'variety' entertainment that popular Hindi cinema usually provides, condemned it as a 'ruthless' and 'claustrophobic' levelling of narrative and dramatic possibilities (1995: 801, 804).

Kailash Nath is a bachelor industrialist, and guardian of his two orphaned nephews: Rajesh (Mohnish Bahl) and Prem (Salman Khan). Through the mediation of the boys' maternal uncle (Ajit Vacchani), a marriage is arranged between Rajesh and Puja (Renuka Shahane), the elder daughter of Prof. S.S. Chowdhury (Anupam Kher) and his lovely wife (Reema Lagoo), both of them, as it happens, old college friends of Kailash Nath's.

Side by side, through a series of life-cycle rituals of engagement, marriage, pregnancy, and childbirth, Rajesh's younger brother, Prem, is attracted to Puja's younger sister, Nisha (Madhuri Dixit), and determines to marry her as soon as he can set up independently in business. He confides in his sister-in-law, who has incidentally been charged with the responsibility of finding a wife for him.

Puja has Prem tie a necklace on Nisha as a token of his love and commitment, but immediately afterwards she falls to her death without communicating this development to the rest of the family. Both families are grief-stricken over Puja's tragic death, and Rajesh is quite distraught worrying over the upbringing of his motherless son.

Unaware of the troth between Prem and Nisha, the elders in the family decide that the best solution to Rajesh's dilemma and sorrow would be for him to marry Nisha, who is already giving her sister's child a mother's love. Nisha agrees to the match, mistakenly believing she is to be married to Prem, while Prem conceals his personal anguish out of love and concern for the well-being of his elder brother and infant nephew, and obedience to the will of senior family members.

As the marriage of Rajesh and Nisha is about to take place, Lallu, the loyal family servant and Prem's confidant and friend, appeals to Lord Krishna to intercede. With the help of Tuffy the dog, the true situation is revealed in the nick of time. Prem and Nisha are united with family blessings.

I. What Makes a 'Clean' Movie?

There are obviously several different components to the widespread categorization of *HAHK* as a clean and morally uplifting movie, suitable for 'family' viewing an contrasted by the same token with the majority of Bollywood *masala* productions. I will deal with these features separately, while suggesting that there is an intrinsic conceptual link uniting them.

(i) The Lack of 'Vulgarity'
For the last several years, the Indian media and the general public have been obsessed with the sexual content—what is euphemistically called 'vulgarity'—in popular cinema, particularly in the song-dance items. The charge of vulgarity is not at all a new one: it has been made from the very early days of Indian cinema (Kakar 1981: 11). But it certainly reached a crescendo in 1993–4 with the notorious (and indubitably catchy) song, '*Choli ke peechey kya hai?*' ('What's she got behind her bodice?'), from Subhash Ghai's film, *Khalnayak*[19] (a song, incidentally, picturized on *HAHK*'s heroine, Madhuri Dixit).

Cinematic vulgarity is popularly believed to stem from two distinct sources, operating in baleful combination: from the culturally alien and morally corrupting influence of Hollywood movies; and from the debased cultural values of the lower classes, on whose patronage the success of any movie ultimately depends (Kakar 1981: 12–13). From its early days, the Bombay movie industry has imitated, indeed often plagiarized, Hollywood movies, but this process of mediated adaptation has recently been threatened by the direct entry of western films into the Indian scene: for the middle classes and urban dwellers through the satellite and cable TV channels; and, more generally, through the dubbing into Hindi of Hollywood films, beginning with the commercially successful, *Jurassic Park*. These developments had caused panic in the Indian film industry, at least momentarily, but *HAHK* now appears to have restored confidence that clean, indigenous, 'vegetarian' products can hold their own commercially while simultaneously stemming the supposedly rising tide of sexual promiscuity and moral depravity. In fact, the Barjatyas are credited with taking 'an explicit position against erotic, abandoned sexuality . . . in favour of a restrained sexuality' (Mayaram n.d.: 12).

In all interviews, my informants were at pains to stress that *HAHK* contained no 'vulgarity'. This is clearly one aspect of its classification as a 'family' film, that is the whole family (grandparents, parents, and children) can watch it together without embarrassment, and it is a criterion that apparently carries great weight in the popular mind (Mishra 1995; Zaveri 1994a). The songs and dances are deemed clean—*saf-suthra*—and 'tasteful' (Zaveri 1994a). Thus, while Salman gets a drenching on two occasions, Madhuri correctly passes up the opportunity to get soaking wet too and 'burst into an obscene number' (Mishra 1995). (Indeed, a sceptical onlooker, presumably a distributor-financier, witnessing the filming of the movie's most spectacular song, '*Didi, tera devar divana*', had declared that such a song would never catch on with the general public unless it had at least a dash of 'rain' to jazz it up [Zaveri 1994a]!) Moreover, as Asha pointed out to me, 'There is no single bedroom scene:' the 'first night scene' and the 'honeymoon scene', those staple ingredients that she insisted were often 'deliberately created' in commercial Hindi cinema—and given the stress on pre-marital virginity, the focus of much sexual fantasy and anxiety[20]—are carefully 'avoided'.

Curiously, Asha's comment ignores the chase after the groom's shoes that fortuitously lands Prem and Nisha together on a bridal-type double bed, to the whistles and applause of the audience. Curiously, too, neither she not anyone else took offence at, or even bothered to remark on, the blatant suggestiveness of Prem's symbolic seduction of Nisha on the billiard table: Prem acknowledges her as the woman he's been waiting for; their eyes meet across the table; and with calculated precision and understated exhilaration, he shoots the billiard ball into the waiting hole.[21]

Asked how she viewed the relationship between Nisha and Prem, 82-year-old Daljit Kaur[22] deemed it a bit 'free' (English term). On investigation, however, it appeared that she was not referring to their romance and its rendering in song and dance, but to the initial joking relationship of the pair as affines, that is as the younger sister and younger brother of the bride and groom respectively. However, as she then went on to explain, the latter relationship was still quite within proper limits. This, she said, was shown by the fact that, when Prem was leaving Nisha's home after the marriage and the customary tussle between the bride's 'sisters' and the groom's party over the groom's shoes, he had whispered to her: 'Please forgive me if I've done anything wrong while having fun,' thereby disarming would-be critics and showing that it really was just good clean fun after all.

Daljit's comment draws attention to an interesting aspect of the relationship of Prem and Nisha as it develops through the course of the film. From a carefree, mischievous, chocolate-licking lass on roller skates, Nisha becomes increasingly demure, soon expressing her growing affection for Prem in rather 'wifely' ways: waiting up for him when he is working late; cooking for him and serving him at table (including paring his apple for him); preparing his favourite *halva*; and sharing with him the baby-sitting of their infant nephew. Simultaneously, she outgrows her adolescent boldness and becomes so bashfully tongue-tied that she finds herself, at the critical moment, unable to confess to her love for Prem and to reject the proposal of marriage to Rajesh (even when she is given a good opening by Rajesh himself). Similarly, Prem matures from a teasing kid brother to a young man in love—'Shit! I love her,' is his exclamation of delighted self-recognition—to an established man-of-the-world with a business of his own, prepared to sacrifice his personal happiness for the higher good of his brother and family. In other words, the blossoming of romantic love and maturing sexuality is not scripted as increasing licence, but as increasing inhibition—the end of playfulness and an induction into the discipline of conjugality, within the larger discipline of joint-family living (cf. Niranjana n.d.: 6, 10).

There seems to be some substance, then, in the disenchanted *Filmfare* reader's observation, already referred to, that both Puja and Nisha are ultimately 'true to their traditional role models' as Hindu wives—domesticated and bashful—despite their liberal upbringing and, in the case of Nisha, apparent boldness.[23] Sunita, an outspoken young woman lecturer, was more explicit. Declaring the film to be 'nauseatingly' conformist, she complained that it had managed to eliminate 'sex' from the very place it should be—the conjugal relationship—while shamelessly celebrating fecundity.

In an anthropological perspective, however, Sunita's reaction appears rather superficial. Sex may not have been foregrounded, but its 'backstage' presence (cf. Das 1976) was nonetheless acknowledged, albeit relatively subtly for a Hindi movie. As film-maker Shohini Ghosh has pointed out (n.d.), in fact *all* the man–woman relationships that are explored in the course of the film disclose a greater or lesser degree of 'erotic tension'.[24] Particularly suggestive, however, are the customary cross-sex 'joking relations' of the north Indian kinship system,[25] which can plausibly be read as playful surrogates for the sexual relation of husband and wife (cf. Kolenda

1990: 144) and which are typically the subject of bawdy songs in exclusively women's rituals at the time of marriage (Kolenda 1990; Hershman 1981: 163–8, 175, 185): the relations of *jija–sali* (sister's husband/wife's younger sister); of *devar–bhabhi* (husband's younger brother/elder brother's wife); and, very often, of *samdhi–samdhan* (cross-sex co-parents-in-law).[26] Each of these relations is explicitly foregrounded in one or another of *HAHK*'s spectacular songs.

The north Indian culture of affinity, with its sexual overtones, is playfully invoked in the shoe-stealing incident and the song ('*Jute do, paise lo*') through which it is articulated. While the choreography pits the boys of the groom's party against the 'sisters' of the bride (a group marriage fantasy?), the libretto makes clear that the relations are of the 'groom's *salis*' and the 'bride's *devars*'. And, as already noted, the song ends with the bride's younger sister, blushing, on a bridal-type bed with the groom's younger brother. As Pauline Kolenda has remarked in reference to the set of cross-sex joking relations between affines in north Indian kinship, this song 'reiterate[s] the purpose of the contact between the two groups—to establish a sexual relationship between a male member of one group and a female member of the other' (1990: 144). Simultaneously, it also hints at the institutions of sororate and levirate, both of which emerge as dramatic possibilities in the unfolding of the film narrative (Kolendo 1990: 130, 140–1; Hershman 1981: 195–6).

Of the many viewers I spoke with who insisted that *HAHK* represents traditional Indian culture (see following pages), not one thought to point out that the content of such women's marriage songs is typically irreverent and bawdy to the point—very often—of obscenity (see S. Singh 1972; Werbner 1990: 260). (In fact, the Arya Samaj and other social organizations have worked hard over the last century to reform or eliminate these undesirable genres—genres which are, incidentally, a specifically *female* form of expression and protest [Chowdhry 1994: 392–7; cf. also Banerjee 1989].) So, while the teasing songs of *HAHK* are themselves innocuous enough, judging by cinema hall reactions, there is every likelihood that for many in the audience they conjure up recall or anticipation of the sexually explicit content of the traditional marriage songs, and of the wider popular culture of affinity in north India (Singh 1972; Srinivasan 1976).

On the surface, Rajesh and Nisha as *jija–sali* appear to have an appropriately restrained relationship, which in fact becomes more inhibited as the *sali* prepares to become the wife. But the erotic potentialities of this relationship in the idiom of popular culture are unmistakably disclosed when, in the course of a party game, Rajesh volunteers a couplet alluding to a three-way relationship of husband, wife, and *sali*: 'Eye your sister-in-law, while chatting with your wife.' The sexual innuendo of this verse was not lost on one young woman, who wrote in her college magazine that the projection of the *sali* as the 'half-wife' was surely 'one of the most offensive concepts still prevalent in Indian society', and she went on to castigate those viewers of *HAHK* 'who find nothing questionable in a man desiring his nubile sister-in-law and then using his wife to satiate his desire' (S. Das 1995: 25).

Similarly, the teasingly affectionate relationship between Puja and Prem,[27] iconicized in the film's most famous song, '*Didi, tera devar divana*' (in the course of which Nisha becomes Puja and the mock *devar*—Rita in drag—is replaced by the real *devar*), would seem to have more than a hint of sexuality—or so the ethnographer believed. For instance, Rajesh is clearly rather miffed when his wife and brother (and Tuffy the dog in sunglasses) gang up against him in a family cricket match. Moreover, at one point the film narrative definitely seems to be leading towards a leviratic outcome: 'I know what will happen,' my companion on one of my viewings hissed to me when Rajesh is suddenly called abroad on business, commending his heavily pregnant wife to the care of his bashful younger brother: 'He's going to die in a plane crash, and she'll have to marry the younger brother.'

But suspicion of sexual overtones in the relation of Puja and Prem was clearly the ethnographer's.[28] Their relationship, she was assured by all and sundry, was exactly as it should be: affectionate and respectful. Though Puja was presumably about Prem's age, she was actually—as the film script explicitly states (overstates?) at several points—expected to be like a *mother* to the orphaned boy who had never known a mother's love. Besides, as Daljit Kaur added on my further probing, it is actually important for family solidarity that the *bhabhi–devar* relationship be close and affectionate. Perhaps she also meant that the joking and teasing may contribute actively to the growth of affection and solidarity in a situation where the bride is initially a stranger in her husband's home (cf. Kolenda 1990: 143–4).

There seems to be no agreement in north Indian ethnographies on whether the relation of cross-sex parents-in-law is typically a flirtatious joking relationship, or one of avoidance (Kolenda 1990: 135, 138–9, 147n.12; Hershman 1981: 203; Vatuk 1976: 181–6).[29] *HAHK* suggests something of both: a restrained relationship when the bride's mother, as her husband's wife, represents the bride-giving party *vis-à-vis* the bride-takers (see Section II.ii in this chapter); and a flirtatious, mock sexual relationship when she identifies with her daughter as an object of marital exchange. This latter, embedded in the song 'Samdhi–samdhan', was variously interpreted by my informants: some saw the relationship as respectfully affectionate, but not at all improper; some, like Mrs Goel (see Section I.iii here), thought the song alluded to a past affair and the 'sacrifice' by one friend for the other. A sophisticated film critic and student of Cultural Studies identified this as the moment of 'transgression' he had been waiting for, while another informant—a student of sociology—thought the song improper by 'traditional' standards. In his opinion, a woman could not, even in jest, admit *in mixed company* to a past love affair, though it might well be the subject of speculation, teasing, or ribald joking in women's gatherings.[30]

To sum up: *HAHK's* supposed elimination of 'vulgarity' seems to carry a double meaning: one, explicitly foregrounded, the avoidance of the *masala* ingredients found in so many contemporary Hindi movies; the second, unacknowledged, the sanitization of a bawdy folk tradition of women's songs, making them fit—or almost fit—for mixed viewing, and for representing Indian culture and tradition. Perhaps this is what has made this film so recognizably one *of* and *for* the Indian middle classes, rather than for the class of '*rickshawwallahs*', i.e. the front-benchers, who are usually regarded as the arbiters of popular cinematic style and taste.[31]

(ii) The Display of Affluence

Judging by several viewers' comments, another notable aspect of *HAHK's* overall impression of decency is its unembarrassed endorsement of upper-class, indeed affluent, lifestyles—no poverty or 'simplicity' here. As Bharucha has pointed out (1995), in terms of its sets, props, and costumes, the film is a veritable parade of fetishized middle-class status symbols; in homes, cars, children's toys, clothes, etc. Even Tuffy the dog, who drew applause and appreciation for his several cameo performances, is the epitome of Indian middle-class aspirations in pet dogs. The two homes on display, including that of the less prosperous professor, were much admired by my companions (my attention was called to the beautiful kitchen, the 'tasteful' marriage decorations, etc.); costumes are gorgeous, and now much copied in the subsidiary industry this film has spawned (Zaveri 1994a: 6–7); lavish gift-giving is a conspicuous feature of all ceremonial occasions; and food is quite mouth-watering (Zaveri 1994a: 802), and frequently deployed to index the quality and intimacy of social relationships. 'Look Papa, they are eating,' said a little girl behind me at regular intervals through the film, reminding one of just how often sumptuous food was offered up for visual and gastronomic consumption.

Viewers were for the most part very appreciative of all this opulence, construing it as evidence of the elite social status of the two families. There were some minor misgivings, however. The picture-book cleanliness of the temple-ashram was thought to be a bit 'unbelievable' (cf. Zaveri 1994a: 803), while the lavish costumes of the maid, Chameli, were deemed 'overdone'. The same could well have been said of the costumes of the village belles and the appurtenances of the rural village through which the romantic pair briefly romp; but none of my informants thought to point that out.[32] Asha was perturbed by one detail, however. She found very worrisome the scene of the bridegroom's party being feasted in a supposedly 'traditional' style, seated on the floor and eating off leaf plates. Rich people might do that in their homes, or in the context of a religious ceremony, she told me authoritatively; but having attended several 'high-class' weddings, she was quite sure that the bride's family would treat the bridegroom's party to a feast laid out formally on tables with all the plates, cutlery, and so on.

Asha's critical comment suggests that the film's effort to meld *haut bourgeois* lifestyles seamlessly with religiosity and with traditionalism in rituals—thereby legitimizing affluence as a value in itself—was not altogether successful. But on the whole the display of opulence was accepted without guilt, and with no indication—in the film narrative or in audience reactions—that affluence might be corrupting or ill-gained, as was so often the case in the Hindi movies of an earlier era, where poverty signalled virtue, and wealth, spiritual depravity (cf. Jayamanne 1992: 150; also Bharucha 1995: esp. 802).

The good breeding of the two families (the word *khandan* was often used in this context, both descriptively and evaluatively) was also thought to be reflected in the gracious treatment of servants—'like family members'.[33] In reverse, the mean-mouthed Mamiji and her silly niece Rita disclose their lack of genuine class by their scornful and inconsiderate attitude to the servants. The manservant Lallu is Prem's friend, co-conspirator, and trusted confidant—even more so than Prem's own elder brother, Rajesh, in whom Prem had hesitated to confide his growing love for Nisha. Symbolically—and the symbolism is very heavily laid on in a tear-jerking ('emotional') soliloquy by Lallu—Puja gives her own life in exchange for that of Lallu's sister-in-law; and she blesses the romance of Lallu and Chameli just as she does that of Prem and Nisha. In other words, fictitious kinship almost succeeds in overriding class differentiation (Bharucha 1995: 803).[34]

The gracious treatment of servants and their incorporation into the family were spontaneously commended by many viewers. Said Satinder,[35] in praise of the film:

The director has given equal importance to all the characters, even to the servants of the house.

Though my socialist feminist friend found the transformation of class differences into family relationships 'phoney', one indication among several others of the film's sinister political agenda, this was not an issue that worried many others. Excepting the comment on Chameli's inappropriate attire, most viewers were content to debate whether this combination of features should be regarded as characterizing the lifestyle of a traditional 'feudal' society, or of the *nouveau riche*—or something of both. In either case, it is clear that *HAHK*'s supposed lack of 'vulgarity' implied a distancing from the carnal desires of the working classes and was metonymically linked in some subtle way to the film's consistent display of the fetishized symbols of middle-class consumerist desire.

(iii) The Spirit of 'Sacrifice'

Though romantic love is a prime ingredient of the popular media in South Asia, as elsewhere, it is obviously deeply problematic (Jayamanne 1992: 150; Singh and Uberoi 1994). *HAHK*, like many other popular Hindi films, sets up, and then seeks to resolve in the course of the unfolding of the film narrative, a tension between the 'desire' of the romantic protagonists for each other, and their '*dharma*' or social responsibility (in this case, to the wider family); between their exercise of free will and choice in the matter of marriage, and social (or cosmic) imperative (Uberoi 1997). And sometimes the attainment of larger social ends requires the sacrifice of immediate personal goals.

Several of my informants assured me that, in one way or another, *HAHK* is essentially a film about 'sacrifice'. As Asha explained to me:

> The story wants to highlight the theme of sacrifice. That's why it makes Puja die in an accident.
> You see it in the scene at Rajesh's bedside. Prem goes out of the room. Then he comes back in—and makes the sacrifice.

Prem's 'sacrifice' was superior to Nisha's, Asha elaborated, because he 'sacrificed his love and will deliberately for the sake of an ideal joint family'. Though Nisha appeared to do the same, she did so only 'under misunderstanding'. In fact, she was initially under the impression that she was to be married to Prem and then, when she realized the truth, simply 'didn't get time or chance to show her reluctance'.[36]

Sacrifice, of course, involves a genuine dilemma: one precious thing has to be given up for another. It is natural, therefore, that viewers should be in two minds about whether in particular instances the sacrifice was, or was not, justified. 'Why did they have to kill Puja?', a young companion asked resentfully after the show. But clearly the tragic death of Puja, a typical Hindi deathbed tableau (cf. Jayamanne 1992: 150), was essential in order to give meaning to the sacrifice that Prem and Nisha were then called upon to make for a greater good than their own love for each other. While none of my informants queried Prem's conduct (with the exception of the visiting British anthropologist, Ronnie, who declared our hero a 'wimp'), Nisha's 'sacrifice' produced mixed reactions. On the one hand was the reaction of Asha, already cited, who thought Nisha's sacrifice involuntary, and thus (compared to Prem's) imperfect; on the other the disappointment of some viewers who felt that *HAHK* still showed women 'in their traditional role models', though Nisha is initially introduced as an emancipated modern girl, with a will and mind of her own.[37] This dissonance of character was obviously felt by the film's leading lady who commented somewhat defensively:

> There is some criticism that Nisha gives in too easily to her family's decision . . . that she's kept in the dark about a major decision like her marriage. But I would like to emphasize that once I come to know what's going on, I try to make amends. But before I can reveal my true feelings, Alok Nath [Kailash Nath] points out my soon-to-be-husband happily playing with the baby and thanks me for giving them a new life. That's when I decide to sacrifice my love to keep my sister's little family together.[38]

For Daljit Kaur, waxing eloquent on what was obviously a favourite theme, this spirit of sacrifice was a value that was now rarely to be found in families. Illustrating her statements with examples, good and bad, from families she knows and from the plots of popular Hindi novels (which she recounted as though they were real personal histories), she spoke at length on the *unselfishness* that several of the film characters displayed. Ignoring the tear-jerking sacrifice that Prem and Nisha intended, but happily were not ultimately required, to make, she pointed instead to the unselfishness of Mamaji (the mother's brother) who took a special quasi-paternal interest in his dead sister's children and was responsible for arranging the match between Rajesh and Puja: 'He wanted to arrange the sort of marriage for Rajesh that would be good for the *khandan*,' she said. (Mamiji, his wife, was quite the opposite in this regard, as we will see [II.iii]).

She was even more admiring of Kailash Nath, the boys' paternal uncle who, while himself remaining a bachelor, had selflessly brought up his elder brother's children as his own: 'Nowadays,' she said authoritatively, 'people only care for their own. Like a *mama* would think, "there's not enough to go round in my home [so why should I take on the burden of someone else's child?]" ' (cf. Das 1976).

Asha also stressed that it requires great nobility of spirit to love another's child like one's own, adding, with her own illustrations from family histories, that once they get married and have children of their own, brothers and sisters cease caring so much for their siblings' children.

Mrs Goel, a 60-year-old housewife, suggested another dimension to the sacrifice theme, and to the nobility of Kailash Nath's character. Inquiring how much I had really understood about the film, she explained it for me as follows:

> It's about 'Indian culture' [English phrase].
> There were these two boys at college.
> They were both in love with the same girl. . . .

When they realised it, they held a competition. One married her and the other stayed a bachelor. But when his nephew's marriage was arranged, it was with that woman's daughter. You get the story from that song, '*Samdhi-samdhan*'. The story begins there.[39]

[P.U.]: The girl's mother had tears in her eyes when she was singing.

[Mrs Goel]: Yes, she was saying, 'Take care of my daughter. Now she's going to your house.'

(iv) The Family as 'Tradition'

Any number of viewers stressed—and, I like to think, not entirely for the benefit of the 'foreign' ethnographer—that *HAHK* is not only a film about the Indian 'joint family' and the sacrifices individual members have to make on its behalf; it is simultaneously a film about Indian 'culture, society and tradition'. Said Asha, summarizing the opinion of her friends:

> Everyone likes and enjoys it. It shows Indian culture and society and tradition. . . . What we see in our families, we see it on the screen.

She then went on to give examples of what she meant, for instance the play of hiding the groom's shoes by the bride's sisters and friends, a practice of which she had earlier said, during a viewing of the film: 'It *was* common; not now.'

The element of nostalgia was even more prominent in the testimony of Daljit Kaur. In her rambling reflections on *HAHK*, she repeatedly emphasized that the film shows domestic rituals and family relationships as they once *were* and as they *should be,* but not as they presently are in a degenerate world. In praise of the film, she noted:

It shows all the *rasmas* [ceremonials], and in a most enjoyable way.

Now this (like Asha's comment) is a rather unexpected perspective on the Indian cultural tradition, for it clearly identifies *folkways,* rather than *Sanskritic rituals,* with the essence of 'tradition'.[40] Indeed, for an anthropologist it is rather striking that *HAHK* focuses, particularly in the spectacular song–dance items, on the *non*-Sanskritic and often exclusively women's rituals that run parallel to, interweave with, and even challenge in gestures of symbolic reversal the hegemony of representation of the Sanskritic life-cycle rituals—the *sanskars* proper—that are performed by the *purohit* following the rules elaborated in the *shastras* (cf. Fruzzetti 1990; Hanchett 1988; Kolenda 1990; Inden and Nicholas 1977: esp. ch. 2; Sharma 1993, etc.). Though this evocation of the folk tradition goes rather against the grain of Indian modernism which, as already noted (I.i in this chapter) has mostly sought to purge the Indian tradition of the excrescences of the folk tradition and restore it to its pristine and uncontaminated form (Chakravarti 1989; Mani 1989; Nandy 1995c), it is consistent with an alternative modernist strategy whereby the folk tradition in its manifold forms is appropriated for nationalist and developmental ends (e.g. Rege 1995: 30–2, 35–6; Singh 1996).

In the unfolding of the story of *HAHK,* a series of life-crisis rituals—betrothal, engagement the *mehndi* and marriage ceremonies, a seventh-month pregnancy ritual, and celebrations of childbirth (including the visit of the *hijras* to bless the newborn child)—are all presented in their non-Sanskritic idioms, albeit purged of the 'obscenity' with which they are often associated. The most remarkable instance is the marriage ceremony itself, the centrepiece and indeed the *raison d'être* of the movie. Here the sacramental *saptapadi* marriage rite, the seven circumambulations of the sacred fire, is no more than a suggestive backdrop for the enactment of the 'teasing' of the young men of the groom's party by the bride's sisters and friends. 'Be careful,' Lallu warns Prem as they enter the wedding reception, 'we're surrounded by our enemies here.' The bride's sisters first try to make fools of Prem and Lallu by persuading them to sit on a specially prepared couch of crackling *papar.* Then, in a long-extended sequence, charted by the exceedingly popular song, '*Jute do, paise lo*' ('Give us the shoes, take the money'), the bride's sisters steal the groom's shoes; the groom's party, aided by the invincible combination of Lord Krishna and Tuffy the dog, recover the shoes; and finally the bride's friends regain the shoes and claim the reward, only then allowing the groom to proceed home with his bride.[41] (Of course we all know that this is a pyrrhic victory, for the extended chase after the shoes has not only landed Prem and Nisha compromisingly in a double bed together, but has given Prem the opportunity to twist Nisha's arm and—if he would—wrest the shoes from her.[42]

The long marriage sequence concludes with the *doli* (*bidai*) ceremony, which expresses most poignantly the anguish of the daughter leaving the love and security of her father's home (see Chowdhry 1994: 310). Many in the audience are now weeping unashamedly, as they do once again when Puja dies—an irrevocable departure. As Veena Das has pointed out, such moments of loss are those where the feminine briefly finds voice to interrogate the normative values of the patriarchal family and the justice of the cosmic order (Das n.d.). Strange indeed that such interrogative moments should be held to *epitomize* the Indian tradition and its ideals of family life!

Judging by the comments of viewers, in sum, it seems that the classification of *HAHK* as a 'clean' movie involves a complex of different features: the avoidance of the routine Bollywood *masala* ingredients of sex, sadism, and violence; the display of affluent lifestyles, effortlessly achieved and maintained; the exploration of the ennobling theme of individual sacrifice on behalf of the family (rather than, for instance, the celebration of violent revenge); and the evocation of ideals of Indian culture and tradition, subtly Hinduized,[43] embourgeoise-ized (to coin a horrible neologism) through the naturalization of affluence and, for that matter Aryanized, for the tradition of Indian kinship that is celebrated is a generalized north Indian one (cf. Uberoi 1990). How these disparate features hang together to constitute a contemporary sense of self and society, and the 'politics' of this construction, are questions to which we will return, but meanwhile it is important, to address the central theme of the film: the Indian family. What are the features of *HAHK*'s construction of the ideal of Indian family life? Is there a 'politics' to this construction, too? And what is the relationship between this ideal and the common assessment of the film as a good, clean movie?

II. The Constitution of the Ideal Indian Family

In an early essay on Indian popular cinema, Sudhir Kakar, had drawn attention to the important role of the family in Bollywood movies—not only in explicitly 'family' and so-called 'social' films, but in 'action' films as well. From his disciplinary perspective as a psychoanalyst, he suggested that the stereotypical roles and narrative structures of these movies are collective projections of the anxieties generated by early childhood or adolescent experiences in the family. The chief locus of this anxiety, according to Kakar, is the mother–son relationship (and to a lesser extent the father–daughter relation), resulting in the splitting of the maternal image between the idealized, self-sacrificing mother and the cruel, rejecting mother-figure,[44] and a parallel splitting between the good and bad aspects of the self. Kakar concedes that the mother–son relation is significantly inflected by the wider context of the Indian joint family, with its underplaying of the husband–wife relation (1978: ch. 3; also Nandy 1980), but the joint family is for him merely the local backdrop for a universal narrative of psycho-sexual maturation, focused on the cross-sex dyadic relations of the nuclear family.

Undoubtedly, *HAHK* would provide some grist to the psychoanalyst's mill, particularly in regard to the interpretation of the *bhabhi–devar* relationship. Thus it is several times stressed that, of the two brothers, Prem had never known a mother's love; Puja, as the new 'lady of the house', was to be like a mother to him (and to the manservant, Lallu).

These and other hints clearly weighed heavily with my informants who, as noted, had erased all suggestion of sexuality from the *bhabhi–devar* relationship despite the familiarity of their horseplay and the unfulfilled fantasy of levirate. Mamiji was of course the very archetype of the bad mother, though neither of the boys seemed to take offence at her conduct.

However, where the psychoanalytic perspective focuses on the elementary relationships of the nuclear family, *HAHK* posits the naturalness or 'just-so' status of the patrilineal joint family within a wider system of kinship and affinity.

(i) The Ideal of the Joint Family

There was one aspect of the film narrative that rather puzzled me. I asked my informants: 'Why did Kailash Nath have to be the *uncle* (*caca* [FyB], of the boys? Wouldn't the story have been the same if he were their real father'? 'It's just a coincidence,' I was told. 'There's no reason!'

On closer look, however, one could say that there was a very good reason for Kailash Nath to be the boys' uncle. Apart from demonstrating his selfless nobility of character (see I.iii here), it is this crucial fact that makes this family a joint *family*, if not a joint *household* in the strict technical sense (see Shah 1974; 1996). As a moral institution, the Indian joint family is one in which the claims of individual members, the sexual relation of husband and wife, and the biological relation of parent and child are subordinated to the larger interests of the family collectivity (Das 1976). Kailash Nath exemplified the values of the joint family for the reason that he was able to renounce his right to an elementary family life of his own, and bring up his orphaned nephews with the same love that a biological father would have shown. As my informants commented, this is a rare attribute, much to be admired.

In turn, in the next generation, the dramatic climax of the film hinges on the crucial questions of (i) whether a stepmother can or cannot give a child a real mother's love; (ii) whether a close blood relation (in this case, the mother's sister) is or is not the obvious and best substitute for the biological mother; and (iii) recalling in a way Kailash Nath's own life history, whether a brother's wife can give her nephew (HBS) the same love that she would have given had she been married to the child's father. *HAHK* rules that a close biological relation is self-evidently a more appropriate foster mother than a distant relation or outsider; but that, ideally speaking, and in the assumed context of the joint family, the fostering can be done equally well by the woman as *caci*. She does not have to become the child's father's wife.

Similarly, though Rajesh and Puja appropriately fall in love with each other after their marriage is arranged, Puja's role is, first, to be the 'house-lady' in a house which has been without one for many years (a part she plays with distinction); and, second, to produce an heir for the family (which she immediately does). And while Rajesh genuinely mourns her death, as does everyone else, including Tuffy the dog, his real worry is the upbringing of his motherless son. It is the pathos of Rajesh's situation that persuades Nisha that she should accept the elders' mandate and marry Rajesh. In caring for 'her sister's little family' more than her own love, Nisha demonstrates her internalization of joint family values; and she has only to be made to publicly acknowledge that she will care for the child as *caci* as much as she would as stepmother, for the film drama to come to a happy-ever-after conclusion.

For the last century and a half, if not longer, public opinion in India has been obsessed with the spectre of the imminent break-up of the Indian joint family system through processes of urbanization, industrialization, westernization, individualization, and the liberation of women. Many professional sociologists of the family are sceptical on this score (e.g. Shah 1974; 1996; Vatuk 1972), but even the most sceptical of them concede that the joint family is, if not a *fact* of traditional Indian society, at least a deeply held traditional *value* that continues to provide the underlying principles of household-building strategies in South Asia, though differently for different regions, castes, and communities. A.M. Shah, in typical 'sociologese', has termed this the principle of 'the residential unity of patrikin and their wives' (1974: 48 ff.).

It is notable that *HAHK*'s cinematic affirmation of joint family ideals has been achieved through the consistent *erasure* of the set of factors that characteristically puts the joint family structure under strain. Thus there is no antagonism between the father (or father-figure, Kailash Nath) and the sons, for Kailash Nath simply does not act like a despotic patriarch (cf. Mukherjee 1995); he is also not in competition with the sons for their mother's love, for their mother is long dead. There is no tension between the two brothers—the younger one willingly sacrifices for the elder when the moment comes. There is no tension between mother-in-law and daughter-in-law: for good measure, the mother-in-law role has been eliminated from the storyline and Puja comes into a home where she is the un-challenged, and very welcome, 'house-lady'. And there is no tension between sisters-in-law: had Puja not died, her *devrani* (HyBW) would have been her own, much-loved sister, a prospect with which she was obviously quite delighted.[45]

All this is almost too good to be true, as my informants remarked with candour, no doubt reflecting on the complexities of their own family situ-ations. The sort of individual sacrifice required to keep the joint family harmoniously functioning 'is not generally found in families', I was told in explanation. Nonetheless, my informants remained convinced that the ideal was possible and worthy of attainment, if not in their own families, due to various contingent reasons, at least in *other* families, or in the Indian family as it had once been. We will address this question again in due course.

(ii) Affinity as a value[46]

Meanwhile, it can hardly be sufficiently emphasized that the joint family of *HAHK* is conceived as only a unit in a system of families linked by mar-riage. The film focuses centrally on the marriage of Rajesh and Puja, on the affinal relationships which this event brings into being, on the projected re-plication of this family alliance through the marriage of Rajesh and Nisha, and on the ultimate happy-ending marriage of the younger siblings, Prem and Nisha. There is a lot of wordplay on the transformation of consanguinity into affinity (the younger sister becomes a *devrani*);[47] and of affinity into consanguinity (the child's *mausi* [MS] becomes a *caci* [FyBW]). The most popular songs are unabashed celebrations of affinity and of the joking rela-tions that affinity creates.[48]

Once again, however, there is a consistent process of erasure at work. The characteristic feature of affinity in north Indian kinship is the inequality of status between the inferior bride-givers and superior bride-takers which is expressed both in ritual and etiquette and in the asymmetrical flow of gifts from the bride's to the groom's family. In *HAHK*, the structural tension (and oftentimes emotional antagonism) between wife-givers and wife-receivers in the north Indian kinship system is happily neutralized by making the fathers-in-law old friends. Professor Chowdhury, the bride-giver, spontaneously says 'Thank you' to Kailash Nath when the latter, now a prosperous industrialist, comes with a proposal for Puja. But this is brushed aside by Kailash Nath who nobly demurs: 'It's I who should thank you' for providing a bride for his home and a 'mother' for Prem. A wealthy man, Kailash Nath makes it clear that he is not seeking material or social gain from his nephew's marriage; he wants only a well-bred, 'simple' (*sidhi-sadi*) girl to preside over the home and care for Prem.

Professor Chowdhury, rather improbably given the tension between wife-givers and wife-takers in north Indian marriage, positively clowns his way through the important *milni* ritual (when the senior men of the bride's side greet the senior men of the groom's party), before the two fathers-in-law embrace as friends. This clowning continues in one form or another through all their interactions, to the great delight of the audience.[49] When Puja's mother demurs that it is not correct to overstay at their daughter's married home (where they have gone to celebrate the birth of their grandson), her husband reminds her that Kailash Nath was his *friend* before he was their daughter's father-in-law. As though to emphasize this non-contradiction, notwithstanding the newly instituted affinal relation, the two 'grandfathers' wear identical costumes—by design, so that the (classificatory) *Dada* (FF) and *Nana* (MF) could be 'as one'. It would be rather difficult to devise a triter symbolic representation of their non-differentiation.

With these highly motivated erasures and structural adjustments, much of the tension that normally invests north Indian marriage is neatly disposed of. Of course, not everyone was convinced of the adequacy of this solution. Asha, as we have seen, was quite perturbed at the informal ('free') treatment of the bridegroom's party. She also felt that a great deal of unpleasantness can occur if the children of friends marry and something goes wrong—it can ruin a friendship for one thing—though she hastened to add that there is usually some other cause of tension in such cases—for instance a breach of affinal etiquette on matters like inquiring after a sick relative, or attending a funeral. Similarly, she insisted, the quantum of dowry becomes an issue in the relations between affines only when there are other sources of tension. On the whole she believed that tensions both *within* joint families and *between* affines were less likely where material resources were ample, and people had no money worries.[50]

Clearly, the credibility of the family ideal constructed in *HAHK* was closely linked, at least in the minds of some viewers, to the affluence of the intermarrying families. Though the professor was reputedly not as well off as Kailash Nath, a fact to which Mamiji rather meanly drew attention, the two families had no material cause to quarrel over anything. In this sense, the film's opulence is functional, removing what is popularly believed to be a major irritant in real family relations, and allowing the free play and development of other elements. The outcome is a highly satisfying and nostalgic fantasy of ideal family life, a mediation of desire and reality which almost, but not completely, succeeds in erasing the unpleasant truth of practical experience. As one viewer summed it up for me: 'It's an ideal nostalgic world. No rich, no poor, no villain, no obstacles. The only problem is an accident'—without which, as it happens, there would have been no story to tell.[51]

(iii) The Truth-telling Voice

There is, however, a truth-telling voice in the film, a comic yet rather unpleasant character who, at every turn in the plot, questions the sanitized ideal of the joint family and of affinal relationships that the film is seeking to construct and project. Perhaps this injection of evil is necessary, lest the film fantasy be just too unreal—all desire and no reality.

The character who takes on this important role is the archetypal 'bad mother'—the childless Mamiji (MBW)—played by a siren of yesteryear, Bindu. Vain, overdressed, selfish, opinionated, she ultimately gets her just reward, a public slap from the long-suffering Mamaji. Thus tamed, she conceives after all, and is co-opted to the possibility of a 'good mother' role; but not before she has had her say, *contra* Mamaji, at all dramatic points in the film narrative.

Mamiji's role, though a small one, clearly demands careful scrutiny. I now take up the more important of Mamiji's unpleasant interventions in the film narrative, in the order of their occurrence:

1. Mamaji and the overdressed Mamiji appear in almost the first scene of the movie, colliding with Mamiji's foolish niece, Rita ('Bum Chum' written across her roundly filled-out teeshirt), at the entrance to Kailash Nath's house. This scene establishes their contrasting characters—Mamaji's goodness and Mamiji's selfishness—in the context of arranging a match for their nephew, Rajesh. Daljit Kaur said:

If a sister dies, the brother has to take care [of her children].

Mamaji's 'character' is very good. He wants to get the sort of girl for Rajesh who would be good for the *khandan*. [Long aside on the plot of a novel of which she is reminded.]

The basic idea is that you need a good girl for the *khandan*.

With this in mind, Mamaji had been doing his own scouting, and had come up with the ideal choice. Mamiji, however, had quite a different agenda— to promote the candidature of Rita's elder sister, Sweety. Sweety's father, Mamiji announces, is a wealthy Delhi businessman, who would surely give his daughter a magnificent wedding. When Mamaji demurs that they want only a simple, well-bred girl for Rajesh, Mamiji accuses him of being out of touch with reality and the ways of the world. As Asha summed up this exchange for me:

Mamaji loved the boys like his own. That's why he took the initiative in arranging Rajesh's wedding. Mamiji was just scheming for her own nieces.

2. Having failed to promote her own candidate, the spiteful Mamiji never passes up an opportunity to point out what Kailash Nath's family are missing by turning down the opportunity of a marital alliance with Sweety's well-heeled family. As preparations for the engagement party are under way, Mamiji arrives fresh from the temple ('from the beauty parlour, more likely', remarks Mamaji in an aside). She volunteers the comment that there cannot have been any worthwhile discussion regarding the 'giving-taking' aspect of the alliance, because a professor would obviously not have been able to put aside very much for his daughter's marriage expenses.

3. Mamiji's spitefulness and bad taste are revealed again when, standing in for the lady-of-the-house, she welcomes the new bride and groom to Kailash Nath's home. After a perfunctory blessing, she taunts Mamaji for his part in arranging a marriage that has brought in so little by way of dowry. Lallu reacts defensively by telling her—rightly or wrongly—that a very ample dowry had actually been given (a TV set, diamond jewellery, an imported car, a VCR, etc.) but that, when weighed against the qualities of the new bride, these items were so paltry that the groom's party had left them all behind. Mamiji is incredulous, and again castigates her husband for his unworldliness. She adds, as Mamaji presents Puja with a copy of the *Ramayana* (a reminder of the conjugal fidelity of Ram and Sita), that if the bride had been her niece Sweety, she would have loaded her with gold.

4. Mamiji's bad taste and *hauteur* are revealed once again in her attitude to the family servants. Puja is about to return for a visit to her parents' home

along with her baby when Lallu receives a telegram that his sister-in-law is seriously ill. Puja spontaneously goes to get him some money to tide over the crisis. Mamiji is infuriated and comments, overheard by the dismayed Lallu, that servants cannot be trusted, that this is the ploy they use to extract money from their employers, and that Puja will never see either Lallu or her money again. (Puja gives Lallu a generous amount nonetheless, and together with Chameli they pray to Lord Krishna for his sister-in-law's recovery. Of course, the prayer succeeds.)

5. Rajesh is unwell, grieving for Puja and worrying over his motherless child. In an impassioned outburst, Mamiji remarks—and this is one of the dramatic high points of the film—that Rajesh would have been better off had he married her niece Sweety in the first place. But Sweety is still available, she says, and would bring a good dowry. Sweety would also be willing to marry Rajesh, on the one condition that an ayah be employed to look after the child. This fuss going on over a child is quite unnecessary, declares Mamiji shrilly. After all, babies keep coming; it's nothing special.

At this point, the normally docile Mamaji slaps her. 'It's probably because of these sort of sentiments that you have never managed to have a child yourself,' he shouts at her. (The audience is thrilled.)[52]

6. In a final brief scene at the wedding of Nisha and Prem, Mamiji appears glowingly happy and roundly pregnant,[53] to the delight of the audience, who seem to find the idea of pregnancy quite funny.

Until the final taming of this overdressed shrew via motherhood, Mamiji has given voice to a range of opinions that strike at the very basis of the joint family as a moral institution. She demonstrates, first, that family members can be selfish, rather than selfless, in arranging matches for the younger generation, and it is probably not irrelevant in her calculations that Kailash Nath's family is exceedingly affluent. She is very conscious of the material transactions that go along with marriage, scorning the match between Rajesh and the less prosperous professor's daughter, mocking the sentimental gift of the *Ramayana* that her husband gives the young bride, and suggesting that Kailash Nath would have had much to gain materially through a marital alliance with Sweety's family. She makes it clear that her husband's high moral sentiments are better suited to the classroom than to real-life situations.

Equally to the point, she sees Rajesh's second marriage as an opportunity to make a materially advantageous new alliance from which she might directly benefit, rather than as the best means of ensuring the physical and psychological welfare of the infant heir to the family, which is the chief concern of all others in the family. She does not concede the biological and social uniqueness of the child, nor his need for genuine 'mothering':—after all, 'babies keep coming, it's nothing special', is her opinion. That is why she endorses Sweety's condition that an ayah should be employed to care for the baby, and fails to appreciate that Puja's closest biological relative, her sister Nisha, a person who is 'exactly like her' and who has been caring for the child day and night, is the only person who would be truly able to bring up the child as her own. It is only consistent with Mamiji's mean character and ill-breeding that she is unable to accept the servants as fictive family members, and insists on redrawing the nearly erased line of class differentiation. Her niece, Rita, is no better in this regard, and the *halva* she attempts to prepare for Prem is salty in consequence. (Naturally, Nisha's *halva* is just right!)

III. The Pleasures of Viewing: Voyeurism, Narcissism and a Happy Ending

HAHK is a film that has given immense pleasure and satisfaction to millions of Indian viewers. It provides the pleasures of *spectacle*, but amazingly does so without the usual formulaic ingredients of Bollywood movies: blood and gore, sex and sadism. And it exploits erotic tension, short of explicit sexuality, right through to the climax. At the same time, as Bharucha convincingly argues (1995), it is very much a product of the Indian liberalized capitalist economy of the 1990s. The old antimonies of south Asian melodrama (Jayamanne 1992: 150):

rural :	urban
poor :	rich
East :	West
good :	bad

—antimonies which, it has been suggested (Kakar 1989; Nandy 1981: 81, 95–6; 1995c) are reflective of the psychic conflicts and existential circumstances of popular cinema audiences—no longer hold good. In *HAHK*, bucolic pastoral scenes are merely romantic interludes between one urban setting and another.[54] The heroines are modern, educated young women (Nisha studies 'computers'), and the heroes successful young businessmen (cf. Mayaram n.d.: 7–9).[55] Wealth is effortlessly acquired, and accepted without guilt, an effect achieved both through the display of the 'fetishized objects' of the capitalist economy, promised in unlimited abundance, and through the consistent erasure of the signs of labour and poverty. Plenitude is convincingly naturalized. The tragic death of Puja, as Bharucha points out, is only a brief interruption in the heady flow of fun and frolic in this 'non-stop roller-coaster of laughter, food, songs and games' (1995: 801). Moreover, the pleasures of consumption are subtly (or not-so-subtly) link-ed with the valorization of the family, reinforcing the opinion held by many of my informants that affluence is an important enabling factor in harmo-nious family life. Similarly, wealth is no longer opposed to, but is metonymi-cally linked in the film with, Indian culture and tradition: indeed, some informants took voyeuristic pleasure in observing life-cycle rituals being celebrated on a scale that their own limited means would never allow:

> It is impossible for a middle class father to celebrate his daughter's wedding on such a scale, so my daughter and I would rather watch it in a film [Mishra 1995].

Needless to say—and the focus on life-crisis rituals naturalizes this elision—the national tradition is assumed Hindu, 'otherness' being either excluded or co-opted through caricature.[56] As Bharucha sarcastically sums up, *HAHK* exemplifies

> the ease with which the market has been embraced within a matrix of upper-class, 'traditional', Hindu cultural values, with an appropriate dose of reli-giosity to keep the 'family' happy, and very discreetly . . . to keep the others out. Of course, if they wish to enter this matrix, they will always be welcomed with a cup of tea and absorbed (1995: 804).

In this interpretation, the pleasure of viewing is effectively the pleasure of voyeurism, that is of being witness to a spectacle of unlimited consumption. This assessment is confirmed by several viewers' comments, and by the participatory reaction of the cinema-hall audiences: when, for instance, the new icon of Indian femininity,[57] Madhuri Dixit, comes down the stairs in her gorgeous purple and gold costume for the '*Didi, tera devar divana*' sequence, she is greeted by sighs and wolf-whistles of appreciation.[58] But the comments of viewers *also* suggest a strong, and very *narcissistic* identifica-tion with the happy family ideal, no matter what their personal family cir-cumstances.

In the defining of 'taste' in Indian cinema, two interrelated criteria are characteristically employed to differentiate the high-brow or parallel cinema from the low-brow commercial cinema: (i) the absence/presence of music, song, and dance (see Beeman 1981); and (ii) realism (e.g. Nandy 1981: 92, 95–6; 1995c; Rajadhyaksha 1993). *HAHK*, as already noted, has an un-usual number of songs—indeed, in a different cultural context it would be classed as a 'musical' or 'operetta'—but the presence of these songs does not apparently detract from the appearance of realism as far as the viewers are concerned. One might argue that this is because the film focuses on a seg-ment of Indian social life—marriage and other life-crisis rituals in their non-Sanskritic aspects—where music, song and dance are always much in evidence, but this of course does not explain why courtship and the declaration of love, or a lovers' phone conversation, should also be rendered in song, as indeed they are.

The deployment of the criterion of realism to discriminate the good from the bad in Indian cinema seems often to imply the rather patronizing assumption that the masses of viewers, like primitives or children, are unable or unwilling (given their individual or collective psychological compulsions) to distinguish fantasy from reality, myth from truth. It comes as something of a surprise, then, to find a wide spectrum of viewers self-consciously complimenting *HAHK* on what they see as its true-to-life, mimetic projection of the realities of Indian family life. (Of course one should not discount the possibility that ordinary Indian viewers have internalized the critique of Indian popular cinema *vis-à-vis* high and middle cinema, or Hollywood productions.) Mr Sharma's[59] comment was typical:

> This is a very good film. Seeing it is like being in one's own living room, with all the family around.

Satinder had something similar to say:

> Although there is no concrete story, the director has very successfully shown an ideal Indian family. While showing the family through their family functions [i.e. domestic rituals], the director has taken the audience along with him. It seems you are moving with the family.

And a middle-aged woman interviewed on television declared:

> It's as though you're watching a video cassette of a marriage in your own home.[60]

Significantly, interviews with the director-scriptwriter, Sooraj Barjatya, also seek to locate the genesis of the film in his real-life experiences in a way that would scarcely be conceivable for the majority of Bollywood films, particularly of the blood-and-gore variety:

> [BARJATYA] When I started out I was conscious that I was going against the accepted norms. Yet the film flowed naturally. *I have lived the kind of life which is shown in the film.* I have lived in a family of wonderful *buas, chachas, chachis,* and other elders. . . .
>
> [QU.] Like the characters in the film, do you stay with a joint family?
> [BARJATYA] Yes, 15 or 16 of us stay together in our house in Worli. There's a sharing, a bond between us.

[QU.] Do you also have a wonder pet dog like Tuffy?

[BARJATYA, smiles] No, but I've seen other families doting on their pets.

[QU.] And what about those home cricket matches?

[BARJATYA] They're straight out of my family life. . . . [emphasis added][61]

Conversely, criticism of the film often focused on details that, in the eyes of viewers, impaired the verisimilitude of the representation. Some of these have already been mentioned: the unbelievable cleanliness of the temple; the maid Chameli's outrageously 'ethnic chic' costume; the careless feasting of the *barat*; the *filmi* 'misunderstanding' that makes Nisha think that she is to be married to Prem until she actually holds the wedding invitation in her hands; to which one might add the detail that most offended Ronnie, Madhuri Dixit's inflexibly pointed breasts, etc.: all minor blemishes really. The intervention of Lord Krishna, though miraculous, was not adversely commented on. Perhaps viewers did not consider the idea of the participation of the deity unrealistic; and in any case this intervention is neatly naturalized through the agency of the wonder-dog, Tuffy.

The appearance of verisimilitude in *HAHK* is artfully enhanced by a number of fantasy scenes, well marked out as such. Nisha's cousin Bhola, smitten by Rita, sees her transformed into the legendary Shakuntala on every encounter. As Prem watches a video of the wedding revelries, Nisha suddenly materializes in the room with him. The '*Didi tera devar divana*' sequence (the pregnancy ritual) has two surprising fantasies—discounting, that is, Prem's swinging from the chandeliers and flipping backwards up onto the balustrade: Prem finds himself suddenly surrounded by half-a-dozen or so infants, and then, inexplicably, appears pregnant in a clinging white shift: a terrible excess of fecundity!

But these little flights of fancy, much relished by the audience, serve only to reinforce the overall impression of the verisimilitude of representation. This was the case even for those, like Daljit Kaur, who insisted that the film portrayed a bygone era more than a contemporary reality; or like Asha, who felt that it portrayed an ideal of harmonious family life that was, as she frankly put it, 'not usually found in families'.

Such is the magical illusion created by *HAHK*, that its picture of ideal family life carries the stamp of authenticity and provokes narcissistic enjoyment even when contradicted by the personal experience of viewers. In other words, it has succeeded in creating what Govind Nihalani has so aptly termed 'believable fantasies', fantasies just within—or just outside—reach (Kazmi 1995b; Gupta 1996): If not one's *own* family life, which is contingently imperfect, viewers see *HAHK* as a truthful rendition of the family life of *others* in the imagined community that is modern India. This 'uto-pian' effect, as I have argued above, is in no small measure achieved by the erasure—or near-erasure—of the harsher realities of Indian family and social life, leaving only the faintest traces in Mamiji's several mean-mouthed comments. This is actually a rather unusual strategy in Indian popular cinema which characteristically (or at least until heroes began to act like thugs, and heroines like vamps) had white and black, good and evil, well differentiated, with little space for shades of grey (Nandy 1981: 89). *HAHK* is almost all white: 'saccharine-sweet', said Sunita dismissively.

Besides the pleasures of voyeurism and narcissistic identification, *HAHK* also affords the pleasure of following a stereotypical romantic story through to its happy ending, though it does so almost at the expense of the sense of realism that it has so carefully built up. This perhaps explains both the cathartic effect of the last-minute resolution of the narrative crisis (and re-lease of 'erotic tension') for many in the audience, for whom such strategies are familiar, and the disappointment of some viewers, the more educated and sophisticated perhaps, who felt that the dramatic twists of the love story (Puja's death and Nisha's 'misunderstanding') made the film, ultimately, rather too much like other commercial movies.

As already noted, the narrative code of the *HAHK* romance is a very res-tricted one—'perfunctory', Bharucha dismissively terms it (1995: 801):

  (i) Prem and Nisha meet in the context of arranging the marriage of their elder siblings;
 (ii) their relationship, though initially teasing, develops slowly into love;
(iii) they pledge themselves to each other;
 (iv) a sudden event occurs (the tragic death of Puja) and a misunderstanding arises (Nisha's misapprehension that she is to be married to Prem) to place obstacles in the way of their happiness;
  (v) a resolution of the crisis occurs through the mediation of Lord Krishna and his instrument, Tuffy the dog;
 (vi) the young couple are united with the blessings of all ('*Hum aapke hain*' [I'm yours] remains on the screen as the *koun* is erased.)

Despite its highly simplified structure, this is a universal love story (Singh and Uberoi 1994; Radway 1987), but it is peculiarly inflected by the mythic conflicts that typically structure the constitution of a romantic narrative in the cultural context of South Asian popular cinema. Following an argument I have developed earlier in reference to Guru Dutt's famous *Sahib, Bibi, aur Ghulam* (1962) (Uberoi 1997; also Jayamanne 1992: 150), these may identified as conflicts between *dharma* (social duty) and desire, and between freedom and destiny—conflicts which have to be reconciled before a love story can be brought to a satisfactory happy ending.

Prem and Nisha nobly renounce their desire for each other out of love for their elder siblings and concern for their infant nephew; in effect, in deference to the wider interests of the joint family as a moral institution. Yet ultimately, thanks to the intervention of Lord Krishna and Tuffy, they are enabled both to do their duty by the family as well as by themselves. Ronnie summed it up in his own English way:

> The film celebrates the power of parents and the power of money.
> Everyone does their duty, and love wins out!

The second conflict is that between the freedom to choose one's own partner, and the need to conform to social expectations or to the force of a higher destiny. When asked by his sister-in-law what sort of marriage he wanted—an arranged or a 'love' marriage— Prem replies without hesitation: 'An arranged-love marriage' (cf. Nandy 1981: 95). And this is what he finally gets, though for a while it seems he would have to forego his own choice of partner in deference to family elders and in the context of an unexpected and tragic turn of fate. Judging by audience reactions, the resolution of this mythic conflict at the very last minute is a source of enormous emotional satisfaction, albeit somewhat undermining the impression of mimetic realism that the film had earlier conveyed.

IV. The Emblematic Family

This chapter began with a reflection on the contemporaneity of a different medium—the moving graffiti of the Delhi roads. Quite coincidentally, Prem, our hero of *HAHK*, drives in a white jeep scrawled all over with graffiti after the style affected by Delhi 'yuppies'. Prominent among these inscriptions is the phrase: 'I love my family,' signed for good measure 'Prem'. Presumably, this unusual graffito is an instruction on how to read the film[62]—as the story of a young man, serendipitously named 'Prem' ('love'), who is prepared to sacrifice his individual love for the sake of his family. This gesture, as we have noted, was interpreted by viewers as an act of great nobility on behalf of an institution which epitomizes at once the singularity, and the excellence, of the Indian tradition.

For quite understandable reasons, a number of recent critiques of the mass media in India have addressed themselves to the ideological implications of the iconicization of women, or of the Hindu tradition, or of both together, as representing the modern Indian nation, and linked these motivated representations in turn to the caste, class, and communal orientation of the governing and non-governing elites of Indian society. In this context, it is interesting to note that the promotion of the joint family ideal as an emblem of Indian culture and tradition—not only in *HAHK*, which is an outstanding contemporary example, but in a large number of movies in the century-long history of Indian cinema—is a question that has hardly been acknowledged, except in so far as it overlaps (as of course it must) with the question of feminine roles and imagery. Nor have changes in the representation of family relations been the object of the same degree of scrutiny as, for instance, have the changing roles of heroes and heroines, linked to the character of the wider social, cultural, and political order of contemporary India.

Why this should be so is a matter on which one can only speculate, given the quite inadequate charting of this field. But it is surely significant that, unlike caste, class, and religion, the family manifests as an especially unifying institution throughout Indian society. There is probably a degree of sociological accuracy in this judgement. While there are significant regional differences in styles of kinship (particularly north versus south), these differences in the culture of kinship, at least in the eyes of some authorities, are underlain by certain unifying principles, and are in any case increasingly being eroded. I have no wish to rehearse here the complex arguments for and against this proposition, but certainly it is possible that the differences across classes, castes, and religions within specific kinship regions are much less than is often supposed—that there is a commonality of underlying structure despite differences in detail at the level of individual features of kinship organization (e.g. Kolenda 1983: esp. 183–92). Perhaps this explains why *HAHK* manages to convey the impression of verisimilitude to a remarkable range of people of different class and caste backgrounds, communities and regional origin living in the city of Delhi.

Sociologist André Béteille has recently commented on the fact that, as compared to class, caste, and religion, there has been remarkably little social critique of the Indian family system. Béteille may not be strictly accurate here,[63] but one can only agree with him that the family is certainly a very important agency for the reproduction of social inequality in contemporary Indian society, not only through the process of child socialization, but also through the system of arranged marriage and through the deployment of 'social capital' to ensure that, in so far as is possible, children inherit or surpass their parents' social class position (1991). The only exceptions to this relative silence regarding the role of the family in modern India are a handful of disgruntled feminists, divided among themselves, whose opinions on this issue are widely seen as testimony to the perfidious influence of an alien culture and a sinister political agenda.

For the rest, as India globalizes, and as the 'imagined economy' can no longer convincingly iconicize the nation (see Deshpande 1993), the family remains, and not merely by default, the sole institution which can signify the unity, the uniqueness, and the moral superiority of Indian culture in a time of change, uncertainty, and crisis.

HAHK, the largest grossing film in the whole history of Indian popular cinema was released in 1994, which was also coincidentally celebrated as the International Year of the Family. It is interesting to note that, albeit in a very different discursive field, this event produced a comparable linking of the family with Indian culture and tradition, similarly underlining its vulnerability in the face of mounting external challenges. As the Minister of State for Welfare remarked, inaugurating the official programmes marking this event (see Uberoi 1994):

> India is proud of its ancient heritage of a united and stable family system. The Indian families have demonstrated a unique strength of keeping themselves together despite the growing stress and strain and external influences on Indian culture. An Indian family is by and large still perceived as a homogen[e]ous unit with strong coping mechanisms.

Notes

1. I owe special thanks to Aradhya Bhardwaj and to my other companions and interlocutors at several viewings of this film in cinema halls in north Delhi between January and May 1995. For this project, I conducted informal interviews with a variety of persons, for the most part of middle- and lower middle-class status, at the theatres before and after shows, and in other settings. Valuable also were responses at presentations at the Indraprastha and Lady Shri Ram Colleges of Delhi University in January and February 1995, and the several inputs of A.M. Shah, Shohini Ghosh, Kajri Jain, Satish Deshpande, and Ravi Vasudevan.

    For various contingent reasons, my informants were mostly female, though I did consciously try to remedy this bias as my study progressed. I was not able to correct the middle class and urban bias of my sample of interviewees, but viewing the film in cinema halls, rather than on video, did give some indication of the responses of the 'front stalls'. However, the reactions of rural viewers remain opaque, as do those of viewers in other regions of the country (see also n.25 here).

2. Contestant at the *Femina* Miss India International contest, asked: 'Are you for or against the joint family system?' (Metro TV, 13 February 1995). Her answer was appreciated by the audience.

3. I retain in this chapter the present tense in which the draft was written in the first half of 1995, though details have subsequently been added or corrected in the course of revision.

4. Over 100 crores of rupees, a figure subsequently equalled by another romantic family drama, Aditya Chopra's *Dilwale Dulhaniya Le Jayenge*. *HAHK* is similarly said to have broken all records for the sale of Hindi film music (Zaveri 1994b), the plagiarization of the music cassette generating also a notable court case.

5. It went on to celebrate its 'jubilee'—i.e. a hundred week run—at Mumbai's Liberty cinema in August 1996.

6. As with other very popular Hindi movies, viewers delight in boasting of how often they have seen the film (cf. Kakar 1981: 11–12; Mukherjee 1995). Such enthusiasts include, for instance, the celebrated octogenarian painter, M.F. Husain, who claimed to have seen the film 24 times, and to be planning another 50 visits while working on a series of paintings of heroine Madhuri Dixit (*Times of India, Delhi Times*, 5 May 1995; *Pioneer*, 10 May 1995). By the time his Madhuri series was completed, Husain was reported to have seen *HAHK* 54 times (*Times of India*, 13 November 1995; also Shahani 1995).

7. Two and a half songs, including the much-loved 'Chocolate—limejuice—icecream—toffees' (said to be a tribute to Madhuri Dixit's 'sweet tooth'), which echoes through the film, finally had to be eliminated to save 11 minutes of running time. These songs have now been restored to 'unabridged' versions of the film, shown selectively (interview with *HAHK*'s producers, Rajshri productions, *Filmfare* 4 [1995]). See also Doraiswamy 1996: 127.

8. Others in the cast include: Renuka Shahane; Mohnish Bahl; Reema Lagoo; Anupam Kher; Alok Nath; Ajit Vacchani; Bindu; and Laxmikant Berde.

9. For the first time in Indian cinema, the Barjatyas made imaginative use of local cable television to promote the film and to publicize the 'family' feeling that went into its making and that purportedly existed between the stars on the sets (Doraiswamy 1996: 127). Rajshri productions had imposed a moratorium on the release of video rights, releasing the film in only a select number of cinema halls: initially at only one cinema in Bombay, followed by the release of 29 prints for India and 6 overseas, to a total eventually of just 450 prints (*Filmfare* 4 [1995], interview with Kamalkumar, Rajkumar, and Ajitkumar Barjatya of Rajshri productions, following the *Filmfare* best film of 1994 Award; see also Doraiswamy 1996; Kazmi 1995b; Majumdar 1995; Sangwan 1996). This strategy of keeping 'control' over the distribution process against the widespread practice of video 'piracy' has meant much greater returns for both the producers and cinema hall owners, some of whom have been able to improve the facilities

in the theatres on the strength of the profits from *HAHK* alone (interview with cinema hall owners and a representative of Rajshri productions in the TV programme, 'Show Biz Masala', Metro Channel, 4 April 1995).

A number of my companions viewing *HAHK* remarked on how many years it was since they had last watched a movie in a suburban cinema hall—and how very shabby the theatres had meanwhile become.

10. Comment of a disappointed reviewer who had found the first half of the film engagingly 'different'.

11. A judgement reiterated by Kazmi several months later in a survey of trends in popular cinema through 1995 (see Kazmi 1995b).

12. Interview with Madhuri Dixit, *Filmfare* 4 (1995).

13. Educated working woman, aged 35. All names of interviewees are pseudonyms.

14. A 'rape' scene is often regarded as compulsory for an 'action' movie, setting the plot in motion. In the present case, Puja's tragic, and in a way inexplicable, death initiates the drama.

15. See, however, Veena Das's analysis of the exceedingly popular Indian soap opera, *Hum Log*, which, though modelled after Mexican soap operas with their proliferation of narrative detail and 'challenge to the ordinary', was on the contrary characterized by its extreme 'ordinariness' (Das, 1995).

16. A similarly resentful reaction was reported to me by a young women who had given a critical lecture at another Delhi women's college on the film, *1942: A love story* (Udita Das, personal communication). Contrariwise, the guilt of the critic who disapproves of *HAHK*'s 'degenerate ideology' yet finds the film pleasurable is the starting point of Shohini Ghosh's deconstruction of the 'pleasure of viewership' in relation to *HAHK* (n.d.). Interestingly, the tone of Bharucha's devasting critique of the banal 'utopia' that *HAHK* presents is notably self-defensive, as though he was anticipating indignation (see 1995: esp. 801, 803).

17. According to one of the artists, Laxmikant Berde, who plays the comic- 'emotional' role of the family servant, Lallu, 'none of the artistes knew where the movie was heading, with the exception of Sooraj Barjatya, the director' (Sharman 1995: 27). Barjatya, who won the 1994 *Filmfare* Award for *HAHK*'s screenplay, felt that the lack of story put a great responsibility on the scriptwriter to construct what he called 'little-little scenes which would absorb the viewer' (interview with Sooraj Barjatya, *Filmfare* 4 [1995]).

18. Interview with Madhuri Dixit, *Filmfare* 4 (1994).

19. Ghai claims now to regret that particular number, which was responsible for spawning a series of even more bawdy songs. In a recent interview, Ghai is reported to have said:

> The profundity of other songs in *Khalnayak* was spoilt by '*Choli ke peechey*'. Sensationalim made my asset a liability. . . . Vices are more habit forming

than virtues, but they have a very short lifespan. Which explains why a 'vegetarian' film like *Hum Aapke Hain Koun* is a total hit (Ghai, 1995).

Ghai's classification of *HAHK* as a 'vegetarian' film may have been an allusion not only to its relative lack of vulgarity, but to the producers' self-imposed taboo on showing non-vegetarian food, and their reluctance to show alcohol 'unless it's relevant to the situation' (*Filmfare*, April 1995, interview with Sooraj Barjatya).

20. For some reflections on the symbolic role of the 'first night' in a very different type of discourse, that is contemporary judicial discourse, see Uberoi (1995: 334–42).

21. The billiard table is an important prop later on in the narrative when, at the conclusion of the love duet, Prem carries Nisha to the same table.

22. Daljit Kaur had visited the cinema house for perhaps the fifth or sixth time in her long life in order to see *HAHK*. She was, however, an *aficionado* of television soaps and serials.

23. Prize-winning reader's letter to *Filmfare* (4 [1995]: 161), concluding with the disillusioned exclamation: 'So much for women's lib!'. See also Manchanda (1996: 86, source not given), endorsing Ashis Nandy's proposition that 'the bolder the Bollywood heroine becomes in dance and dress, the more submissive they are required to be as wife and daughter-in-law after marriage' also Ravinder Kaur's comparison of two contemporary cinematic heroines—the submissive Nisha of *HAHK*, and the rebellious 'bandit queen' (1996).

24. She lists the relations of; Prem/Puja; Nisha/Rajesh; Kailash Nath/the girls' mother/ the manservant Lallu/maidservant Chameli; Bhola/Rita; Prem/Rita; Mama/Mamiji; Prem/Chachijan (the Muslim doctor's wife).

25. As some critical south Indian informants pointed out, *HAHK* presents a typically *north* Indian perspective on the kinship system (see also Bharucha 1995: 802). Understandably, north Indian viewers see it as simply a film about the Indian family. This naturalization of the values of north Indian kinship may be seen as consistent with a larger historical process of cultural hegemonization of the northern over the southern culture of kinship, a process that has probably intensified in modern times (see Uberoi 1993: 33–4; 45–9; Trautmann 1979).

26. Strictly speaking, the terms may refer to *either* set of cross-sex co-parents-in-law, but the joking relation, if at all, pertains especially between the groom's father and the bride's mother. One could speculate that the opposite would suggest an inappropriate reversal of the hierarchical relations of wife-takers and wife-givers. On the etiquette of avoidance between the *samdhis* and the *samdhans* see Vatuk (1976).

27. Bharucha likens it to the bantering between Renuka Shahane and Siddharth Kak on the popular TV cultural magazine programme, *Surabhi*, on which Renuka first established her media reputation, and patented her famous smile (1995: 804 n. 3).

28. Shohini Ghosh is the only critic I know of who has commented on the eroticism of this relationship (n.d.: 4–5). In fact, she virtually derives the romantic relationship of Prem and Nisha from that of *devar* and *bhabhi*.

29. Note that for anthropologists both avoidance and joking relationships are evidence of nodes of structural tension in the kinship system.

30. Similarly, he insisted, an unmarried girl would not dance and express longing in public as Nisha does in the '*Mae-ni-mae*' number, though she might express her feelings in confidence to her girlfriends or to her mother.

31. Film director Vinod Chopra, pronouncing on the success of *HAHK* and the successor blockbuster, *Dilwale Dulhaniya Le Jayenge*, in interview with Nikhat Kazmi (1995b).

32. See, however, Gavaskar (1995: 35) who notes how the film erases all signs of 'work' and makes 'alienating features of the outside world . . . hospitable for relaxation and enjoyment'. One of the examples he cites is the 'toy-like yellow' handcart in the village scene, a handcart being 'otherwise a symbol of drab exclusion'.

33. Kajri Jain (personal communication) has suggested that the presence of servants in the home is one of the important markers of India as the 'homeland' for diasporic Indians. This comment points to the need for an independent *diasporic* reading of this film and its representation of notions of national 'culture' and 'tradition'.

34. Shohini Ghosh (n.d.: 2) interestingly interprets *HAHK*'s erasure of the master-servant distinction as an instance of what she terms the film's 'carnivalesque egalitarianism'. Similarly included as 'family', she notes, are Tuffy the dog, a Muslim couple who are family friends, and the family gods. This is obviously a theme that could be further developed. For another example of the erasure of class differentiation in contemporary commercial cinema, see Tejaswini Niranjana's critique of Mani Ratnam's *Geetanjali* (n.d.: 4).

35. Thirty-five year old research assistant.

36. Such 'misunderstandings' according to Asha, are typical of Hindi film dramas.

37. See here n.23.

38. Interview with Madhuri Dixit, *Filmfare* 4 (1995). Note the change from third to first person here.

39. Mrs Goel may have overinterpreted this song and the scene it which in occurs, but her reading is endorsed by Ghosh (n.d.: 3–4): 'Fleeting references to college days, looks that linger longer than usual and double entendres evoke images of unrequited love. The song they are made to sing for each other during the engagement ceremony, . . . 'There is a strange dilemma in our hearts today', can be reread as a re-working of their failed relationship and the forging of a new one. For two people who are denied the exclusive space to 'rework' their feelings the song becomes a vehicle for renegotiation. The 'carnivalesque' suspends

judgement set by moral and social norms, thereby provoking space for the play of unconscious desires'.

40. A similar observation has been made by Pnina Werbner in reference to the wedding rituals of UK Pakistanis (1990: 260).

41. For an anthropological interpretation of the 'joke bargaining' between the bride's sisters and the groom (in UK Pakistani marriage rituals), see Werbner (1990: esp. 278–9).

42. That he chivalrously passes up this opportunity and thereby earns Nisha's love and gratitude provoked adverse comment from a college student who considered this scene to be 'as blatant a reinforcement of the myth that a woman needs to look up to a man as is possible' (S. Das 1995: 25).

43. A point made by several critics, notably Bharucha (1995) and Mukherjee (1995). See also Section III in this chapter.

44. Presumably the wife/vamp dichotomy of popular movies is another encoding of this anxiety (see e.g. O'Flaherty 1981; Nandy 1981: 93–4).

45. Not everyone found the idea of two brothers marrying two sisters a proper solution to the typical joint family problem of the hostility between sister-in-law. Some said it would ruin the relationship between sisters, rather than consolidate that between brothers (cf. Kolenda 1978).

46. From the title of Louis Dumont's collection of essays on marriage alliance in South Asia and Australia (1983).

47. The indignant young college student, whose condemnation of the culture of the *bibi-sali* jokes has already been noted, saw a sinister plot here to valorize the affinal relations of sisters-in-law over the biological relation of sisterhood. Quoting the title line of the song sung by Puja in celebration of the wedding plans of her younger brother-in-law and her sister—'*Lo, chali main, apne devar ki barat leke*' (Look, here I go in the groom's party of my brother-in-law) she remarks that Puja is now 'totally the "*bhabhi*", never the "*didi*" [older sister]', a role which both expresses her total alienation from her parental home and which gives her 'someone to rule over' (i.e. a junior sister-in-law) in her new home (S. Das 1995: 24).

48. '*Samdhi-samdhan*'; '*Jute lo, paise do*'; '*Didi, tera devar divana*'.

49. Anupam Kher, who plays the role of Professor Chowdhury, is highly rated as a comedian, and has received four *Filmfare* best comedian awards. Audiences were delighted with his many comic acts in *HAHK*, particularly his parody of a scene from *Sholay* during a game of 'pass the cushion'; and his loving-teasing equation with his wife.

50. A certain empirical support for her views comes from Promilla Kapur's study of the marital adjustment of urban educated women (1970: esp. 423–33).

51. Comment by a woman journalist. Her statement echoes Barjatya's own understanding: 'Since I was going to talk of love, warmth and family relationships

in my film, there was no place for a well-defined villain. You can say that circumstances and fate are villains in my film' (1995).

52. After this outburst, and the threat of a stepmother neglecting Puja's child, the onlookers to the scene come round to the view that it would be best if Rajesh were married to Nisha. The initiative in this is taken by the professor, who recognizes a need, and an obligation, to strengthen the family alliance already made, and to protect the interests of Puja's child.

53. My informants could give no explanation for this unanticipated development, 'and so quickly, too!'. On the other hand, a feminist-conscientized student thought it highly significant that Mamiji conceived only after being literally slapped into place by her husband. Alternatively, Shohini Ghosh points out (n.d.: 3) that Mamaji's slap marks the belated assertion of his manhood *vis-à-vis* his shrewish wife. This explanation is endorsed by the audience's enthusiastic applause of Mamaji's conduct. There was altogether little sympathy for Mamiji, though a student complained that her character was 'a grotesque caricature of the director's notion of a childless woman', . . . 'as though her childlessness was a result of some innate essential flaw in her nature' (S. Das 1995: 25).

54. Indeed, as Shohini Ghosh remarks (n.d.: 2), most scenes are set in the private space of the two homes of the intermarrying families, and there is quite minimal engagement with the outside world.

55. Interestingly, the original film on which *HAHK* was based, Rajshri productions' moderately successful '*Nadia Ke Paar*', had the heroine as a village not city girl (interview with Sooraj Barjatya, *Filmfare* 4 [1995]).

56. For instance, the role of the poetry-spouting Muslim doctor in the film.

57. The reference is to publicity around M.F. Husain's paintings of Madhuri Dixit (*Times of India*, Delhi Times section, 5 May 1995).

58. It is relevant that in this song Prem is first a voyeur on a desirable spectacle ('gentlemen not allowed'), then witness to a parody of himself within the spectacle, and finally a participant in the spectacle, taking the lead and vanquishing the false '*devar*'.

59. Fifty-five year old administrative officer.

60. 'Show Biz Masala', Metro TV, 2 May 1995. Videotaping the marriage ceremony is almost *de rigueur* in urban areas now, even for the working classes.

61. Interview with Sooraj Barjatya, *Filmfare* 4 (1995).

62. After all, Prem might well have used that favourite among motorized graffiti— the bleeding arrow-pierced heart (*zakhmi dil*)!

63. See e.g. Madan (1993: esp. 415–18) for a summary of critiques of the Indian joint family as an impediment to economic and social development. The remarkable women who were the pioneers of the Indian women's movement were also very outspoken on the evils of the Indian family system (see e.g. Chaudhuri 1995: 227–32).

REFERENCES

Anderson, B., 1983, *Imagined Communities: Reflections on the Origin and Spread of Nationalism*, London: Verso.

Banerjee, S., 1989, 'Marginalization of Women's Popular Culture in Nineteenth-century Bengal', in Kumkum Sangari and Sudesh Vaid (eds), *Recasting Women: Essays in Colonial History*, New Delhi: Kali for Women: 127–79.

Barjatya, S., 1995, 'I am a Romantic', interview with Sooraj Barjatya, *Hindustan Times*, Infotainment section, 27 January 1995.

Beeman, W.O., 1981, 'The Use of Music in Popular Film: East and West', *India International Centre Quarterly*, Special Issue on Indian Popular Cinema: Myth, Meaning and Metaphor, 8 (1): 77–87.

Béteille, A., 1991, 'The Reproduction of Inequality: Occupation, Caste and Family', *Contributions to Indian Sociology*, n.s. 25 (1): 3–28.

Bharucha, R., 1995, 'Utopia in Bollywood: "Hum Aapke Hain Koun . . .!." ', *Economic and Political Weekly*, 15 April: 801–904.

Chakravarti, U., 1989, 'Whatever Happened to the Vedic *Dasi*? Orientalism, Nationalism, and a Script for the Past', in Kumkum Sangari and Sudesh Vaid (eds), *Recasting Women: Essays in Colonial History*, New Delhi: Kali for Women, 27–87.

Chaudhuri, M., 1995, 'Citizens, Workers and Emblems of Culture: An Analysis of the First Plan Document on Women', *Contributions to Indian Sociology*, n.s. 29 (1 & 2): 211–35.

Chowdhry, Prem, 1994, *The Veiled Women: Shifting Gender Equations in Rural Haryana, 1880–1990*, Delhi: Oxford University Press.

Das, S., 1995, 'Cine-osure: Hum Aapke Hain Koun', *Lady Shri Ram College Journal*, 24–5.

Das, V., 1976, 'Masks and Faces: An Essay on Punjabi Kinship', *Contributions to Indian Sociology*, n.s. 10 (1): 1–30.

——, 1995, 'On Soap Opera: What Kind of Anthropological Object is It?', in Daniel Miller (ed.), *Worlds Apart*, London: Routledge.

——, (n.d.), 'Narrativizing the Male and Female in Tulasidas' *Ramayana*'. Paper presented at the Workshop on 'The Female Body and Gender Identity'. Centre for the Study of Social Systems, Jawaharlal Nehru University, New Delhi, 18–19 January 1989. (Forthcoming in a collection to be edited by Ashis Nandy.)

Deshpande, S., 1993, 'Imagined Economies: Styles of Nation-building in Twentieth-Century India', *Journal of Arts and Ideas*, 25–26: 5–35.

Doraiswamy, R., 1996, 'The Home and the World: Images of Self-perception', *India International Centre Quarterly*, Summer: 123–9.

Dumont, L., 1983, *Affinity as a Value: Marriage Alliance in South India, with Comparative Essays on Australia*, Chicago: University of Chicago Press.

Fruzzetti, L.M., 1990, *The Gift of a Virgin: Women, Marriage and Ritual in a Bengali Society*, Delhi: Oxford University Press.

Gavaskar, M., 1995, '*Hum Aapke Hain Koun:* Family as Bouquet', *Manushi*, 88: 34–6.

Ghai, S., 1995, 'I Hate to See My Movies'. Personality of the week: Subhash Ghai. *Pioneer* (Pulse section), 19 March 1995.

Ghosh, S., n.d., 'Hum Apke Hain Kaun? Pluralizing Pleasures of Viewership', unpublished MS.

Gupta, D., 1996, 'Ritualism and Fantasy in Hindi Cinema', *Pioneer*, 28 August 1996.

Hanchett, S., 1988, *Coloured Rice: Symbolic Structure in Hindu Family Festivals*, Delhi: Hindustan.

Hershman, P., 1981, *Punjabi Kinship and Marriage*, Delhi: Hindustan.

Inden, R.B. and R.W. Nicholas, 1977, *Kinship in Bengali Culture*, Chicago: University of Chicago Press.

Jayamanne, L., 1992, 'Sri Lankan Family Melodrama: A Cinema of Primitive Attractions', *Screen* 33 (2): 145–53.

Kakar, S., 1978, *The Inner World: A Psychoanalytic Study of Childhood and Society in India*, Delhi: Oxford University Press.

———, 1981, 'The Ties That Bind: Family Relationships in the Mythology of Hindi Cinema', *India International Centre Quarterly*, Special Issue on Indian Popular Cinema: Myth, Meaning and Metaphor, 8 (1): 11–21.

———, 1989, *Intimate Relations: Exploring Indian Sexuality*, New York: Penguin.

Kapur, Promilla, 1970, *Marriage and the Working Woman in India*, New Delhi: Vikas.

Kaur, R., 1996, 'Two Faces of Women: HAHK and Bandit Queen', *Times of India*, 18 May 1996.

Kazmi, Nikhat, 1995a, 'The Lure of the Low Brow', *Times of India*, Delhi, 2 April 1995.

———, 1995b, 'The Film as Hero: Bollywood's Big Comeback', *Sunday Times*, 24 December 1995: 17.

Kolenda, P., 1978, 'Sibling-set Marriage, Collateral-set Marriage, and Deflected Affinity Among Annana Jats of Jaipur District, Rajasthan', in Sylvia Vatuk (ed.), *American Studies in the Anthropology of India*, Delhi: Manohar, 242–77.

———, 1983, 'Widowhood Among the "Untouchable" Chuhras', in Akos Ostor, Lina Fruzzetti, and Steve Barnett (eds), *Concepts of Person: Kinship, Caste and Marriage in India*, Delhi: Oxford University Press: 172–220.

———, 1990, 'Untouchable Chuhras through Their Humour: "Equalizing" Marital Ties Through Teasing, Pretence and Farce', in Owen Lynch (ed.), *Divine Passions: The Social Construction of Emotion in India*, Delhi: Oxford University Press: 116–53.

Madan, T.N., 1993, 'The Hindu Family and Development', in Patricia Uberoi (ed.), *Family, Kinship and Marriage in India*, Delhi: Oxford University Press: 416–34.

Majumdar, V., 1995, 'Reel Rights', *Hindustan Times*, Sunday edn, 2 April 1995.

Manchanda, R., 1996, 'Icons of Indian Womanhood', *India International Centre Quarterly*, Summer: 85–94.

Mani, Lata, 1989, 'Contentious Traditions: The Debate on *Sati* in Colonial India', in Kumkum Sangari and Sudesh Vaid (eds), *Recasting Women: Essays in Colonial History*, New Delhi: Kali for Women: 88–126.

Mayaram, S., n.d., 'Love, Marriage and Sexuality in Hindi-Urdu Popular Cinema and Literary Writing', unpublished MS.

Mishra, P., 1995, 'A Film for the Family', *Pioneer*, Delhi, 19 April 1995.

Mukherjee, M., 1995, 'The HAHK Phenomenon: Appeal of Permanence and Stability', *Times of India*, 22 May 1995.

Nandy, A., 1980, 'Woman *versus* Womanliness in India: An Essay in Cultural and Political Psychology', in *At the Edge of Psychology: Essays in Politics and Culture*, Delhi: Oxford University Press: 32–46.

———, 1981, 'The Popular Hindi Film: Ideology and First Principles', *India International Centre Quarterly*, Special Issue on Indian Popular Cinema: Myth, Meaning and Metaphor, 8 (1): 89–96.

———, 1995a, 'Popular Cinema: A Slum's Eye View of Indian Politics', *Times of India*, Delhi, 9 January 1995.

———, 1995b, 'Popular Cinema: The Politics of Triviality', *Times of India*, Delhi, 11 February 1995.

———, 1995c, 'An Intelligent Critic's Guide to Indian Cinema', in *The Savage Freud, and Other Essays on Possible and Retrievable Selves*, Delhi: Oxford University Press: 196–236.

Niranjana, T., 1994, 'Integrating Whose Nation? Tourists and Terrorists in *Roja*', *Economic and Political Weekly*, 15 January: 79–82.

———, n.d., 'Femininity, "Indianness" and Modernity'. Paper presented at the seminar on 'Femininity, the Female Body and Sexuality', Nehru Memorial Museum and Library, 1994.

O'Flaherty, W.D., 1981, 'The Mythological in Disguise: An Analysis of *Karz*', *India International Centre Quarterly*, Special Issue on Indian Popular Cinema: Myth, Meaning and Metaphor, 8 (1): 23–9.

Radway, J.A., 1987, *Reading the Romance: Women, Patriarchy and Popular Literature*, London: Verso.

Rajadhyaksha, A., 1993, 'The Epic Melodrama: Themes of Nationality in Indian Cinema', *Journal of Arts and Ideas* (25–6): 55–70.

Rege, S., 1995, 'The Hegemonic Appropriation of Sexuality: The Case of the *Lavani*

Performers of Maharashtra', *Contributions to Indian Sociology*, n.s. 29 (1 & 2): 23–38.

Sangwan, S., 1996, 'Selling Celluloid', *Pioneer*, 3 February 1996.

Shah, A.M., 1974, *The Household Dimension of the Family in India*, Delhi: Orient Longman.

———, 1996, 'Is the Joint Household Disintegrating?', *Economic and Political Weekly*, 31 (9): 537–42.

Shahani, R., 1995, 'Art for Heart's Sake: M.F. Husain-Madhuri Dixit', *Filmfare* 44 (7): 32–8.

Sharma, A.K., 1993, 'Symbols of Kinship Identity in a Village in Bihar', Ph.D. dissertation, Jawaharlal Nehru University, New Delhi.

Sharman, D., 1995, 'Jest a Minute: Interview with Laxmikant Berde', *E-times*, 31 March–6 April 1995: 26–7.

Singh, A.T and P. Uberoi, 1994, 'Learning to "Adjust": Conjugal Relations in Indian Popular Fiction', *Indian Journal of Gender Studies*, 1 (1): 93–120.

Singh, K., 1996, 'Changing the Tune: Bengali *Pata* Painting's Encounter with the Modern', *India International Centre Quarterly*, Summer: 60–78.

Singh, S., 1972, 'An Introduction to the Structural Analysis of *Sithnian*', in S.S. Noor (ed.), *Structuralism and Literature*, Patiala: Vidwan Press: 14–20.

Srinivasan, A., 1976, 'Obscenity, Address and the Vocabulary of Kinship', *Journal of the School of Language, J.N.U.*: 71–7.

Trautmann, T.R., 1979, 'The Study of Dravidian Kinship', in Madhav M. Deshpande and Peter Edwin Hook (eds), *Aryan and Non-Aryan in India*, Ann Arbor: University of Michigan Press: 153–73.

Uberoi, P., 1990, 'Feminine Identity and National Ethos in Indian Calendar Art', *Economic and Political Weekly*, 25 (17): WS41–8.

———, ed., 1993, *Family, Kinship and Marriage in India*, New Delhi: Oxford University Press.

———, 1994, 'Mixed Signals', *Seminar*, 424: 14–19.

———, 1995, 'When is a Marriage Not a Marriage? Sex, Sacrament and Contract in Hindu Marriage', *Contributions to Indian Sociology*, n.s. 29 (1 & 2): 319–45.

———, 1997, '*Dharma* and Desire, Freedom and Destiny: Rescripting the Man-Woman Relationship in Popular Hindi Cinema', in Meenakshi Thapan (ed.), *Embodiment: Essays on Gender and Identity*, Delhi: Oxford University Press: 145–71.

Vasudevan, R., 1995, ' "You Cannot Live in Society—and Ignore It": Nationhood and Female Modernity in *Andaz*', *Contributions to Indian Sociology* 30 (1 & 2): 83–108.

Vatuk, S., 1972, *Kinship and Urbanization: White Collar Workers in North India*, London: University of California Press.

————, 1976, 'Gifts and Affines in North India', *Contributions to Indian Sociology*, n.s. 9 (2): 155–96.

Werbner, P., 1990, *The Migration Process: Capital, Gifts and Offerings among Muslim Pakistanis*, New York: Berg.

Zaveri, S., 1994a, '*Madhuri ka Hai Zamana*', *E-times*, 25 November–1 December 1994: 4–7.

————, 1994b, 'Heart Busters', *E-times*, 30 December–5 January 1994: 4–7.

Index